SEC Corporate Disclosure Reforms

Compendium

Related CCH Titles

SEC Handbook: Rules and Forms for Financial Statements and Related Disclosures

SEC Handbook II: Preparing Annual SEC Disclosure Documents

U.S. Master™ Federal Securities Law Guide

Responsibilities of Corporate Officers and Directors

SEC Filings Insight

Significant SEC Filings Reporter

Informal Corporate Disclosure Under Federal Securities Law

Sarbanes-Oxley Manual: A Handbook for the Act and SEC Rules

SEC Corporate Disclosure Reforms

Compendium

James Hamilton, J.D., LL.M.
Ted Trautmann, J.D.

CCH INCORPORATED
Chicago

A WoltersKluwer Company

Editorial Staff

James Hamilton, J.D., LL.M.

Ted Trautmann, J.D.

ISBN: 0-8080-0996-6

4025 W. Peterson Ave.
Chicago, IL 60645-6085
1-800-248-3248
http://business.cch.com

FOREWORD

SEC Corporate Disclosure Reforms: Compendium offers guidance on three important and distinct reforms adopted by the Securities and Exchange Commission designed to improve issuer disclosure. These reforms address: current reporting on Form 8-K; CEO/CFO certification of financial statements; and accelerated filing of financial statements.

Form 8-K Reporting.—Responding to the real time issuer disclosure mandate of Sarbanes-Oxley Act Section 409, the Commission significantly revised Form 8-K to increase the number of material corporate events that must be currently disclosed. The SEC also shortened the Form 8-K filing deadline to four business days after the triggering event.

In addition to retaining, and sometimes broadening, existing Form 8-K disclosure items, the SEC added several new items to the current disclosure mandate, including: entry into a material agreement and termination of such an agreement; material impairments; delisting; and exit or disposal activities.

Certification of Financial Statements.—The Sarbanes-Oxley Act and SEC rules implementing it require senior executive and financial officers to certify the accuracy of the company's quarterly and annual financial statements, and provides criminal penalties for their failure to do so.

Among other things, the designated senior officers must certify that the financial statements fairly present in all material respects the company's financial condition, results of operations and cash flows for the reporting period. In addition, the certifying officers are responsible for establishing corporate disclosure controls and procedures designed to ensure that material information is made known to them.

Accelerated Filing.—The SEC also accelerated the filing deadlines for annual reports on Form 10-K and quarterly reports on Form 10-Q. The new deadlines apply to larger companies with a prior reporting history. The Form 10-K filing deadline will accelerate over time from 90 to 60 days after the company's fiscal year end, while the Form 10-Q deadline will accelerate over time from 45 days to 30 days after the quarter ends.

In the same release, and for the same community of companies, the SEC also adopted rules requiring Form 10-K disclosures concerning website access to periodic reports. Companies must tell investors where they can obtain access to corporate filings and whether the company makes its periodic reports available on or through its website.

April 2004

Table of Contents

PART I. EXPLANATION

Chapter 1—Form 8-K Reforms

PART II. TEXT OF AMENDMENTS

Form 8-K Reforms

CEO/CFO Certification

Accelerated Filing Deadlines

PART III. ADOPTING RELEASES

Form 8-K Amendments

CEO/CFO Certification

Accelerated Filing Deadlines

Part I. Explanation

Chapter 1

Form 8-K Reforms

Overview

¶ 101 Introduction

The SEC, in response to the real-time issuer disclosure mandate in Sarbanes-Oxley Act Section 409, substantially expanded the items triggering a filing on Form 8-K and transformed the report into a true current reporting form. Effective August 23, 2004, the amendments:

- add eight new disclosure items to Form 8-K;
- transfer two existing items from the periodic reports;
- expand disclosures under two existing Form 8-K requirements;
- reorganize the Form 8-K items into topical categories;
- shorten the Form 8-K filing deadline for most items to four business days after the occurrence of an event triggering disclosure;
- provide a new limited safe harbor from liability under Exchange Act Section antifraud provisions for failure to file certain of the required Form 8-K reports; and
- provide limited relief from loss of eligibility to use Forms S-2 and S-3 stemming from a company's failure to timely file a Form 8-K report.

Extraordinary Events

In the new Form 8-K, the SEC identified extraordinary events as specific disclosure items because they are presumptively so important to investors that prompt disclosure is necessary. In identifying these events, the Commission considered the relative importance of different types of corporate events to investors. (See "proposing" Release No. 34-46084.)

Specifically, the Commission considered various factors to gauge, among other things: (1) the extent to which investors would consider the event important in making an investment or voting decision; (2) the frequency of occurrence of the event; (3) the likely market reaction to the event; and (4) the potential impact of the event on a company's operations and financial statements.

The SEC encourages companies to continue to use Form 8-K to disclose any other information that may be material or otherwise important to investors. Specifically, it encourages companies to file voluntary reports on Form 8-K pursuant to Item 8.01 (formerly Item 5).

Items From Periodic Reports

The two items that the SEC transferred and modified from existing disclosure requirements in periodic reports and included in Form 8-K are Item 3.02 (Unregistered Sales of Equity Securities) and Item 3.03 (Material Modifications to Rights of Security Holders), each of which the SEC previously required to be reported pursuant to Forms 10-Q, 10-QSB, 10-K and 10-KSB. However, the Commission retained in these applicable periodic reports a requirement to disclose any sales of unregistered equity securities that do not meet the numeric thresholds of the new Form 8-K item.

Filing Deadline

Companies ordinarily must file required current reports on Form 8-K within four business days of a triggering event. For example, if a reportable event occurred on a Wednesday, the Form 8-K filing deadline would typically be the following Tuesday. The amendments do not, however, affect the filing deadline for disclosures under Regulation FD (Item 7.01), voluntary disclosures (Item 8.01) and certain exhibits.

The four-business-day deadline for Form 8-K contains no provision for extension under Exchange Act Rule 12b-25.

Numbering System

As part the amendments, the SEC reorganized Form 8-K topically and renumbered the items accordingly. The new numbering system avoids re-use of the former single-digit item numbering system to prevent confusion about the subject of particular items.

Consequently, the Form 8-K item permitting voluntary disclosure of other events that was formerly designated as Item 5 now appears as Item 8.01. Thus, anyone searching the EDGAR database for such filings made before and after the change will need to search for both Items 5 and 8.01.

In addition, a company amending a Form 8-K that it filed before the effective date of the new rules must file the amendment using the form's new numbering system. For example, a company amending a Form 8-K previously filed under former Item 2, Acquisition or Disposition of Assets, to add the required financial statements must reference new Item 9.01, Financial Statements and Exhibits, when filing the amendment.

The following table indicates the new items to Form 8-K, items imported from Forms 10-Q and 10-K, and items that are substantively the same as former items or broadened former items:

Form 8-K Item	Source or History
1.01 (Entry Into Material Agreements)	New Item
1.02 (Termination of Material Agreement)	New Item
1.03 (Bankruptcy)	Former Item 3
2.01 (Acquisition—Disposition of Assets)	Former Item 2
2.02 (Results of Operations—Financial Condition)	Former Item 12
2.03 (Financial Obligations—Off-Balance Sheet)	New Item
2.04 (Acceleration of Financial Obligations)	New Item
2.05 (Exit or Disposal Activities)	New Item
2.06 (Material Impairments)	New Item
3.01 (Delisting—Listing Standards)	New Item
3.02 (Unregistered Sales)	Form 10-Q Item 2(c), Form 10-K Item 5(a)
3.03 (Shareholder Rights Modification)	Form 10-Q Item 2(a) and (b)
4.01 (Change in Accountants)	Former Item 4
4.02 (Non-Reliance on Financial Statements)	New Item
5.01 (Change in Control)	Former Item 1
5.02 (Director Resignation—Principal Officers)	Former Item 6
5.03 (By-Law Amendments—Fiscal Year Change)	Former Item 8
5.04 (Trading Suspension—Employee Benefit Plans)	Former Item 11
5.05 (Code of Ethics)	Former Item 10
7.01 (Regulation FD)	Former Item 9
8.01 (Voluntary Disclosure of Other Events)	Former Item 5
9.01 (Exhibits)	Former Item 7

¶ 102 Background

The SEC created Form 8-K in 1936 as the form on which companies must file current reports when specific extraordinary corporate events occur. As originally adopted, companies could file Form 8-K as late as 10 days after the end of the month in which an event requiring disclosure occurred. This meant that, for covered events occurring on the first day of the month, the company would not have to report the event until 40 days later.

In 1977, the SEC significantly amended Form 8-K and provided filing deadlines that require reporting of some corporate events within five business days after their occurrence and others within 15 calendar days after their occurrence. In the intervening years, the Commission amended Form 8-K at various times to add or delete items.

Under the previous Form 8-K regime, companies had to report only a very few significant corporate events. The limited number of Form 8-K disclosure items permitted a company to delay disclosure of many significant events until the due date for its next periodic report. During such a delay, the market was unable to assimilate this undisclosed information into the value of a company's securities.

Sarbanes-Oxley and Real Time Disclosure

Sarbanes-Oxley Act Section 409 requires public companies to disclose "on a rapid and current basis" material information regarding changes in a company's financial condition or operations as the SEC determines to be necessary or useful for the protection of investors and in the public interest. In furtherance of the Act's goals, the SEC significantly revised Form 8-K to increase the number of unquestionably or presumptively material events that must be disclosed currently and provide investors with more timely disclosure of important events.

The Form 8-K changes represent the first steps in the SEC's planned move to a disclosure system that relies more on affirmative obligations for current disclosure. Commission official Alan Beller had noted earlier that, in this era of investor access to sophisticated trading and information technology, investors demand and require more current information regarding the most important events about a company. In the current environment, preventing unfair informational advantage is not enough. Affirmative current disclosure must be promoted to enable investors to make the best capital allocation and investment decisions, and expanded Form 8-K disclosure requirements are a big step in this area. (See remarks of Alan Beller, Director of Division of Corporation Finance, July 11, 2002, before the American Society of Corporate Secretaries National Conference.)

Impact of Sarbanes-Oxley Certification

Sarbanes-Oxley Act Section 906 requires that periodic reports be accompanied by a written statement by the company's chief executive officer and chief financial officer certifying that information contained in the report fairly presents the company's financial condition and operations.

The Department of Justice and the SEC have jointly concluded that Section 906 does not apply to Form 8-K. The SEC was concerned that extending the statutory certifications to Form 8-K could potentially chill the disclosure of information by companies.

Business and Operations

¶ 103 Entry into Material Agreement

New Form 8-K Item 1.01 requires the disclosure of material definitive agreements entered into by a company that are not made in the ordinary course of business. The item parallels Regulation S-K Item 601(b)(10) with regard to the types of agreements that are material to a company, a standard already familiar to reporting companies.

These agreements will include, for example, those on which the company's business depends substantially, such as continuing contracts to sell the major part of the company's products or services. Another example of a material contract is one calling for the acquisition or sale of any property, plant or equipment for a consideration exceeding 15% of the company's fixed assets. (See Instruction 1 to Item 1.01 and Item 610(b)(10)(ii).)

Under Item 1.01, a company must also disclose any material amendment to a material definitive agreement. Disclosure of a material amendment may be required even if the underlying agreement previously has not been disclosed by the company. This could occur if, for example, the agreement was entered into prior to the effective date of Item 1.01, or the amendment results in the agreement becoming a material definitive agreement of the company.

Scope of Disclosure

A company must disclose the following information upon entry into, or material amendment of, a material definitive agreement:

- The date on which the agreement was entered into or amended, the identity of the parties to the agreement and a brief description of any material relationship between the company or its affiliates and any of the parties, other than in respect of the material definitive agreement or amendment; and

● A brief description of the terms and conditions of the agreement or amendment that are material to the company.

Under the definition of "material definitive agreement" in Item 1.01(b), only agreements providing for obligations that are material to and enforceable against a company, or rights that are material to the company and enforceable by the company against one or more other parties to the agreement by the company, are required to be disclosed, regardless of whether the material definitive agreement is enforceable subject to stated conditions.

Thus, for example, a material definitive agreement that is subject to customary closing conditions, such as the delivery of legal opinions or comfort letters, completion of due diligence or regulatory approval, must be disclosed under Item 1.01 when such agreement is enforceable against or by the company despite the fact that such conditions have not yet been satisfied.

However, if a company enters into a non-binding letter of intent or memorandum of understanding that also contains some binding, but non-material elements, such as a confidentiality agreement or a no-shop agreement, the letter or memorandum does not need to be filed because the binding provisions are not material.

The SEC does not require disclosure of each party's rights and obligations under the material definitive agreement and the duration and termination provisions of the agreement. To the extent that any of these provisions is material to the company, however, it must be briefly described under Item 1.01(a)(2), which requires a brief description of the agreement's material terms and conditions.

Exhibits

The SEC also does not require that the material agreement be filed as an exhibit to Form 8-K. However, the Commission does encourage companies to file the exhibit with Form 8-K when feasible, particularly when no confidential treatment is requested.

In addition, under Item 601 of Regulation S-K, the agreement must be filed as an exhibit to the company's next periodic report or registration statement.

Business Combinations

Item 1.01 requires disclosure of all material definitive agreements specified by the item, including business combination agreements and other agreements that relate to extraordinary corporate transactions. The filing of the Form 8-K may constitute the first public announcement for purposes of Rule 165 under the Securities Act and Rule 14d-2(b) or Rule 14a-12 under the Exchange Act, and thereby trigger a filing obligation under those rules.

Rule 165 provides an exemption from Section 5 of the Securities Act for communications relating to the business combination made before the filing of a registration statement in connection with that business combination if all written communications are filed under Securities Act Rule 425.

Rule 14d-2(b) allows communications by the bidder before the commencement of a tender offer provided that all written communications are filed. Rule 14a-12 allows solicitations to be made before a proxy statement meeting the requirements of Rule 14a-3(a) is furnished to shareholders if the written solicitations are filed.

To avoid duplicative filings, Form 8-K includes boxes on the cover page enabling the filer to indicate that the Form 8-K filing also satisfies a separate filing obligation under Rule 165, Rule 14d-2(b) and/or Rule 14a-12. Thus, a company should check one or more of the boxes to indicate that it is simultaneously satisfying its filing obligations under the above rules, provided that the Form 8-K contains all of the information required by those rules.

The Form 8-K filing must generally include the substantive information and legends required by the above rules. The appropriate EDGAR tag will also be needed, specifically "425", "TO-C", or "DEFA14A".

Under an interpretation of the Division of Corporation Finance, a company that files information regarding a business combination on Form 8-K may have to make a separate filing under Rule 425. (See Q&A No. I.B.13, Manual of Publicly Available Telephone Interpretations, Third Supplement, July 2001.) As of the August 23, 2004 compliance date for these amendments, however, a separate filing no longer will be necessary if the company indicates on the cover of the Form 8-K report that it intends the filing to satisfy the requirements of Rule 425.

¶ 104 Termination of Material Agreement

Item 1.02 requires disclosure of the termination of certain agreements. Specifically, a company must report on Form 8-K the termination of a material definitive agreement not made in the ordinary course of business to which a company is a party if the termination is: (1) other than by expiration of the agreement on a stated termination date or as a result of all parties completing their obligations under such agreement; and (2) material to the company. In such an event, the company must disclose the following information:

- The date of the termination of the material definitive agreement, the identity of the parties to the agreement and a brief description of any material relationship between the company or its affiliates and any of the parties other than in respect of the material definitive agreement;

- A brief description of the terms and conditions of the agreement that are material to the company;

- A brief description of the material circumstances surrounding the termination; and

- Any material early termination penalties incurred by the company.

Note that disclosure of the termination of a material definitive agreement may be required under this item even if the agreement was not disclosed previously because, for example, the agreement was entered into prior to the effectiveness of Item 1.01.

In Instruction 1 to Item 1.02, the SEC clarifies that no disclosure is required under the item during negotiations or discussions regarding termination of a material definitive agreement unless and until the agreement has been terminated. This clarification was to allay fears that one party to an agreement could use the item as a negotiating tool to induce another party to modify the agreement or else potentially suffer a negative market reaction to disclosure about the agreement's termination.

Moreover, Instruction 2 clarifies that the Item does not require disclosure if the company believes, in good faith, that the agreement has not been terminated, unless the company has received a notice of termination pursuant to the agreement's terms.

If a company believes in good faith that a material definitive agreement has not been terminated, but determines nevertheless to make disclosure under Item 1.02, the company could disclose under this item a statement of its good faith belief as to any relevant matter, including, for example, that not all conditions to termination have been satisfied or that a termination has otherwise not occurred. In that instance, an amendment under Item 1.02 may be required if the company's conclusions as to termination changes due to a loss of, or change in, its good faith belief. In that situation, the company will have to amend the Form 8-K to provide this updated information within four business days from the date that conclusion changes.

"Mini MD&A"

The SEC decided not to require a "mini MD&A" disclosure of management's analysis of the effects of termination based on a recognition that such may be difficult to provide within the abbreviated Form 8-K filing period. However, the SEC cautioned that disclosure made in a report on Form 8-K must include all other material information, if any, that is necessary to make the required disclosure not misleading. (See Exchange Act Rule 12b-20.)

¶ 105 Bankruptcy or Receivership

Item 1.03 retains the basic substantive requirements formerly included in Item 3 of Form 8-K regarding a company's entry into bankruptcy or receivership. The SEC did, however, adopt minor changes to make the item more readable, such as breaking out embedded lists from the text and moving some language currently included in the text into an instruction to the item. Thus, a company in bankruptcy or receivership must disclose the following on Form 8-K:

- the name or other identification of the proceeding;
- the identity of the court or governmental authority;
- the date that jurisdiction was assumed; and
- the identity of the receiver, fiscal agent or similar officer and the date of his or her appointment.

If an order confirming a plan of reorganization, arrangement or liquidation has been entered, the following must be disclosed:

- the identity of the court or governmental authority;
- the date that the order confirming the plan was entered by the court or governmental authority;
- a summary of the material features of the plan and, pursuant to Item 9.01 (Financial Statements and Exhibits), a copy of the plan as confirmed;
- the number of shares or other units issued and outstanding, the number reserved for future issuance in respect of claims and interests filed and allowed under the plan, and the aggregate total of such numbers; and
- information as to the assets and liabilities of the company or its parent as of the date that the order confirming the plan was entered, or a date as close thereto as practicable. The information may be presented in the form in which it was furnished to the court. (See Instruction to Item 1.03.)

Financial Information

¶ 106 Acquisition; Disposition of Assets

Item 2.01 retains most of the substantive requirements included in former Item 2 of Form 8-K. In that spirit, Item 2.01 requires the same basic disclosure formerly required by Item 2, except that disclosure no longer is required regarding the nature of the business in which the acquired assets were used and whether the company acquiring the assets intends to continue such use.

Specifically, Item 2.01 requires disclosure if a company, or any of its majority-owned subsidiaries, has acquired or disposed of a significant amount of assets, otherwise than in the ordinary course of business. Thus, a company that has completed the acquisition or disposition of a significant amount of assets, otherwise than in the ordinary course of business, must disclose the following information:

- the date of completion of the transaction;
- a brief description of the assets involved;
- the identity of the person(s) from whom the assets were acquired or to whom they were sold and the nature of any material relationship, other than in respect of the transaction, between such person(s) and the company or any of its affiliates, or any corporate director or officer, or their associates;
- the nature and amount of consideration given or received for the assets and, if any material relationship is disclosed, the formula or principle followed in determining the amount of such consideration; and
- the source of funding for an acquisition but only where a material relationship exists between the company and the funding source, unless all or any part of the consideration used is a loan made in the ordinary course of business by a bank, in which case the identity of the bank may be omitted.

The SEC believes that Congress intended for certain procedures to be present with regard to the disclosure of the identity of a bank involved in such a transaction when the bank is loaning funds in the ordinary course of its business. (See Exchange Act Section 13(d)(1)(B), which allows omission of a bank's name as a source of funds for beneficial ownership reporting under Section 13(d)(1).)

The SEC has indicated, in Instruction 1 of Item 2.01, that no information need be given as to: (1) any transaction between any person and any wholly-owned subsidiary; (2) any transaction between two or more wholly-owned subsidiaries of any person; or (3) the company's redemption or other acquisition of securities from the public, or the sale or other disposition of securities to the public.

The SEC defines "acquisition" to include every purchase, acquisition by lease, exchange, merger, consolidation, succession or other acquisition, except that the term does not include the construction or development of property by or for the company or its subsidiaries or the acquisition of materials for such purpose. Similarly, "disposition" is defined to include every sale, disposition by lease, exchange, merger, consolidation, mortgage, assignment or hypothecation of assets, whether for the benefit of creditors or otherwise, abandonment, destruction, or other disposition. (See Instruction 2 of Item 2.01.)

It can be seen that disclosure under Item 2.01 is related to the disclosure of entry into a material agreement under Item 1.01. Typically, a company will report its entry into a material definitive agreement to acquire or dispose of assets under Item 1.01, and then later disclose the closing of the acquisition or disposition transaction under Item 2.01.

Reporting Threshold

However, a company will not necessarily have to provide disclosure regarding every material definitive acquisition or disposition agreement disclosed under Item 1.01, since Item 2.01 includes a bright-line reporting threshold not found in Item 1.01.

Under this threshold, a company need only report a completed acquisition or disposition of assets if the transaction meets the significant asset test as set forth in the item. This test is identical to the test in former Item 2 of Form 8-K. It states that an acquisition or disposition is deemed significant if:

- the company's and its other subsidiaries' equity in the net book value of the assets or the amount paid or received for the assets exceeded 10% of the total assets of the company and its consolidated subsidiaries; or

- the transaction involved a business that is significant under Regulation S-X, specifically 210.11-01(b).

Acquisitions of individually insignificant businesses need not be reported unless they are related businesses and are significant in the aggregate. (See Instruction 4 to Item 2.01.) In determining if the acquired businesses are related, Instruction 4 refers to the test in Regulation S-X, which looks to factors such as common control and conditioning the acquisition of one business on the acquisition of each other business. (See 17 CFR § 210.3-05(a)(3).)

The information called for by Item 2.01 is required for each transaction or series of related transactions of the size indicated. In addition, the acquisition or disposition of securities is deemed the indirect acquisition or disposition of the assets represented by such securities if it results in the acquisition or disposition of control of such assets. (See Instruction 3 to Item 2.01.)

Exhibits

Finally, filers should consult the requirements in Item 9.01 (Financial Statements and Exhibits) with respect to the filing of: (1) financial statements of businesses acquired; (2) pro forma financial information; and (3) copies of the plans of acquisition or disposition as exhibits to the report.

¶ 107 Results of Operations and Financial Condition

Item 2.02 retains all of the substantive requirements of former Item 12 of Form 8-K regarding public announcements or releases of material non-public information regarding a company's results of operations or financial condition. Thus, if a company or any person acting on its behalf makes any public announcement or release, including any update of an earlier announcement or release, that discloses material inside information regarding the company's results of operations or financial condition for a completed quarterly or annual fiscal period, the company must:

- disclose the date of the announcement or release;
- briefly identify the announcement or release; and
- include the text of that announcement or release as an exhibit.

An exception exists for certain broadly-disseminated communications that complement a preceding disclosure. Specifically, a Form 8-K need not be furnished to the SEC in the case of disclosure of material inside information that is disclosed orally, telephonically, by webcast, by broadcast, or by similar means if:

- the information is provided as part of a presentation that is complementary to, and initially occurs within 48 hours after, a related, written announcement or release that has been furnished on Form 8-K pursuant to Item 2.02 prior to the presentation;
- the presentation is broadly accessible to the public by dial-in conference call, by webcast, by broadcast or by similar means;
- the financial and other statistical information contained in the presentation is provided on the company's website; and
- the presentation was announced by a widely disseminated press release, that included instructions as to when and how to access the presentation and the location on the company's website.

Note that the Item 2.02 requirements are triggered by the disclosure of material inside information regarding a completed fiscal year or quarter. Release of additional or updated material inside information regarding a completed fiscal year or quarter would trigger an additional Item 2.02 requirement. (See Instruction 1 to Item 2.02.)

In addition, companies that make earnings announcements or other disclosures of material inside information regarding a completed fiscal year or quarter in an interim or annual report to shareholders are permitted to specify which portion of the report contains the information required to be furnished under the item. (See Instruction 3 to Item 2.02.)

Also note that Item 2.02 does not apply in the case of disclosure made in Form 10-Q or Form 10-K reports filed with the SEC. (See Instruction 4 to Item 2.02.)

Furnished or Filed

The information in a report furnished pursuant to Item 2.02 will not be deemed to be "filed" for purposes of Exchange Act Section 18 or otherwise subject to the liabilities of that section, unless the company specifically states that the information is to be considered "filed" under the Exchange Act or incorporates it by reference into a filing under the Securities Act or the Exchange Act. (See General Instruction B.2 to Form 8-K.)

Similarly, if a report on Form 8-K contains disclosures under Item 2.02, whether or not the report contains disclosures regarding other items, all exhibits to such report relating to Item 2.02 will be deemed furnished, and not filed, unless the company specifies which exhibits, or portions of exhibits, are intended to be deemed filed rather than furnished. (See General Instruction B.2 to Form 8-K.)

¶ 108 Direct or Off-Balance Sheet Obligation

New Item 2.03 requires disclosure of two events: the creation of a direct financial obligation and an obligation under an off-balance sheet arrangement. If a company comes under a direct material financial obligation, the following information must be disclosed:

- the date on which the company becomes obligated and a brief description of the transaction or agreement creating the obligation;

- the amount of the obligation, including the terms of its payment and, if applicable, a brief description of the material terms under which it may be accelerated or increased and the nature of any recourse provisions that would enable the company to recover from third parties; and

- a brief description of the other terms and conditions of the transaction or agreement that are material to the company.

Item 2.03 defines a "direct financial obligation" as any: (1) long-term debt obligation, as defined in Item 303(a)(5)(ii)(A) of Regulation S-K; (2) capital lease obligation, as defined in Item 303(a)(5)(ii)(B) of Regulation S-K; (3) operating lease obligation, as defined in Item 303(a)(5)(ii)(C) of Regulation

S-K; or (4) short-term debt obligation that arises other than in the ordinary course of business.

Item 2.03 itself defines "short-term debt obligation" as a payment obligation under a borrowing arrangement scheduled to mature within one year, or for companies using the operating cycle concept of working capital, within a company's operating cycle that is longer than one year.

Item 2.03 clarifies that a company need not file a report until it enters into an agreement enforceable against it, whether or not subject to conditions, under which the direct financial obligation will arise or be created or issued. If there is no such agreement, the company must provide the disclosure within four business days after the occurrence of the closing or settlement of the transaction or arrangement under which the direct financial obligation arises or is created. (See Instruction 1 to Item 2.03.)

Further, under Instruction 3, if a company enters into a facility, program or similar arrangement that creates or may give rise to direct financial obligations in connection with multiple transactions, the company must disclose:

- the entering into of the facility, program or similar arrangement; and
- its material obligations as they arise or are created under the facility or program (including when a series of previously undisclosed individually immaterial obligations become material in the aggregate).

Off-Balance Sheet Arrangements

If the company becomes directly or contingently liable for an material obligation arising out of an off-balance sheet arrangement, it must provide the following information:

- the date on which the company becomes directly or contingently liable on the obligation and a brief description of the transaction or agreement creating the arrangement and obligation;
- a brief description of the nature and amount of the obligation of the company under the arrangement, including the material terms under which it may become a direct obligation, if applicable, or may be accelerated or increased and the nature of any recourse provisions that would enable the company to recover from third parties;
- a brief description of the other material terms and conditions of the obligation or arrangement; and
- the maximum potential amount of future payments (undiscounted) that the company may have to make, if different.

The maximum amount of future payments cannot be reduced by the effect of any amounts that a company may possibly recover under recourse or collateralization provisions in any guarantee agreement, transaction or arrangement. (See Instruction 4 to Item 2.03.)

For a definition of "off-balance sheet arrangement, Item 2.03 refers to Item 303(a)(4)(ii) of Regulation S-K.

A company must provide the disclosure required regarding off-balance sheet arrangements, whether or not the company is also a party to the transaction or agreement creating the contingent obligation arising under the off-balance sheet arrangement. (See Instruction 2 of Item 2.03.)

In the event that neither the company nor any affiliate of the company is also a party to the transaction or agreement creating the contingent obligation arising under the off-balance arrangement in question, the four-business-day period for reporting the event would begin on the earlier of: (i) the fourth business day after the contingent obligation is created or arises, and (ii) the day on which an executive officer of the company becomes aware of the contingent obligation.

For example, assume Company A enters into an agreement with Bank B pursuant to which Company A agrees with Bank B that Company C, an unconsolidated subsidiary of Company A, will maintain equity of at least $1. Six months later, Company C borrows $100 million from Bank B. Three months later, Company C defaults on its debt obligation to Bank B.

In this fact pattern, upon entering into the initial agreement with Bank B, Company A would generally have no disclosure requirement under Item 2.03 on Form 8-K. However, when Company C borrows $100 million from Bank B, Company A will be required to file a Form 8-K under Item 2.03 as Company A has become contingently liable for an obligation arising out of an off-balance sheet arrangement, assuming such contingent obligation is material to Company A.

Upon Company C's default on it debt obligation to Bank B, a further Form 8-K filing obligation will be required under Item 2.04 (discussed at ¶ 109) as a contingent obligation of Company A has become a direct financial obligation, assuming such direct financial obligation is material to Company A.

Obligation as Security

If the obligation required to be disclosed under Item 2.03 is a security, or a term of a security, that has been or will be sold pursuant to an effective registration statement, the company need not file a Form 8-K, provided that the prospectus relating to the sale contains the information required by this item and is filed within the required time period under Securities Act Rule 424. (See Instruction 5 to Item 2.03.)

¶ 109 Acceleration of Direct or Off-Balance Sheet Obligation

New item 2.04 requires a company to file a Form 8-K report if a triggering event causing the increase or acceleration of a direct financial obligation of the company occurs and the consequences of the event are material. The company must provide the following information:

- the date of the triggering event and a brief description of the agreement or transaction under which the direct financial obligation was created and is increased or accelerated;
- a brief description of the triggering event;
- the amount of the direct financial obligation, as increased if applicable, and the terms of payment or acceleration that apply; and
- any other material obligations of the company that may arise, increase, be accelerated or become direct financial obligations as a result of the triggering event or the increase or acceleration of the direct financial obligation.

Item 2.04 defines the term "direct financial obligation" by reference to the definition provided in Item 2.03, but adds for purposes of Item 2.04 that such term includes an obligation arising out of an off-balance sheet arrangement that is accrued under the FASB Statement of Financial Accounting Standards No. 5, Accounting for Contingencies as a probable loss contingency.

Off-Balance Sheet Arrangements

Similarly, if a triggering event occurs causing a company's obligation under an off-balance sheet arrangement to increase or be accelerated, or causing a company's contingent obligation under an off-balance sheet arrangement to become a direct financial obligation of the company, and the consequences of that event are material, it must disclose:

- the date of the triggering event and a brief description of the off-balance sheet arrangement;
- a brief description of the triggering event;
- the nature and amount of the obligation, as increased if applicable, and the terms of payment or acceleration that apply; and
- any other material obligations of the company that may arise, increase, be accelerated or become direct financial obligations as a result of the triggering event or the increase or acceleration of the obligation under the off-balance sheet arrangement or its becoming a direct financial obligation of the company.

Item 2.04 defines "off-balance sheet arrangement" by reference to the definition provided in Item 2.03 (see ¶ 108).

The SEC has clarified that disclosure is required if a triggering event occurs in respect of the company's obligation under an off-balance sheet arrangement and the consequences are material to the company, whether or not the company is also a party to the transaction or agreement under which the triggering event occurs. (See Instruction 1 to Item 2.04.)

If a company is subject to an obligation arising out of an off-balance sheet arrangement, whether or not disclosed pursuant to Item 2.03, if a triggering event occurs as a result of which under that obligation an accrual for a probable loss is required under SFAS No. 5, the obligation arising out of the off-balance sheet arrangement becomes a direct financial obligation for purposes of Item 2.04. In this situation, if the consequences as determined are material to the company, Item 2.04 requires disclosure. (See Instruction 4 to Item 2.04.)

Triggering Event

Item 2.04 defines "triggering event" as an event, including an event of default, event of acceleration or similar event, as a result of which a direct financial obligation of the company or an obligation of the company arising under an off-balance sheet arrangement is increased or becomes accelerated or as a result of which a contingent obligation of the company arising out of an off-balance sheet arrangement becomes a direct financial obligation of the company.

Item 2.04 does not require disclosure unless and until a triggering event has occurred in accordance with the terms of the relevant agreement, transaction or arrangement, including, if required, the sending to the company of notice of the occurrence of a triggering event under the terms of the agreement, transaction or arrangement and the satisfaction of all conditions to such occurrence, except the passage of time. (See Instruction 2 to Item 2.04.)

In addition, no disclosure is required if the company believes, in good faith, that no triggering event has occurred, unless the company has received a notice. A company may wish to disclose a statement of its good faith belief as to any relevant matter, including, for example, that not all conditions to occurrence of a triggering event have been satisfied or that a triggering event otherwise has not occurred. In such event, an amendment under Item 2.04 may be required if the company's conclusion as to the triggering event changes due to a loss of, or change in, its good faith. In such event, the company would have to amend the Form 8-K to provide this updated information within four business days from the date that its conclusion changes. (See Instruction 3 to Item 2.04.)

The SEC decided not to impose a "mini-MD&A" under Item 2.04, which would have required disclosure of management's analysis of the effect of the triggering event on the company.

The SEC reminded companies, however, that any disclosure made in a report on Form 8-K must include all other material information, if any, that is necessary to make the required disclosure, in the light of the circumstances under which it is made, not misleading. (See Exchange Act Rule 12b-20.)

¶ 110 Exit or Disposal Activity Costs

New item 2.05 requires disclosure when directors or authorized officers commit the company to an exit or disposal plan or otherwise dispose of a long-lived asset or terminate employees under a plan of termination described in relevant FASB standards, under which material charges will be incurred under GAAP. Specifically, the item requires a company to disclose:

- the date of the commitment to the course of action and a description of the course of action, including the facts and circumstances leading to the expected action and the expected completion date;

- for each major type of cost associated with the course of action—for example, one-time termination benefits, contract termination costs and other associated costs—an estimate of the total amount or range of amounts expected to be incurred in connection with the action;

- an estimate of the total amount or range of amounts expected to be incurred in connection with the action; and

- the company's estimate of the amount or range of amounts of the charge that will result in future cash expenditures.

Estimates

If at the time of filing the company is unable to make a good faith estimate of the amount of the charges, it need not disclose an estimate at that time, but must nevertheless file the Form 8-K report describing the company's commitment to a course of action under which it will incur a material charge. Within four business days after the company formulates an estimate, the company must amend its earlier Form 8-K filing to include the estimate.

"Mini-MD&A"

The SEC decided not to impose a "mini-MD&A" under Item 2.05, which would have required disclosure of management's analysis of the effect of these events on the company. The SEC reminded companies, however, that any disclosure made in a report on Form 8-K must include all other material information, if any, that is necessary to make the required disclosure, in the light of the circumstances under which it is made, not misleading. (See Exchange Act Rule 12b-20.)

¶ 111 Material Impairments

New Item 2.06 requires disclosure when a company's directors or authorized officers conclude that a material charge for impairment to one or more of its assets—including, without limitation, an impairment of securities or goodwill—is required under applicable generally accepted accounting principles. Specifically, the company must disclose:

- the date of the conclusion that a material charge is required and describe the impaired asset or assets and the facts and circumstances leading to the conclusion that the charge for impairment is required;

- the company's estimates of the amount or range of amounts of the impairment charge; and

- the company's estimates of the amount or range of amounts of the impairment charge that will result in future cash expenditures.

Tests for impairment or recoverability often occur in conjunction with the preparation, review or audit of financial statements.

In light of the fact that a periodic report with complete financial statements will be made publicly available, no Form 8-K disclosure is required pursuant to Item 2.06 if the conclusion regarding the material charge is made in connection with the preparation, review or audit of financial statements at the end of a fiscal quarter or year and the plan is disclosed in the company's Exchange Act report for that period. (See Instruction to Item 2.06.)

"Mini-MD&A"

The SEC decided not to impose a "mini-MD&A" under Item 2.06, which would have required disclosure of management's analysis of the effect of material impairments on the company. The SEC has reminded companies, however, that any disclosure made in a report on Form 8-K must include all other material information, if any, that is necessary to make the required disclosure, in the light of the circumstances under which it is made, not misleading. (See Exchange Act Rule 12b-20.)

Securities and Trading Markets

¶ 112 Delisting; SRO Rule Violation

New Item 3.01(a) requires disclosure concerning self-regulatory organization (SRO) delisting or rule violations. Specifically, the item requires a company to report its receipt of a notice from the national securities exchange or national securities association (i.e., NASD) that maintains the principal listing for any class of the company's common equity, indicating that:

- the company or such class of its securities does not satisfy a rule or standard for continued listing on the exchange or association;

- the exchange has submitted an application under Exchange Act Rule 12d2-2 to the Commission to delist such class of the company's securities; or

- the association has taken all necessary steps under its rules to delist the security from its automated inter-dealer quotation system.

A company that receives this type of a notice must disclose the following information: (1) the date that it received the notice; (2) the rule or standard for continued listing on the national securities exchange or Nasdaq that the company fails, or has failed, to satisfy; and (3) any action or response that, at the time of filing, the company has determined to take in response to the notice.

Similarly, under Item 3.01(b), if the company has notified the national securities exchange or NASD that the company is aware of any material noncompliance with a rule or standard for continued listing on the exchange or association, the company must disclose: (1) the date that the company provided such notice to the exchange or association; (2) a rule or standard for continued listing on the exchange or association that the company fails, or has failed, to satisfy; and (3) any action or response that, at the time of filing, the company has determined to take regarding its noncompliance.

Note that Item 3.01(b) requires disclosure if a particular exchange or association rule specifically provides that a particular officer or other authorized individual, such as the chief executive officer, must provide the notice to the exchange or association, rather than the company itself.

Note also that the element requiring disclosure of any action the company has determined to take in response to a notice of delisting or failure to satisfy a listing standard requires only identification of the company's anticipated action or response as of the date the Form 8-K is filed. This is based on a recognition that, in light of the short Form 8-K filing deadline, a company may not have sufficient time to determine its course of action or to fully analyze the effect of such delisting on the company.

A company may, of course, voluntarily file an amendment to the previously filed Form 8-K regarding any changes to the anticipated action or response.

Companies do not have to file the actual written notice received from the exchange as an Form 8-K exhibit.

Letters of Reprimand

If the exchange or association, in lieu of suspending trading in or delisting such class of the company's securities, issues a public reprimand letter or similar communication indicating that the company has violated a rule or standard, the company must state the date and summarize the contents of the letter or communication. (See Item 3.01(c).)

Corporate Action

If the company's directors or authorized officers have taken definitive action to cause the listing of a class of its common equity to be withdrawn from the national securities exchange, or terminated from the automated inter-dealer quotation system of a registered national securities association (i.e., Nasdaq), where such exchange or association maintains the principal listing for such class of securities, the company must describe the action taken and state the date of the action. (See Item 3.01(d).)

This requirement includes disclosure of action taken by a company to transfer such a listing or quotation of its securities to another securities exchange or quotation system. The definitive action taken by the company may also include the adoption of a resolution by the board of directors, or committee of the board, to delist the class of securities.

Effect of Grace Period

A company must provide disclosure regarding any failure to satisfy a rule or standard for continued listing on the national securities exchange or national securities association even if the company has the benefit of a grace period or similar extension period during which it may cure the deficiency that triggers the disclosure mandate. (See Instruction 2 to Item 3.01.)

Relevant Listing Standards

The SEC has clarified that the relevant listing requirements or standards for this item are the rules or standards for continued listing on the exchange or association. Typically, exchanges and quotation systems have different standards for determining whether a security is qualified to enter the exchange or quotation system than for determining whether a security can remain listed. Because the entry standards are not relevant to whether the securities may continue trading on such exchange or quotation system, the SEC clarified the item.

Item 3.01 Reporting Regime

The SEC generally anticipates two filings in the typical involuntary delisting process under Item 3.01. An initial filing will be made when the company receives the first notice that it does not comply with a rule or standard for continued listing, or when it notifies the exchange or association that it no longer complies with a rule or standard for continued listing on the exchange or association. A second Form 8-K filing will be required upon the company's receipt of a notice regarding the actual delisting of a class of the company's securities.

Note that Item 3.01 refers to a national securities exchange or a national securities association. Thus, for example, a notification by The Nasdaq Stock Market that a company does not satisfy a rule or standard for continued listing on Nasdaq, if Nasdaq maintains the principal listing of any class of the company's common equity, would be subject to Item 3.01.

Finally, subsequent notices or other communications that continue to indicate that the company does not comply with the same rule or standard for continued listing that was the subject of the initial notice are not required to be filed, but may be filed voluntarily. (See Instruction 3 to Item 3.01.)

Bulletin Board; Pink Sheets

Companies whose securities are quoted exclusively on automated inter-dealer quotation systems, such as the over-the-counter bulletin board, or OTCBB, and the electronic pink sheets, are not subject to Item 3.01. Thus, these companies will not be required to file a Form 8-K if the securities cease to be quoted on such quotation system. (See Instruction 4 to Item 3.01.)

These quotation systems do not provide companies with the ability to list their securities, but, rather, serve as a medium for the over-the-counter securities market by collecting and distributing market maker quotes to subscribers. These automated inter-dealer quotation systems do not maintain or impose listing standards, nor do they have a listing agreement or arrangement with the companies whose securities are quoted through them. Although market makers may be required to review and maintain specified information about a company and to furnish that information to the inter-dealer quotation system, the companies whose securities are quoted on such systems do not have any filing or reporting requirements imposed by the system.

In some cases, however, a security that is listed on an exchange or association may also be quoted on such an automated inter-dealer quotation system. In that case, the company is subject to Item 3.01 if any of the events specified in Item 3.01 occur.

Exceptions to Disclosure

The company need not disclose any information when the delisting is a result of one of the following:

- the entire class of the security has been called for redemption, maturity or retirement and, if required by the terms of the securities, funds sufficient for the payment of all such securities have been deposited with an agency authorized to make such payments and such funds have been made available to security holders;

- the entire class of the security has been redeemed or paid at maturity or retirement;

- the instruments representing the entire class of securities have come to evidence, by operation of law or otherwise, other securities in substitution therefor and represent no other right, except, if true, the right to receive an immediate cash payment; or

- all rights pertaining to the entire class of the security have been extinguished. (See Instruction 1 to Item 3.01.)

These exceptions are specifically referenced in Rule 12d2-2, the rule pursuant to which national securities exchanges file applications with the Commission to delist a security from the exchange.

Early Warning Notice

A company's receipt of an early warning notice does not trigger disclosure, since such a notice merely informs the company that it is in danger of falling out of compliance with a rule or standard for continued listing on the exchange or association. It is not a notice that the company no longer satisfies that rule or standard.

However, if the warning notice informs the company that it is out of compliance with a rule or standard for continued listing, but that the company will not be delisted if it cures the problem within a specified time, such a notice will trigger a Form 8-K filing requirement.

¶ 113 Unregistered Sale of Securities

Item 3.02 is a new Form 8-K item that the SEC imported from periodic filing requirements. More specifically, this disclosure was previously required in Item 2(c) of Forms 10-Q an 10-QSB and Item 5(a) of Forms 10-K and 10-KSB.

Under Item 3.02, a company must disclose the information specified in Regulation S-K Item 701(a) and (c)–(e) regarding its sale of equity securities in a transaction not registered under the Securities Act. Thus, the company must disclose:

- the date of sale and the title and amount of securities sold (Item 701(a));

- if the securities were sold for cash, the aggregate offering price and the aggregate underwriting discounts or commissions (Item 701(c));

- if sold other than for cash, the nature of the transaction and the nature and aggregate amount of consideration received (Item 701(c));

- the section of the Securities Act or SEC rule under which exemption from registration was claimed and a brief statement of the facts relied on to make the exemption available (Item 701(d));

- the terms of conversion or exercise when the securities sold are convertible or exchangeable into equity securities or are warrants or options representing equity securities (Item 701(e)).

The SEC believes that more timely disclosure of such issuances will benefit investors due to the fact that unregistered sales of equity securities can have a significant effect on the capital structure of the company and the security holdings of existing investors. Issuances not reported on Form 8-K, however, will continue to be required to be reported in periodic reports.

A company has no obligation to disclose information under Item 3.02 until the company enters into an agreement enforceable against it, whether or not subject to conditions, under which the equity securities are to be sold. If there is no such agreement, the company must provide the disclosure within four business days after the occurrence of the closing or settlement of the transaction or arrangement under which the equity securities are sold.

De Minimis Exception

In a de minimus amelioration of the disclosure mandate, Item 3.02(b) provides that no Form 8-K need be filed if the equity securities sold in the aggregate since the company's last report filed under the item or the last periodic report, whichever is more recent, constitute less than 1% of its outstanding securities of that class.

Small Businesses

With regard to the small business issuer, no Form 8-K need be filed if the equity securities sold in the aggregate since the issuer's last report filed under the item or the last periodic report, whichever is more recent, constitute less than 5% of its outstanding securities of that class.

For purposes of Item 3.02, the "number of shares outstanding" refers to the actual number of shares of equity securities of the class outstanding and does not include outstanding securities convertible into or exchangeable for such equity securities. (See Instruction 1 to Item 3.01.)

¶ 114 Modifications to Shareholder Rights

Another item imported into Form 8-K from periodic reports is Item 3.03, which requires disclosure of material modifications to shareholder rights and a brief description of the general effect of the modification on those rights. The substance of the disclosure is the same as previously required by Items 2(a) and (b) of Forms 10-Q and 10-QSB.

Working capital restrictions and other limitations on the payment of dividends must be reported under Item 3.03. (See Instruction 1 to Item 3.03.)

Once a company has reported a material modification to the rights of its shareholders on Form 8-K, the company need not make any duplicative disclosure about the modification in any of its subsequently filed periodic reports. (See General Instruction B.3 to Form 8-K.)

Accountants and Financial Statements

¶ 115 Change in Accountants

Item 4.01 is substantively identical to former Item 4 of Form 8-K, requiring disclosure of the resignation, dismissal or engagement of an independent accountant. The only revision made to the substantive requirements of former Item 4 was to delete the phrase "and the related instructions to Item 304" since a company routinely needs to consider and comply with the instructions to all disclosure items.

Thus, the information required by Item 304 of Regulation S-K must be disclosed if an independent accountant engaged as the principal accountant to audit the company's financial statements, or an independent accountant on whom the principal accountant expressed reliance in its report regarding a significant subsidiary, resigns or is dismissed.

Similar disclosure is required if a new independent accountant has been engaged as either the principal accountant to audit the financial statements or as an independent accountant on whom the principal accountant is expected to express reliance in its report regarding a significant subsidiary.

Note that the resignation or dismissal of an independent accountant is a reportable event separate from the engagement of a new independent accountant. (See Instruction to Item 4.01.) Thus, on some occasions, two reports on Form 8-K are required for a single change in accountants: (1) on the resignation or dismissal of the former accountant; and (2) when the new accountant is engaged. However, information required in the second Form 8-K in such situations need not be provided to the extent that it has been reported previously in the first Form 8-K. (See Instruction to Item 4.01.)

¶ 116 Non-Reliance on Financial Statements or Audit

New Item 4.02 requires a company to file a Form 8-K if and when its directors or authorized officers conclude that any of the company's previously issued financial statements covering one or more years or interim periods no longer should be relied on because of an error in those financial statements. Specifically, the company must disclose:

- the date of the conclusion regarding the non-reliance and an identification of the financial statements and years or periods covered that should no longer be relied on;
- a brief description of the facts underlying the conclusion to the extent known to the company at the time of filing; and
- a statement of whether the audit committee, or the board in the absence of an audit committee, or authorized officers, discussed with the company's independent accountant the subject matter giving rise to the conclusion.

With regard to the requirement that the company disclose a brief description of the facts underlying the conclusion to the extent known to it at the time of filing, the SEC has noted that the company may voluntarily file an amendment to the previously filed Form 8-K regarding any changes to the facts underlying the conclusion.

Note that there is no requirement for the company to disclose its plan to address the issue. This is because the SEC agreed with concerns that, within the short Form 8-K filing deadline, the company may not have sufficient time to complete its analysis regarding the impact of the error on the company's financial statements, which could require discussions with numerous parties.

Notice from Accountant

If the company is advised by, or receives notice from, its independent accountant that disclosure should be made or action should be taken to prevent future reliance on a previously issued audit report or completed interim review related to previously issued financial statements, it must disclose the following information:

- The date on which the company was so advised or notified;
- Identification of the financial statements that should no longer be relied on;

- A brief description of the information provided by the accountant; and

- A statement of whether the audit committee, or the board in the absence of an audit committee, or authorized officers, discussed with the independent accountant the subject matter giving rise to the notice.

In addition, if the company receives such advice or notice from its independent accountant, the company must provide the independent accountant with a copy of the disclosures it is making under Item 4.02(b) no later than the same day it files these disclosures with the SEC.

The company also must request the independent accountant to furnish to the company as promptly as possible a letter addressed to the SEC stating whether the accountant agrees with the statements made by the company and, if not, stating the respects in which it does not agree. The company must then amend its previously filed Form 8-K by filing the independent accountant's letter as an exhibit to the filed Form 8-K within two business days of the company's receipt of the letter.

Corporate Governance and Management

¶ 117 Changes in Control

Item 5.01 on changes in control of the company is substantively the same as prior Item 1 of Form 8-K. The SEC has streamlined the disclosure by, for example, breaking out lists and rearranging the requirements set forth in the item. If a change in control of the company has occurred, the following information must be disclosed:

- The identity of the person(s) who acquired control;

- The date and a description of the transaction(s) that resulted in the change in control;

- The basis of the control, including the percentage of voting securities of the company now beneficially owned directly or indirectly by the person(s) who acquired control;

- The amount of the consideration used;

- The source of funds used, unless all or any part of the consideration used is a loan made in the ordinary course of business by a bank, in which case the identity of the bank may be omitted provided a request for confidentiality and report states that the identity of the bank has been so omitted and filed separately with the SEC;

- The identity of the person(s) from whom control was assumed; and

- Any arrangements or understandings among members of both the former and new control groups and their associates with respect to election of directors or other matters.

In addition, the company must describe any known arrangements the operation of which may later result in a change of control of the company, including any pledge of company securities. (See Item 5.01(b), which mandates that information required by Regulation S-K Item 403(c) must be furnished.)

¶ 118 Events Concerning Directors and Principal Officers

Item 5.02 requires disclosure of certain events concerning directors and principal officers. Under Item 5.02(a), if a director has resigned or refuses to stand for re-election to the board because of a disagreement with the company, known to an executive officer, on any matter relating to corporate operations, policies or practices, or if a director has been removed for cause from the board, the company must disclose:

- the date of the director's resignation, refusal to stand for re-election or removal;

- any positions held by the director on any board committee at the time of the director's resignation, refusal to stand for re-election or removal; and

- a brief description of the circumstances representing the disagreement that management believes caused, in whole or in part, the director's resignation, refusal to stand for re-election or removal.

The inclusion of the requirement that the disagreement be known to a company executive officer reinforces the fact that the company must be aware that the director departed because of a disagreement. The term "executive officer" is defined in Exchange Act Rule 3b-7.

Exhibits

In addition, if directors furnish the company with any written correspondence concerning the circumstances surrounding their resignation, refusal or removal, the company must file a copy of the correspondence as an exhibit to the report on Form 8-K regardless of whether the director requests that the company take such action. The company must also:

- provide the director with a copy of the disclosures it is making in response to this item no later than the day that the company files the disclosures with the SEC;

- provide directors with the opportunity to furnish a letter addressed to the company as promptly as possible stating whether they agree with the company's disclosures in response to this item and, if not, the respects in which they do not agree; and

- file any letter it receives from the director with the Commission as an exhibit by amendment to the previously filed Form 8-K within two business days after receipt by the company.

Officer's Retirement, Resignation or Termination

Companies must also disclose the fact that a principal corporate officer has retired, resigned, or been terminated, as well as the date that event occurred. (Item 5.02(b).) The officers covered by this requirement are the company's principal executive officer, president, principal financial officer, principal accounting officer, principal operating officer or any person performing similar functions. The reason for the officer's departure need not be disclosed.

Item 5.02(b) also requires disclosure when a director retires, resigns, is removed or declines to stand for re-election and the company is not required to provide disclosure under Item 5.02(a).

Note an important difference between disclosure under this item and disclosure about a director's departure because of a disagreement under Item 5.02(a), which is that if an officer resigns, is terminated or reassigned, as the result of a disagreement with the company, the company would not be obligated to disclose the reasons for, or seek the officer's explanation of, the departure as it would be if a director departed under similar circumstances.

The SEC believes that the nature of the relationship between a director and the company's shareholders is sufficiently different to justify the expanded procedures for directors. The function of directors is to oversee the company for the shareholders to whom they are directly answerable. (See "proposing" Release No. 34-46084.)

Appointment/Election of Officers and Directors

If a new principal officer is appointed, the company must disclose the officer's name and position, the date of the appointment, information regarding the background of the officer and certain related transactions with the company, and also provide a brief description of the material terms of any employment agreement between the company and the officer. (See Item 5.02(c).)

A company can delay disclosure of a new officer's appointment until the day on which the company first makes public announcement of the appointment if the company intends to make a public announcement of the appointment other than by means of a report on Form 8-K. (See Instruction to Item 5.01(c).)

This provision is designed to give companies time to make proper introductions within the organization before publicly announcing such appointments and thereby facilitate a smooth transition of authority.

Similarly, if a new director is elected to the board, except by shareholder vote at an annual or special meeting, a company must disclose the new director's name, the election date, a brief description of any arrangement or understanding pursuant to which the new director was selected as a director, any committees to which the new director has been, or at the time of the disclosure is expected to be, named, and information regarding certain related transactions between the new director and the company. (See Item 5.02(d).)

To the extent that information regarding an employment contract of a newly-appointed executive officer, or the board committee or related party transaction information associated with a newly-elected director, is not determined or is unavailable at the time of the required Form 8-K filing, a company must include a statement to this effect in the filing and then must file an amendment to the filing containing the information within four business days after the information is determined or becomes available. (See Instruction 2 to Item 5.02.)

Exemption for Subsidiaries

A company that is a wholly-owned subsidiary of a reporting company is excluded from the reporting requirements of Item 5.02 pursuant to Instruction 2.

¶ 119 Articles or Bylaws Amendment; Fiscal Year Change

Item 5.03 requires disclosure of amendments to a company's charter or bylaws, as well as changes to its fiscal year. Under Item 5.03(a), a company must disclose any amendment to its articles of incorporation or bylaws if the company did not propose the amendment in a previously filed proxy statement or information statement. The company must disclose the effective date of the amendment and a description of the provision adopted or changed by amendment and, if applicable, the previous provision. (See Item 5.03(a).)

The SEC intended the provision to ensure that shareholders are kept apprised of changes to these documents. The item presumes that any amendment that is subject to shareholder approval will be adequately disclosed in the company's proxy statement.

Under Item 5.02(b), if the company determines to change the fiscal year from that used in its most recent SEC filing by means other than a submission to shareholder vote, or by an amendment to its articles of incorporation or bylaws, the company must state the date of that determination, the date of the new fiscal year end, and the form on which the report covering the transition period will be filed.

Item 5.03 is limited to companies with a class of equity securities registered under Exchange Act Section 12. The limitation reflects the fact that companies with no equity securities registered under the Exchange Act are typically debt issuers, and the rights of holders of such securities are reflected in the debt documents and changes to those rights would typically be reflected under Item 3.03.

Regulation S-K Item 601 requires a company to file a complete copy of its articles of incorporation or bylaws as amended. Thus, if an amendment to the articles or bylaws is reported on Form 8-K, the company need only file the text of the amendment as an exhibit to the Form 8-K filing. If it does so, it must file the restated articles of incorporation or bylaws as an exhibit to its next periodic report. (See Instruction to Item 5.03.)

The SEC recognizes that a company potentially would have to report changes to its articles and bylaws that affect the rights of shareholders under both this item and Item 3.03, "Material Modification to Rights of Security Holders." However, General Instruction D to Form 8-K states that a company need only file one report listing all relevant item numbers. Therefore, the company could file a single Form 8-K and include the disclosure in a single place under the captions for both items. (See Release No. 34-46084.)

¶ 120 Suspension of Benefit Plan Trading

Item 5.04, redesignated from former Item 11, requires disclosure concerning the temporary suspension of trading under a company's employee benefit plan during a blackout period.

Sarbanes-Oxley Act Section 306(a) prohibits any director or executive officer from trading in company stock during a pension plan blackout period that temporarily prevents plan participants from engaging in stock transactions through their plan accounts, if the directors or executive officers acquired the stock in connection with their service or employment. Further, a company must provide timely notice to its directors and executive officers, and to the SEC, of the imposition of a blackout period triggering the trading prohibition. (See Section 306(a)(6).)

The SEC believes that Form 8-K is an appropriate vehicle for ensuring both timely notice to the Commission and widespread dissemination of information of a blackout period triggering the Section 306(a) trading prohibition. (See Release No. 34-47225.)

The due date for the Form 8-K filing under Item 5.04 is generally four business days after the company receives notice of the impending blackout period from the benefit plan administrator, as required by ERISA. If the notice is not received by the company, the Form 8-K filing must be on the same date by which the company transmits a timely notice to the affected officer or director within the time period set forth in SEC Regulation BTR.

The company must provide the information specified in Rule 104(b) of Regulation BTR and, if applicable, the date it received the notice required by ERISA. Pursuant to SEC Rule 104(b), the following information must be provided:

- The reason or reasons for the blackout period;

- A description of the plan transactions to be suspended during, or otherwise affected by, the blackout period;

- A description of the class of equity securities subject to the blackout period;

- The length of the blackout period by reference to the actual or expected beginning date and ending date of the blackout period or the calendar week during which the period is expected to begin and the calendar week during which it is expected to end.

- The name, address and telephone number of the person designated by the issuer to respond to inquiries about the blackout period, or, in the absence of such a designation, the issuer's human resources director or person performing equivalent functions.

Change in Blackout Period Dates

SEC rules provide that, if there is a subsequent change in the beginning or ending dates of the blackout period, the company must provide directors and executive officers with an updated notice explaining the reasons for the change in the date or dates and identifying all material changes in the information contained in the prior notice. The updated notice must be provided as soon as reasonably practicable, unless such notice in advance of the termination of a blackout period is impracticable. (See Rule 104(b)(2)(iii) of Regulation BTR.)

Item 5.04(b) requires that, on the same day that the company transmits a timely updated notice to an affected officer or director, it must provide a Form 8-K containing the updated beginning or ending dates of the blackout period, explaining the reasons for the change in the date or dates, and identifying all material changes in the information contained in the prior report. (See also Rule 104(b)(3)(iii) of Regulation BTR.)

¶ 121 Ethics Code Amendment or Waiver

Item 5.05 dealing with disclosure about the company's code of ethics is essentially the same as previous Item 10, which was adopted as part of the implementation of the Sarbanes-Oxley Act. Section 406(b) of the Act directed the SEC to require a company to make immediate disclosure on Form 8-K or via Internet dissemination of any change to, or waiver from, the company's code of ethics for its senior financial officers. Earlier, in Release No. 34-47235, the SEC adopted Item 10 of Form 8-K, which the overall comprehensive reform has renumbered as Item 5.05.

Under Item 5.05, the company must briefly describe the date and nature of any amendment to its ethics code that applies to its principal executive officer, principal financial officer, principal accounting officer or controller, or persons performing similar functions and that relates to any elements of the code of ethics definition found in Regulation S-K Item 406(b). Under Item 406(b), the term "code of ethics" means written standards that are reasonably designed to deter wrongdoing and to promote:

- Honest and ethical conduct, including the ethical handling of actual or apparent conflicts of interest between personal and professional relationships;
- Full, fair, accurate, timely, and understandable disclosure in reports and documents that a company files with, or submits to, the Commission and in other public communications made by the company;
- Compliance with applicable governmental laws, rules and regulations;
- The prompt internal reporting of violations of the code to an appropriate person or persons identified in the code; and
- Accountability for adherence to the code.

Note that a company need not disclose technical, administrative or other non-substantive amendments to the code of ethics. (See Instruction 1 to Item 5.05.)

Waivers from Ethics Code

If the company has granted a waiver, including an implicit waiver, from an ethics code provision to one of the specified senior officers, it must disclose: (1) the nature of the waiver; (2) the name of the person who received the waiver; and (3) the date of the waiver. Note that only amendments or waivers relating to the specified elements of the code of ethics and the specified officers must be disclosed.

This clarification is intended to allow and encourage companies to retain broad-based business codes. For example, if a company has a code of ethics that applies to its directors, as well as its principal executive officer and senior financial officers, an amendment to a provision affecting only directors would not require Form 8-K or Internet disclosure. (See Release No. 34-47235.)

A company choosing to provide the required disclosure on Form 8-K must do so within four business days after it amends its ethics code or grants a waiver.

As an alternative to reporting this information on Form 8-K, a company may use its Internet website as a method of disseminating this disclosure, but only if it previously has disclosed in its most recently filed annual report the company's: (1) intention to disclose these events on its Internet website; and (2) Internet website address. If a company elects to disclose this information on its website, it must do so within the same four-business day period as required for a Form 8-K that includes this type of disclosure.

In addition, a company electing to provide disclosure in this manner must make the disclosure available on its website for at least 12 months after it initially posts the disclosure. Although a company may remove information from its website after the 12-month posting period, the company must retain this disclosure for a period of not less than five years and make it available to the Commission or its staff upon request. (See Item 5.05(c).)

Definitions

Item 5.05 defines "waiver" to mean the approval by the company of a material departure from a provision of the code of ethics. The term "implicit waiver" means the company's failure to take action within a reasonable period of time regarding a material departure from a provision of the code of ethics that has been made known to a company executive officer, as defined in Exchange Act Rule 3b-7.

Other Matters

¶ 122 Regulation FD

Item 7.01 provides for Form 8-K disclosure of information that the company elects to disclose under Regulation FD. Alternatively, the company may file a report under Item 8.01 to satisfy the disclosure mandate of Regulation FD.

Regulation FD (17 CFR §§243.100 et seq.) is a company disclosure regime that addresses selective disclosure. It provides that when a company discloses material non-public information to securities market professionals, or company shareholders who may well trade on the basis of such information, the company must make public disclosure of that information.

The SEC provides great flexibility under Regulation FD to allow companies to select the most appropriate means to satisfy the disclosure requirement. Companies can file or furnish a Form 8-K or disseminate information through another method of disclosure that is reasonably designed to provide broad, non-exclusionary distribution of information to the public.

The time period for filing or furnishing a Form 8-K report satisfying the mandate of Regulation FD is not the generally applicable four business days. Rather, reference must be made to Regulation FD for the appropriate filing deadline. (See General Instruction B.1 to Form 8-K.)

Under Regulation FD, the timing of the required public disclosure depends on whether the company has made an intentional selective disclosure or an non-intentional selective disclosure. (See Rule 101(a).) For an intentional selective disclosure, the company must publicly disclose the same information simultaneously. A selective disclosure is intentional when the company or the person acting on its behalf making the disclosure either knows or is reckless in not knowing that the information is both material and non-public.

For a non-intentional disclosure, the company must make public disclosure promptly. Regulation FD defines "promptly" to mean as soon as reasonably practicable after a senior company official learns that there has been a non-intentional disclosure of information that the official knows or is reckless in not knowing is both material and non-public. The regulation further states that "promptly" can in no event be the later of 24 hours or the commencement of the next day's trading on the New York Stock Exchange.

The definition recognizes that sometimes non-intentional selective disclosures will arise close to or over a weekend or holiday. Thus, the rules provide for an outer boundary for prompt disclosure. For example, if a non-intentional selective disclosure is discovered after the close of trading on Friday, the outer boundary for making public disclosure is the beginning of trading on the NYSE on Monday.

In addition, the 24-hour period takes into account a company's potential difficulty in making the disclosure any sooner due to the need to marshal all the information necessary and reach the appropriate personnel. In other cases, however, the company may well be able to make public disclosure before the maximum allowable 24-hour disclosure period. In such cases, the requirement to disclose as soon as reasonably practicable means that the company should act sooner than 24 hours.

Filing or furnishing

If the company chooses to file the required Regulation FD disclosure on Form 8-K under Item 8.01, the information will be subject to the liabilities of Section 18 of the Exchange Act, and will also be subject to automatic incorporation by reference into the company's Securities Act registration statements.

If a company chooses instead to furnish the information under Item 7.01, it will not be deemed to be filed for purposes of Section 18 unless the company specifically states that the information is to be considered filed or incorporates it by reference into a filing under the 1933 Act or 1934 Act, such as a proxy statement or registration statement. (See General Instruction B.2 to Form 8-K.)

Exhibits

Similarly, if a report on Form 8-K contains disclosures under Item 7.01, whether or not the report contains disclosures regarding other items, all exhibits to that report relating to Item 7.01 will be deemed furnished, and not filed, unless the company specifies exhibits, or portions of exhibits, that are intended to be deemed filed rather than furnished. (See General Instruction B.2 to Form 8-K.)

Admission of Materiality

Filing or furnishing information on Form 8-K solely to satisfy Regulation FD will not, by itself, be deemed an admission as to the materiality of the information. (See General Instruction B.6 to Form 8-K.)

¶ 123 Voluntary Disclosure of Other Events

At its option, the company may disclose under Item 8.01 any events with respect to which information is not otherwise called for by Form 8-K that the company deems important to shareholders. There is no filing deadline under this provision.

Also at its option, the company may file a report disclosing the non-public information required by Regulation FD. (See ¶ 122 for additional discussion of using Form 8-K to satisfy Regulation FD disclosure requirements.)

¶ 124 Safe Harbor

The SEC has adopted a new limited safe harbor from public and private claims under Exchange Act antifraud provisions, particularly Rule 10b-5, for a failure to timely file a Form 8-K for those disclosure items that may require management to quickly assess the materiality of an event or to determine whether a disclosure obligation has been triggered. The safe harbor applies to the following items:

- Item 1.01 Entry into a Material Definitive Agreement

- Item 1.02 Termination of a Material Definitive Agreement

- Item 2.03 Creation of a Direct Financial Obligation or an Obligation under an Off-Balance Sheet Arrangement

- Item 2.04 Triggering Events that Accelerate or Increase a Direct Financial Obligation under an Off-Balance Sheet Arrangement

- Item 2.05 Costs Associated with Exit or Disposal Activities

- Item 2.06 Material Impairments

- Item 4.02(a) Non-Reliance on Previously Issued Financial Statements or a Related Audit Report or Completed Interim Review (in the case where a company makes the determination and does not receive a notice described in Item 4.02(b) from its accountant)

The safe harbor for these items states that no failure to file a report on Form 8-K that is required solely pursuant to the provisions of Form 8-K will be deemed to be a violation of Rule 10b-5.

Note that the safe harbor only applies to a failure to file a report on Form 8-K. Thus, material misstatements or omissions in a Form 8-K will continue to be subject to Rule 10b-5 liability. In addition, if the company has a duty to disclose information that is the subject of any of the Form 8-K items covered by the safe harbor for any reason apart from the Form 8-K requirement, the safe harbor will not provide protection from Rule 10b-5 that may arise from the company's failure to satisfy such separate disclosure obligation.

For example, if a company publicly sells or repurchases its own securities while in possession of material non-public information that is required to be disclosed in a Form 8-K report pursuant to an item that is covered by the safe harbor, the safe harbor will not protect the company from antifraud rule liability regarding its separate disclosure obligation pursuant to the offering of securities.

The SEC amended Forms 10-Q and 10-K to provide that the new safe harbor extends only until the due date of the periodic report of the company for the relevant period in which the Form 8-K was not timely filed. Thus, for example, if an event occurs that required the filing of a Form 8-K during a particular quarter, but the company fails to make the required timely disclosure, the company must provide the disclosure prescribed by the relevant Form 8-K item in its Form 10-Q filed for the quarter during which that event occurred. Failure to make such disclosure in the periodic report will subject a company to potential liability under the antifraud rule, in addition to the potential liability under Section 13(a) or 15(d).

In response to commenters who feared that failure to timely file all required Form 8-K reports could disqualify companies from being eligible to use Securities Act Form S-2 and S-3 registration statements, the SEC revised instructions to those forms to indicate that companies failing to timely file 8-K reports required by the disclosure items covered by the safe harbor will not lose their eligibility to use Form S-2 and S-3.

The SEC's carve-out of the same list of items as covered by the antifraud rule safe harbor, in addition to providing a beneficial measure of regulatory consistency, recognizes that the significant burden resulting from a company's sudden loss of eligibility to use Form S-2 or S-3 under these circumstances could be a disproportionately large negative consequence of an untimely Form 8-K filing.

Moreover, similar to the reasoning behind the safe harbor, the carve-out is based on the SEC's belief that these items may require management to make rapid materiality and similar judgments within the compressed Form 8-K filing timeframe.

The SEC cautioned, however, that a company must be current in its Form 8-K filings with respect to the covered items at the actual time of a Form S-2 or S-3 filing. Thus, a company must have filed the disclosure required by any of these Form 8-K items on or before the date that it files a Form S-2 or Form S-3 registration statement to satisfy the eligibility requirements of these forms.

For example, if a company fails to file a Form 8-K regarding the entry into a material definitive agreement, the company must include the disclosure required by Item 1.01 in the periodic report filed for the period in which the company failed to timely file the Form 8-K.

This disclosure must be made before the company files a later Form S-3 registration statement (assuming that the registration statement is filed within 12 months of the missed Form 8-K) in order for the company to be current in its periodic reports and thus eligible to use Form S-3.

If the company fails to include such disclosure in its quarterly report or annual report, as applicable, the company must amend the report to include the Item 1.01 information before filing the Form S-3 registration statement.

With respect to the other Form 8-K items that were not carved out, a company's failure to timely file Form 8-K pursuant to any of these items will result in a loss of Form S-2 or S-3 eligibility for the 12 months following the Form 8-K due date. Many of these items are currently required Form 8-K disclosure items and are thus familiar to companies, while the other new Form 8-K items not included above generally do not require the same degree of analysis. For example, if a company fails to timely file an Item 3.01 Form 8-K regarding a delisting notice received from a national securities association, the company would be ineligible to use Form S-2 or S-3 for the next 12 months.

Rule 144

A company's failure to timely file a Form 8-K report would not affect a shareholder's ability to rely on Rule 144 to resell securities. Rule 144 eligibility is conditioned on, among other things, the availability of current public information about the company.

Because of the significant burden that would be placed on selling shareholders if eligibility to rely on Rule 144 were conditioned on a company's satisfaction of the new Form 8-K requirements, the SEC amended the rule to clarify that a company need not have filed all required Form 8-K reports during the 12 months preceding a sale of securities pursuant to Rule 144 to satisfy its current public information condition.

As required by Rule 144(h), however, shareholders will continue to be required to represent that they do not have inside information.

Regulation FD

Although Item 7.01 dealing with Regulation FD disclosures did not receive a Form 8-K safe harbor, note that it is already subject to a safe harbor from Rule 10b-5. Similarly, because Item 8.01 dealing with other events is designated for voluntary filings, it does not, by itself, impose a duty to disclose for purposes of Rule 10b-5.

CHAPTER 2

CEO/CFO CERTIFICATION

¶ 201 Introduction

Signed into law on July 30, 2002, the Sarbanes-Oxley Act of 2002 required the SEC to adopt rules under which the principal corporate executive officer or officers and the principal financial officer or officers, or persons providing similar functions, each must certify the information contained in the company's quarterly and annual reports. Section 302 of the Act also requires these officers to certify that: they are responsible for establishing, maintaining and regularly evaluating the effectiveness of the company's internal controls; they have made certain disclosures to the company's auditors and the audit committee about the internal controls; and they have included information in the company's quarterly and annual reports about their evaluation and whether there have been significant changes in the internal controls

Effective August 29, 2002, the SEC adopted the certification rules mandated by Sarbanes-Oxley. (See Release No. 34-46427 (SEC 2002), reproduced at ¶ 1101 et seq.) The new rules cover the more expansive reach of Section 302 and contain additional collection of information requirements. The purpose of the certification and disclosure controls and procedures requirements embodied in the new rules is to ensure that the information that is collected and disclosed in Exchange Act reports is complete and accurate. Consequently, the SEC envisions that the senior officer certification, as well as the periodic evaluations of internal reporting systems, required by the rules will become part of the process in which companies engage in order to comply with Exchange Act reporting requirements.

The mandate to certify financial reports had its genesis in a concern over whether senior corporate officials were devoting sufficient attention to the preparation of their companies' quarterly and annual reports and to the internal procedures that generate the data from which they are prepared. A related concern was that investor confidence suffered because of a real or perceived absence of such participation. The certification statute and rules are based on a belief that it is important both to the quality of disclosure, and hence to investor confidence, that senior executives provide assurance that they have reviewed and evaluated the information contained in the quarterly and annual reports.

Background

The Sarbanes-Oxley Act of 2002 is intended to address systemic and structural weaknesses affecting the capital markets that have been revealed in recent months and that show failures of audit effectiveness and a breakdown in corporate financial and broker-dealer responsibility. The legislation will fundamentally change the way public companies do business and how the accounting profession performs its statutorily required audit function.

The Act establishes a comprehensive framework to modernize and reform the oversight of public company auditing, improve quality and transparency in financial reporting by those companies, and strengthen the independence of auditors. It promotes competition among service providers, enhances accurate investor decisionmaking throughout the capital markets, and seeks to correct shortcomings that have threatened the reputation of those markets for integrity.

In further response to recent corporate failures, Title III of the Act makes a number of changes to improve the responsibility of public companies for their financial disclosures. At the center of this initiative is Section 302 (reproduced at ¶ 1101), which requires that senior corporate officers certify the material accuracy and fair presentation of their company's financial statements.

¶ 202 Sarbanes-Oxley Provisions

Congress believes that management should be held responsible for the financial representations of their companies. The Act therefore clearly establishes that CEOs and CFOs are responsible for the presentation of material in their company's financial reports. Under one of the recommendations put forward by the President in March 2002, CEOs would personally attest each quarter that the financial statements and company disclosures accurately and fairly disclose the information of which the CEO is aware that a reasonable investor should have to make an informed investment decision.

In effect, the Act adopts this proposal by requiring CEOs and CFOs to certify, in periodic reports containing financial statements filed with the Commission, the appropriateness of financial statements and disclosures contained therein, and that those financials and disclosures fairly present the company's operations and financial condition. These provisions reflect concern regarding the reliability of companies' audited financial statements.

Foreign reincorporations will have no effect on the certification required from CEOs and CFOs. It will still be required after the transfer of a company's domicile from inside the U.S. to outside the U.S.

More specifically, the Act requires the principal executive officer and the principal financial officer to certify in each annual or quarterly report that:

- the signing officer has reviewed the report;
- based on the officer's knowledge, the report does not contain any untrue statement of a material fact or omit to state a material fact necessary in order to make the statements made, in light of the circumstances under which such statements were made, not misleading;
- based on such officer's knowledge, the financial statements, and other financial information included in the report, fairly present in all material respects the financial condition and results of operations of the issuer as of, and for, the periods presented in the report;
- the signing officers are responsible for establishing and maintaining internal controls and have designed such internal controls to ensure that material information relating to the company and its consolidated subsidiaries is made known to such officers by others within those entities, particularly during the period in which the periodic reports are being prepared. They must also have evaluated the effectiveness of the company's internal controls as of a date within 90 days prior to the report and presented their conclusions about the effectiveness of their internal controls based on their evaluation as of that date.
- the signing officers have disclosed to the company's auditors and the audit committee all significant deficiencies in the design or operation of internal controls that could adversely affect the company's ability to record, process, summarize, and report financial data and have identified for the auditors any material weaknesses in internal controls; and any fraud, whether or not material, that involves management or other employees who have a significant role in the issuer's internal controls; and
- the signing officers have indicated in the report whether or not there were significant changes in internal controls or in other factors that could significantly affect internal controls subsequent to the date of their evaluation, including any corrective actions with regard to significant deficiencies and material weaknesses.

Regarding statutory certification requirements, Congress recognizes that results presented in financial statements often necessarily require accompanying disclosures in order to apprise investors of the company's true financial condition and results of operations. The supplemental information contained in these additional disclosures increases transparency for investors. Thus, the signing officers must certify that the financial statements together with the disclosures contained in the periodic report, taken as a whole, are appropriate and fairly represent, in all material respects, the company's operations and financial condition. (See remarks of Sen. Mike Enzi, Cong. Rec., July 25, 2002, p. S7356.)

Criminal Penalties

In Section 906 of the Act (reproduced at ¶ 1102), Congress provides that the periodic reports must be accompanied by a written statement by the company's chief executive officer and chief financial officer (or equivalent thereof) certifying that information contained in the periodic report fairly presents, in all material respects, the company's financial condition and results of operations. A person certifying a statement knowing that the periodic report accompanying the statement does not comport with all the requirements set forth in this section will be fined not more than $1,000,000 or imprisoned not more than 10 years, or both. In addition, willfully certifying a statement knowing that the periodic report accompanying the statement does not comport with all the requirements set forth in this section carries a fine of up to $5,000,000, or 20-years imprisonment, or both.

The Department of Justice and the SEC have jointly concluded that Section 906 does not apply to current reports filed on Form 8-K. (See Release No. 34-49424 (SEC 2004), Part II.F.5, reproduced at ¶ 2002.) The SEC was concerned that extending the statutory certifications to Form 8-K could potentially chill the disclosure by companies,

¶ 203 SEC Rulemaking

As directed under Sarbanes-Oxley Act Section 302, the SEC adopted rules implementing the Act's certification requirement. (See Release No. 33-8124 (SEC 2002), 2002 CCH Dec. ¶ 86,720, reproduced at ¶ 2101 et seq.) The rules are intended to enhance investor confidence in the quality of the information available in quarterly and annual reports filed under the Exchange Act. The SEC believes that requiring a company's principal executive and financial officers to provide the required certification will enhance investor confidence in the securities markets.

In particular, new Exchange Act Rules 13a-14 (see ¶ 1103) and 15d-14 (see ¶ 1105) require a company's principal executive officer or officers and the principal financial officer or officers, or persons performing similar functions, each to certify in each quarterly and annual report that:

- they have reviewed the report;

- based on their knowledge, the report does not contain any untrue statement of a material fact or omit to state a material fact necessary to make the statements made, in light of the circumstances under which such statements were made, not misleading with respect to the period covered by this report;

- based on their knowledge, the financial statements, and other financial information included in the report, fairly present in all material respects the financial condition, results of operations and cash flows of the company as of, and for, the periods presented in the report;

- they and the other certifying officers are responsible for establishing and maintaining disclosure controls and procedures and internal control over financial reporting and have:

- designed such disclosure controls and procedures to ensure that material information relating to the company, including its consolidated subsidiaries, is made known, particularly during the period in which this report is being prepared;

- designed such internal control over financial reporting to provide reasonable assurance regarding the reliability of financial reporting and the preparation of financial statements for external purposes in accordance with generally accepted accounting principles;

- evaluated the effectiveness of the disclosure controls and procedures and presented in this report their conclusions about the effectiveness of the disclosure controls and procedures, as of the end of the period covered by this report based on such evaluation;

- disclosed in this report any change in the internal control over financial reporting that occurred during the most recent fiscal quarter (the fourth fiscal quarter in the case of an annual report) that has materially affected, or is reasonably likely to materially affect, the internal control over financial reporting; and

- They and the other certifying officers have disclosed, based on their most recent evaluation of internal control over financial reporting, to the company's auditors and the audit committee all significant deficiencies and material weaknesses in the design or operation of internal control over financial reporting which are reasonably likely to adversely affect the company's ability to record, process, summarize and report financial information; and any fraud, whether or not material, that involves management or other employees who have a significant role in the company's internal control over financial reporting.

In addition, the SEC expects that certifying officers who become aware of a significant deficiency, material weakness or fraud requiring disclosure outside of the formal evaluation process, or after the management's most recent evaluation of internal controls, they will disclose it to the auditors and audit committee. (Release No. 33-8238.)

Note that, while the evaluation date for disclosure controls is as of the end of the period covered by the quarterly or annual report, the SEC did not specify the point at which management must evaluate changes to the company's internal controls.

Although an evaluation of the effectiveness of disclosure controls and procedures must be undertaken on a quarterly basis, the SEC expect that for purposes of disclosure by domestic companies, the traditional relationship between disclosure in annual reports and intervening quarterly reports will continue. This means that disclosure in an annual report that continues to be accurate need not be repeated.

Rather, disclosure in quarterly reports may make appropriate reference to disclosures in the most recent annual report, and where appropriate intervening quarterly reports, and disclose subsequent developments required to be disclosed in the quarterly report.

Given that the rules do not require a company to state the conclusions of the certifying officers regarding the effectiveness of the company's internal controls as of a particular date on a quarterly basis, as the company must with respect to disclosure controls, the SEC felt it unnecessary to specify a date for the quarterly evaluation of changes in internal control over financial reporting. The rules do not require that the evaluation take place on the last day of the period, but that the statement of effectiveness of the disclosure controls and internal controls be as of the end of the period.

Note also that a company must disclose any change in its internal controls that occurred during the fiscal quarter covered by the quarterly report, or the last fiscal quarter in the case of an annual report, that has materially affected, or is reasonably likely to materially affect, the company's internal controls. Similarly, the management of a foreign private issuer must disclose in the annual report any change in the internal controls that occurred during the period covered by the annual report and that materially affected, or is reasonably likely to affect, this internal control.

Although SEC rules do not explicitly require the company to disclose the reasons for any change that occurred during a fiscal quarter, or to otherwise elaborate about the change, a company will have to determine, on a facts and circumstances basis, whether the reasons for the change, or other information about the circumstances surrounding the change, constitute material information necessary to make the disclosure about the change not misleading.

Signature and Execution

The principal executive and financial officers must sign the certification. To further emphasize the importance of the required certification, a principal executive officer or principal financial officer is not permitted to have the certification signed on his or her behalf pursuant to a power of attorney or other form of confirming authority.

Co-principal executive officers or co-principal financial officers should each execute separate certifications. (See Division of Corporation Finance FAQ of Nov. 8, 2002.)

If the same individual is both the principal executive officer and principal financial officer, the individual may provide one certification and provide both titles underneath the signature.

If a CEO resigned after the end of the quarter but before the filing of the upcoming Form 10-Q, and the company appointed a new CEO prior to the filing, the new CEO signs the certification because he or she is the principal executive officer at the time of the filing. (See Division of Corporation Finance FAQ of Nov. 8, 2002.)

If a company has a CEO who is resigning at the end of the year and is no longer performing the function of CEO although still employed, and in the interim another individual is performing the function of CEO, the person performing the function of CEO at the time of the filing should provide the certification. If it is not the person with the title of CEO, the company should disclose in the filing that the other individual is performing that function. (See Division of Corporation Finance FAQ of Nov. 8, 2002.)

If Section 302 certifications are not included in a Form 10-K or 10-Q filing, and an amendment will be filed to include the certifications, the amendment should include the entire filing. It cannot just include the signature pages because the certification relates to the entire Form 10-K or 10-Q filing. Further, if the amendment is not filed within the time period required for the periodic report, the periodic report will not be deemed timely for purposes of form eligibility and the company will not be deemed current until the amended periodic report containing the certification is filed. (See Division of Corporation Finance FAQ of Nov. 8, 2002.)

Internal Control Over Financial Reporting

The term "internal control over financial reporting" is defined as a process designed by, or under the supervision of, the principal executive and principal financial officers, or persons performing similar functions, and effected by the board of directors, management and other personnel, to provide reasonable assurance regarding the reliability of financial reporting and the preparation of financial statements for external purposes in accordance with generally accepted accounting principles and includes those policies and procedures that:

- Pertain to the maintenance of records that in reasonable detail accurately and fairly reflect the transactions and dispositions of company assets;

- Provide reasonable assurance that transactions are recorded as necessary to permit preparation of financial statements in accordance with generally accepted accounting principles, and that receipts and expenditures of the company are being made only in accordance with authorizations of management and directors; and

- Provide reasonable assurance regarding prevention or timely detection of unauthorized acquisition, use or disposition of the company's assets that could have a material effect on the financial statements.

The concept of reasonable assurance is built into the definition of internal control over financial reporting. This conforms to the standard contained in the internal accounting control provisions of Section 13(b)(2) of the Exchange Act and current auditing literature.

If management decides to include a discussion of reasonable assurance in the internal control report, the discussion must be presented in a manner that neither makes the disclosure in the report confusing nor renders management's assessment concerning the effectiveness of the company's internal control over financial reporting unclear. (Release No. 33-8238.)

Components of Certification

The required certification contains several statements and components. The certification statement concerning the material accuracy and completeness of the periodic reports that are covered by the statement generally mirrors the existing statutory disclosure standards for material accuracy and completeness of information contained in reports.

The component of the certification statement regarding fair presentation of financial statements and other financial information included in the report separately addresses the presentation of a company's financial disclosure, including financial statements, along with footnote disclosure, selected financial data, management's discussion and analysis of financial condition and results of operations, and other financial information in a report.

The certification will state that the overall financial disclosure fairly presents, in all material respects, the company's financial condition, results of operations and cash flows. The SEC added a specific reference to cash flows even though Section 302 does not include such because the Commission believes that it is consistent with congressional intent to include both income or loss and cash flows within the concept of fair presentation of the results of operations.

It is important to note that the certification statement regarding fair presentation of financial statements is not limited to a representation that the financial statements and other financial information have been presented in accordance with generally accepted accounting principles and is not otherwise limited by reference to generally accepted accounting principles.

The SEC believes that Congress intended this statement to provide assurances that the financial information disclosed in a report, viewed in its entirety, meets a standard of overall material accuracy and completeness that is broader than financial reporting requirements under generally accepted accounting principles.

Federal courts have ruled that presenting financial information in conformity with generally accepted accounting principles may not necessarily satisfy obligations under the antifraud provisions of the federal securities laws. (See *United States v. Simon* (CA-2 1969), 1969-1970 CCH Dec. ¶ 92,511.)

In the SEC's view, a fair presentation of a company's financial condition, results of operations and cash flows encompasses the selection of appropriate accounting policies, proper application of appropriate accounting policies, disclosure of financial information that is informative and reasonably reflects the underlying transactions and events and the inclusion of any additional disclosure necessary to provide investors with a materially accurate and complete picture of an issuer's financial condition, results of operations and cash flows.

In addition, both International Accounting Standard IAS 1, 14 and 15 and AICPA, Codification of Statements on Auditing Standards, AU 411.04 speak to the essential elements that must be considered, within the framework of generally accepted accounting principles, in evaluating whether financial statements fairly present a company's financial condition and results of operations.

According to the SEC, these statements, without being limited by reference to generally accepted accounting principles, provide guidance as to what elements should be considered in determining whether a company's financial information, taken as a whole, provides a fair presentation of its financial condition and results of operations. These elements include, without limitation, whether the accounting principles selected are appropriate in the circumstances and whether the disclosure is informative and reasonably reflects the underlying transactions and events.

Knowledge of Certifying Officers

The components of the certification statement dealing with material accuracy and fair presentation are based on the knowledge of the certifying officer. In the SEC's view, this is not meant to change the current obligations of corporate officers in connection with the discharge of their duties.

Both certification statements are made in the context of the requirements of the reports in which they are included. In particular, quarterly reports have less extensive disclosure and financial statement and footnote requirements than annual reports. The certification requirement is not intended to require expansion of quarterly reports to satisfy the requirements of annual reports. Rather, completeness of disclosure will be determined through application of standards derived from existing SEC rules, forms and interpretations.

¶ 204 Disclosure Controls and Procedures

Although Sarbanes-Oxley Act Section 302(a)(4) requires a company's principal executive and financial officers to make specific certifications regarding their responsibilities to establish and maintain internal controls, it does not directly address the company's responsibility for controls and procedures related to the company's Exchange Act reporting obligations. The SEC has adopted requirements that companies maintain sufficient procedures to provide reasonable assurances that they are able to timely collect, process and disclose the information required to be disclosed in their Exchange Act reports.

The SEC rules require companies to maintain disclosure controls and procedures in order to assist principal executive and financial officers in the discharge of their duties in making the required certifications, as well as to discharge their duties in providing accurate and complete information to shareholders. In this regard, companies must ensure that their internal communications and other procedures operate so that important information flows to the appropriate collection and disclosure points in a timely manner.

For purposes of the new rules, "disclosure controls and procedures" are defined as corporate controls and other procedures designed to ensure that information required to be disclosed in the reports filed or submitted by it under the Exchange Act is recorded, processed, summarized and reported, within the time periods specified in the SEC's rules and forms. Disclosure controls and procedures include, without limitation, controls and procedures designed to ensure that information required to be disclosed by a company in the reports that it files or submits is accumulated and communicated to management, including the principal executive and financial officers, as appropriate to allow timely decisions regarding required disclosure.

Thus, for purposes of the certification required by Section 302(a)(4) of the Act, the SEC has defined disclosure controls and procedures to incorporate a broader concept of controls and procedures designed to ensure compliance with disclosure requirements generally. This definition is included in the SEC rules and applies to the portion of the certification required by Section 302(a)(4) of the Act.

Disclosure controls and procedures have been so defined as to make it explicit that the controls contemplated by Section 302(a)(4) of the Act are intended to embody controls and procedures addressing the quality and timeliness of disclosure. The SEC also included this definition to differentiate this concept of disclosure controls and procedures from the pre-existing concept of internal controls that pertains to a company financial reporting and control of its assets, as currently embodied in Section 13(b) of the Exchange Act and as addressed in Sections 302(a)(5) and (a)(6) and Section 404 of the Act.

The rules also require the company, under the supervision of the principal executive and financial officers, to conduct an evaluation of the effectiveness of the design and operation of its disclosure controls and procedures. While the new rules do not provide detailed procedures for such an evaluation, the evaluation must, at a minimum, address the matters specified by the rules. The SEC expects that this evaluation would be carried out in a manner that would form the basis for the certification statements required by Section 302 of Sarbanes-Oxley regarding disclosure controls and procedures required by SEC rules in the quarterly and annual reports.

The periodic review and evaluation of information collection and reporting procedures required by the new rules involves a performance standard. The new rules do not mandate how companies should conduct this review and evaluation. The SEC believes that this flexibility will enable small and large entities to develop approaches for the review and evaluation that are appropriate to their individual circumstances.

For example, some companies may need to institute appropriate controls and procedures, while others may need to enhance existing informal or ad hoc controls and procedures. In any event, each company is expected to develop a process that is consistent with its business and internal management and supervisory practices.

The SEC does, however, recommend that a company create a committee with responsibility for considering the materiality of information and determining disclosure obligations on a timely basis. Officers and employees who have an interest in, and the expertise to serve on, such a committee could include the principal accounting officer (or the controller), the general counsel or other senior legal official with responsibility for disclosure matters who reports to the general counsel, the principal risk management officer, the chief investor relations officer (or an officer with equivalent responsibilities) and such other officers or employees, including individuals associated with corporate business units, as the company deems appropriate.

As is implicit in Sarbanes-Oxley Act Section 302(a)(4), such a committee would report to senior management, including the principal executive and financial officers, who bear express responsibility for designing, establishing, maintaining, reviewing and evaluating the issuer's disclosure controls and procedures.

A company that failed to maintain adequate procedures, review them and otherwise comply with the rule could be subject to Commission action for violating Exchange Act Section 13(a) even where the failure did not lead to flawed disclosure.

The new SEC rules are viewed as being entirely complementary to the objectives of Section 302. While Section 302 requires the principal executive and financial officers to make specific statements in their certifications and to take the actions satisfying the representations made in the statements as to the company's disclosure controls and procedures, it does not directly address the company's obligations with respect to these controls and procedures. The new rules are designed to ensure that a company also has a responsibility to maintain adequate disclosure controls and procedures, so that its principal executive and financial officers can supervise and review these periodic evaluations and report the results to security holders through the Exchange Act reports.

While acknowledging that mandatory requirements regarding disclosure controls and procedures may raise several issues for foreign private issuers, the SEC noted that Section 302 does not provide any exception to the certification requirement for foreign private issuers. Because the SEC believes that the maintenance of disclosure controls and procedures is an important part of satisfying the certification requirement, the agency feels that it is appropriate to require foreign private issuers to comply with the new rules with respect to the implementation of the controls

Disclosure Controls/Internal Controls Compared

There has been some confusion as to the differences between a company's disclosure controls and procedures and a company's internal control over financial reporting. The SEC defines disclosure controls and procedures to mean controls and procedures designed to ensure that information required to be disclosed is recorded, processed, summarized and reported within the time periods specified.

The definition further states that disclosure controls and procedures include, without limitation, controls and procedures designed to ensure that the information required to be disclosed is accumulated and communicated to the company's management, including its principal executive and principal financial officers, or persons performing similar functions, as appropriate to allow timely decisions regarding required disclosure.

While there is substantial overlap between a company's disclosure controls and procedures and its internal control over financial reporting, there are both some elements of disclosure controls and procedures that are not subsumed by internal control over financial reporting and some elements of internal control that are not subsumed by the definition of disclosure controls and procedures. With respect to the latter point, the broad COSO description of internal control, which includes the efficiency and effectiveness of a company's operations and the company's compliance with laws and regulations, not restricted to the federal securities laws, would not be wholly subsumed within the definition of disclosure controls and procedures.

According to the SEC, some components of internal control over financial reporting will be included in disclosure controls and procedures for all companies. In particular, disclosure controls and procedures will include those components of internal control that provide reasonable assurances that transactions are recorded as necessary to permit preparation of financial statements in accordance with GAAP.

However, in designing their disclosure controls and procedures, companies can be expected to make judgments regarding the processes on which they will rely to meet applicable requirements. In doing so, some companies might design their disclosure controls and procedures so that certain components of internal control pertaining to the accurate recording of transactions and disposition of assets or to the safeguarding of assets are not included.

For example, a company might have developed internal controls that include as a component of safeguarding of assets dual signature requirements or limitations on signature authority on checks. That company could nonetheless determine that this component is not part of disclosure controls and procedures. Thus, the SEC believes that, while there is substantial overlap between internal control and disclosure controls and procedures, many companies will design their disclosure controls and procedures so that they do not include all components of internal control over financial reporting.

The SEC rules requiring quarterly evaluations of disclosure controls and procedures and disclosure of the conclusions regarding their effectiveness, include the elements of internal control over financial reporting that are subsumed within disclosure controls and procedures.

While the evaluation is of effectiveness overall, a company's management has the ability to make judgments that evaluations, particularly quarterly evaluations, should focus on developments since the most recent evaluation, areas of weakness or continuing concern or other aspects of disclosure controls and procedures that merit attention.

The nature of the quarterly evaluations of those components of internal controls that are subsumed within disclosure controls and procedures should be informed by the purposes of disclosure controls and procedures. For example, when a component of internal control over financial reporting is subsumed within disclosure controls and procedures, even where systems testing of that component would clearly be required as part of the annual evaluation of internal controls, management could make a different determination of the appropriate nature of the evaluation of that component for purposes of a quarterly evaluation of disclosure controls and procedures.

¶ 205 Scope of Certification Requirement

Section 302(a) of Sarbanes-Oxley states that the certification requirement is to apply to each company filing periodic reports under Exchange Act Section 13(a) or 15(d). Accordingly, the rules apply to the principal executive officers and principal financial officers, or persons performing similar functions, of any company that files quarterly and annual reports with the Commission under either Section 13(a) or 15(d), including foreign private issuers, banks and savings associations, issuers of asset-backed securities and small business issuers.

The certification requirement does not apply to annual reports on Form 11-K, which is used by employee benefit plans.

Because Congress has directed the senior officers of all companies, regardless of size, to certify corporate quarterly and annual reports, the SEC reasoned it would be inconsistent with that mandate to exempt small issuers from the new rules.

In addition, the new rules are designed to achieve the objective of Section 302(b) because they apply to all companies without regard to their jurisdiction of incorporation or domicile. Section 302(b) states that the provision is not to be applied to allow any company to lessen the legal force of the certification requirement by a company that has reincorporated or engaged in any other transaction resulting in the transfer of the corporate domicile or offices from inside United States to outside the United States.

Foreign Private Issuers

Sarbanes-Oxley Act Section 302 makes no distinction between domestic and foreign issuers and, by its terms, clearly applies to foreign private issuers. The SEC rules, therefore, apply the certification requirement to the principal executive officers and principal financial officers of foreign private issuers that file reports under Exchange Act Section 13(a) or 15(d).

For purposes of the Exchange Act, a "foreign private issuer" is any foreign issuer (other than a foreign government) except an issuer meeting the following conditions: (1) more than 50% of the issuer's outstanding voting securities are directly or indirectly held of record by residents of the U.S.; and (2) the majority of the executive officers or directors are U.S. citizens or residents; or more than 50% of the assets of the issuer are located in the U.S.; or the business of the issuer is administered principally in the U.S. (See Exchange Act Rule 3b-4(c).) The new rules do not apply to foreign private issuers that furnish materials to the Commission pursuant to Exchange Act Rule 12g3-2(b).

The new rules apply the certification requirement to foreign private issuers filing annual reports on Form 20-F and Canadian issuers filing annual reports on Form 40-F under the multi-jurisdictional disclosure system. Although Form 20-F is not required to be signed by any specific executive officer of a foreign registrant, the SEC believes that it is the clear intent of Congress to require that the appropriate officers execute and submit the required certification in an annual report filed under the Exchange Act on Form 20-F or 40-F.

The management of a foreign private issuer that has Exchange Act reporting obligations must also, like its domestic counterparts, report any material changes to the internal control over financial reporting. However, because foreign private issuers are not required to file quarterly reports under Exchange Act Section 13(a) or 15(d), the rules clarify that a foreign private issuer's management need only disclose in the annual report the material changes to its internal control over financial reporting that have occurred in the period covered by the annual report.

A foreign private issuer must furnish under cover of Form 6-K material information that it makes public or is required to make public under its home country laws or the rules of its home country stock exchange or that it distributes to shareholders. While foreign private issuers may submit interim financial information under cover of Form 6-K, they do so pursuant to their home country requirements and not because of a Commission requirement to submit updated financial information for specified periods and according to specified standards. Therefore, a Form 6-K does not constitute a "periodic" report analogous to a quarterly report on Form 10-Q or 10-QSB for which certification is required.

The inclusion of foreign private issuers under the certification mandate was not without some controversy. In a letter to the SEC, a group of Germany's largest New York Stock Exchange-listed companies asked the Commission not to apply the financial certification provisions of the Sarbanes-Oxley Act to them. While supporting efforts to restore investor confidence in the integrity of the U.S. markets, the German foreign private issuers pointed out that German corporate law differs significantly from the U.S. corporate legal regime, but at the same time offers equivalent safeguards for stakeholders. Similarly, in a comment letter of Aug. 15, 2002, the American Bar Association, Section of Business Law, urged the Commission to make some accommodations for foreign private issuers.

In the tradition of extending comity, the German companies urged the SEC to exercise its broad discretion and exempt foreign private issuers from the certification requirements of Section 302 of Sarbanes-Oxley. The letter was submitted on behalf of, among others, Deutsche Telekom AG, Daimler-Chrysler AG, and Allianz AG. While noting that Section 302 appears on its face to cover foreign private issuers that file reports with the SEC, the German group contended that statutory construction and legislative history mandate the interpretation that the certification requirement was not intended to apply to foreign private issuers. They also noted that imposing the certification requirements on foreign private issuers will make U.S. public capital markets less attractive.

The ABA urged the Commission to exclude foreign private issuers from the internal procedures requirements of Section 302 included in Paragraphs (a)(4) (internal controls), (a)(5) (auditor and audit committee communications) and (a)(6) (changes to internal controls) of Section 302 of the Act, and, Rules 13a-15 and 15d-15.

Both letters cited Section 302(b), which specifically applies the certification requirement to U.S. companies that reincorporate outside the U.S. in order to evade the certification requirements. Were Section 302(a) read to apply identically to both domestic and foreign issuers, reasoned the German companies, there would have been no reason for Congress to include Section 302(b) to prevent domestic issuers from circumventing the rules.

Similarly, the bar group believes Section 302(b) contemplates that the Commission will make accommodations for foreign private issuers. Subsection (b) requires the Commission to continue to treat any domestic issuers as such even if the issuer reincorporates outside the United States. For this provision to have meaning, reasoned the group, it must be the case that Congress expected the Commission to afford different treatment to foreign private issuers that have not previously been domestic issuers.

Both letters also cited remarks by Sen. Mike Enzi during consideration of the conference bill on July 25, 2002. Sen. Enzi said, in part, that the SEC historically has permitted a company's home country to implement corporate governance standards. He added that foreign issuers are not part of the current problems being seen in the U.S. capital markets, and it was not the intent of the conferees to export U.S. standards disregarding the sovereignty of other countries as well as their regulators. (See Cong. Rec., July 25, 2002, p. S7356.)

Senator Enzi said that Sarbanes-Oxley gives the SEC wide authority to enact implementing regulations that are necessary or appropriate in the public interest. He said that the conferees intended to permit the Commission wide latitude in using its rulemaking authority to deal with technical matters such as the scope of the definitions and their applicability to foreign issuers. He encouraged the SEC to use its authority to make the act as workable as possible consistent with longstanding SEC interpretations. (See Cong. Rec., July 25, 2002, p. S7356.)

Banks and Savings Associations

The certification requirement also applies to principal executive officers and principal financial officers of banks and savings associations that file periodic reports under Exchange Act Section 13(a) or 15(d). The Act amended Exchange Act Section 12(i) to clarify that the federal banking agencies have the authority to administer and enforce various provisions of the Act, including the certification required by Section 302.

Issuer of Asset-Backed Securities

Issuers of asset-backed securities in public offerings have a reporting obligation under either Exchange Act Section 13(a) or 15(d), at least for a period of time. Asset-backed issuers also sometimes voluntarily file Exchange Act reports in order to comply with provisions in the indenture or pooling and servicing agreements. Because of the nature of asset-backed issuers, the staff of the Division of Corporation Finance has historically granted requests allowing asset-backed issuers to file modified reports under the Exchange Act.

The modified reporting structure for asset-backed issuers allows issuers or depositors to file modified annual reports on Form 10-K and to file reports tied to payments on the underlying assets in the trust. These reports include a copy of the servicing or distribution report required by the issuer's governing documents and information on the performance of the assets, payments on the asset-backed securities and any other material developments that affect the issuer. Because the reported information for asset-backed issuers differs significantly from that for other issuers, the certification requirement of Section 302 of the Act must be specifically tailored for asset-backed issuers. The new rules require asset-backed issuers to certify their reports.

The staff of the Division of Corporation Finance has provided guidance for asset-backed issuers regarding compliance with the certification requirement.

Because asset-backed issuers do not typically have a principal executive officer or principal financial officer, the staff recognizes that the signature requirements for the certifications relating to asset-backed issuers differ from those for other issuers. Thus, SEC rules will require the certification to be signed by the trustee of the trust (if the trustee signs the periodic report) or the senior officer in charge of securitization of the depositor (if the depositor signs the periodic report). Alternatively, the senior officer in charge of the servicing function of the master servicer (or entity performing equivalent functions) may sign the certificate.

¶ 206 Investment Companies

The SEC rules require investment companies to file a report with the Commission on new Form N-CSR, essentially a certified shareholder report, containing: (1) a copy of any required shareholder report; (2) additional information regarding disclosure controls and procedures; and (3) the certification required by the Sarbanes-Oxley Act.

Form N-CSR requires certified shareholder reports to contain the exact form of the certification prescribed by the form. The certification is required of each principal executive officer and financial officer, and the form of this certification parallels the form of the certification prescribed for other Exchange Act reporting forms, such as Forms 10-K and 10-Q.

The Section 302 certification must be filed as an exhibit to a report on Form N-CSR. Similarly, the Section 906 certification to accompany periodic reports containing financial statements must be filed as an exhibits.

Because the Section 906 certification requirement applies to periodic reports containing financial statements that are filed pursuant to Exchange Act Section 13(a) or 15(d), the exhibit requirement will only apply to reports on Form N-CSR filed under these sections and not to reports on Form N-CSR that are filed under the Investment Company Act only.

In addition to the signature required on the certification, the report must be signed by the company, and on behalf of the company by its principal executive officer or officers and its principal financial officer or officers. The certification requirement will also apply to amendments of certified shareholder reports on Form N-CSR. Rule 30d-1 under the Investment Company

Act designates reports on Form N-CSR as periodic reports filed with the Commission under Exchange Act Section 13(a) or 15(d).

Note that unlike other companies, the SEC does not require the evaluation by an investment company's management of the effectiveness of its disclosure controls and procedures to be as of the end of the period covered by each report on Form N-CSR. Rather, the evaluation will be within 90 days prior to the filing date of the report.

Commenters noted that requiring evaluation as of the end of the period covered by each report would have required investment company complexes that have funds with staggered fiscal year ends to perform evaluations of their disclosure controls and procedures as many as twelve times per year. They argued that requiring such frequent evaluations would be extremely costly, inefficient, and operationally disruptive, and would not provide any benefits to shareholders.

The SEC agreed that the costs of requiring investment company complexes to perform evaluations of their disclosure controls and procedures twelve times per year would outweigh the benefits to investors. The certification rules thus require an investment company complex to perform at most four such evaluations per year.

The Commission has also noted that in the case of a series fund or family of investment companies in which the disclosure controls and procedures for each fund in the series or family are the same, a single evaluation of the effectiveness of the disclosure controls for the series or family could be used in multiple certifications for the funds in the series or family, as long as the evaluation has been performed within 90 days of the report on Form N-CSR. (See Release No. IC-25914.)

¶ 207 Incorporation by Reference

As permitted under SEC rules, a company may satisfy its disclosure obligations under Part III of Forms 10-K and 10-KSB by incorporating the required information by reference from its definitive proxy or information statement, if that statement involves the election of directors and is filed not later than 120 days after the end of the fiscal year covered by the annual report. For purposes of certifying that the report does not contain any untrue statement of a material fact or omit to state a necessary material fact, the certification in the annual report on Form 10-K or 10-KSB would be considered to cover the Part III information in a registrant's proxy or information statement as and when filed.

¶ 208 Location of Certification

Companies must file the certifications required by Sarbanes-Oxley Act Section 302 as an exhibit to the periodic reports to which they relate. Placing the certifications in the "Exhibits" section rather than in the text of quarterly and annual reports is designed to enhance the ability of investors and the SEC staff to verify that the certifications have, in fact, been submitted with the Exchange Act reports to which they relate and to review the contents of the certifications to ensure compliance.

Similarly, the Section 906 certifications must accompany periodic reports containing financial statements as exhibits.

Section 906 requires that the certifications accompany the periodic report to which they relate, which is in contrast to Section 302, which requires the certifications to be included in the periodic report. In recognition of this difference, the SEC allows companies to furnish, rather than file, the Section 906 certifications. Thus, the certifications would not be subject to liability under Section 18 of the Exchange Act. Moreover, the certifications would not be subject to automatic incorporation by reference into a company's Securities Act registration statements, which are subject to liability under Section 11 of the Securities Act, unless the company takes steps to include the certifications in a registration statement.

Although Section 906 does not explicitly require the certifications to be made public, the SEC believes it is appropriate to require certifications that accompany a publicly filed periodic report to be provided publicly. Indeed, the SEC has indicated that Congress intended for Section 906 certifications to be publicly provided. Civil liability already exists under the signature requirements and the Section 302 certifications. In addition, any Section 906 certification submitted to the Commission as correspondence is subject to the Freedom of Information Act.

In addition, the requirement to furnish Section 906 certifications as exhibits serves a number of important functions. First, the exhibit requirement enhances compliance by allowing the Commission, the Department of Justice and the public to monitor the certifications effectively. Second, by subjecting the Section 906 certifications to the signature requirements of Regulation S-T, companies must retain a manually signed signature page or other authenticating document for a five-year period, which helps preserve evidence in the event of prosecution.

It should also be noted that, unlike the Section 302 certifications, the Section 906 certifications are required only in periodic reports that contain financial statements. Thus, amendments to periodic reports that do not contain financial statements would not require a new Section 906 certification, but would require a new Section 302 certification to be filed with the amendment. In addition, unlike the Section 302 certifications, the Section 906 certifications may take the form of a single statement signed by a company's chief executive and financial officers.

¶ 209 Liability

A company's principal executive and financial officers already are responsible as signatories for corporate disclosures under Exchange Act liability provisions and can be liable for material misstatements or omissions under general antifraud standards, as well as under the SEC's authority to seek redress against those who cause or aid or abet securities law violations. An officer providing a false certification potentially could be subject to Commission action for violating Exchange Act Section 13(a) or 15(d) and to both Commission and private actions for violating Rule 10b-5.

Federal courts have ruled that corporate officer who sign an SEC filing containing representations make the statement in the filing and can be liable as primary violators of Rule 10b-5. Courts have reasoned that investor protection from misleading information is enhanced by giving corporate officers the responsibility to ensure the validity of filings. (See *Howard v. Everix Systems, Inc.* (CA-9 2000), 2000-2001 CCH Dec. ¶ 91,217.)

A false certification also may have liability consequences under Sections 11 and 12(a)(2) of the Securities Act where a quarterly or annual report is incorporated by reference into a registration statement on Form S-3 or F-3 or into a prospectus filed pursuant to Securities Act Rule 424(b).

Thus, the SEC sees the certification requirement as reinforcing the duty of these officers to shareholders for the content of quarterly and annual reports. Similarly, the certification rules are not intended to affect other existing bases of liability for principal executive officers and principal financial officers or to increase, decrease, or otherwise alter the potential liability of other corporate officers and directors, whether or not signatories, who are not required to provide the proposed certification. (See the proposing release, Release No. 34-46079.)

Materiality

The certification also reflects the current disclosure standards for material information. The SEC does not intend to establish for the certification a standard of materiality that does not already exist under current law. The certification faithfully follows the standard of materiality set forth in the leading U.S. Supreme Court opinions: *TSC Industries, Inc. v. Northway, Inc.* (US Sup Ct 1976), 1976-1977 CCH Dec. ¶ 95,615; and *Basic, Inc. v. Levinson* (US Sup Ct 1988), 1987-1988 CCH Dec. ¶ 93,645.

As developed by the Court, information is material if there is a substantial likelihood that a reasonable shareholder would consider it important in making an investment decision. To fulfill the materiality requirement, there must be a substantial likelihood that a fact would have been viewed by the reasonable investor as having significantly altered the total mix of information made available. Materiality with regard to contingent or speculative events depends on a balancing of both the indicated probability that the event will occur and the anticipated magnitude of the event in light of the totality of company activity.

In addition, the certification follows the general materiality standard contained in Exchange Act Rule 12b-20, which states that there must be added any further material information needed to make the required statements, in light of the circumstances under which they are made, not misleading. The certification would, however, speak in terms of the officers' knowledge and belief.

CHAPTER 3

ACCELERATED FILING DEADLINES

WEBSITE ACCESS

ACCELERATED FILING DEADLINES

WEBSITE ACCESS

Accelerated Filing Deadlines

¶ 301 Introduction

The Securities and Exchange Commission (SEC) accelerated for certain companies the deadlines for filing annual reports on Forms 10-K and quarterly reports on Form 10-Q. As discussed elsewhere (see ¶ 303), the new deadlines apply only to companies that meet certain "accelerated filer" thresholds as to size and reporting history. These accelerated filers must now comply with a phased-in filing schedule over the next three years (see ¶ 304), with no deadline changes in the first year and incrementally shorter deadlines in the second and third year. In all, the timeframe for filing Form 10-K will diminish from 90 to 60 days after the company's fiscal year end; for Form 10-Q, the timeframe will diminish from 45 to 35 days after the fiscal quarter end.

Background

The Securities Exchange Act of 1934 ("Exchange Act") requires public companies to file periodic reports with the SEC disclosing information to investors on an ongoing basis to help them in making investment and voting decisions. Certain established reporting companies can incorporate information from their Exchange Act reports into their registration statements under the Securities Act of 1933. Thus, investors purchasing securities in public offerings also rely on Exchange Act disclosure.

SEC rules under the Exchange Act require disclosure at quarterly and annual intervals, with specified material events reported on a more current basis. Specifically, domestic reporting companies must file the following reports:

- An annual report on Form 10-K (or 10-KSB for small business issuers) no later than 90 calendar days after the end of its fiscal year;

- Quarterly reports on Form 10-Q (or Form 10-QSB for small business issuers) no later than 45 calendar days after the end of the first three quarters of its fiscal year; and

- Current reports on Form 8-K for a number of specified events generally within five or 15 days after their occurrence.

The SEC in April 2002 proposed to accelerate the Form 10-K and Form 10-Q filing deadlines for certain companies in an effort to improve the usefulness of periodic reports to investors. (See Release No. 34-45741 (SEC 2002), 2001-2002 CCH Dec. ¶ 86,626.) Those deadlines had not been changed since 1970 and, the Commission reasoned, had become obsolete in light of technology and communications advances, investor needs, and other factors (see ¶ 302). In response, over 300 persons submitted public comments. The majority of them opposed the extent of acceleration and length of the transition period as too burdensome. Based on those comments, the SEC modified the rules to include a phased-in acceleration schedule that it deemed less burdensome to the affected companies.

Effect of Noncompliance

The consequences of missing a filing deadline, however, remain quite severe. Apart from the negative market reaction, filing an untimely report will render a company ineligible for short-form registration for at least one year after the late filing. A missed deadline could also make Securities Act Rule 144 temporarily unavailable for shareholder resales of restricted and control securities, and make new filings on Form S-8 temporarily unavailable for resales of employee benefit plan securities. Moreover, many if not most indentures and credit agreements require public companies to provide periodic reports to the trustee or lender within specified timeframes. Failure to comply with these covenants can result in default. In addition, SEC enforcement action against late filers is possible.

All of these risks become more likely as compliance with the tighter deadlines becomes more difficult. Companies subject to the new filing deadlines should therefore take immediate steps to review and streamline their disclosure processes. Indeed, against the backdrop of other recent and impending disclosure requirements—concerning CEO/CFO certification, critical accounting estimates, off-balance sheet transactions, assessments of internal controls, pro forma earnings, Section 16(a) reports, and current reporting on Form 8-K—the need to improve these disclosure processes becomes all the more evident.

¶ 302 Purpose

The purpose of the new filing deadlines is simply to provide investors with quicker access to the important information contained in periodic reports. The SEC noted that commentators have long complained that, because the current filing deadlines are so lengthy, the information disclosed often becomes stale by the time the company files the report. Elaborating, the Commission stated:

> While quarterly and annual reports at present generally reflect historical information, it is important that a lengthy delay before that information becomes available does not make the information less valuable to investors.

(Release No. 34-45741 (SEC 2002), Part II.A.1, 2001-2002 CCH Dec. ¶ 86,626 (proposing release).) By shortening the delay between the close of the reporting period and the time of filing, the accelerated deadlines help ensure that periodic reports contain meaningful, timely information about the issuer.

The demand and need for quicker access to periodic reports has grown for several reasons. These reasons include advances in technology. As discussed below, the ability of companies to gather, organize, and disseminate information rapidly has raised investor expectations about prompt disclosure. The fact that many companies issue press releases containing "pro forma" earnings results well before filing the applicable report, as discussed further below, reflects this growing demand for timely information. These press releases, however, are not a substitute for periodic reports. Their inconsistent formats and non-GAAP methodologies simply underscore the need for timely, structured, and GAAP-compliant periodic reports.

Technological Advances

Compliance with the accelerated deadlines has become more possible with improved technology. As the SEC observed, significant technological advances over the last three decades have both increased the market's demand for more timely disclosure and the ability of companies to capture, process, and disseminate this information. Contrasting the tools available to companies today with those available when the original deadlines were adopted, the Commission stated:

> Computers, sophisticated financial software, electronic mail, teleconferencing, videoconferencing and other technologies available today have replaced the paper and pencil, typewriter, adding machines, carbon paper, mail system, travel and face-to-face meetings relied on in 1970.

(Release No. 34-45741, supra, Part II.A.1.) In sum, vast improvements in technology have enabled companies to prepare and file their reports more efficiently, and to that extent have eased the burden of complying with accelerated deadlines.

Pro Forma Earnings Results

The widespread practice of issuing pro forma results in press releases well before the company files its reports is further evidence that accelerated filing is possible. Assuming that companies collect and evaluate information before issuing pro forma results, "the availability of this information also suggests that much of the process involved in preparing the financial information contained in periodic reports is substantially complete." (Release No. 34-46464 (SEC 2002), Part II.A.1, at ¶ 2202 (adopting release).)

Prompt dissemination of pro forma results does not, however, obviate the need for more timely periodic reports. As the Commission observed:

> [E]arnings announcements . . . are generally less complete in their disclosure than quarterly or annual reports, and they can emphasize information that is less prominent in quarterly or annual reports. Investors often must wait for the periodic reports to receive financial statements and the accompanying notes prepared in accordance with generally accepted accounting principles, management's discussion and analysis, or MD&A, and other vitally important financial disclosures.

Moreover, the required information in periodic reports "provides a verification function against other statements made by the company in press releases and other public announcements." (Release No. 34-46464 (SEC 2002), supra.) In sum, periodic reports offer a balanced, structured, and GAAP-compliant presentation of results, and a delay in filing such reports long after a company issues pro forma earnings figures deprives investors of information necessary to a more complete understanding of the company's results.

¶ 303 Covered Issuers

The accelerated filing deadlines apply only to "accelerated filers," i.e., companies that meet certain conditions as to size and reporting history.

Specifically, the new filing deadlines apply to a company when it first meets the following conditions as of the end of its fiscal year:

- Its common equity "public float" (defined below) was $75 million or more as of the last business day of its most recently completed second quarter;

- The company has been subject to Exchange Act Section 13(a) or 15(d) reporting requirements for at least 12 calendar months;

- The company has previously filed at least one annual report under Exchange Act Section 13(a) or 15(d); and

- The company is not eligible to use Forms 10-KSB and 10-QSB.

(Exchange Act Rule 12b-2, at ¶ 1203.)

The SEC intended the accelerated filing deadlines to cover only those companies that are least likely to find compliance overly burdensome. The Commission based the public float and reporting history requirements on the current eligibility requirements for registration on Form S-3. Elaborating, the SEC stated:

> As these companies can take advantage of short-form registration, including the resultant benefits of incorporation by reference and quick access to the capital markets through "shelf registration," a shortening of the [periodic report] deadlines for these companies seems appropriate. In identifying companies that would be subject to this new requirement, we thought it would be appropriate to use a pre-existing threshold to reduce regulatory complexity.

(Release No. 34-45741 (SEC 2002), Part II.A.3, 2001-2002 CCH Dec. ¶ 86,626 (proposing release).)

Many companies are exempt. The definition, with its $75 million public float threshold, excludes nearly half of all publicly-traded companies, as well as all companies eligible for the Commission's small business issuer reporting system, all foreign private issuers that file on Form 20-F, and all companies that do not have a common equity public float. (Release No. 34-46464 (SEC 2002), Part II.B.3, at ¶ 2202 (adopting release).)

Public Float

As mentioned, the accelerated filing deadlines apply to companies with a public float of $75 million or more as of the last business day of its most recently completed second quarter. "Public float" generally means the total value of the common equity held by non-affiliates of the company. More precisely, the term means the aggregate market value of the company's outstanding voting and non-voting common equity (i.e., market capitalization), minus the value of common equity held by the company's affiliates. (Release No. 34-46464, supra, n. 24.)

The SEC clarified how to calculate the public float. In computing the aggregate market value of outstanding common equity, a company must use the price at which the equity was last sold, or the average of that equity's bid and asked prices, in the principal market for the equity as of the last business day of the company's most recently completed second quarter. (Note to Rule 12b-2, at ¶ 1203.)

Disclosure in Form 10-K

Reporting companies must indicate their public float on the cover of Form 10-K. Under prior rules, companies had to disclose their public float as of a specified date within 60 days before filing the report. To assist the SEC and investors in evaluating whether a company is subject to accelerated deadlines, the Commission revised this requirement. Now all companies (regardless of whether they are accelerated filers) must state the public float by reference to the price at which the common equity was last sold, or the average bid and asked price, as of the last business day of the company's most recently completed second quarter. The SEC acknowledged that this reduces the disclosure's currency, but reasoned that the change will ease the burden for companies by requiring them to calculate only one public float amount. (Release No. 34-46464, supra, Part II.B.3.)

Also, to clarify further a company's filing status, the company now must check a box on the cover of its quarterly and annual reports to indicate whether it is an accelerated filer. (See Form 10-Q, at ¶ 1204; Form 10-K, at ¶ 1204.)

Determination Date

Companies must, as mentioned, determine whether they meet the conditions for accelerated filer status as of the end of their fiscal year. A company that does not fall within the "accelerated filer" definition at the close of its first fiscal year ending on or after December 15, 2002 will have to reevaluate its status at the end of each subsequent fiscal year. (Release No. 34-46464, supra, Part II.B.3.)

Although the determination date is a company's fiscal year-end, the company can predict in advance whether it will qualify for accelerated filer status by reference to the public float test. As indicated, the operative date for that key test is the end of the company's second fiscal quarter. This enables companies to know further in advance whether they will be subject to accelerated reporting, and to begin making the necessary preparations. (Release No. 34-46464, supra, Part II.B.3.)

The determination of whether a company becomes an accelerated filer as of the end of its fiscal year governs the filing of the annual report for that fiscal year, quarterly reports for the subsequent fiscal year, and annual and quarterly reports thereafter. (Exchange Act Rule 12b-2.) Thus, for example:

> [I]f a calendar year-end company meets the public float requirement, but has not filed its first annual report as of December 31, 2002, it does not become an accelerated filer and remains subject to existing deadlines for its 2002 annual report and its 2003 quarterly reports. However, if on December 31, 2003, the company meets the public float test as of the last business day of its second fiscal quarter ending June 30, 2003 and meets the other requirements of the accelerated filer definition, the company becomes an accelerated filer subject to the accelerated deadlines for its 2003 annual report, 2004 quarterly reports and all periodic reports thereafter.

(Release No. 34-46464, supra, Part II.B.3.)

Loss of Status

A company loses accelerated filer status if it becomes eligible to file reports on Forms 10-KSB and 10-QSB. In other words, once a company becomes an accelerated filer, it will remain so unless the company becomes eligible to use Forms 10-KSB and 10-QSB for its annual and quarterly reports. In that event, the company will not become an accelerated filer again unless it subsequently becomes ineligible to use Forms 10-KSB and 10-QSB and once again meets the test for accelerated filer status. (Exchange Act Rule 12b-2, at ¶ 1203.)

¶ 304 Filing Deadlines

Companies that meet the test for accelerated filer status (see ¶ 303) must file their periodic reports by the new deadlines. In response to public comments, the SEC decided to phase-in the deadlines over several years to reduce the compliance burden. The final rules leave the deadlines unchanged the first year, and accelerate them incrementally over the subsequent three years. Specifically, the following deadlines apply for fiscal years ending on or after:

- *December 15, 2002*—Form 10-K is due 90 days after the fiscal year end; Form 10-Q is due 45 days after the fiscal quarter end.

- *December 15, 2003*—Form 10K is due 75 days after the fiscal year end; Form 10-Q is due 45 days after the fiscal quarter end.

- *December 15, 2004*—Form 10K is due 60 days after the fiscal year end; Form 10-Q is due 40 days after the fiscal quarter end.

- *December 15, 2005*—Form 10K is due 60 days after the fiscal year end; Form 10-Q is due 35 days after the fiscal quarter end.

(17 CFR 249.308a(a), 249.310(b); General Instruction A.2 to Form 10-K, General Instruction A.1 to Form 10-Q; see ¶ 1204.)

Illustration

Thus, for example, a company that follows a fiscal calendar year and that meets the "accelerated filer" definition as of December 31, 2002 must file its Form 10-K report for that year by the existing 90-day deadline (i.e., by March 31, 2003). Each Form 10-Q report for the 2003 fiscal year will be due by the existing 45-day deadline (e.g., by May 15, 2003 for quarter ending March 31, 2003). The next Form 10-K report—for the fiscal year ending December 31, 2003—will be due within 75 days (i.e., by March 15, 2004). Each of the Form 10-Q reports for the 2004 fiscal year will be due within 40 days (e.g., by May 10, 2004 for the first quarter). The Form 10-K report for the fiscal year ending December 31, 2004 will be due within 60 days (i.e., by March 1, 2005). Each of the Form 10-Q reports for the 2005 fiscal year will be due within 35 days (e.g., by May 5, 2005 for the first quarter). All subsequent reports on Form 10-K and Form 10-Q will be subject to a 60- and 35-day deadline, respectively. (Release No. 34-46464 (SEC 2002), Part II.A.3, at ¶ 2202.)

Presenting the above example in tabular format, an accelerated filer that follows a fiscal calendar year must file Form 10-Q accordingly:

Reporting Period	Filing Deadline	Due Date
1Q - March 31, 2003	45 Days (Prior rule)	May 15, 2003
2Q - June 30, 2003	45 Days	August 14, 2003
3Q - Sept. 30, 2003	45 Days	November 14, 2003
1Q - March 31, 2004	40 Days (Phase 1)	May 10, 2004
2Q - June 30, 2004	40 Days	August 9, 2004
3Q - Sept. 30, 2004	40 Days	November 9, 2004
1Q - March 31, 2005	35 Days (Phase 2)	May 5, 2005
2Q - June 30, 2005	35 Days	August 4, 2005
3Q - Sept. 30, 2005	35 Days	November 4, 2005

The same company must file Form 10-K as follows:

Reporting Period	Filing Deadline	Due Date
YE - Dec. 31, 2002	90 Days (Prior rule)	March 31, 2003
YE - Dec. 31, 2003	75 Days (Phase 1)	March 15, 2004
YE - Dec. 31, 2004	60 Days (Phase 2)	March 1, 2005

Transition Reports

The same deadlines apply to an accelerated filer's transition reports. For accelerated filers that change their fiscal year, transition reports filed on Form 10-K and Form 10-Q are due according to the above deadline schedule. (Exchange Act Rule 13a-10(j)(1) and (2), Rule 15d-10(j)(1) and (2), at ¶ 1203.)

Phased-in Approach

The SEC chose to phase in the accelerated deadlines to ease the burden of compliance. The Commission concluded that a phased-in approach would allow a greater transition period for companies to adjust their procedures and to develop efficiencies to ensure that quality of their reports will not suffer. The approach will also enable companies to adapt to the various new reporting requirements imposed by the Sarbanes-Oxley Act of 2002. (Release No. 34-46464, supra, Part II.A.3.)

The SEC acknowledged that, even with the phase-in period, accelerated filing deadlines may cause more companies to file their reports late or seek an extension. Filing an untimely report will, moreover, render the company ineligible for short-form registration for at least one year after the late filing. A missed deadline could also render Securities Act Rule 144 temporarily unavailable for shareholder resales of restricted and control securities, and make new filings on Form S-8 temporarily unavailable for resales of employee benefit plan securities. The SEC considered, but ultimately rejected, suggestions from some commenters to extend the filing extension periods in Exchange Act Rule 12b-25 to alleviate these risks. As the Commission reasoned, "[W]e think a lengthy phase-in period adequately addresses these concerns." Moreover, Rule 12b-25 in its existing form still will allow companies facing extenuating circumstances to obtain a filing extension of five calendar days for quarterly reports and 15 calendar days for annual reports. (Release No. 34-46464, supra, Part II.A.3.)

¶ 305 Conforming Amendments

The SEC amended various other rules to conform them to the new filing deadlines. These consist of amendments to the Regulation S-X timeliness requirements for financial statements in other SEC filings, such as registration statements and proxy statements. Under the conforming amendments, as discussed below, financial statements included in a registration statement or proxy statement must continue to be at least as current as any financial statements filed under the Exchange Act. (Release No. 34-46464 (SEC 2002), Part II.C.1, at ¶ 2202.)

The purpose of these conforming amendments is to facilitate the integrated reporting system by simplifying existing rules, the Commission explained. Parallel requirements also improve overall disclosure as investors are assured consistent requirements for the timeliness of information regardless of the document received. Without the conforming amendments, the SEC reasoned, "a filing could conceivably be filed under the Securities Act with financial information less current than that filed under the Exchange Act." (Release No. 34-46464, supra, Part II.C.1.)

Filings Within 90 Days of Year-End

One conforming amendment concerns the inclusion of audited financial statements for filings within 90 days of the company's fiscal year-end. Currently, a reporting company need not include audited financial statements for the most recent fiscal year until the 90th day after the year-end if the company:

- Has filed all required Exchange Act reports;
- Reasonably and in good faith expects to report income (after taxes but before extraordinary items and a cumulative effect of a change in accounting principle) for its most recent fiscal year; and
- Has reported income (after taxes but before extraordinary items and a cumulative effect of a change in accounting principle) for at least one of the two immediately preceding fiscal years.

(Regulation S-X Rule 3-01(c), at ¶ 1201.) Unless the company meets all three conditions, registration statements filed or declared effective or proxy statements mailed after the 45th day following the fiscal year-end must include audited financial statements for the most recent fiscal year. (Rule 3-01(d), at ¶ 1201.)

The SEC shortened the 90-day deadline to conform to the phase-in periods for accelerated filers. Thus, in year one of the phase-in period, the deadline will remain at 90 days. In year two, the deadline will accelerate to 75 days. In year three and thereafter, the deadline will accelerate to 60 days. For companies that are not accelerated filers, however, the deadline will remain unchanged at 90 days. (See Regulation S-X Rule 3-01(i)(1)(i), at ¶ 1201; Release No. 34-46464, supra, Part II.C.1.a.)

Filings 135 Days After Year-End

Another conforming amendment affects registration statements filed more than 134 days after the company's fiscal year-end. Currently, the registrant must include with such a filing an interim balance sheet as of a date within 135 days of the filing date. Under the conforming amendments, the SEC reduced incrementally the time period after which interim balance sheets become necessary for accelerated filers. (See Regulation S-X Rule 3-01(e)(1) and (i)(2), at ¶ 1201.)

The new time periods parallel the phase-in schedule for accelerated filing of periodic reports. Thus, in year one of the phase-in, the period after which an interim balance sheet becomes necessary will remain 134 days for accelerated filers. In year two of the phase-in, the period is shortened to 129 days. In other words, an accelerated filer that files or declares a registration statement effective during this period must include updated financial statements as of an interim date within 130 days after the filing date. For year three and subsequent years, the period is reduced further to 124 days. In other words, an accelerated filer that files or declares a registration statement effective during this period must include updated financial statements as of an interim date within 125 days after the filing date. (See Rule 3-01(e)(1) and (i)(2), at ¶ 1201; Release No. 34-46464, supra, Part II.C.1.b.)

Age at Filing's Effective Date

The SEC imposed similar changes to Rule 3-12, which requires companies to update financial statements that will reach a specified age as of the filing's effective date. Specifically, where financial statements in a filing are as of a date 135 days or more before the filing's expected effective date, or its proposed mailing date in the case of a proxy statement, the company must update the financial statements with: (1) a balance sheet as of an interim date within 135 days; and (2) statements of income and cash flows on a comparative basis for the interim period between the end of the most recent fiscal year and the date of the interim balance sheet provided and for the corresponding period of the preceding fiscal year. (Regulation S-X Rule 3-12(a), at ¶ 1201.)

The conforming amendments revise the updating rule to parallel the phase-in schedule for accelerated filing of periodic reports. Thus, in year one of the phase-in, the updating period will remain at 135 days for accelerated filers. In year two of the phase-in, the period is shortened to 130 days for accelerated filers. In year three and subsequent years, the period reduces further to 125 days. The SEC also shortened, for accelerated filers, the operative time period in the Rule 3-12(b) exception to the updating requirement. (See Rule 3-12(g)(2)(i), at ¶ 1201; Release No. 34-46464, supra, Part II.C.1.c.)

Non-Wholly Owned Entities

The SEC also made conforming amendments to Regulation S-X Rule 3-09, which governs financial statements of unconsolidated subsidiaries and 50 percent or less owned persons. Several commenters had urged the Commission not to accelerate the Rule 3-09 due date for including these financial statements to conform to the investor registrant's accelerated filing deadlines. The commenters reasoned that accelerating the filing of these financial statements could require a company without accelerated filer status to file its financial statements before otherwise necessary solely because of the investor registrant's minority ownership stake in the company. Moreover, for its part, the investor registrant may have difficulty obtaining financial statements from such non-wholly owned entities within the applicable timeframe. This may lead a registrant to sell its investment, not for business reasons, but to remain timely and current in its filing requirements, or cause the investor registrant to file late and suffer adverse consequences, such as the loss of short-form registration. (Release No. 34-46464, supra, Part II.C.1.d.)

The SEC amended Rule 3-09 to address these concerns. Under the amendment, separate financial statements of unconsolidated subsidiaries and 50 percent or less owned persons required by Rule 3-09 will not be accelerated for inclusion in a company's Form 10-K if the subsidiary or 50-percent or less owned person is not an accelerated filer. In that instance, the financial statements can be filed by amendment within the existing time periods. (Rule 3-09(b)(1), at ¶ 1201.) Moreover, the SEC also made conforming amendments to continue providing companies with additional time to file the required financial statements if the fiscal years of the investor registrant and the non-wholly owned entity differ. (See Rule 3-09(b)(2), at ¶ 1201.)

Schedules Amending Form 10-K

Finally, the SEC made a conforming change to the deadline for schedules required by Regulation S-X Article 12 filed as an amendment to the annual report. The Commission changed this date to maintain the 30-day period after the report's due date to file the schedules. (Release No. 34-46464, supra, Part II.C.3.) Under the revised provision, "all schedules required by Article 12 of Regulation S-X . . . may, at the option of the registrant, be filed as an amendment to the report not later than 30 days after the applicable due date of the report." (17 CFR § 249.310(d); General Instruction A(4) to Form 10-K, at ¶ 1204.)

Website Access

¶ 306 Introduction

The SEC also adopted website disclosure requirements for accelerated filers. As discussed more fully elsewhere (see ¶ 307), the Commission amended Regulation S-K to require accelerated filers to disclose in their annual reports on Form 10-K where investors can obtain access to their filings, including whether the company provides access to its Forms 10-K, 10-Q, and 8-K reports on the company's Internet website, free of charge, as soon as reasonably practicable after it files those reports. If the company does not make its filings available in this manner, the company must disclose why it does not do so and whether it will voluntarily provide electronic or paper copies free of charge upon request. (Regulation S-K Item 101(e)(4), at ¶ 1202.)

The SEC reasoned that Internet websites are an efficient and ideal means for companies to disclose information about themselves to investors. In addition to other existing sources of corporate information, such as the Commission website, a company's own website is often an obvious place for investors to go first. (Release No. 34-46464 (SEC 2002), Part II.D.1, at ¶ 2202.) Moreover, despite the availability of corporate reports in the EDGAR database, the SEC concluded that parallel disclosure in a company's website furthers the Commission's objectives to encourage the availability of information in a variety of locations and to foster best practices for making that information broadly accessible. (Release No. 34-46464, supra, Part II.D.3.)

Scope of Requirement

The disclosure requirement applies to annual reports of covered issuers filed on Form 10-K. Compliance with the rule must begin with the Form 10-K for fiscal years ending on or after December 15, 2002. (Release No. 34-46464, supra, Part II.D.3.)

The disclosure requirement creates duties only under Exchange Act Sections 13(a) and 15(d). It is not an antifraud rule. The SEC did not intend the rule to create new duties under existing antifraud provisions or in private rights of action, or to alter any existing liability provisions. The rule does not, moreover, separately create or otherwise affect a company's duty to update its prior statements. (Release No. 34-46464, supra, Part II.D.3.)

Covered Issuers

The website disclosure rule applies only to companies subject to the new accelerated filing deadlines. Thus, companies that meet the Rule 12b-2 test for "accelerated filer" status must disclose certain information in Form 10-K concerning website access to their Exchange Act reports. These accelerated filers, as discussed elsewhere (see ¶ 303), are companies: (1) with at least a $75 million public float as of the end of their second fiscal quarter; (2) that have been subject to Exchange Act reporting requirements for at least one year; (3) that have filed at least at least one annual report; and (4) that are ineligible to use Forms 10-KSB and 10-QSB.

Background and Purpose

The obvious and fundamental purpose of the website disclosure rule is to ensure broad, public access to timely corporate information. Such access promotes the efficient functioning of the secondary markets by enabling investors to make informed investment decisions. Moreover, it helps to "democratize" the capital markets by giving small investors access to the same corporate information that is readily available to large institutional investors. (Release No. 34-45741 (SEC 2002), Part II.B.1, 2001-2002 CCH Dec. ¶ 86,626 (proposing release).)

A related, but narrower, goal of the website disclosure rule is to facilitate short-form registration. Broad and timely access to Exchange Act information, the Commission noted, is critical to short-form registration of offerings by seasoned reporting companies. As the SEC elaborated:

Our system of short-form registration, which is available in varying degrees for domestic issuers on Forms S-2, S-3, and S-8, allows certain information about the company conducting the offering to be incorporated by reference from the company's Exchange Act reports without, in many instances, separate delivery of these reports. One rationale for these abbreviated registration forms is that the information in a company's Exchange Act reports already has been adequately disseminated and evaluated by the marketplace.

(Release No. 34-45741, supra, Part II.B.1.)

The new rule is consistent with the SEC's efforts to modernize its disclosure requirements. Those efforts reflect a recognition of the Internet's importance in fostering prompt and widespread dissemination of information. The SEC believes that corporate disclosure should be more readily available to investors on a timely basis in a variety of locations to facilitate investor access to that information. In addition, the Commission believes that companies should make investors aware of the different sources that provide access to corporate information. (Release No. 34-45741, supra, Part II.B.1.)

The new rule is also consistent with industry practice. A substantial number of companies already provide access to their SEC filings through their websites. According to a survey conducted by the SEC's Office of Economic Analysis, which examined 152 companies with at least a $75 million public float, 83 percent of those companies provided some form of access to their Commission filings through their websites. These companies provided such access by several means, including: hyperlinking to a third-party service providing real-time access to the filings (45 percent); posting the filings directly on their websites (29 percent); and hyperlinking to the EDGAR database (15 percent). (Release No. 34-46464 (SEC 2002), Part II.D.1, at ¶ 2202 (adopting release).)

¶ 307 Required Website Disclosure

Companies subject to the website disclosure rule (i.e., accelerated filers) must disclose in their Form 10-K several new items concerning Internet access to periodic reports. Specifically, Regulation S-K Item 101(e) now requires accelerated filers to disclose in their Form 10-K:

- The company's website address, if it has one;
- Whether the company makes available at no charge on or through its website (if it has one) its Forms 10-K, 10-Q, and 8-K, and all amendments to those reports, as soon as reasonably practicable after the company electronically files that information with, or otherwise furnishes it to, the SEC;

- If the company does not make its filings available in this manner, the reasons why it does not do so (including, if applicable, that it does not have a website); and

- If the company does not make its filings available in this manner, whether it voluntarily will provide electronic or paper copies of its filings free of charge upon request.

(Regulation S-K Item 101(e)(3) and (4), at ¶ 1202.) Accelerated filers must begin complying with this disclosure requirement starting with their annual reports on Form 10-K filed for fiscal years ending on or after December 15, 2002. (Release No. 34-46464 (SEC 2002), Part II.D.3, at ¶ 2202.)

The website access contemplated by the rule includes access to all exhibits and supplemental schedules electronically filed with the reports or amendments. The SEC does not require companies to post separately information incorporated by reference, but does encourages them to do so if it will aid investor access to that information. (Release No. 34-46464, supra, Part II.D.3.)

The Commission interprets the "as soon as reasonably practicable" standard to mean that the report would be posted, barring unforeseen circumstances, on the same day as filing. The SEC cautioned that it might revisit this requirement if posting on the same day does not generally occur. (Release No. 34-46464, supra, Part II.D.3.)

Format

The website disclosure rule does not require that the filings appear in any particular format. Some companies, the SEC noted, display their reports in electronic formats (for example, PDF) other than the official HTML format used to transmit the filing to the Commission's EDGAR system. The SEC in fact encourages companies to do so if alternative formats improve the report's readability and accessibility, so long as all of the information in the report is retrievable. The Commission cautioned, however, against using a particular medium that is so burdensome as to prevent the intended recipients from effectively accessing the information provided. (Release No. 34-46464, supra, Part II.D.3.)

Duration of Access

The rule does not state how long a report must be available electronically. In the adopting release, however, the SEC urged companies to provide website access to their previous reports for at least a 12-month period. In addition, the Commission recommended that companies maintain on their website an archive of reports "over an even longer timeframe," and that they expand the range of available documents to include other SEC filings, such as filings under the proxy rules and the Securities Act. (Release No. 34-46464, supra, Part II.D.3.)

Site Address Requirement

The adopting release discussed certain issues concerning the requirement that companies disclose their website address. For example, the Commission acknowledged that companies may have multiple websites for various purposes, such as investor relations, product information, and business-to-business activities. The SEC clarified that it interprets the website address requirement to mean the website that the company normally uses for investor relations functions. (Release No. 34-46464, supra, Part II.D.3.)

The Commission also discussed whether disclosing the website address would unintentionally incorporate all of the site's content by reference. Some commenters had expressed concern that "including the website address in the filing would constitute incorporation by reference of any website information into the filing." Dispelling this concern, the SEC stated:

> If a company is complying with this disclosure item in its annual report on Form 10-K, the inclusion of the company's website address will not, by itself, include or incorporate by reference the information on the site into the company's Commission filing, unless the company otherwise acts to incorporate the information by reference.

(Release No. 34-46464, supra, Part II.D.3.)

¶ 308 Practical Considerations

The SEC's adopting release addressed two practical issues raised by the website access requirement. The first involves a company's reliance on a third-party website to provide access to the company's periodic reports. The second involves hyperlinking to the Commission's EDGAR database as a means of timely satisfying the website access requirement. These matters are discussed separately below.

Third-Party websites

Some companies currently provide Internet access to their periodic reports by establishing a hyperlink to the reports via a third-party service in lieu of maintaining the reports themselves. Reliance on these third-party services will satisfy the website access requirement, the SEC advised, so long as the reports are available within the appropriate timeframe and access to them is free of charge. To clarify that hyperlinks to these services is acceptable, the Commission modified the rule's language as proposed to specify that a company can provide access to its reports "on *or through*" its website. (Release No. 34-46464 (SEC 2002), Part II.D.3, at ¶ 2202 (adopting release); see Regulation S-K Item 101(e)(4)(i), at ¶ 1202.)

Companies that rely on third-party services to satisfy the website access rule may face unique issues. One such issue is investor confusion. To avoid this confusion, the SEC advises companies to hyperlink directly to their reports (or to a list of the reports) rather than just to the home page or a general search page of the third-party service. (Release No. 34-46464, supra, Part II.D.3.)

Also, the Commission has previously noted various liability risks associated with hyperlinking to a third-party site. (See Release No. 34-42728 (SEC 2000), 2000 CCH Dec. ¶ 86,304.) A principal risk is that the company may incur liability for any statements made in the hyperlinked document, as if the company had made those statements itself. Thus, when hyperlinking to third-party information, the company should ensure that all the information appearing in the hyperlinked page is accurate and not misleading.

Hyperlinks to EDGAR

The adopting release discusses hyperlinking to the SEC's EDGAR database. Hyperlinking to EDGAR will enable a company to state, under Regulation S-K Item 101(e)(4)(i), that it provides website access to its reports "as soon as reasonably practicable" after filing. In the Commission's words:

> As we now provide real-time access to Exchange Act reports through our website, hyperlinking directly to a company's reports (or to a list of its reports) on our EDGAR website will allow a company to state that it provides website access to its reports as soon as reasonably practicable after those reports are filed.

This, the SEC noted, will help to decrease further any incremental burdens or costs imposed by the new requirement. (Release No. 34-46464 (SEC 2002), Part II.D.3., at ¶ 2202.)

Companies that currently offer hyperlinks to their reports on EDGAR will need to revise their hyperlink scripts soon, the Commission noted. As a result of adding real-time EDGAR filing data to the SEC website, new searches located on new web pages are now available on the website that provide access to this real-time data. Companies that currently hyperlink to the EDGAR database therefore must update their hyperlink scripts to refer to the new search pages providing real-time data. The Commission will eliminate the older search pages "in the near future." (Release No. 34-46464, supra, n. 134.)

The availability of reports on EDGAR does not obviate the need to make reports available on the company's own website. The SEC concluded that disclosure on a company's website is still desirable because one of the Commission's objectives is to encourage the availability of information in a variety of locations and to foster best practices for making that information broadly accessible. (Release No. 34-46464, supra, Part II.D.3.)

PART II. TEXT OF AMENDMENTS

FORM 8-K REFORMS

¶ 1001 Securities Act Rules

PART 230—GENERAL RULES AND REGULATIONS, SECURITIES ACT OF 1933

5. The authority citation for part 230 continues to read in part as follows:

Authority: 15 U.S.C. 77b, 77c, 77d, 77f, 77g, 77h, 77j, 77r, 77s, 77z-3, 77sss, 78c, 78d, 78j, 78*l*, 78m, 78n, 78o, 78t, 78w, 78*ll*(d), 78mm, 79t, 80a-8, 80a-24, 80a-28, 80a-29, 80a-30, and 80a-37, unless otherwise noted.

* * * * * *

6. Amend § 230.144 by revising paragraph (c)(1) to read as follows:

§ 230.144 Persons deemed not to be engaged in a distribution and therefore not underwriters.

* * * * *

(c) * * *

(1) *Filing of reports.* The issuer has securities registered pursuant to section 12 of the Securities Exchange Act of 1934, has been subject to the reporting requirements of section 13 of that Act for a period of at least 90 days immediately preceding the sale of the securities and has filed all the reports required to be filed thereunder during the 12 months preceding such sale (or for such shorter period that the issuer was required to file such reports), other than Form 8-K reports (§ 249.308 of this chapter); or has securities registered pursuant to the Securities Act of 1933, has been subject to the reporting requirements of section 15(d) of the Securities Exchange Act of 1934 for a period of at least 90 days immediately preceding the sale of the securities and has filed all the reports required to be filed thereunder during the 12 months preceding such sale (or for such shorter period that the issuer was required to file such reports), other than Form 8-K reports (§ 249.308 of this chapter). The person for whose account the securities are to be sold shall be entitled to rely upon a statement in whichever is the most recent report, quarterly or annual, required to be filed and filed by the issuer that such issuer has filed all

reports required to be filed by section 13 or 15(d) of the Securities Exchange Act of 1934 during the preceding 12 months (or for such shorter period that the issuer was required to file such reports), other than Form 8-K reports (§ 249.308 of this chapter), and has been subject to such filing requirements for the past 90 days, unless he knows or has reason to believe that the issuer has not complied with such requirements. Such person shall also be entitled to rely upon a written statement from the issuer that it has complied with such reporting requirements unless he knows or has reasons to believe that the issuer has not complied with such requirements.

* * * * *

¶ 1002 Securities Act Forms

PART 239—FORMS PRESCRIBED UNDER THE SECURITIES ACT OF 1933

7. The authority citation for part 239 continues to read in part as follows:

Authority: 15 U.S.C. 77f, 77g, 77h, 77j, 77s, 77z-2, 77sss, 78c, 78*l*, 78m, 78n, 78o(d), 78u-5, 78w(a), 78*ll*(d), 79e, 79f, 79g, 79j, 79*l*, 79m, 79n, 79q, 79t, 80a-8, 80a-24, 80a-26, 80a-29, 80a-30, and 80a-37, unless otherwise noted.

* * * * *

8. Amend § 239.12 by revising paragraph (c)(2) to read as follows:

§ 239.12 Form S-2, for registration under the Securities Act of 1933 of securities of certain issuers.

* * * * *

(c) * * *

(2) Has filed in a timely manner all reports required to be filed during the twelve calendar months and any portion of a month immediately preceding the filing of the registration statement, other than a report that is required solely pursuant to Item 1.01, 1.02, 2.03, 2.04, 2.05, 2.06 or 4.02(a) of Form 8-K (§ 249.308 of this chapter). If the registrant has used (during the twelve calendar months and any portion of a month immediately preceding the filing of the registration statement) § 240.12b-25(b) of this chapter with respect to a report or a portion of a report, that report or portion thereof has actually been filed within the time period prescribed by that section; and

* * * * *

9. Amend Form S-2 (referenced in § 239.12) by revising General Instruction I.(C) to read as follows:

Note—The text of Form S-2 does not, and this amendment will not, appear in the Code of Federal Regulations.

FORM S-2

REGISTRATION STATEMENT UNDER THE SECURITIES ACT OF 1933

* * * * *

GENERAL INSTRUCTIONS

I. * * *

C. The registrant:

(1) has been subject to the requirements of Section 12 or 15(d) of the Exchange Act and has filed all the material required to be filed pursuant to Section 12, 14 or 15(d) for a period of at least thirty-six calendar months immediately preceding the filing of the registration statement on this Form; and

(2) has filed in a timely manner all reports required to be filed during the twelve calendar months and any portion of a month immediately preceding the filing of the registration statement, other than a report that is required solely pursuant to Item 1.01, 1.02, 2.03, 2.04, 2.05, 2.06 or 4.02(a) of Form 8-K (§ 249.308 of this chapter). If the registrant has used (during the twelve calendar months and any portion of a month immediately preceding the filing of the registration statement) Rule 12b-25(b) (§ 240.12b-25(b) of this chapter) under the Exchange Act with respect to a report or a portion of a report, that report or portion thereof has actually been filed within the time period prescribed by that rule.

* * * * *

10. Amend § 239.13 by removing the authority citation following the section and revising paragraph (a)(3)(ii) to read as follows:

§ 239.13 Form S-3, for registration under the Securities Act of 1933 of securities of certain issuers offered pursuant to certain types of transactions.

* * * * *

(a) * * *

(3) * * *

(ii) Has filed in a timely manner all reports required to be filed during the twelve calendar months and any portion of a month immediately preceding the filing of the registration statement, other than a report that is required solely pursuant to Item 1.01, 1.02, 2.03, 2.04, 2.05, 2.06 or 4.02(a) of Form 8-K (§ 249.308 of this chapter). If the registrant has used (during the twelve calendar months and any portion of a month immediately preceding the filing of the registration statement) § 240.12b-25(b) of this chapter with respect to a report or a portion of a report, that report or portion thereof has actually been filed within the time period prescribed by that section; and

* * * * *

11. Amend Form S-3 (referenced in § 239.13) by revising General Instruction I.A.3 to read as follows:

Note—The text of Form S-3 does not, and this amendment will not, appear in the Code of Federal Regulations.

FORM S-3

REGISTRATION STATEMENT UNDER THE SECURITIES ACT OF 1933

* * * * *

GENERAL INSTRUCTIONS

I. * * *

A. * * *

3. The registrant:

(a) has been subject to the requirements of Section 12 or 15(d) of the Exchange Act and has filed all the material required to be filed pursuant to Section 12, 14 or 15(d) for a period of at least twelve calendar months immediately preceding the filing of the registration statement on this Form; and

(b) has filed in a timely manner all reports required to be filed during the twelve calendar months and any portion of a month immediately preceding the filing of the registration statement, other than a report that is required solely pursuant to Item 1.01, 1.02, 2.03, 2.04, 2.05, 2.06 or 4.02(a) of Form 8-K (§ 249.308 of this chapter). If the registrant has used (during the twelve calendar months and any portion of a month immediately preceding the filing of the registration statement) Rule 12b-25(b) (§ 240.12b-25(b) of this chapter) under the Exchange Act with respect to a report or a portion of a report, that report or portion thereof has actually been filed within the time period prescribed by that rule.

* * * * *

¶ 1003 Exchange Act Rules

PART 240—GENERAL RULES AND REGULATIONS, SECURITIES EXCHANGE ACT OF 1934

12. The authority citation for part 240 continues to read in part as follows:

Authority: 15 U.S.C. 77c, 77d, 77g, 77j, 77s, 77z-2, 77z-3, 77eee, 77ggg, 77nnn, 77sss, 77ttt, 78c, 78d, 78e, 78f, 78g, 78i, 78j, 78j-1, 78k, 78k-1, 78*l*, 78m, 78n, 78o, 78p, 78q, 78s, 78u-5, 78w, 78x, 78*ll*, 78mm, 79q, 79t, 80a-20, 80a-23, 80a-29, 80a-37, 80b-3, 80b-4, 80b-11, and 7201 *et seq.*; and 18 U.S.C. 1350, unless otherwise noted.

* * * * *

13. Amend § 240.12b-23 by revising paragraphs (a)(3)(i) and (ii) and adding paragraph (a)(3)(iii) to read as follows:

§ 240.12b-23 Incorporation by reference.

* * * * *

(a) * * *

(3) * * *

(i) A proxy or information statement incorporated by reference in response to Part III of Form 10-K and Form 10-KSB (17 CFR 249.310 and 249.310b);

(ii) A form of prospectus filed pursuant to 17 CFR 230.424(b) incorporated by reference in response to Item 1 of Form 8-A (17 CFR 249.208a); and

(iii) Information filed on Form 8-K (17 CFR 249.308) need not be filed as an exhibit.

* * * * *

14. Amend § 240.13a-10 by revising Note 1 at the end of the section to read as follows:

§ 240.13a-10 Transition reports.

* * * * *

Note 1: In addition to the report or reports required to be filed pursuant to this section, every issuer, except a foreign private issuer or an investment company required to file reports pursuant to § 270.30b1-1 of this chapter, that changes its fiscal closing date is required to file a Form 8-K (§ 249.308 of this chapter) report that includes the information required by Item 5.03 of Form 8-K within the period specified in General Instruction B.1. to that form.

* * * * *

15. Amend § 240.13a-11 by adding paragraph (c) to read as follows:

§ 240.13a-11 Current reports on Form 8-K (§ 249.308 of this chapter).

* * * * *

(c) No failure to file a report on Form 8-K that is required solely pursuant to Item 1.01, 1.02, 2.03, 2.04, 2.05, 2.06 or 4.02(a) of Form 8-K shall be deemed to be a violation of 15 U.S.C. 78j(b) and § 240.10b-5.

16. Amend § 240.15d-10 by revising Note 1 at the end of the section to read as follows:

§ 240.15d-10 Transition reports.

* * * * *

Note 1: In addition to the report or reports required to be filed pursuant to this section, every issuer, except a foreign private issuer or an investment company required to file reports pursuant to § 270.30b1-1 of this chapter, that changes its fiscal closing date is required to file a Form 8-K (§ 249.308 of this chapter) report that includes the information required by Item 5.03 of Form 8-K within the period specified in General Instruction B.1. to that form.

* * * * *

17. Amend § 240.15d-11 by adding paragraph (c) to read as follows:

§ 240.15d-11 Current reports on Form 8-K (§ 249.308 of this chapter).

* * * * *

(c) No failure to file a report on Form 8-K that is required solely pursuant to Item 1.01, 1.02, 2.03, 2.04, 2.05, 2.06 or 4.02(a) of Form 8-K shall be deemed to be a violation of 15 U.S.C. 78j(b) and § 240.10b-5.

¶ 1004 Exchange Act Forms

PART 249—FORMS, SECURITIES EXCHANGE ACT OF 1934

18. The authority citation for part 249 continues to read in part as follows:

Authority: 15 U.S.C. 78a *et seq.* and 7201 *et seq.;* and 18 U.S.C. 1350, unless otherwise noted.

* * * * *

19. Amend Form 8-K (referenced in § 249.308) by:

a. Adding the "check the appropriate box" paragraph directly above the General Instructions on the cover page;

b. Revising the heading for General Instruction A, designating the current text as paragraph 1 and adding paragraph 2;

c. Revising General Instruction B; and

d. Revising all of the items appearing under the caption "Information to Be Included in the Report" after the General Instructions.

The revisions and addition read as follows:

Note—The text of Form 8-K does not, and this amendment will not, appear in the Code of Federal Regulations.

Form 8-K

Current Report

Pursuant to Section 13 or 15(d) of the Securities Exchange Act of 1934

* * * * *

Check the appropriate box below if the Form 8-K filing is intended to simultaneously satisfy the filing obligation of the registrant under any of the following provisions (*see* General Instruction A.2. below):

[ ] Written communications pursuant to Rule 425 under the Securities Act (17 CFR 230.425)

[ ] Soliciting material pursuant to Rule 14a-12(b) under the Exchange Act (17 CFR 240.14a-12(b))

[ ] Pre-commencement communications pursuant to Rule 14d-2(b) under the Exchange Act (17 CFR 240.14d-2(b))

GENERAL INSTRUCTIONS

A. Rules as to Use of Form 8-K.

1. * * *

2. Form 8-K may be used by a registrant to satisfy its filing obligations pursuant to Rule 425 under the Securities Act, regarding written communications related to business combination transactions, or Rules 14a-12(b) or Rule 14d-2(b) under the Exchange Act, relating to soliciting materials and pre-commencement communications pursuant to tender offers, respectively, provided that the Form 8-K filing satisfies all the substantive requirements of those rules (other than the Rule 425(c) requirement to include certain specified information in any prospectus filed pursuant to such rule). Such filing is also deemed to be filed pursuant to any rule for which the box is checked. A registrant is not required to check the box in connection with Rule 14a-12(b) or Rule 14d-2(b) if the communication is filed pursuant to Rule 425. Communications filed pursuant to Rule 425 are deemed filed under the other applicable sections. See Note 2 to Rule 425, Rule 14a-12(b) and Instruction 2 to Rule 14d-2(b)(2).

B. Events to be Reported and Time for Filing of Reports.

1. A report on this form is required to be filed or furnished, as applicable, upon the occurrence of any one or more of the events specified in the items in Sections 1 - 6 and 9 of this form. Unless otherwise specified, a report is to be filed or furnished within four business days after occurrence of the event. If the event occurs on a Saturday, Sunday or holiday on which the Commission is not open for business, then the four business day period shall begin to run on, and include, the first business day thereafter. A registrant either furnishing a report on this form under Item 7.01 (Regulation FD Disclosure) or electing to file a report on this form under Item 8.01 (Other Events) solely to satisfy its obligations under Regulation FD (17 CFR 243.100 and 243.101) must furnish such report or make such filing, as applicable, in accordance with the requirements of Rule 100(a) of Regulation FD (17 CFR 243.100(a)), including the deadline for furnishing or filing such report.

2. The information in a report furnished pursuant to Item 2.02 (Results of Operations and Financial Condition) or Item 7.01 (Regulation FD Disclosure) shall not be deemed to be "filed" for purposes of Section 18 of the Exchange Act or otherwise subject to the liabilities of that

section, unless the registrant specifically states that the information is to be considered "filed" under the Exchange Act or incorporates it by reference into a filing under the Securities Act or the Exchange Act. If a report on Form 8-K contains disclosures under Item 2.02 or Item 7.01, whether or not the report contains disclosures regarding other items, all exhibits to such report relating to Item 2.02 or Item 7.01 will be deemed furnished, and not filed, unless the registrant specifies, under Item 9.01 (Financial Statements and Exhibits), which exhibits, or portions of exhibits, are intended to be deemed filed rather than furnished pursuant to this instruction.

3. If the registrant previously has reported substantially the same information as required by this form, the registrant need not make an additional report of the information on this form. To the extent that an item calls for disclosure of developments concerning a previously reported event or transaction, any information required in the new report or amendment about the previously reported event or transaction may be provided by incorporation by reference to the previously filed report. The term *previously reported* is defined in Rule 12b-2 (17 CFR 240.12b-2).

4. Copies of agreements, amendments or other documents or instruments required to be filed pursuant to Form 8-K are not required to be filed or furnished as exhibits to the Form 8-K unless specifically required to be filed or furnished by the applicable Item. This instruction does not affect the requirement to otherwise file such agreements, amendments or other documents or instruments, including as exhibits to registration statements and periodic reports pursuant to the requirements of Item 601 of Regulation S-K or Item 601 of Regulation S-B, as applicable.

5. When considering current reporting on this form, particularly of other events of material importance pursuant to Item 7.01 (Regulation FD Disclosure) and Item 8.01(Other Events), registrants should have due regard for the accuracy, completeness and currency of the information in registration statements filed under the Securities Act which incorporate by reference information in reports filed pursuant to the Exchange Act, including reports on this form.

6. A registrant's report under Item 7.01 (Regulation FD Disclosure) or Item 8.01 (Other Events) will not be deemed an admission as to the materiality of any information in the report that is required to be disclosed solely by Regulation FD.

* * * * *

Information to Be Included in the Report

Section 1—Registrant's Business and Operations

Item 1.01 Entry into a Material Definitive Agreement.

(a) If the registrant has entered into a material definitive agreement not made in the ordinary course of business of the registrant, or into any amendment of such agreement that is material to the registrant, disclose the following information:

(1) the date on which the agreement was entered into or amended, the identity of the parties to the agreement or amendment and a brief description of any material relationship between the registrant or its affiliates and any of the parties, other than in respect of the material definitive agreement or amendment; and

(2) a brief description of the terms and conditions of the agreement or amendment that are material to the registrant.

(b) For purposes of this Item 1.01, a *material definitive agreement* means an agreement that provides for obligations that are material to and enforceable against the registrant, or rights that are material to the registrant and enforceable by the registrant against one or more other parties to the agreement, in each case whether or not subject to conditions.

Instructions.

1. Any material definitive agreement of the registrant not made in the ordinary course of the registrant's business must be disclosed under this Item 1.01. An agreement is deemed to be not made in the ordinary course of a registrant's business even if the agreement is such as ordinarily accompanies the kind of business conducted by the registrant if it involves the subject matter identified in Item 601(b)(10)(ii)(A)—(D) of Regulation S-K (17 CFR 229.601(b)(10)(ii)(A)—(D)). An agreement involving the subject matter identified in Item 601(b)(10)(iii)(A) or (B) also must be disclosed unless Item 601(b)(10)(iii)(C) would not require the registrant to file a material agreement involving the same subject matter as an exhibit.

2. A registrant must provide disclosure under this Item 1.01 if the registrant succeeds as a party to the agreement or amendment to the agreement by assumption or assignment (other than in connection with a merger or acquisition or similar transaction).

Item 1.02 Termination of a Material Definitive Agreement.

(a) If a material definitive agreement which was not made in the ordinary course of business of the registrant and to which the registrant is a party is terminated otherwise than by expiration of the agreement on its stated termination date, or as a result of all parties completing their obligations under such agreement, and such termination of the agreement is material to the registrant, disclose the following information:

(1) the date of the termination of the material definitive agreement, the identity of the parties to the agreement and a brief description of any material relationship between the registrant or its affiliates and any of the parties other than in respect of the material definitive agreement;

(2) a brief description of the terms and conditions of the agreement that are material to the registrant;

(3) a brief description of the material circumstances surrounding the termination; and

(4) any material early termination penalties incurred by the registrant.

(b) For purposes of this Item 1.02, the term *material definitive agreement* shall have the same meaning as set forth in Item 1.01(b).

Instructions.

1. No disclosure is required solely by reason of this Item 1.02 during negotiations or discussions regarding termination of a material definitive agreement unless and until the agreement has been terminated.

2. No disclosure is required solely by reason of this Item 1.02 if the registrant believes in good faith that the material definitive agreement has not been terminated, unless the registrant has received a notice of termination pursuant to the terms of agreement.

Item 1.03 Bankruptcy or Receivership.

(a) If a receiver, fiscal agent or similar officer has been appointed for a registrant or its parent, in a proceeding under the Bankruptcy Act or in any other proceeding under state or federal law in which a court or governmental authority has assumed jurisdiction over substantially all of the assets or business of the registrant or its parent, or if such jurisdiction has been assumed by leaving the existing directors and officers in possession but subject to the supervision and orders of a court or governmental authority, disclose the following information:

(1) the name or other identification of the proceeding;

(2) the identity of the court or governmental authority;

(3) the date that jurisdiction was assumed; and

(4) the identity of the receiver, fiscal agent or similar officer and the date of his or her appointment.

(b) If an order confirming a plan of reorganization, arrangement or liquidation has been entered by a court or governmental authority having supervision or jurisdiction over substantially all of the assets or business of the registrant or its parent, disclose the following;

(1) the identity of the court or governmental authority;

(2) the date that the order confirming the plan was entered by the court or governmental authority;

(3) a summary of the material features of the plan and, pursuant to Item 9.01 (Financial Statements and Exhibits), a copy of the plan as confirmed;

(4) the number of shares or other units of the registrant or its parent issued and outstanding, the number reserved for future issuance in

respect of claims and interests filed and allowed under the plan, and the aggregate total of such numbers; and

(5) information as to the assets and liabilities of the registrant or its parent as of the date that the order confirming the plan was entered, or a date as close thereto as practicable.

Instruction.

The information called for in paragraph (b)(5) of this Item 1.03 may be presented in the form in which it was furnished to the court or governmental authority.

Section 2—Financial Information

Item 2.01 Completion of Acquisition or Disposition of Assets.

If the registrant or any of its majority-owned subsidiaries has completed the acquisition or disposition of a significant amount of assets, otherwise than in the ordinary course of business, disclose the following information:

(a) the date of completion of the transaction;

(b) a brief description of the assets involved;

(c) the identity of the person(s) from whom the assets were acquired or to whom they were sold and the nature of any material relationship, other than in respect of the transaction, between such person(s) and the registrant or any of its affiliates, or any director or officer of the registrant, or any associate of any such director or officer;

(d) the nature and amount of consideration given or received for the assets and, if any material relationship is disclosed pursuant to paragraph (c) of this Item 2.01, the formula or principle followed in determining the amount of such consideration; and

(e) if the transaction being reported is an acquisition and if any material relationship is disclosed pursuant to paragraph (c) of this Item 2.01, the source(s) of the funds used *unless* all or any part of the consideration used is a loan made in the ordinary course of business by a bank as defined by Section 3(a)(6) of the Act, in which case the identity of such bank may be omitted provided the registrant:

(1) has made a request for confidentiality pursuant to Section 13(d)(1)(B) of the Act; and

(2) states in the report that the identity of the bank has been so omitted and filed separately with the Commission.

Instructions.

1. No information need be given as to:

(i) any transaction between any person and any wholly-owned subsidiary of such person;

(ii) any transaction between two or more wholly-owned subsidiaries of any person; or

(iii) the redemption or other acquisition of securities from the public, or the sale or other disposition of securities to the public, by the issuer of such securities or by a wholly-owned subsidiary of that issuer.

2. The term *acquisition* includes every purchase, acquisition by lease, exchange, merger, consolidation, succession or other acquisition, except that the term does not include the construction or development of property by or for the registrant or its subsidiaries or the acquisition of materials for such purpose. The term *disposition* includes every sale, disposition by lease, exchange, merger, consolidation, mortgage, assignment or hypothecation of assets, whether for the benefit of creditors or otherwise, abandonment, destruction, or other disposition.

3. The information called for by this Item 2.01 is to be given as to each transaction or series of related transactions of the size indicated. The acquisition or disposition of securities is deemed the indirect acquisition or disposition of the assets represented by such securities if it results in the acquisition or disposition of control of such assets.

4. An acquisition or disposition shall be deemed to involve a significant amount of assets:

(i) if the registrant's and its other subsidiaries' equity in the net book value of such assets or the amount paid or received for the assets upon such acquisition or disposition exceeded 10% of the total assets of the registrant and its consolidated subsidiaries; or

(ii) if it involved a business (see 17 CFR 210.11-01(d)) that is significant (see 17 CFR 210.11-01(b)).

Acquisitions of individually insignificant businesses are not required to be reported pursuant to this Item 2.01 unless they are related businesses (see 17 CFR 210.3-05(a)(3)) and are significant in the aggregate.

5. Attention is directed to the requirements in Item 9.01 (Financial Statements and Exhibits) with respect to the filing of:

(i) financial statements of businesses acquired;

(ii) *pro forma* financial information; and

(iii) copies of the plans of acquisition or disposition as exhibits to the report.

Item 2.02 Results of Operations and Financial Condition.

(a) If a registrant, or any person acting on its behalf, makes any public announcement or release (including any update of an earlier announcement or release) disclosing material non-public information regarding the registrant's results of operations or financial condition for a completed quarterly or annual fiscal period, the registrant shall disclose the date of the announcement or release, briefly identify the announcement or release and include the text of that announcement or release as an exhibit.

(b) A Form 8-K is not required to be furnished to the Commission under this Item 2.02 in the case of disclosure of material non-public information that is disclosed orally, telephonically, by webcast, by broadcast, or by similar means if:

(1) the information is provided as part of a presentation that is complementary to, and initially occurs within 48 hours after, a related, written announcement or release that has been furnished on Form 8-K pursuant to this Item 2.02 prior to the presentation;

(2) the presentation is broadly accessible to the public by dial-in conference call, by webcast, by broadcast or by similar means;

(3) the financial and other statistical information contained in the presentation is provided on the registrant's website, together with any information that would be required under 17 CFR 244.100; and

(4) the presentation was announced by a widely disseminated press release, that included instructions as to when and how to access the presentation and the location on the registrant's website where the information would be available.

Instructions.

1. The requirements of this Item 2.02 are triggered by the disclosure of material non-public information regarding a completed fiscal year or quarter. Release of additional or updated material non-public information regarding a completed fiscal year or quarter would trigger an additional Item 2.02 requirement.

2. The requirements of paragraph (e)(1)(i) of Item 10 of Regulation S-K (17 CFR 229.10(e)(1)(i)) (or paragraph (h)(1)(i) of Item 10 of Regulation S-B (17 CFR 228.10(h)(1)(i)) in the case of a small business issuer) shall apply to disclosures under this Item 2.02.

3. Issuers that make earnings announcements or other disclosures of material non-public information regarding a completed fiscal year or quarter in an interim or annual report to shareholders are permitted to specify which portion of the report contains the information required to be furnished under this Item 2.02.

4. This Item 2.02 does not apply in the case of a disclosure that is made in a quarterly report filed with the Commission on Form 10-Q (17 CFR 249.308a) (or Form 10-QSB (17 CFR 249.308b)) or an annual report filed with the Commission on Form 10-K (17 CFR 249.310) (or Form 10-KSB (17 CFR 249.310b)).

Item 2.03 Creation of a Direct Financial Obligation or an Obligation under an Off-Balance Sheet Arrangement of a Registrant.

(a) If the registrant becomes obligated on a direct financial obligation that is material to the registrant, disclose the following information:

(1) the date on which the registrant becomes obligated on the direct financial obligation and a brief description of the transaction or agreement creating the obligation;

(2) the amount of the obligation, including the terms of its payment and, if applicable, a brief description of the material terms under which it may be accelerated or increased and the nature of any recourse provisions that would enable the registrant to recover from third parties; and

(3) a brief description of the other terms and conditions of the transaction or agreement that are material to the registrant.

(b) If the registrant becomes directly or contingently liable for an obligation that is material to the registrant arising out of an off-balance sheet arrangement, disclose the following information:

(1) the date on which the registrant becomes directly or contingently liable on the obligation and a brief description of the transaction or agreement creating the arrangement and obligation;

(2) a brief description of the nature and amount of the obligation of the registrant under the arrangement, including the material terms whereby it may become a direct obligation, if applicable, or may be accelerated or increased and the nature of any recourse provisions that would enable the registrant to recover from third parties;

(3) the maximum potential amount of future payments (undiscounted) that the registrant may be required to make, if different; and

(4) a brief description of the other terms and conditions of the obligation or arrangement that are material to the registrant.

(c) For purposes of this Item 2.03, *direct financial obligation* means any of the following:

(1) a long-term debt obligation, as defined in Item 303(a)(5)(ii)(A) of Regulation S-K (17 CFR 229.303(a)(5)(ii)(A));

(2) a capital lease obligation, as defined in Item 303(a)(5)(ii)(B) of Regulation S-K (17 CFR 229.303(a)(5)(ii)(B));

(3) an operating lease obligation, as defined in Item 303(a)(5)(ii)(C) of Regulation S-K (17 CFR 229.303(a)(5)(ii)(C)); or

(4) a short-term debt obligation that arises other than in the ordinary course of business.

(d) For purposes of this Item 2.03, *off-balance sheet arrangement* has the meaning set forth in Item 303(a)(4)(ii) of Regulation S-K (17 CFR 229.303(a)(4)(ii)) or Item 303(c)(2) of Regulation S-B (17 CFR 228.303(c)(2)), as applicable.

(e) For purposes of this Item 2.03, *short-term debt obligation* means a payment obligation under a borrowing arrangement that is scheduled to mature within one year, or, for those registrants that use the operating cycle concept of working capital, within a registrant's operating cycle that is longer than one year, as discussed in Accounting Research Bulletin No. 43, Chapter 3A, *Working Capital.*

Instructions.

1. A registrant has no obligation to disclose information under this Item 2.03 until the registrant enters into an agreement enforceable against the registrant, whether or not subject to conditions, under which the direct financial obligation will arise or be created or issued. If there is no such agreement, the registrant must provide the disclosure within four business days after the occurrence of the closing or settlement of the transaction or arrangement under which the direct financial obligation arises or is created.

2. A registrant must provide the disclosure required by paragraph (b) of this Item 2.03 whether or not the registrant is also a party to the transaction or agreement creating the contingent obligation arising under the off-balance sheet arrangement. In the event that neither the registrant nor any affiliate of the registrant is also a party to the transaction or agreement creating the contingent obligation arising under the off-balance sheet arrangement in question, the four business day period for reporting the event under this Item 2.03 shall begin on the earlier of (i) the fourth business day after the contingent obligation is created or arises, and (ii) the day on which an executive officer, as defined in 17 CFR 240.3b-7, of the registrant becomes aware of the contingent obligation.

3. In the event that an agreement, transaction or arrangement requiring disclosure under this Item 2.03 comprises a facility, program or similar arrangement that creates or may give rise to direct financial obligations of the registrant in connection with multiple transactions, the registrant shall:

(i) disclose the entering into of the facility, program or similar arrangement if the entering into of the facility is material to the registrant; and

(ii) as direct financial obligations arise or are created under the facility or program, disclose the required information under this Item 2.03 to the extent that the obligations are material to the registrant (including when a series of previously undisclosed individually immaterial obligations become material in the aggregate).

4. For purposes of Item 2.03(b)(3), the maximum amount of future payments shall not be reduced by the effect of any amounts that may possibly be recovered by the registrant under recourse or collateralization provisions in any guarantee agreement, transaction or arrangement.

5. If the obligation required to be disclosed under this Item 2.03 is a security, or a term of a security, that has been or will be sold pursuant to an effective registration statement of the registrant, the registrant is not required

to file a Form 8-K pursuant to this Item 2.03, *provided* that the prospectus relating to that sale contains the information required by this Item 2.03 and is filed within the required time period under Securities Act Rule 424 (§ 230.424 of this chapter).

Item 2.04 Triggering Events That Accelerate or Increase a Direct Financial Obligation or an Obligation under an Off-Balance Sheet Arrangement.

(a) If a triggering event causing the increase or acceleration of a direct financial obligation of the registrant occurs and the consequences of the event, taking into account those described in paragraph (a)(4) of this Item 2.04, are material to the registrant, disclose the following information:

(1) the date of the triggering event and a brief description of the agreement or transaction under which the direct financial obligation was created and is increased or accelerated;

(2) a brief description of the triggering event;

(3) the amount of the direct financial obligation, as increased if applicable, and the terms of payment or acceleration that apply; and

(4) any other material obligations of the registrant that may arise, increase, be accelerated or become direct financial obligations as a result of the triggering event or the increase or acceleration of the direct financial obligation.

(b) If a triggering event occurs causing an obligation of the registrant under an off-balance sheet arrangement to increase or be accelerated, or causing a contingent obligation of the registrant under an off-balance sheet arrangement to become a direct financial obligation of the registrant, and the consequences of the event, taking into account those described in paragraph (b)(4) of this Item 2.04, are material to the registrant, disclose the following information:

(1) the date of the triggering event and a brief description of the off-balance sheet arrangement;

(2) a brief description of the triggering event;

(3) the nature and amount of the obligation, as increased if applicable, and the terms of payment or acceleration that apply; and

(4) any other material obligations of the registrant that may arise, increase, be accelerated or become direct financial obligations as a result of the triggering event or the increase or acceleration of the obligation under the off-balance sheet arrangement or its becoming a direct financial obligation of the registrant.

(c) For purposes of this Item 2.04, the term *direct financial obligation* has the meaning provided in Item 2.03 of this form, but shall also include an obligation arising out of an off-balance sheet arrangement that is accrued under FASB Statement of Financial Accounting Standards No. 5 *Accounting for Contingencies* (SFAS No. 5) as a probable loss contingency.

(d) For purposes of this Item 2.04, the term *off-balance sheet arrangement* has the meaning provided in Item 2.03 of this form.

(e) For purposes of this Item 2.04, a *triggering event* is an event, including an event of default, event of acceleration or similar event, as a result of which a direct financial obligation of the registrant or an obligation of the registrant arising under an off-balance sheet arrangement is increased or becomes accelerated or as a result of which a contingent obligation of the registrant arising out of an off-balance sheet arrangement becomes a direct financial obligation of the registrant.

Instructions.

1. Disclosure is required if a triggering event occurs in respect of an obligation of the registrant under an off-balance sheet arrangement and the consequences are material to the registrant, whether or not the registrant is also a party to the transaction or agreement under which the triggering event occurs.

2. No disclosure is required under this Item 2.04 unless and until a triggering event has occurred in accordance with the terms of the relevant agreement, transaction or arrangement, including, if required, the sending to the registrant of notice of the occurrence of a triggering event pursuant to the terms of the agreement, transaction or arrangement and the satisfaction of all conditions to such occurrence, except the passage of time.

3. No disclosure is required solely by reason of this Item 2.04 if the registrant believes in good faith that no triggering event has occurred, unless the registrant has received a notice described in Instruction 2 to this Item 2.04.

4. Where a registrant is subject to an obligation arising out of an off-balance sheet arrangement, whether or not disclosed pursuant to Item 2.03 of this form, if a triggering event occurs as a result of which under that obligation an accrual for a probable loss is required under SFAS No. 5, the obligation arising out of the off-balance sheet arrangement becomes a direct financial obligation as defined in this Item 2.04. In that situation, if the consequences as determined under Item 2.04(b) are material to the registrant, disclosure is required under this Item 2.04.

Item 2.05 Costs Associated with Exit or Disposal Activities.

If the registrant's board of directors, a committee of the board of directors or the officer or officers of the registrant authorized to take such action if board action is not required, commits the registrant to an exit or disposal plan, or otherwise disposes of a long-lived asset or terminates employees under a plan of termination described in paragraph 8 of FASB Statement of Financial Accounting Standards No. 146 *Accounting for Costs Associated with Exit or Disposal Activities* (SFAS No. 146), under which material charges will be incurred under generally accepted accounting principles applicable to the registrant, disclose the following information:

(a) the date of the commitment to the course of action and a description of the course of action, including the facts and circumstances leading to the expected action and the expected completion date;

(b) for each major type of cost associated with the course of action (for example, one-time termination benefits, contract termination costs and other associated costs), an estimate of the total amount or range of amounts expected to be incurred in connection with the action;

(c) an estimate of the total amount or range of amounts expected to be incurred in connection with the action; and

(d) the registrant's estimate of the amount or range of amounts of the charge that will result in future cash expenditures, *provided, however*, that if the registrant determines that at the time of filing it is unable in good faith to make a determination of an estimate required by paragraphs (b), (c) or (d) of this Item 2.05, no disclosure of such estimate shall be required; *provided further, however*, that in any such event, the registrant shall file an amended report on Form 8-K under this Item 2.05 within four business days after it makes a determination of such an estimate or range of estimates.

Item 2.06 Material Impairments.

If the registrant's board of directors, a committee of the board of directors or the officer or officers of the registrant authorized to take such action if board action is not required, concludes that a material charge for impairment to one or more of its assets, including, without limitation, impairments of securities or goodwill, is required under generally accepted accounting principles applicable to the registrant, disclose the following information:

(a) the date of the conclusion that a material charge is required and a description of the impaired asset or assets and the facts and circumstances leading to the conclusion that the charge for impairment is required;

(b) the registrant's estimate of the amount or range of amounts of the impairment charge; and

(c) the registrant's estimate of the amount or range of amounts of the impairment charge that will result in future cash expenditures, *provided, however*, that if the registrant determines that at the time of filing it is unable in good faith to make a determination of an estimate required by paragraphs (b) or (c) of this Item 2.06, no disclosure of such estimate shall be required; *provided further, however*, that in any such event, the registrant shall file an amended report on Form 8-K under this Item 2.06 within four business days after it makes a determination of such an estimate or range of estimates.

Instruction.

No filing is required under this Item 2.06 if the conclusion is made in connection with the preparation, review or audit of financial statements required to be included in the next periodic report due to be filed under the Exchange Act, the periodic report is filed on a timely basis and such conclusion is disclosed in the report.

Section 3—Securities and Trading Markets

Item 3.01 Notice of Delisting or Failure to Satisfy a Continued Listing Rule or Standard; Transfer of Listing.

(a) If the registrant has received notice from the national securities exchange or national securities association (or a facility thereof) that maintains the principal listing for any class of the registrant's common equity (as defined in Exchange Act Rule 12b-2 (17 CFR 240.12b-2)) that:

- the registrant or such class of the registrant's securities does not satisfy a rule or standard for continued listing on the exchange or association;
- the exchange has submitted an application under Exchange Act Rule 12d2-2 (17 CFR 240.12d2-2) to the Commission to delist such class of the registrant's securities; or
- the association has taken all necessary steps under its rules to delist the security from its automated inter-dealer quotation system, the registrant must disclose:

(i) the date that the registrant received the notice;

(ii) the a rule or standard for continued listing on the national securities exchange or national securities association that the registrant fails, or has failed to, satisfy; and

(iii) any action or response that, at the time of filing, the registrant has determined to take in response to the notice.

(b) If the registrant has notified the national securities exchange or national securities association (or a facility thereof) that maintains the principal listing for any class of the registrant's common equity (as defined in Exchange Act Rule 12b-2 (17 CFR 240.12b-2) that the registrant is aware of any material noncompliance with a rule or standard for continued listing on the exchange or association, the registrant must disclose:

(i) the date that the registrant provided such notice to the exchange or association;

(ii) the rule or standard for continued listing on the exchange or association that the registrant fails, or has failed, to satisfy; and

(iii) any action or response that, at the time of filing, the registrant has determined to take regarding its noncompliance.

(c) If the national securities exchange or national securities association (or a facility thereof) that maintains the principal listing for any class of the registrant's common equity (as defined in Exchange Act Rule 12b-2 (17 CFR 240.12b-2)), in lieu of suspending trading in or delisting such class of the registrant's securities, issues a public reprimand letter or similar communication indicating that the registrant has violated a rule or standard for continued listing on the exchange or association, the registrant must state the date, and summarize the contents of the letter or communication.

(d) If the registrant's board of directors, a committee of the board of directors or the officer or officers of the registrant authorized to take such action if board action is not required, has taken definitive action to cause the listing of a class of its common equity to be withdrawn from the national securities exchange, or terminated from the automated inter-dealer quotation system of a registered national securities association, where such exchange or association maintains the principal listing for such class of securities, including by reason of a transfer of the listing or quotation to another securities exchange or quotation system, describe the action taken and state the date of the action.

Instructions.

1. The registrant is not required to disclose any information required by paragraph (a) of this Item 3.01 where the delisting is a result of one of the following:

- the entire class of the security has been called for redemption, maturity or retirement; appropriate notice thereof has been given; if required by the terms of the securities, funds sufficient for the payment of all such securities have been deposited with an agency authorized to make such payments; and such funds have been made available to security holders;

- the entire class of the security has been redeemed or paid at maturity or retirement;

- the instruments representing the entire class of securities have come to evidence, by operation of law or otherwise, other securities in substitution therefor and represent no other right, except, if true, the right to receive an immediate cash payment (the right of dissenters to receive the appraised or fair value of their holdings shall not prevent the application of this provision); or

- all rights pertaining to the entire class of the security have been extinguished; *provided, however,* that where such an event occurs as the result of an order of a court or other governmental authority, the order shall be final, all applicable appeal periods shall have expired and no appeals shall be pending.

2. A registrant must provide the disclosure required by paragraph (a) or (b) of this Item 3.01, as applicable, regarding any failure to satisfy a rule or standard for continued listing on the national securities exchange or national securities association (or a facility thereof) that maintains the principal listing for any class of the registrant's common equity (as defined in Exchange Act

Rule 12b-2 (17 CFR 240.12b-2)) even if the registrant has the benefit of a grace period or similar extension period during which it may cure the deficiency that triggers the disclosure requirement.

3. Notices or other communications subsequent to an initial notice sent to, or by, a registrant under Item 3.01(a), (b) or (c) that continue to indicate that the registrant does not comply with the same rule or standard for continued listing that was the subject of the initial notice are not required to be filed, but may be filed voluntarily.

4. Registrants whose securities are quoted exclusively (i.e., the securities are not otherwise listed on an exchange or association) on automated inter-dealer quotation systems are not subject to this Item 3.01 and such registrants are thus not required to file a Form 8-K pursuant to this Item 3.01 if the securities are no longer quoted on such quotation system. If a security is listed on an exchange or association and is also quoted on an automated inter-dealer quotation system, the registrant is subject to the disclosure obligations of Item 3.01 if any of the events specified in Item 3.01 occur.

Item 3.02 Unregistered Sales of Equity Securities.

(a) If the registrant sells equity securities in a transaction that is not registered under the Securities Act, furnish the information set forth in paragraphs (a) and (c) through (e) of Item 701 of Regulation S-K or Regulation S-B, as applicable (17 CFR 229.701(a) and (c) through (e) and 228.701(a) and (c) through (e), respectively). For purposes of determining the required filing date for the Form 8-K under this Item 3.02(a), the registrant has no obligation to disclose information under this Item 3.02 until the registrant enters into an agreement enforceable against the registrant, whether or not subject to conditions, under which the equity securities are to be sold. If there is no such agreement, the registrant must provide the disclosure within four business days after the occurrence of the closing or settlement of the transaction or arrangement under which the equity securities are to be sold.

(b) No report need be filed under this Item 3.02 if the equity securities sold, in the aggregate since its last report filed under this Item 3.02 or its last periodic report, whichever is more recent, constitute less than 1% of the number of shares outstanding of the class of equity securities sold. In the case of a small business issuer, no report need be filed if the equity securities sold, in the aggregate since its last report filed under this Item 3.02 or its last periodic report, whichever is more recent, constitute less than 5% of the number of shares outstanding of the class of equity securities sold.

Instructions.

1. For purposes of this Item 3.02, "the number of shares outstanding" refers to the actual number of shares of equity securities of the class outstanding and does not include outstanding securities convertible into or exchangeable for such equity securities.

2. Small business issuer is defined under Item 10(a)(1) of Regulation S-B (17 CFR 228.10(a)(1)).

Item 3.03 Material Modification to Rights of Security Holders.

(a) If the constituent instruments defining the rights of the holders of any class of registered securities of the registrant have been materially modified, disclose the date of the modification, the title of the class of securities involved and briefly describe the general effect of such modification upon the rights of holders of such securities.

(b) If the rights evidenced by any class of registered securities have been materially limited or qualified by the issuance or modification of any other class of securities by the registrant, briefly disclose the date of the issuance or modification, the general effect of the issuance or modification of such other class of securities upon the rights of the holders of the registered securities.

Instruction.

Working capital restrictions and other limitations upon the payment of dividends must be reported pursuant to this Item 3.03.

Section 4—Matters Related to Accountants and Financial Statements

Item 4.01 Changes in Registrant's Certifying Accountant.

(a) If an independent accountant who was previously engaged as the principal accountant to audit the registrant's financial statements, or an independent accountant upon whom the principal accountant expressed reliance in its report regarding a significant subsidiary, resigns (or indicates that it declines to stand for re-appointment after completion of the current audit) or is dismissed, disclose the information required by Item 304(a)(1) of Regulation S-K or Item 304(a)(1) of Regulation S-B, as applicable, including compliance with Item 304(a)(3) of Regulation S-K or Item 304(a)(3) of Regulation S-B (17 CFR 229.304(a)(1) and (a)(3) or 228.304(a)(1) and (a)(3), respectively).

(b) If a new independent accountant has been engaged as either the principal accountant to audit the registrant's financial statements or as an independent accountant on whom the principal accountant is expected to express reliance in its report regarding a significant subsidiary, the registrant must disclose the information required by Item 304(a)(2) of Regulation S-K or Item 304(a)(2) of Regulation S-B, as applicable (17 CFR 229.304(a)(2) or 228.304(a)(2), respectively).

Instruction.

The resignation or dismissal of an independent accountant, or its refusal to stand for re-appointment, is a reportable event separate from the engagement of a new independent accountant. On some occasions, two reports on Form 8-K are required for a single change in accountants, the first on the resignation (or refusal to stand for re-appointment) or dismissal of the former accountant and the second when the new accountant is engaged. Information required in the second Form 8-K in such situations need not be provided to the extent that it has been reported previously in the first Form 8-K.

Item 4.02 Non-Reliance on Previously Issued Financial Statements or a Related Audit Report or Completed Interim Review.

(a) If the registrant's board of directors, a committee of the board of directors or the officer or officers of the registrant authorized to take such action if board action is not required, concludes that any previously issued financial statements, covering one or more years or interim periods for which the registrant is required to provide financial statements under Regulation S-X (17 CFR 210) or Regulation S-B (17 CFR 228), should no longer be relied upon because of an error in such financial statements as addressed in Accounting Principles Board Opinion No. 20, as may be modified, supplemented or succeeded, disclose the following information:

(1) the date of the conclusion regarding the non-reliance and an identification of the financial statements and years or periods covered that should no longer be relied upon;

(2) a brief description of the facts underlying the conclusion to the extent known to the registrant at the time of filing; and

(3) a statement of whether the audit committee, or the board of directors in the absence of an audit committee, or authorized officer or officers, discussed with the registrant's independent accountant the matters disclosed in the filing pursuant to this Item 4.02(a).

(b) If the registrant is advised by, or receives notice from, its independent accountant that disclosure should be made or action should be taken to prevent future reliance on a previously issued audit report or completed interim review related to previously issued financial statements, disclose the following information:

(1) the date on which the registrant was so advised or notified;

(2) identification of the financial statements that should no longer be relied upon;

(3) a brief description of the information provided by the accountant; and

(4) a statement of whether the audit committee, or the board of directors in the absence of an audit committee, or authorized officer or officers, discussed with the independent accountant the matters disclosed in the filing pursuant to this Item 4.02(b).

(c) If the registrant receives advisement or notice from its independent accountant requiring disclosure under paragraph (b) of this Item 4.02, the registrant must:

(1) provide the independent accountant with a copy of the disclosures it is making in response to this Item 4.02 that the independent accountant shall receive no later than the day that the disclosures are filed with the Commission;

(2) request the independent accountant to furnish to the registrant as promptly as possible a letter addressed to the Commission stating whether the independent accountant agrees with the statements made by the registrant in response to this Item 4.02 and, if not, stating the respects in which it does not agree; and

(3) amend the registrant's previously filed Form 8-K by filing the independent accountant's letter as an exhibit to the filed Form 8-K no later than two business days after the registrant's receipt of the letter.

Section 5—Corporate Governance and Management

Item 5.01 Changes in Control of Registrant.

(a) If, to the knowledge of the registrant's board of directors, a committee of the board of directors or authorized officer or officers of the registrant, a change in control of the registrant has occurred, furnish the following information:

(1) the identity of the person(s) who acquired such control;

(2) the date and a description of the transaction(s) which resulted in the change in control;

(3) the basis of the control, including the percentage of voting securities of the registrant now beneficially owned directly or indirectly by the person(s) who acquired control;

(4) the amount of the consideration used by such person(s);

(5) the source(s) of funds used by the person(s), *unless* all or any part of the consideration used is a loan made in the ordinary course of business by a bank as defined by Section 3(a)(6) of the Act, in which case the identity of such bank may be omitted provided the person who acquired control:

(1) has made a request for confidentiality pursuant to Section 13(d)(1)(B) of the Act; and

(2) states in the report that the identity of the bank has been so omitted and filed separately with the Commission.

(6) the identity of the person(s) from whom control was assumed; and

(7) any arrangements or understandings among members of both the former and new control groups and their associates with respect to election of directors or other matters.

(b) Furnish the information required by Item 403(c) of Regulation S-K (17 CFR 229.403(c)) or Item 403(c) of Regulation S-B (17 CFR 228.403(c)), as applicable.

Item 5.02 Departure of Directors or Principal Officers; Election of Directors; Appointment of Principal Officers.

(a)(1) If a director has resigned or refuses to stand for re-election to the board of directors since the date of the last annual meeting of shareholders because of a disagreement with the registrant, known to an executive officer of the registrant, as defined in 17 CFR 240.3b-7, on any matter relating to the registrant's operations, policies or practices, or if a director has been removed for cause from the board of directors, disclose the following information:

(i) the date of such resignation, refusal to stand for re-election or removal;

(ii) any positions held by the director on any committee of the board of directors at the time of the director's resignation, refusal to stand for re-election or removal; and

(iii) a brief description of the circumstances representing the disagreement that the registrant believes caused, in whole or in part, the director's resignation, refusal to stand for re-election or removal.

(2) If the director has furnished the registrant with any written correspondence concerning the circumstances surrounding his or her resignation, refusal or removal, the registrant shall file a copy of the document as an exhibit to the report on Form 8-K.

(3) The registrant also must:

(i) provide the director with a copy of the disclosures it is making in response to this Item 5.02 no later than the day the registrant file the disclosures with the Commission;

(ii) provide the director with the opportunity to furnish the registrant as promptly as possible with a letter addressed to the registrant stating whether he or she agrees with the statements made by the registrant in response to this Item 5.02 and, if not, stating the respects in which he or she does not agree; and

(iii) file any letter received by the registrant from the director with the Commission as an exhibit by an amendment to the previously filed Form 8-K within two business days after receipt by the registrant.

(b) If the registrant's principal executive officer, president, principal financial officer, principal accounting officer, principal operating officer or any person performing similar functions retires, resigns or is terminated from that position, or if a director retires, resigns, is removed, or refuses to stand for re-election (except in circumstances described in paragraph (a) of this Item 5.02), disclose the fact that the event has occurred and the date of the event.

(c) If the registrant appoints a new principal executive officer, president, principal financial officer, principal accounting officer, principal operating officer or person performing similar functions, disclose the following information with respect to the newly appointed officer:

(1) the name and position of the newly appointed officer and the date of the appointment;

(2) the information required by Items 401(b), (d), (e) and Item 404(a) of Regulation S-K (17 CFR 229.401(b), (d), (e) and 229.404(a)), or, in the case of a small business issuer, Items 401(a)(4), (a)(5), (c), and Items 404(a) and (b) of Regulation S-B (17 CFR 228.401(a)(4), (a)(5), (c), and 228.404(a) and (b), respectively); and

(3) a brief description of the material terms of any employment agreement between the registrant and that officer.

Instruction to paragraph (c).

If the registrant intends to make a public announcement of the appointment other than by means of a report on Form 8-K, the registrant may delay filing the Form 8-K containing the disclosures required by this Item 5.02(c) until the day on which the registrant otherwise makes public announcement of the appointment of such officer.

(d) If the registrant elects a new director, except by a vote of security holders at an annual meeting or special meeting convened for such purpose, disclose the following information:

(1) the name of the newly elected director and the date of election;

(2) a brief description of any arrangement or understanding between the new director and any other persons, naming such persons, pursuant to which such director was selected as a director;

(3) the committees of the board of directors to which the new director has been, or at the time of this disclosure is expected to be, named; and

(4) the information required by Item 404(a) of Regulation S-K or Item 404(a) of Regulation S-B, as applicable (17 CFR 229.404(a) or 228.404(a), respectively).

Instructions to Item 5.02.

1. The disclosure requirements of this Item 5.02 do not apply to a registrant that is a wholly-owned subsidiary of an issuer with a class of securities registered under Section 12 of the Exchange Act (15 U.S.C. 78l), or that is required to file reports under Section 15(d) of the Exchange Act (15 U.S.C. 78o(d)).

2. To the extent that any information called for in Item 5.02(c)(3) or Item 5.02(d)(3) or Item 5.02(d)(4) is not determined or is unavailable at the time of the required filing, the registrant shall include a statement this effect in the filing and then must file an amendment to its Form 8-K filing under this Item 5.02 containing such information within four business days after the information is determined or becomes available.

Item 5.03 Amendments to Articles of Incorporation or Bylaws; Change in Fiscal Year.

(a) If a registrant with a class of equity securities registered under Section 12 of the Exchange Act (15 U.S.C. 78l) amends its articles of incorporation or bylaws and a proposal for the amendment was not disclosed in a proxy statement or information statement filed by the registrant, disclose the following information:

(1) the effective date of the amendment; and

(2) a description of the provision adopted or changed by amendment and, if applicable, the previous provision.

(b) If the registrant determines to change the fiscal year from that used in its most recent filing with the Commission other than by means of:

(1) a submission to a vote of security holders through the solicitation of proxies or otherwise; or

(2) an amendment to its articles of incorporation or bylaws, disclose the date of such determination, the date of the new fiscal year end and the form (for example, Form 10-K, Form 10-KSB, Form 10-Q or Form 10-QSB) on which the report covering the transition period will be filed.

Instruction to Item 5.03.

Refer to Item 601(b)(3) of Regulation S-K or Regulation S-B (17 CFR 229.601(b)(3) and 228.601(b)(3)), as applicable, regarding the filing of exhibits to this Item 5.03.

Item 5.04 Temporary Suspension of Trading Under Registrant's Employee Benefit Plans.

(a) No later than the fourth business day after which the registrant receives the notice required by section 101(i)(2)(E) of the Employment Retirement Income Security Act of 1974 (29 U.S.C. 1021(i)(2)(E)), or, if such notice is not received by the registrant, on the same date by which the registrant transmits a timely notice to an affected officer or director within the time period prescribed by Rule 104(b)(2)(i)(B) or 104(b)(2)(ii) of Regulation BTR (17 CFR 245.104(b)(2)(i)(B) or 17 CFR 245.104(b)(2)(ii)), provide the information specified in Rule 104(b) (17 CFR 245.104(b)) and the date the registrant received the notice required by section 101(i)(2)(E) of the Employment Retirement Income Security Act of 1974 (29 U.S.C. 1021(i)(2)(E)), if applicable.

(b) On the same date by which the registrant transmits a timely updated notice to an affected officer or director, as required by the time period under Rule 104(b)(2)(iii) of Regulation BTR (17 CFR 245.104(b)(2)(iii)), provide the information specified in Rule 104(b)(3)(iii) (17 CFR 245.104(b)(2)(iii)).

Item 5.05 Amendments to the Registrant's Code of Ethics, or Waiver of a Provision of the Code of Ethics.

(a) Briefly describe the date and nature of any amendment to a provision of the registrant's code of ethics that applies to the registrant's principal executive officer, principal financial officer, principal accounting officer or controller or persons performing similar functions and that relates to any element of the code of ethics definition enumerated in Item 406(b) of Regulations S-K and S-B (17 CFR 229.406(b) and 228.406(b), respectively).

(b) If the registrant has granted a waiver, including an implicit waiver, from a provision of the code of ethics to an officer or person described in paragraph (a) of this Item 5.05, and the waiver relates to one or more of the elements of the code of ethics definition referred to in paragraph (a) of this Item 5.05, briefly describe the nature of the waiver, the name of the person to whom the waiver was granted, and the date of the waiver.

(c) The registrant does not need to provide any information pursuant to this Item 5.05 if it discloses the required information on its Internet website within four business days following the date of the amendment or waiver and the registrant has disclosed in its most recently filed annual report its Internet address and intention to provide disclosure in this manner. If the registrant elects to disclose the information required by this Item 5.05 through its website, such information must remain available on the website for at least a 12-month period. Following the 12-month period, the registrant must retain the information for a period of not less than five years. Upon request, the registrant must furnish to the Commission or its staff a copy of any or all information retained pursuant to this requirement.

Instructions.

1. The registrant does not need to disclose technical, administrative or other non-substantive amendments to its code of ethics.

2. For purposes of this Item 5.05:

(i) The term *waiver* means the approval by the registrant of a material departure from a provision of the code of ethics; and

(ii) The term *implicit waiver* means the registrant's failure to take action within a reasonable period of time regarding a material departure from a provision of the code of ethics that has been made known to an executive officer, as defined in Rule 3b-7 (17 CFR 240.3b-7) of the registrant.

Section 6—[Reserved]

Section 7—Regulation FD

Item 7.01 Regulation FD Disclosure.

Unless filed under Item 8.01, disclose under this item only information that the registrant elects to disclose through Form 8-K pursuant to Regulation FD (17 CFR 243.100 through 243.103).

Section 8—Other Events

Item 8.01 Other Events.

The registrant may, at its option, disclose under this Item 8.01 any events, with respect to which information is not otherwise called for by this form, that the registrant deems of importance to security holders. The registrant may, at its option, file a report under this Item 8.01 disclosing the nonpublic information required to be disclosed by Regulation FD (17 CFR 243.100 through 243.103).

Section 9—Financial Statements and Exhibits

Item 9.01 Financial Statements and Exhibits.

List below the financial statements, pro forma financial information and exhibits, if any, filed as a part of this report.

(a) *Financial statements of businesses acquired.*

(1) For any business acquisition required to be described in answer to Item 2.01 of this form, financial statements of the business acquired shall be filed for the periods specified in Rule 3-05(b) of Regulation S-X (17 CFR 210.3-05(b)).

(2) The financial statements shall be prepared pursuant to Regulation S-X except that supporting schedules need not be filed. A manually signed accountant's report should be provided pursuant to Rule 2-02 of Regulation S-X (17 CFR 210.2-02).

(3) With regard to the acquisition of one or more real estate properties, the financial statements and any additional information specified by Rule 3-14 of Regulation S-X (17 CFR 210.3-14) shall be filed.

(4) Financial statements required by this item may be filed with the initial report, or by amendment not later than 71 calendar days after the date that the initial report on Form 8-K must be filed. If the financial statements are not included in the initial report, the registrant should so indicate in the Form 8-K report and state when the required financial statements will be filed. The registrant may, at its option, include unaudited financial statements in the initial report on Form 8-K.

(b) *Pro forma financial information.*

(1) For any transaction required to be described in answer to Item 2.01 of this form, furnish any pro forma financial information that would be required pursuant to Article 11 of Regulation S-X (17 CFR 210).

(2) The provisions of paragraph (a)(4) of this Item 9.01 shall also apply to pro forma financial information relative to the acquired business.

(c) *Exhibits.* The exhibits shall be deemed to be filed or furnished, depending on the relevant item requiring such exhibit, in accordance with the provisions of Item 601 of Regulation S-K (17 CFR 229.601), or Item 601 of Regulation S-B (17 CFR 228.601) and Instruction B.2 to this form.

Instruction.

During the period after a registrant has reported a business combination pursuant to Item 2.01 of this form, until the date on which the financial statements specified by this Item 9.01 must be filed, the registrant will be deemed current for purposes of its reporting obligations under Section 13(a) or 15(d) of the Exchange Act (15 U.S.C. 78m or 78o(d)). With respect to filings under the Securities Act, however, registration statements will not be declared effective and post-effective amendments to registrations statements will not be declared effective unless financial statements meeting the requirements of Rule 3-05 of Regulation S-X (17 CFR 210.3-05) are provided. In addition, offerings should not be made pursuant to effective registration statements, or pursuant to Rules 505 and 506 of Regulation D (17 CFR 230.505 and 230.506) where any purchasers are not accredited investors under Rule 501(a) of that Regulation, until the audited financial statements required by Rule 3-05 of Regulation S-X (17 CFR 210.3-05) are filed; *provided, however,* that the following offerings or sales of securities may proceed notwithstanding that financial statements of the acquired business have not been filed:

(a) offerings or sales of securities upon the conversion of outstanding convertible securities or upon the exercise of outstanding warrants or rights;

(b) dividend or interest reinvestment plans;

(c) employee benefit plans;

(d) transactions involving secondary offerings; or

(e) sales of securities pursuant to Rule 144 (17 CFR 230.144).

* * * * *

20. Amend Form 10-Q (referenced in § 249.308a) by:

a. Revising the heading for Item 2 in Part II—Other Information;

b. Removing Items 2(a), 2(b) and 6(b);

c. Redesignating paragraphs (c), (d) and (e) in Item 2 as paragraphs (a), (b) and (c);

d. Revising newly redesignated paragraph (a) in Item 2;

e. Revising the Instructions to Item 3;

f. Revising Item 5;

g. Removing the words "and Reports on Form 8-K (§ 249.308 of this chapter)" from the heading of Item 6; and

h. Removing the paragraph (a) designation in Item 6.

The revisions read as follows:

Note—The text of Form 10-Q does not, and this amendment will not, appear in the Code of Federal Regulations.

Form 10-Q

* * * * *

PART II—OTHER INFORMATION

* * * * *

Item 2. Unregistered Sales of Equity Securities and Use of Proceeds.

(a) Furnish the information required by Item 701 of Regulation S-K (17 CFR 229.701) as to all equity securities of the registrant sold by the registrant during the period covered by the report that were not registered under the Securities Act. If the Item 701 information previously has been included in a Current Report on Form 8-K (17 CFR 249.308), however, it need not be furnished.

* * * * *

Item 3. Defaults Upon Senior Securities.

* * * * *

Instructions to Item 3

1. Item 3 need not be answered as to any default or arrearage with respect to any class of securities all of which is held by or for the account of the registrant or its totally held subsidiaries.

2. The information required by Item 3 need not be made if previously disclosed on a report on Form 8-K (17 CFR 249.308).

* * * * *

Item 5. Other Information.

The registrant must disclose under this item any information required to be disclosed in a report on Form 8-K during the period covered by this Form 10-Q, but not reported, whether or not otherwise required by this Form 10-Q. If disclosure of such information is made under this item, it need not be repeated in a report on Form 8-K which would otherwise be required to be filed with respect to such information or in a subsequent report on Form 10-Q.

* * * * *

21. Amend Form 10-QSB (referenced in § 249.308b) by:

a. Revising the heading for Item 2 in Part II—Other Information;

b. Removing Items 2(a), 2(b) and 6(b);

c. Redesignating paragraphs (c), (d) and (e) in Item 2 as paragraphs (a), (b) and (c);

d. Revising newly redesignated paragraph (a) in Item 2;

e. Revising the Instructions to Item 3;

f. Revising Item 5;

g. Removing the words "and Reports on Form 8-K" from the heading of Item 6; and

h. Removing the paragraph (a) designation in Item 6.

The revisions read as follows:

Note—The text of Form 10-QSB does not, and this amendment will not, appear in the Code of Federal Regulations.

Form 10-QSB

* * * * *

PART II—OTHER INFORMATION

* * * * *

Item 2. Unregistered Sales of Equity Securities and Use of Proceeds.

(a) Furnish the information required by Item 701 of Regulation S-B (17 CFR 228.701) as to all equity securities of the small business issuer sold by the small business issuer during the period covered by the report that were not registered under the Securities Act. If the Item 701 information previously has been included in a Current Report on Form 8-K (17 CFR 249.308), however, it need not be furnished.

* * * * *

Item 3. Defaults Upon Senior Securities.

* * * * *

Instructions to Item 3

1. Item 3 need not be answered as to any default or arrearage with respect to any class of securities all of which is held by or for the account of the small business issuer or its totally held subsidiaries.

2. The information required by Item 3 need not be made if previously disclosed on a report on Form 8-K (17 CFR 249.308).

* * * * *

Item 5. Other Information.

The small business issuer must disclose under this item any information required to be disclosed in a report on Form 8-K during the period covered by this Form 10-QSB, but not reported, whether or not otherwise required by this Form 10-QSB. If disclosure of such information is made under this item, it need not be repeated in a report on Form 8-K which would otherwise be required to be filed with respect to such information or in a subsequent report on Form 10-QSB.

* * * * *

22. Amend Form 10-K (referenced in § 249.310) by:

a. Revising Items 5(a) and 9;

b. Adding Item 9B;

c. Revising the heading of Item 15 to read "Exhibits and Financial Statement Schedules.";

d. Removing paragraph (b) of Item 15; and

e. Redesignating paragraphs (c) and (d) in Item 15 as paragraphs (b) and (c).

The revisions read as follows:

Note—The text of Form 10-K does not, and this amendment will not, appear in the Code of Federal Regulations.

Form 10-K

Annual Report Pursuant to Section 13 or 15(d) of the Securities Exchange Act of 1934

* * * * *

Item 5. Market for Registrant's Common Equity and Related Stockholder Matters.

(a) Furnish the information required by Item 201 of Regulation S-K (17 CFR 229.201) and Item 701 of Regulation S-K (17 CFR 229.701) as to all equity securities of the registrant sold by the registrant during the period covered by the report that were not registered under the Securities Act other than unregistered sales made in reliance on Regulation S (17 CFR 230.901 through 230.905). If the Item 701 information previously has been included in a Quarterly Report on Form 10-Q or 10-QSB (17 CFR 249.308a or 249.308b), or in a Current Report on Form 8-K (17 CFR 249.308), it need not be furnished.

* * * * *

Item 9. Changes in and Disagreements With Accountants on Accounting and Financial Disclosure.

Furnish the information required by Item 304(b) of Regulation S-K (§ 229.304(b) of this chapter).

* * * * *

Item 9B. Other Information.

The registrant must disclose under this item any information required to be disclosed in a report on Form 8-K during the fourth quarter of the year covered by this Form 10-K, but not reported, whether or not otherwise required by this Form 10-K. If disclosure of such information is made under this item, it need not be repeated in a report on Form 8-K which would otherwise be required to be filed with respect to such information or in a subsequent report on Form 10-K.

* * * * *

23. Amend Form 10-KSB (referenced in § 249.310a) by:

a. Revising Items 5(a) and 8 in Part II;

b. Adding Item 8B in Part II;

c. Removing the words "and Reports on Form 8-K" from the heading to Item 13;

d. Removing paragraph (b) of Item 13 in Part III;

e. Removing the paragraph (a) designation in Item 13;

f. Revising Item 3 in Part II of "Information Required in Annual Report of Transitional Small Business Issuers"; and

g. Removing Item 6 in Part II of "Information Required in Annual Report of Transitional Small Business Issuers".

The revisions read as follows:

Note—The text of Form 10-KSB does not, and this amendment will not, appear in the Code of Federal Regulations.

Form 10-KSB

(Check one)

[ ] Annual Report Pursuant to Section 13 or 15(d) of the Securities Exchange Act of 1934

* * * * *

PART II

Item 5. Market for Common Equity and Related Stockholder Matters.

(a) Furnish the information required by Item 201 of Regulation S-B and Item 701 of Regulation S-B as to all equity securities of the small business issuer sold by the small business issuer during the period covered by the report that were not registered under the Securities Act. If the Item 701 information previously has been included in a Quarterly Report on Form 10-Q or 10-QSB, or on a Current Report on Form 8-K, however, it need not be furnished.

* * * * *

Item 8. Changes In and Disagreements With Accountants on Accounting and Financial Disclosure.

Furnish the information required by Item 304(b) of Regulation S-B.

* * * * *

Item 8B. Other Information

The small business issuer must disclose under this item any information required to be disclosed in a report on Form 8-K during the fourth quarter of the year covered by this Form 10-KSB, but not reported, whether or not otherwise required by this Form 10-KSB. If disclosure of such information is made under this item, it need not be repeated in a report on Form 8-K which would otherwise be required to be filed with respect to such information or in a subsequent report on Form 10-KSB.

* * * * *

INFORMATION REQUIRED IN ANNUAL REPORT OF TRANSITIONAL SMALL BUSINESS ISSUERS

* * * * *

PART II

Item 3. Changes In and Disagreements With Accountants

Furnish the information required by Item 304(b) of Regulation S-B, if applicable.

* * * * *

CEO/CFO CERTIFICATION

¶ 1101 Sarbanes-Oxley Act Sections

Section 302—CORPORATE RESPONSIBILITY FOR FINANCIAL REPORTS.

(a) REGULATIONS REQUIRED—The Commission shall, by rule, require, for each company filing periodic reports under section 13(a) or 15(d) of the Securities Exchange Act of 1934 (15 U.S.C. 78m, 78o(d)), that the principal executive officer or officers and the principal financial officer or officers, or persons performing similar functions, certify in each annual or quarterly report filed or submitted under either such section of such Act that—

(1) the signing officer has reviewed the report;

(2) based on the officer's knowledge, the report does not contain any untrue statement of a material fact or omit to state a material fact necessary in order to make the statements made, in light of the circumstances under which such statements were made, not misleading;

(3) based on such officer's knowledge, the financial statements, and other financial information included in the report, fairly present in all material respects the financial condition and results of operations of the issuer as of, and for, the periods presented in the report;

(4) the signing officers—

(A) are responsible for establishing and maintaining internal controls;

(B) have designed such internal controls to ensure that material information relating to the issuer and its consolidated subsidiaries is made known to such officers by others within those entities, particularly during the period in which the periodic reports are being prepared;

(C) have evaluated the effectiveness of the issuer's internal controls as of a date within 90 days prior to the report; and

(D) have presented in the report their conclusions about the effectiveness of their internal controls based on their evaluation as of that date;

(5) the signing officers have disclosed to the issuer's auditors and the audit committee of the board of directors (or persons fulfilling the equivalent function)—

(A) all significant deficiencies in the design or operation of internal controls which could adversely affect the issuer's ability to record, process, summarize, and report financial data and have identified for the issuer's auditors any material weaknesses in internal controls; and

(B) any fraud, whether or not material, that involves management or other employees who have a significant role in the issuer's internal controls; and

(6) the signing officers have indicated in the report whether or not there were significant changes in internal controls or in other factors that could significantly affect internal controls subsequent to the date of their evaluation, including any corrective actions with regard to significant deficiencies and material weaknesses.

(b) FOREIGN REINCORPORATIONS HAVE NO EFFECT—Nothing in this section 302 shall be interpreted or applied in any way to allow any issuer to lessen the legal force of the statement required under this section 302, by an issuer having reincorporated or having engaged in any other transaction that resulted in the transfer of the corporate domicile or offices of the issuer from inside the United States to outside of the United States.

(c) DEADLINE—The rules required by subsection (a) shall be effective not later than 30 days after the date of enactment of this Act.

Section 906—CORPORATE RESPONSIBILITY FOR FINANCIAL REPORTS.

(a) IN GENERAL—Chapter 63 of title 18, United States Code, is amended by inserting after section 1349, as created by this Act, the following:

'Sec. 1350. Failure of corporate officers to certify financial reports

(a) CERTIFICATION OF PERIODIC FINANCIAL REPORTS—Each periodic report containing financial statements filed by an issuer with the Securities Exchange Commission pursuant to section 13(a) or 15(d) of the Securities Exchange Act of 1934 (15 U.S.C. 78m(a) or 78o(d)) shall be accompanied by a written statement by the chief executive officer and chief financial officer (or equivalent thereof) of the issuer.

'(b) CONTENT—The statement required under subsection (a) shall certify that the periodic report containing the financial statements fully complies with the requirements of section 13(a) or 15(d) of the Securities Exchange Act of 1934 (15 U.S.C. 78m or 78o(d)) and that information contained in the periodic report fairly presents, in all material respects, the financial condition and results of operations of the issuer.

'(c) CRIMINAL PENALTIES—Whoever—

'(1) certifies any statement as set forth in subsections (a) and (b) of this section knowing that the periodic report accompanying the statement does not comport with all the requirements set forth in this section shall be fined not more than $1,000,000 or imprisoned not more than 10 years, or both; or

'(2) willfully certifies any statement as set forth in subsections (a) and (b) of this section knowing that the periodic report accompanying the statement does not comport with all the requirements set forth in this section shall be fined not more than $5,000,000, or imprisoned not more than 20 years, or both.'.

(b) CLERICAL AMENDMENT—The table of sections at the beginning of chapter 63 of title 18, United States Code, is amended by adding at the end the following:

'1350. Failure of corporate officers to certify financial reports.'.

¶ 1102 Regulation S-B

Part 228—INTEGRATED DISCLOSURE SYSTEM FOR SMALL BUSINESS ISSUERS

1. The authority citation for Part 228 is amended by adding the following citation to read as follows:

Authority: 15 U.S.C. 77e, 77f, 77g, 77h, 77j, 77k, 77s, 77z-2, 77z-3, 77aa(25), 77aa(26), 77ddd, 77eee, 77ggg, 77hhh, 77jjj, 77nnn, 77sss, 78l, 78m, 78n, 78o, 78u-5, 78w, 78ll, 78mm, 80a-8, 80a-29, 80a-30, 80a-37 and 80b-11.

Section 228.307 is also issued under secs. 3(a) and 302, Pub.L.No. 107-204, 116 Stat. 745.

2. By adding 228.307 to read as follows:

228.307 Controls and Procedures.

(a) Evaluation of disclosure controls and procedures. Disclose the conclusions of the small business issuer's principal executive officer or officers and principal financial officer or officers, or persons performing similar functions, about the effectiveness of the small business issuer's disclosure controls and procedures (as defined in 240.13a-14(c) and 240.15d-14(c)) based on their evaluation of these controls and procedures as of a date within 90 days of the filing date of the quarterly or annual report that includes the disclosure required by this paragraph.

(b) Changes in internal controls. Disclose whether or not there were significant changes in the small business issuer's internal controls or in other factors that could significantly affect these controls subsequent to the date of their evaluation, including any corrective actions with regard to significant deficiencies and material weaknesses.

(c) Asset-Backed Issuers. A small business issuer that is an Asset-Backed Issuer (as defined in Rule 13a-14(g) and Rule 15d-14(g) under the Securities Exchange Act of 1934 [17 CFR 240.13a-14(g) and 17 CFR 240.15d-14(g)] is not required to disclose the information required by this Item.

¶ 1103 Regulation S-K

Part 229—STANDARD INSTRUCTIONS FOR FILING FORMS UNDER SECURITIES ACT OF 1933, SECURITIES EXCHANGE ACT OF 1934 AND ENERGY POLICY AND CONSERVATION ACT OF 1975—REGULATION S-K

3. The authority citation for Part 229 is amended by adding the following citation to read as follows:

Authority: 15 U.S.C. 77e, 77f, 77g, 77h, 77j, 77k, 77s, 77z-2, 77z-3, 77aa(25), 77aa(26), 77ddd, 77eee, 77ggg, 77hhh, 77iii, 77jjj, 77nnn, 77sss, 78c, 78i, 78j, 78l, 78m, 78n, 78o, 78u-5, 78w, 78ll(d), 78mm, 79e, 79n, 79t, 80a-8, 80a-29, 80a-30, 80a-31(c), 80a-37, 80a-38(a) and 80b-11, unless otherwise noted.

Section 229.307 is also issued under secs. 3(a) and 302, Pub.L.No. 107-204, 116 Stat. 745.

4. By adding 229.307 to read as follows:

229.307 Controls and Procedures.

(a) Evaluation of disclosure controls and procedures. Disclose the conclusions of the registrant's principal executive officer or officers and principal financial officer or officers, or persons performing similar functions, about the effectiveness of the registrant's disclosure controls and procedures (as defined in 240.13a-14(c) and 240.15d-14(c)) based on their evaluation of these controls and procedures as of a date within 90 days of the filing date of the quarterly or annual report that includes the disclosure required by this paragraph.

(b) Changes in internal controls. Disclose whether or not there were significant changes in the registrant's internal controls or in other factors that could significantly affect these controls subsequent to the date of their evaluation, including any corrective actions with regard to significant deficiencies and material weaknesses.

(c) Asset-Backed Issuers. A registrant that is an Asset-Backed Issuer (as defined in 240.13a-14(g) and 240.15d-14(g)) is not required to disclose the information required by this Item.

¶ 1104 Regulation S-T

PART 232—REGULATION S-T—GENERAL RULES AND REGULATIONS FOR ELECTRONIC FILINGS

5. The authority citation for Part 232 is amended by adding the following citation to read as follows:

Authority: 15 U.S.C. 77f, 77g, 77h, 77j, 77s(a), 77sss(a), 78c(b), 78l, 78m, 78n, 78o(d), 78w(a), 78ll(d), 79t(a), 80a-8, 80a-29, 80a-30 and 80a-37.

Section 232.302 is also issued under secs. 3(a) and 302, Pub.L.No. 107-204, 116 Stat. 745.

6. By amending 232.302 by revising paragraphs (a) and (b) to read as follows:

232.302 Signatures.

(a) Required signatures to, or within, any electronic submission (including, without limitation, signatories within the certifications required by 240.13a-14, 240.15d-14 and 270.30a-2 of this chapter) must be in typed form rather than manual format. Signatures in an HTML document that are not required may, but are not required to, be presented in an HTML graphic or image file within the electronic filing, in compliance with the formatting requirements of the EDGAR Filer Manual. When used in connection with an electronic filing, the term "signature" means an electronic entry in the form of a magnetic impulse or other form of computer data compilation of any letters or series of letters or characters comprising a name, executed, adopted or authorized as a signature. Signatures are not required in unofficial PDF copies submitted in accordance with 232.104.

(b) Each signatory to an electronic filing (including, without limitation, each signatory to the certifications required by 240.13a-14, 240.15d-14 and 270.30a-2 of this chapter) shall manually sign a signature page or other document authenticating, acknowledging or otherwise adopting his or her signature that appears in typed form within the electronic filing. Such document shall be executed before or at the time the electronic filing is made and shall be retained by the filer for a period of five years. Upon request, an electronic filer shall furnish to the Commission or its staff a copy of any or all documents retained pursuant to this section.

* * * * *

¶ 1105 Exchange Act Rules

PART 240—GENERAL RULES AND REGULATIONS, SECURITIES EXCHANGE ACT OF 1934

7. The authority citation for Part 240 is amended by adding the following citations in numerical order to read as follows:

Authority: 15 U.S.C. 77c, 77d, 77g, 77j, 77s, 77z-2, 77z-3, 77eee, 77ggg, 77nnn, 77sss, 77ttt, 78c, 78d, 78e, 78f, 78g, 78i, 78j, 78j-1, 78k, 78k-1, 78l, 78m, 78n, 78o, 78p, 78q, 78s, 78u-5, 78w, 78x, 78ll, 78mm, 79q, 79t, 80a-20, 80a-23, 80a-29, 80a-37, 80b-3, 80b-4 and 80b-11, unless otherwise noted.

* * * * *

Section 240.12b-15 is also issued under secs. 3(a) and 302, Pub.L.No. 107-204, 116 Stat. 745.

Section 240.13a-10 is also issued under secs. 3(a) and 302, Pub.L.No. 107-204, 116 Stat. 745.

Section 240.13a-14 is also issued under secs. 3(a) and 302, Pub.L.No. 107-204, 116 Stat. 745.

Section 240.13a-15 is also issued under secs. 3(a) and 302, Pub.L.No. 107-204, 116 Stat. 745.

Section 240.15d-10 is also issued under secs. 3(a) and 302, Pub.L.No. 107-204, 116 Stat. 745.

Section 240.15d-14 is also issued under secs. 3(a) and 302, Pub.L.No. 107-204, 116 Stat. 745.

Section 240.15d-15 is also issued under secs. 3(a) and 302, Pub.L.No. 107-204, 116 Stat. 745.

* * * * *

8. By revising 240.12b-15 to read as follows:

240.12b-15 Amendments.

All amendments must be filed under cover of the form amended, marked with the letter "A" to designate the document as an amendment, e.g., "10-K/A," and in compliance with pertinent requirements applicable to statements and reports. Amendments filed pursuant to this section must set forth the complete text of each item as amended. Amendments must be numbered sequentially and be filed separately for each statement or report amended. Amendments to a statement may be filed either before or after registration becomes effective. Amendments must be signed on behalf of the registrant by a duly authorized representative of the registrant. In addition, each principal executive officer and principal financial officer of the registrant must provide a new certification as specified in 240.13a-14 or 240.15d-14. The requirements of the form being amended will govern the number of copies to be filed in connection with a paper format amendment. Electronic filers satisfy the provisions dictating the number of copies by filing one copy of the amendment in electronic format. See Rule 309 of Regulation S-T (232.309 of this chapter).

9. By amending 240.13a-10 to add an "Additional Note" after the "Note" at the end of the section to read as follows:

240.13a-10 Transition reports.

* * * * *

Additional Note: The report or reports to be filed pursuant to this section must include the certification required by 240.13a-14.

10. By adding 240.13a-14 to read as follows:

240.13a-14 Certification of disclosure in annual and quarterly reports.

(a) Each report, including transition reports, filed on Form 10-Q, Form 10-QSB, Form 10-K, Form 10-KSB, Form 20-F or Form 40-F (249.308a, 249.308b, 249.310, 249.310b, 249.220f and 249.240f of this chapter) under section 13(a) of the Act (15 U.S.C. 78m(a)), other than a report filed by an Asset-Backed Issuer (as defined in paragraph (g) of this section), must include a certification containing the information set forth in paragraph (b) of this section in the form specified in the report. Each principal executive officer or officers and principal financial officer or officers of the issuer, or persons performing similar functions, at the time of filing of the report must sign the certification.

(b) The certification included in each report specified in paragraph (a) of this section must be in the form specified in the report and consist of a statement of the certifying officer that:

(1) He or she has reviewed the report being filed;

(2) Based on his or her knowledge, the report does not contain any untrue statement of a material fact or omit to state a material fact necessary to make the statements made, in light of the circumstances under which such statements were made, not misleading with respect to the period covered by the report;

(3) Based on his or her knowledge, the financial statements, and other financial information included in the report, fairly present in all material respects the financial condition, results of operations and cash flows of the issuer as of, and for, the periods presented in the report;

(4) He or she and the other certifying officers are responsible for establishing and maintaining disclosure controls and procedures (as such term is defined in paragraph (c) of this section) for the issuer and have:

(i) Designed such disclosure controls and procedures to ensure that material information relating to the issuer, including its consolidated subsidiaries, is made known to them by others within those entities, particularly during the period in which the periodic reports are being prepared;

(ii) Evaluated the effectiveness of the issuer's disclosure controls and procedures as of a date within 90 days prior to the filing date of the report ("Evaluation Date"); and

(iii) Presented in the report their conclusions about the effectiveness of the disclosure controls and procedures based on their evaluation as of the Evaluation Date;

(5) He or she and the other certifying officers have disclosed, based on their most recent evaluation, to the issuer's auditors and the audit committee of the board of directors (or persons fulfilling the equivalent function):

(i) All significant deficiencies in the design or operation of internal controls which could adversely affect the issuer's ability to record, process, summarize and report financial data and have identified for the issuer's auditors any material weaknesses in internal controls; and

(ii) Any fraud, whether or not material, that involves management or other employees who have a significant role in the issuer's internal controls; and

(6) He or she and the other certifying officers have indicated in the report whether or not there were significant changes in internal controls or in other factors that could significantly affect internal controls subsequent to the date of their most recent evaluation, including any corrective actions with regard to significant deficiencies and material weaknesses.

(c) For purposes of this section and 240.13a-15 of this chapter, the term "disclosure controls and procedures" means controls and other procedures of an issuer that are designed to ensure that information required to be disclosed by the issuer in the reports that it files or submits under the Act (15 U.S.C. 78a et seq.) is recorded, processed, summarized and reported, within the time periods specified in the Commission's rules and forms. Disclosure controls and procedures include, without limitation, controls and procedures designed to ensure that information required to be disclosed by an issuer in the reports that it files or submits under the Act is accumulated and communicated to the issuer's management, including its principal executive officer or officers and principal financial officer or officers, or persons performing similar functions, as appropriate to allow timely decisions regarding required disclosure.

(d) A person required to provide the certification specified in paragraph (a) of this section may not have the certification signed on his or her behalf pursuant to a power of attorney or other form of confirming authority.

(e) Each annual report filed by an Asset-Backed Issuer (as defined in paragraph (g) of this section) under section 13(a) of the Act (15 U.S.C. 78m(a)) must include a certification addressing the following items:

(1) Review by the certifying officer of the annual report and other reports containing distribution information for the period covered by the annual report;

(2) The absence in these reports, to the best of the certifying officer's knowledge, of any untrue statement of material fact or omission of a material fact necessary to make the statements made, in light of the circumstances under which such statements were made, not misleading;

(3) The inclusion in these reports, to the best of the certifying officer's knowledge, of the financial information required to be provided to the trustee under the governing documents of the issuer; and

(4) Compliance by the servicer with its servicing obligations and minimum servicing standards.

(f) With respect to Asset-Backed Issuers, the certification required by paragraph (e) of this section must be signed by the trustee of the trust (if the trustee signs the annual report) or the senior officer in charge of securitization of the depositor (if the depositor signs the annual report). Alternatively, the senior officer in charge of the servicing function of the master servicer (or entity performing the equivalent functions) may sign the certification.

(g) For purposes of this section, the term Asset-Backed Issuer means any issuer whose reporting obligation results from the registration of securities it issued that are primarily serviced by the cash flows of a discrete pool of receivables or other financial assets, either fixed or revolving, that by their terms convert into cash within a finite time period plus any rights or other assets designed to assure the servicing or timely distribution of proceeds to security holders.

11. By adding 240.13a-15 to read as follows:

240.13a-15 Issuer's disclosure controls and procedures related to preparation of required reports.

(a) Every issuer that has a class of securities registered pursuant to section 12 of the Act (15 U.S.C. 78l), other than an Asset-Backed Issuer (as defined in 240.13a-14(g) of this chapter), must maintain disclosure controls and procedures (as defined in 240.13a-14(c) of this chapter).

(b) Within the 90-day period prior to the filing date of each report requiring certification under 240.13a-14 and 270.30a-2 of this chapter, an evaluation must be carried out under the supervision and with the participation of the issuer's management, including the issuer's principal executive officer or officers and principal financial officer or officers, or persons performing similar functions, of the effectiveness of the design and operation of the issuer's disclosure controls and procedures.

12. By amending 240.15d-10 to add an "Additional Note" after the "Note" at the end of the section to read as follows:

240.15d-10 Transition reports.

* * * * *

Additional Note: The report or reports to be filed pursuant to this section must include the certification required by 240.15d-14.

13. By adding 240.15d-14 to read as follows:

240.15d-14 Certification of disclosure in annual and quarterly reports.

(a) Each report, including transition reports, filed on Form 10-Q, Form 10-QSB, Form 10-K, Form 10-KSB, Form 20-F or Form 40-F (249.308a, 249.308b, 249.310, 249.310b, 249.220f and 249.240f of this chapter) under section 15(d) of the Act (15 U.S.C. 78o(d)), other than a report filed by an Asset-Backed Issuer (as defined in paragraph (g) of this section), must include a certification containing the information set forth in paragraph (b) of this section in the form specified in the report. Each principal executive officer or officers and principal financial officer or officers of the issuer, or persons performing similar functions, at the time of filing of the report must sign the certification.

(b) The certification included in each report specified in paragraph (a) of this section must be in the form specified in the report and consist of a statement of the certifying officer that:

(1) He or she has reviewed the report being filed;

(2) Based on his or her knowledge, the report does not contain any untrue statement of a material fact or omit to state a material fact necessary to make the statements made, in light of the circumstances under which such statements were made, not misleading with respect to the period covered by the report;

(3) Based on his or her knowledge, the financial statements, and other financial information included in the report, fairly present in all material respects the financial condition, results of operations and cash flows of the issuer as of, and for, the periods presented in the report;

(4) He or she and the other certifying officers are responsible for establishing and maintaining disclosure controls and procedures (as such term is defined in paragraph (c) of this section) for the issuer and have:

(i) Designed such disclosure controls and procedures to ensure that material information relating to the issuer, including its consolidated subsidiaries, is made known to them by others within those entities, particularly during the period in which the periodic reports are being prepared;

(ii) Evaluated the effectiveness of the issuer's disclosure controls and procedures as of a date within 90 days prior to the filing date of the report (the "Evaluation Date"); and

(iii) Presented in the report their conclusions about the effectiveness of the disclosure controls and procedures based on their evaluation as of the Evaluation Date;

(5) He or she and the other certifying officers have disclosed, based on their most recent evaluation, to the issuer's auditors and the audit committee of the board or directors (or persons fulfilling the equivalent function):

(i) All significant deficiencies in the design or operation of internal controls which could adversely affect the issuer's ability to record, process, summarize and report financial data and have identified for the issuer's auditors any material weaknesses in internal controls; and

(ii) Any fraud, whether or not material, that involves management or other employees who have a significant role in the issuer's internal controls; and

(6) He or she and the other certifying officers have indicated in the report whether or not there were significant changes in internal controls or in other factors that could significantly affect internal controls subsequent to the date of their most recent evaluation, including any corrective actions with regard to significant deficiencies and material weaknesses.

(c) For purposes of this section and 240.15d-15 of this chapter, the term "disclosure controls and procedures" means controls and other procedures of an issuer that are designed to ensure that information required to be disclosed by the issuer in the reports that it files or submits under the Act (15 U.S.C. 78a et seq.) is recorded, processed, summarized and reported, within the time periods specified in the Commission's rules and forms. Disclosure controls and procedures include, without limitation, controls and procedures designed to ensure that information required to be disclosed by an issuer in the reports that it files or submits under the Act is accumulated and communicated to the issuer's management, including its principal executive officer or officers and principal financial officer or officers, or persons performing similar functions, as appropriate to allow timely decisions regarding required disclosure.

(d) A person required to provide the certification specified in paragraph (a) of this section may not have the certification signed on his or her behalf pursuant to a power of attorney or other form of confirming authority.

(e) Each annual report filed by an Asset-Backed Issuer (as defined in paragraph (g) of this section) under section 13(a) of the Act (15 U.S.C. 78m(a)) must include a certification addressing the following items:

(1) Review by the certifying officer of the annual report and other reports containing distribution information for the period covered by the annual report;

(2) The absence in these reports, to the best of the certifying officer's knowledge, of any untrue statement of material fact or omission of a material fact necessary to make the statements made, in light of the circumstances under which such statements were made, not misleading;

(3) The inclusion in these reports, to the best of the certifying officer's knowledge, of the financial information required to be provided to the trustee under the governing documents of the issuer; and

(4) Compliance by the servicer with its servicing obligations and minimum servicing standards.

(f) With respect to Asset-Backed Issuers, the certification required by paragraph (e) of this section must be signed by the trustee of the trust (if the trustee signs the annual report) or the senior officer in charge of securitization of the depositor (if the depositor signs the annual report). Alternatively, the senior officer in charge of the servicing function of the master servicer (or entity performing the equivalent functions) may sign the certification.

(g) For purposes of this section, the term Asset-Backed Issuer means any issuer whose reporting obligation results from the offering of securities it issued that are primarily serviced by the cash flows of a discrete pool of receivables or other financial assets, either fixed or revolving, that by their terms convert into cash within a finite time period plus any rights or other assets designed to assure the servicing or timely distribution of proceeds to security holders.

14. By adding 240.15d-15 to read as follows:

240.15d-15 Issuer's disclosure controls and procedures related to preparation of required reports.

(a) Every issuer that files reports under section 15(d) of the Act (15 U.S.C. 78o(d)), other than an Asset-Backed Issuer (as defined in 240.15d-14(g) of this chapter), must maintain disclosure controls and procedures (as defined in 240.15d-14(c) of this chapter).

(b) Within the 90-day period prior to the filing date of each report requiring certification under 240.13a-14 and 270.30a-2 of this chapter, an evaluation must be carried out under the supervision and with the participation of the issuer's management, including the issuer's principal executive officer or officers and principal financial officer or officers, or persons performing similar functions, of the effectiveness of the design and operation of the issuer's disclosure controls and procedures.

¶ 1106 Exchange Act Forms

PART 249—FORMS, SECURITIES EXCHANGE ACT OF 1934

15. The authority citation for Part 249 is amended by adding the following citations in numerical order to read as follows:

Authority: 15 U.S.C. 78a et seq., unless otherwise noted.

* * * * *

Section 249.308a is also issued under secs. 3(a) and 302, Pub.L.No. 107-204, 116 Stat. 745.

Section 249.308b is also issued under secs. 3(a) and 302, Pub.L.No. 107-204, 116 Stat. 745.

Section 249.310 is also issued under secs. 3(a) and 302, Pub.L.No. 107-204, 116 Stat. 745.

Section 249.310b is also issued under secs. 3(a) and 302, Pub.L.No. 107-204, 116 Stat. 745.

Section 249.220f is also issued under secs. 3(a) and 302, Pub.L.No. 107-204, 116 Stat. 745.

Section 249.240f is also issued under secs. 3(a) and 302, Pub.L.No. 107-204, 116 Stat. 745.

* * * * *

16. By amending Form 10-Q (referenced in 249.308a) by revising General Instruction G, by adding new Item 4 to "Part I—Financial Information" and by adding a "Certifications" section after the "Signatures" section to read as follows:

Note: The text of Form 10-Q does not, and this amendment will not, appear in the Code of Federal Regulations.

FORM 10-Q

* * * * *

GENERAL INSTRUCTIONS

* * * * *

G. Signature and Filing of Report.

If the report is filed in paper pursuant to a hardship exemption from electronic filing (see Item 201 et seq. of Regulation S-T (17 CFR 232.201 et seq.), three complete copies of the report, including any financial statements, exhibits or other papers or documents filed as a part thereof, and five additional copies which need not include exhibits must be filed with the Commission. At least one complete copy of the report, including any financial statements, exhibits or other papers or documents filed as a part thereof, must be filed with each exchange on which any class of securities of the registrant is registered. At least one complete copy of the report filed with the Commission and one such copy filed with each exchange must be manually signed on the registrant's behalf by a duly authorized officer of the registrant and by the principal financial or chief accounting officer of the registrant. (See Rule 12b-11(d) (17 CFR 240.12b-11(d).) Copies not manually signed must bear typed or printed signatures. In the case where the principal executive officer, principal financial officer or chief accounting officer is also duly authorized to sign on behalf of the registrant, one signature is acceptable provided that the registrant clearly indicates the dual responsibilities of the signatory. In addition, each principal executive officer and principal financial officer of the registrant must provide the certification required by Rule 13a-14 (17 CFR 240.13a-14) or Rule 15d-14 (17 CFR 240.15d-14) exactly as specified in this form.

* * * * *

PART I—FINANCIAL INFORMATION

* * * * *

Item 4. Controls and Procedures.

Furnish the information required by Item 307 of Regulation S-K (229.307 of this chapter).

* * * * *

SIGNATURES

* * * * *

CERTIFICATIONS*

I, [identify the certifying individual], certify that:

1. I have reviewed this quarterly report on Form 10-Q of [identify registrant];

2. Based on my knowledge, this quarterly report does not contain any untrue statement of a material fact or omit to state a material fact necessary to make the statements made, in light of the circumstances under which such statements were made, not misleading with respect to the period covered by this quarterly report;

3. Based on my knowledge, the financial statements, and other financial information included in this quarterly report, fairly present in all material respects the financial condition, results of operations and cash flows of the registrant as of, and for, the periods presented in this quarterly report;

4. The registrant's other certifying officers and I are responsible for establishing and maintaining disclosure controls and procedures (as defined in Exchange Act Rules 13a-14 and 15d-14) for the registrant and we have:

a) designed such disclosure controls and procedures to ensure that material information relating to the registrant, including its consolidated subsidiaries, is made known to us by others within those entities, particularly during the period in which this quarterly report is being prepared;

b) evaluated the effectiveness of the registrant's disclosure controls and procedures as of a date within 90 days prior to the filing date of this quarterly report (the "Evaluation Date"); and

c) presented in this quarterly report our conclusions about the effectiveness of the disclosure controls and procedures based on our evaluation as of the Evaluation Date;

5. The registrant's other certifying officers and I have disclosed, based on our most recent evaluation, to the registrant's auditors and the audit committee of registrant's board of directors (or persons performing the equivalent function):

a) all significant deficiencies in the design or operation of internal controls which could adversely affect the registrant's ability to record, process, summarize and report financial data and have identified for the registrant's auditors any material weaknesses in internal controls; and

b) any fraud, whether or not material, that involves management or other employees who have a significant role in the registrant's internal controls; and

6. The registrant's other certifying officers and I have indicated in this quarterly report whether or not there were significant changes in internal controls or in other factors that could significantly affect internal controls

subsequent to the date of our most recent evaluation, including any corrective actions with regard to significant deficiencies and material weaknesses.

Date:

[Signature]

[Title]

Provide a separate certification for each principal executive officer and principal financial officer of the registrant. See Rules 13a-14 and 15d-14. The required certification must be in the exact form set forth above.

17. By amending Form 10-QSB (referenced in 249.308b) by revising General Instruction F, by adding new Item 3 to "Part I—Financial Information" and by adding a "Certifications" section after the "Signatures" section to read as follows:

Note: The text of Form 10-QSB does not, and this amendment will not, appear in the Code of Federal Regulations.

FORM 10-QSB

* * * * *

GENERAL INSTRUCTIONS

* * * * *

F. Signature and Filing of Report

1. If the report is filed in paper pursuant to a hardship exemption from electronic filing (see Item 201 et seq. of Regulation S-T (17 CFR 232.201 et seq.), file three "complete" copies and five "additional" copies of the report with the Commission and file at least one complete copy with each exchange on which any class of securities of the small business issuer is registered. A "complete" copy includes financial statements, exhibits and all other papers and documents. An "additional" copy excludes exhibits.

2. Manually sign at least one complete copy of the report filed with the Commission and with each exchange; other copies should have typed or printed signatures. (See Rule 12b-11(d) (17 CFR 240.12b-11(d).) In the case where the principal executive officer, principal financial officer or chief accounting officer is also duly authorized to sign on behalf of the small business issuer, one signature is acceptable provided that the issuer clearly indicates the dual responsibilities of the signatory. Each principal executive officer and principal financial officer of the small business issuer must provide the certification required by Rule 13a-14 (17 CFR 240.13a-14) or Rule 15d-14 (17 CFR 240.15d-14) exactly as specified in this form.

* * * * *

PART I—FINANCIAL INFORMATION

* * * * *

Item 3. Controls and Procedures.

Furnish the information required by Item 307 of Regulation S-B (228.307 of this chapter).

* * * * *

SIGNATURES

* * * * *

CERTIFICATIONS*

I, [identify the certifying individual], certify that:

1. I have reviewed this quarterly report on Form 10-QSB of [identify registrant];

2. Based on my knowledge, this quarterly report does not contain any untrue statement of a material fact or omit to state a material fact necessary to make the statements made, in light of the circumstances under which such statements were made, not misleading with respect to the period covered by this quarterly report;

3. Based on my knowledge, the financial statements, and other financial information included in this quarterly report, fairly present in all material respects the financial condition, results of operations and cash flows of the registrant as of, and for, the periods presented in this quarterly report;

4. The registrant's other certifying officers and I are responsible for establishing and maintaining disclosure controls and procedures (as defined in Exchange Act Rules 13a-14 and 15d-14) for the registrant and have:

a) designed such disclosure controls and procedures to ensure that material information relating to the registrant, including its consolidated subsidiaries, is made known to us by others within those entities, particularly during the period in which this quarterly report is being prepared;

b) evaluated the effectiveness of the registrant's disclosure controls and procedures as of a date within 90 days prior to the filing date of this quarterly report (the "Evaluation Date"); and

c) presented in this quarterly report our conclusions about the effectiveness of the disclosure controls and procedures based on our evaluation as of the Evaluation Date;

5. The registrant's other certifying officers and I have disclosed, based on our most recent evaluation, to the registrant's auditors and the audit committee of registrant's board of directors (or persons performing the equivalent functions):

a) all significant deficiencies in the design or operation of internal controls which could adversely affect the registrant's ability to record, process, summarize and report financial data and have identified for the registrant's auditors any material weaknesses in internal controls; and

b) any fraud, whether or not material, that involves management or other employees who have a significant role in the registrant's internal controls; and

6. The registrant's other certifying officers and I have indicated in this quarterly report whether or not there were significant changes in internal controls or in other factors that could significantly affect internal controls subsequent to the date of our most recent evaluation, including any corrective actions with regard to significant deficiencies and material weaknesses.

Date:

[Signature]

[Title]

Provide a separate certification for each principal executive officer and principal financial officer of the registrant. See Rules 13a-14 and 15d-14. The required certification must be in the exact form set forth above.

* * * * *

18. By amending Form 10-K (referenced in 249.310):

a. by revising General Instruction D(2)(a),

b. by redesignating Item 14 as Item 15 in Part IV,

c. adding new Item 14 to Part III, and

d. by adding a "Certifications" section after the "Signatures" section and before the reference to "Supplemental information to be Furnished With Reports Filed Pursuant to Section 15(d) of the Act by Registrants Which Have Not Registered Securities Pursuant to Section 12 of the Act." The revisions read as follows:

Note: The text of Form 10-K does not, and this amendment will not, appear in the Code of Federal Regulations.

FORM 10-K

* * * * *

GENERAL INSTRUCTIONS

* * * * *

D. Signature and Filing of Report.

(1) * * *

(2)(a) The report must be signed by the registrant, and on behalf of the registrant by its principal executive officer or officers (who also must provide the certification required by Rule 13a-14 (17 CFR 240.13a-14) or Rule 15d-14 (17 CFR 240.15d-14) exactly as specified in this form), its principal financial officer or officers (who also must provide the certification required by Rule 13a-14 (17 CFR 240.13a-14) or Rule 15d-14 (17 CFR 240.15d-14) exactly as specified in this form), its controller or principal accounting officer, and by at least the majority of the board of directors or persons performing similar functions. Where the registrant is a limited partnership, the report must be signed by the majority of the board of directors of any corporate general partner who signs the report.

* * * * *

Annual Report Pursuant to Section 13 or 15(d) of the Securities Exchange Act of 1934

* * * * *

PART III

* * * * *

Item 14. Controls and Procedures.

Furnish the information required by Item 307 of Regulation S-K (229.307 of this chapter).

* * * * *

SIGNATURES

* * * * *

CERTIFICATIONS*

I, [identify the certifying individual], certify that:

1. I have reviewed this annual report on Form 10-K of [identify registrant];

2. Based on my knowledge, this annual report does not contain any untrue statement of a material fact or omit to state a material fact necessary to make the statements made, in light of the circumstances under which such statements were made, not misleading with respect to the period covered by this annual report;

3. Based on my knowledge, the financial statements, and other financial information included in this annual report, fairly present in all material respects the financial condition, results of operations and cash flows of the registrant as of, and for, the periods presented in this annual report;

4. The registrant's other certifying officers and I are responsible for establishing and maintaining disclosure controls and procedures (as defined in Exchange Act Rules 13a-14 and 15d-14) for the registrant and have:

a) designed such disclosure controls and procedures to ensure that material information relating to the registrant, including its consolidated subsidiaries, is made known to us by others within those entities, particularly during the period in which this annual report is being prepared;

b) evaluated the effectiveness of the registrant's disclosure controls and procedures as of a date within 90 days prior to the filing date of this annual report (the "Evaluation Date"); and

c) presented in this annual report our conclusions about the effectiveness of the disclosure controls and procedures based on our evaluation as of the Evaluation Date;

5. The registrant's other certifying officers and I have disclosed, based on our most recent evaluation, to the registrant's auditors and the audit committee of registrant's board of directors (or persons performing the equivalent functions):

a) all significant deficiencies in the design or operation of internal controls which could adversely affect the registrant's ability to record, process, summarize and report financial data and have identified for the registrant's auditors any material weaknesses in internal controls; and

b) any fraud, whether or not material, that involves management or other employees who have a significant role in the registrant's internal controls; and

6. The registrant's other certifying officers and I have indicated in this annual report whether there were significant changes in internal controls or in other factors that could significantly affect internal controls subsequent to the date of our most recent evaluation, including any corrective actions with regard to significant deficiencies and material weaknesses.

Date:

[Signature]

[Title]

Provide a separate certification for each principal executive officer and principal financial officer of the registrant. See Rules 13a-14 and 15d-14. The required certification must be in the exact form set forth above.

* * * * *

19. By amending Form 10-KSB (referenced in 249.310b):

a. by revising General Instruction C.2.,

b. by adding new Item 14 to Part III, and

c. by adding a "Certifications" section after the "Signatures" section and before the reference to "Supplemental information to be Furnished With Reports Filed Pursuant to Section 15(d) of the Exchange Act By Non-reporting Issuers." The revisions read as follows:

Note: The text of Form 10-KSB does not, and this amendment will not, appear in the Code of Federal Regulations.

FORM 10-KSB

* * * * *

GENERAL INSTRUCTIONS

* * * * *

PART III

* * * * *

Item 14. Controls and Procedures.

Furnish the information required by Item 307 of Regulation S-B (228.307 of this chapter).

* * * * *

C. Signature and Filing of Report.

1. * * *

2. Who must sign. The small business issuer, its principal executive officer or officers (who also must provide the certification required by Rule 13a-14 (17 CFR 240.13a-14) or Rule 15d-14 (17 CFR 240.15d-14) exactly as specified in this form), its principal financial officer (who also must provide the certification required by Rule 13a-14 (17 CFR 240.13a-14) or Rule 15d-14 (17 CFR 240.15d-14) exactly as specified in this form), its controller or principal accounting officer and at least a majority of the board of directors or persons

performing similar functions. If the small business issuer is a limited partnership, then the general partner and a majority of its board of directors if a corporation must sign the report. Any person who occupies more than one of the specified positions must indicate each capacity in which he or she signs the report. See Rule 12b-11 concerning manual signatures under powers of attorney.

* * * * *

SIGNATURES

* * * * *

CERTIFICATIONS*

I, [identify the certifying individual], certify that:

1. I have reviewed this annual report on Form 10-KSB of [identify registrant];

2. Based on my knowledge, this annual report does not contain any untrue statement of a material fact or omit to state a material fact necessary to make the statements made, in light of the circumstances under which such statements were made, not misleading with respect to the period covered by this annual report;

3. Based on my knowledge, the financial statements, and other financial information included in this annual report, fairly present in all material respects the financial condition, results of operations and cash flows of the registrant as of, and for, the periods presented in this annual report;

4. The registrant's other certifying officers and I are responsible for establishing and maintaining disclosure controls and procedures (as defined in Exchange Act Rules 13a-14 and 15d-14) for the registrant and have:

a) designed such disclosure controls and procedures to ensure that material information relating to the registrant, including its consolidated subsidiaries, is made known to us by others within those entities, particularly during the period in which this annual report is being prepared;

b) evaluated the effectiveness of the registrant's disclosure controls and procedures as of a date within 90 days prior to the filing date of this annual report (the "Evaluation Date"); and

c) presented in this annual report our conclusions about the effectiveness of the disclosure controls and procedures based on our evaluation as of the Evaluation Date;

5. The registrant's other certifying officers and I have disclosed, based on our most recent evaluation, to the registrant's auditors and the audit committee of registrant's board of directors (or persons performing the equivalent functions):

a) all significant deficiencies in the design or operation of internal controls which could adversely affect the registrant's ability to record, process, summarize and report financial data and have identified for the registrant's auditors any material weaknesses in internal controls; and

b) any fraud, whether or not material, that involves management or other employees who have a significant role in the registrant's internal controls; and

6. The registrant's other certifying officers and I have indicated in this annual report whether there were significant changes in internal controls or in other factors that could significantly affect internal controls subsequent to the date of our most recent evaluation, including any corrective actions with regard to significant deficiencies and material weaknesses.

Date:

[Signature]

[Title]

Provide a separate certification for each principal executive officer and principal financial officer of the registrant. See Rules 13a-14 and 15d-14. The required certification must be in the exact form set forth above.

* * * * *

20. By amending Form 20-F (referenced in 249.220f):

a. by adding a new paragraph (e) to General Instruction B,

b. by adding new Item 15, and

c. by adding a "Certifications" section after the "Signatures" section and before the section referencing "Instructions as to Exhibits." The revisions read as follows:

Note: The text of Form 20-F does not, and this amendment will not, appear in the Code of Federal Regulations.

FORM 20-F

* * * * *

GENERAL INSTRUCTIONS

* * * * *

B. General Rules and Regulations That Apply to this Form.

* * * * *

(e) Where the Form is being used as an annual report filed under Section 13(a) or 15(d) of the Exchange Act, provide the certification required by Rule 13a-14 (17 CFR 240.13a-14) or Rule 15d-14 (17 CFR 240.15d-14) exactly as specified in this form.

* * * * *

PART II

* * * * *

Item 15. Controls and Procedures.

(a) Where the Form is being used as an annual report filed under Section 13(a) or 15(d) of the Exchange Act, disclose the conclusions of the registrant's principal executive officer or officers and principal financial officer or officers, or persons performing similar functions, about the effectiveness of the registrant's disclosure controls and procedures (as defined in 240.13a-15(c) and 240.15d-15(c)) based on their evaluation the controls and procedures as of a date within 90 days prior to the filing date of the report.

(b) Where the Form is being used as an annual report filed under Section 13(a) or 15(d) of the Exchange Act, disclose whether or not there were significant changes in the registrant's internal controls or in other factors that could significantly affect these controls subsequent to the date of their evaluation, including any corrective actions with regard to significant deficiencies and material weaknesses.

* * * * *

SIGNATURES

* * * * *

CERTIFICATIONS*

I, [identify the certifying individual], certify that:

1. I have reviewed this annual report on Form 20-F of [identify registrant];

2. Based on my knowledge, this annual report does not contain any untrue statement of a material fact or omit to state a material fact necessary to make the statements made, in light of the circumstances under which such statements were made, not misleading with respect to the period covered by this annual report;

3. Based on my knowledge, the financial statements, and other financial information included in this annual report, fairly present in all material

respects the financial condition, results of operations and cash flows of the registrant as of, and for, the periods presented in this annual report;

4. The registrant's other certifying officers and I are responsible for establishing and maintaining disclosure controls and procedures (as defined in Exchange Act Rules 13a-14 and 15d-14) for the registrant and have:

a) designed such disclosure controls and procedures to ensure that material information relating to the registrant, including its consolidated subsidiaries, is made known to us by others within those entities, particularly during the period in which this annual report is being prepared;

b) evaluated the effectiveness of the registrant's disclosure controls and procedures as of a date within 90 days prior to the filing date of this annual report (the "Evaluation Date"); and

c) presented in this annual report our conclusions about the effectiveness of the disclosure controls and procedures based on our evaluation as of the Evaluation Date;

5. The registrant's other certifying officers and I have disclosed, based on our most recent evaluation, to the registrant's auditors and the audit committee of registrant's board of directors (or persons performing the equivalent function):

a) all significant deficiencies in the design or operation of internal controls which could adversely affect the registrant's ability to record, process, summarize and report financial data and have identified for the registrant's auditors any material weaknesses in internal controls; and

b) any fraud, whether or not material, that involves management or other employees who have a significant role in the registrant's internal controls; and

6. The registrant's other certifying officers and I have indicated in this annual report whether or not there were significant changes in internal controls or in other factors that could significantly affect internal controls subsequent to the date of our most recent evaluation, including any corrective actions with regard to significant deficiencies and material weaknesses.

Date:

[Signature]

[Title]

Provide a separate certification for each principal executive officer and principal financial officer of the registrant. See Rules 13a-14 and 15d-14. The required certification must be in the exact form set forth above.

* * * * *

21. By amending Form 40-F (referenced in 249.240f) by adding a new paragraph (6) to General Instruction B and by adding a "Certifications" section after the "Signatures" section to read as follows:

Note: The text of Form 40-F does not, and this amendment will not, appear in the Code of Federal Regulations.

FORM 40-F

* * * * *

GENERAL INSTRUCTIONS

* * * * *

B. Information To Be Filed on this Form.

* * * * *

(6) Where the Form is being used as an annual report filed under Section 13(a) or 15(d) of the Exchange Act:

(a) Provide the certification required by Rule 13a-14 (17 CFR 240.13a-14) or Rule 15d-14 (17 CFR 240.15d-14) exactly as specified in this form.

(b) Disclose the conclusions of the registrant's principal executive officer or officers and principal financial officer or officers, or persons performing similar functions, about the effectiveness of the registrant's disclosure controls and procedures (as defined in 240.13a-15(c) and 240.15d-15(c)) based on their evaluation the controls and procedures as of a date within 90 days prior to the filing date of the report.

(c) Disclose in the report whether or not there were significant changes in the registrant's internal controls or in other factors that could significantly affect these controls subsequent to the date of their evaluation, including any corrective actions with regard to significant deficiencies and material weaknesses.

* * * * *

SIGNATURES

* * * * *

CERTIFICATIONS*

I, [identify the certifying individual], certify that:

1. I have reviewed this annual report on Form 40-F of [identify registrant];

2. Based on my knowledge, this annual report does not contain any untrue statement of a material fact or omit to state a material fact necessary to make the statements made, in light of the circumstances under which such statements were made, not misleading with respect to the period covered by this annual report;

3. Based on my knowledge, the financial statements, and other financial information included in this annual report, fairly present in all material respects the financial condition, results of operations and cash flows of the registrant as of, and for, the periods presented in this annual report;

4. The registrant's other certifying officers and I are responsible for establishing and maintaining disclosure controls and procedures (as defined in Exchange Act Rules 13a-14 and 15d-14) for the registrant and have:

a) designed such disclosure controls and procedures to ensure that material information relating to the registrant, including its consolidated subsidiaries, is made known to us by others within those entities, particularly during the period in which this annual report is being prepared;

b) evaluated the effectiveness of the registrant's disclosure controls and procedures as of a date within 90 days prior to the filing date of this annual report (the "Evaluation Date"); and

c) presented in this annual report our conclusions about the effectiveness of the disclosure controls and procedures based on our evaluation as of the Evaluation Date;

5. The registrant's other certifying officers and I have disclosed, based on our most recent evaluation, to the registrant's auditors and the audit committee of registrant's board of directors (and persons performing the equivalent function):

a) all significant deficiencies in the design or operation of internal controls which could adversely affect the registrant's ability to record, process, summarize and report financial data and have identified for the registrant's auditors any material weaknesses in internal controls; and

b) any fraud, whether or not material, that involves management or other employees who have a significant role in the registrant's internal controls; and

6. The registrant's other certifying officers and I have indicated in this annual report whether there were significant changes in internal controls or in other factors that could significantly affect internal controls subsequent to the date of our most recent evaluation, including any corrective actions with regard to significant deficiencies and material weaknesses.

Date:

[Signature]

[Title]

Provide a separate certification for each principal executive officer and principal financial officer of the registrant. See Rules 13a-14 and 15d-14. The required certification must be in the exact form set forth above.

¶ 1107 Investment Company Act Rules

PART 270—RULES AND REGULATIONS, INVESTMENT COMPANY ACT OF 1940

22. The authority citation for part 270 is amended by adding the following citation in numerical order to read as follows:

Authority: 15 U.S.C. 80a-1, et seq., 80a-34(d), 80a-37, 80a-39, unless otherwise noted;

* * * * *

Section 270.30a-2 is also issued under 15 U.S.C. 78m, 78o(d), and 80a-29, and secs. 3(a) and 302, Pub. L. No. 107-204, 116 Stat. 745.

* * * * *

23. By adding 270.30a-2 to read as follows:

270.30a-2 Certification of disclosure in annual and semi-annual reports.

(a) Each report, including transition reports, filed on Form N-SAR (referenced in 249.330 and 274.101) by a registered management investment company or unit investment trust must include a certification containing the information set forth in paragraph (b) of this section in the form specified in the report, except that a report of a unit investment trust or small business investment company on Form N-SAR may omit paragraph (b)(3) of this section. Each principal executive officer or officers and principal financial officer or officers of the investment company, or persons performing similar functions, at the time of filing of the report must sign the certification.

(b) The certification included in each report specified in paragraph (a) of this section must be in the form specified in the report and consist of a statement of the certifying officer that:

(1) He or she has reviewed the report being filed;

(2) Based on his or her knowledge, the report does not contain any untrue statement of a material fact or omit to state a material fact necessary to make the statements made, in light of the circumstances under which such statements were made, not misleading with respect to the period covered by the report;

(3) Based on his or her knowledge, the financial information included in the report, and the financial statements on which the financial information is based, fairly present in all material respects the financial condition, results of operations, changes in net assets, and cash flows (if the financial statements are required to include a statement of cash flows) of the investment company as of, and for, the periods presented in the report;

(4) He or she and the other certifying officers are responsible for establishing and maintaining disclosure controls and procedures (as such term is defined in paragraph (c) of this section) for the investment company and have:

(i) Designed such disclosure controls and procedures to ensure that material information relating to the investment company, including its consolidated subsidiaries, is made known to them by others within those entities, particularly during the period in which the periodic reports are being prepared;

(ii) Evaluated the effectiveness of the investment company's disclosure controls and procedures as of a date within 90 days prior to the filing date of the report (the "Evaluation Date"); and

(iii) Presented in the report their conclusions about the effectiveness of the disclosure controls and procedures based on their evaluation as of the Evaluation Date;

(5) He or she and the other certifying officers have disclosed, based on their most recent evaluation, to the investment company's auditors and the audit committee of the board of directors (or persons fulfilling the equivalent function):

(i) All significant deficiencies in the design or operation of internal controls which could adversely affect the investment company's ability to record, process, summarize, and report financial data and have identified for the investment company's auditors any material weaknesses in internal controls; and

(ii) Any fraud, whether or not material, that involves management or other employees who have a significant role in the investment company's internal controls; and

(6) He or she and the other certifying officers have indicated in the report whether or not there were significant changes in internal controls or in other factors that could significantly affect internal controls subsequent to the date of their most recent evaluation, including any correc-

tive actions with regard to significant deficiencies and material weaknesses.

(c) For purposes of this section, the term "disclosure controls and procedures" means controls and other procedures of an investment company that are designed to ensure that information required to be disclosed by the investment company in the reports that it files or submits under the Securities Exchange Act of 1934 is recorded, processed, summarized, and reported, within the time periods specified in the Commission's rules and forms. Disclosure controls and procedures include, without limitation, controls and procedures designed to ensure that information required to be disclosed by an investment company in the reports that it files or submits under the Securities Exchange Act of 1934 is accumulated and communicated to the investment company's management, including its principal executive officer or officers and principal financial officer or officers, or persons performing similar functions, as appropriate to allow timely decisions regarding required disclosure.

(d) A person required to provide the certification specified in paragraph (a) of this section may not have the certification signed on his or her behalf pursuant to a power of attorney or other form of confirming authority.

24. Section 270.30b1-3 is amended by adding a sentence at the end of the section to read as follows:

270.30b1-3 Transition reports.

* * * A report filed pursuant to this section must include the certification required by 270.30a-2.

¶ 1108 Investment Company Act Forms

PART 274—FORMS PRESCRIBED UNDER THE INVESTMENT COMPANY ACT OF 1940

25. The authority citation for Part 274 is revised to read as follows:

Authority: 15 U.S.C. 77f, 77g, 77h, 77j, 77s, 78c(b), 78l, 78m, 78n, 78o(d), 80a-8, 80a-24, 80a-26, and 80a-29, and secs. 3(a) and 302, Pub. L. No. 107-204, 116 Stat. 745, unless otherwise noted.

26. By amending Form N-SAR (referenced in 249.330 and 274.101) by:

a. Revising the reference "132" in item 6 to read "133";

b. Adding item 133;

c. Revising the reference "132" in the fifth paragraph of General Instruction A to read "133";

d. Revising General Instructions D and G, and the Instructions to sub-items 77Q3 and 102P3;

e. Adding an Instruction to item 133; and

f. Revising the reference "132" in the Instructions to the Signature Page to read "133."

These additions and revisions read as follows:

Note: The text of Form N-SAR does not, and these amendments will not, appear in the Code of Federal Regulations.

FORM N-SAR

* * * * *

133. Include the certifications required by rule 30a-2 under the Investment Company Act (17 CFR 270.30a-2).

* * * * *

GENERAL INSTRUCTIONS

* * * * *

D. Preparation of Report

(1) No item of the form except items 77 and 102 shall be answered by incorporating any information by reference. No exhibits or supplemental information are required or permitted, except in response to these items and item 133.

* * * * *

G. Submitting an Amendment to Form N-SAR on Paper or Electronically

* * * * *

(5) In an exhibit to the amendment, each principal executive officer and principal financial officer must provide the certification required by Item 133, instruction (a) for sub-item 77Q3, and instruction (a) for sub-item 102P3. A registrant that is a unit investment trust or a small business investment company may omit paragraph 3 of the certification required by instruction 77Q3(a)(iii).

* * * * *

INSTRUCTIONS TO SPECIFIC ITEMS

* * * * *

SUB-ITEM 77Q3:

Subject to Rule 201.24 of the General Rules of Practice regarding incorporation by reference, the rules applicable to electronic submission of filings, and General Instruction F of this form, the following exhibits shall be filed as part of this form, if not previously filed:

(a) If the form is filed under Section 13(a) or 15(d) of the 1934 Act, include the following information:

(i) Disclose the conclusions of the registrant's principal executive officer or officers and principal financial officer or officers, or persons performing similar functions, about the effectiveness of the registrant's disclosure controls and procedures (as defined in rule 30a-2(c) under the Act (17 CFR 270.30a-2(c)) based on their evaluation of these controls and procedures as of a date within 90 days of the filing date of the report that includes the disclosure required by this paragraph.

(ii) Disclose whether or not there were significant changes in the registrant's internal controls or in other factors that could significantly affect these controls subsequent to the date of their evaluation, including any corrective actions with regard to significant deficiencies and material weaknesses.

(iii) Include the certification of each principal executive officer and principal financial officer required by Rule 30a-2 under the Act (17 CFR 270.30a-2). Provide a separate certification for each principal executive officer and principal financial officer, or person performing similar functions, in the exact form set forth below:

CERTIFICATIONS

I, [identify the certifying individual], certify that:

1. I have reviewed this report on Form N-SAR of [identify registrant];

2. Based on my knowledge, this report does not contain any untrue statement of a material fact or omit to state a material fact necessary to make the statements made, in light of the circumstances under which such statements were made, not misleading with respect to the period covered by this report;

3. Based on my knowledge, the financial information included in this report, and the financial statements on which the financial information is based, fairly present in all material respects the financial condition, results of operations, changes in net assets, and cash flows (if the financial statements

are required to include a statement of cash flows) of the registrant as of, and for, the periods presented in this report;

4. The registrant's other certifying officers and I are responsible for establishing and maintaining disclosure controls and procedures (as defined in rule 30a-2(c) under the Investment Company Act) for the registrant and have:

a) designed such disclosure controls and procedures to ensure that material information relating to the registrant, including its consolidated subsidiaries, is made known to us by others within those entities, particularly during the period in which this report is being prepared;

b) evaluated the effectiveness of the registrant's disclosure controls and procedures as of a date within 90 days prior to the filing date of this report (the "Evaluation Date"); and

c) presented in this report our conclusions about the effectiveness of the disclosure controls and procedures based on our evaluation as of the Evaluation Date;

5. The registrant's other certifying officers and I have disclosed, based on our most recent evaluation, to the registrant's auditors and the audit committee of the registrant's board of directors (or persons performing the equivalent functions):

a) all significant deficiencies in the design or operation of internal controls which could adversely affect the registrant's ability to record, process, summarize, and report financial data and have identified for the registrant's auditors any material weaknesses in internal controls; and

b) any fraud, whether or not material, that involves management or other employees who have a significant role in the registrant's internal controls; and

6. The registrant's other certifying officers and I have indicated in this report whether or not there were significant changes in internal controls or in other factors that could significantly affect internal controls subsequent to the date of our most recent evaluation, including any corrective actions with regard to significant deficiencies and material weaknesses.

Date:

[Signature]

[Title]

(b) Furnish any other information required to be included as an exhibit pursuant to such rules and regulations as the Commission may prescribe.

* * * * *

SUB-ITEM 102P3

See instructions for sub-item 77Q3. The registrant may omit paragraph 3 of the certification required by instruction (a)(iii).

* * * * *

ITEM 133

Include the exhibit required by instruction (a) for sub-item 77Q3. The registrant may omit paragraph 3 of the certification required by instruction (a)(iii).

Accelerated Filing Deadlines*

¶ 1201 Regulation S-X

PART 210—FORM AND CONTENT OF AND REQUIREMENTS FOR FINANCIAL STATEMENTS, SECURITIES ACT OF 1933, SECURITIES EXCHANGE ACT OF 1934, PUBLIC UTILITY HOLDING COMPANY ACT OF 1935, INVESTMENT COMPANY ACT OF 1940, INVESTMENT ADVISERS ACT OF 1940, AND ENERGY POLICY AND CONSERVATION ACT OF 1975

1. The authority citation for Part 210 continues to read as follows:

Authority: 15 U.S.C. 77f, 77g, 77h, 77j, 77s, 77z-2, 77z-3, 77aa(25), 77aa(26), 78c, 78j-1, 78l, 78m, 78n, 78o(d), 78q, 78u-5, 78w(a), 78ll, 78mm, 79e(b), 79j(a), 79n, 79t(a), 80a-8, 80a-20, 80a-29, 80a-30, 80a-37(a), 80b-3, 80b-11 unless otherwise noted.

2. Section 210.3-01 is amended by:

a. Removing the phrase "90 days of the end of the registrant's fiscal year" and adding, in its place, the phrase "the number of days of the end of the registrant's fiscal year specified in paragraph (i) of this section" in the introductory text of paragraph (c) and paragraph (d); and

b. Revising paragraph (e) and adding paragraph (i) to read as follows:

§ 210.3-01 Consolidated balance sheets.

* * * * *

(e) For filings made after the number of days specified in paragraph (i) of this section, the filing shall also include a balance sheet as of an interim date within the following number of days of the date of filing:

(1) For accelerated filers (as defined in § 240.12b-2 of this chapter):

(i) 135 days for fiscal years ending on or after December 15, 2002 and before December 15, 2003;

(ii) 130 days for fiscal years ending on or after December 15, 2003 and before December 15, 2004; and

* The rule amendments reproduced here reflect technical amendments adopted in Release No. 34-46464A (SEC 2003), FED. SEC. L. REP. ¶ 86,901. In that release, the SEC amended the deadlines for statements filed by accelerated filers under Regulation S-X Rules 3-01 and 3-12 to conform to the corresponding deadlines for Forms 10-K and 10-Q.

(iii) 125 days for fiscal years ending on or after December 15, 2004; and

(2) 135 days for all other registrants.

* * * * *

(i)(1) For purposes of paragraph (c) and (d) of this section, the number of days shall be:

(i) For accelerated filers (as defined in § 240.12b-2 of this chapter):

(A) 90 days for fiscal years ending on or after December 15, 2002 and before December 15, 2003;

(B) 75 days for fiscal years ending on or after December 15, 2003 and before December 15, 2004; and

(C) 60 days for fiscal years ending on or after December 15, 2004; and

(ii) 90 days for all other registrants.

(2) For purposes of paragraph (e) of this section, the number of days shall be:

(i) For accelerated filers (as defined in § 240.12b-2 of this chapter):

(A) 134 days subsequent to the end of the registrant's most recent fiscal year for fiscal years ending on or after December 15, 2002 and before December 15, 2003;

(B) 129 days subsequent to the end of the registrant's most recent fiscal year for fiscal years ending on or after December 15, 2003 and before December 15, 2004; and

(C) 124 days subsequent to the end of the registrant's most recent fiscal year for fiscal years ending on or after December 15, 2004; and

(ii) 134 days subsequent to the end of the registrant's most recent fiscal year for all other registrants.

3. Section 210.3-09 is amended by:

a. Removing the authority citation following § 210.3-09;

b. Removing the phrase "§ 210.1-02(v)" and adding, in its place, the phrase "§ 210.1-02(w)" in the first sentence of paragraph (a); and

c. Revising the last sentence of paragraph (b) and adding paragraphs (b)(1), (b)(2), (b)(3) and (b)(4) to read as follows:

§ 210.3-09 Separate financial statements of subsidiaries not consolidated and 50 percent or less owned persons.

* * * * *

(b) * * * For purposes of a filing on Form 10-K (§ 249.310 of this chapter):

(1) If the registrant is an accelerated filer (as defined in § 240.12b-2 of this chapter) but the 50 percent or less owned person is not an accelerated filer, the required financial statements may be filed as an amendment to the report within 90 days, or within six months if the 50 percent or less owned person is a foreign business, after the end of the registrant's fiscal year.

(2) If the fiscal year of any 50 percent or less owned person ends within the registrant's number of filing days before the date of the filing, or if the fiscal year ends after the date of the filing, the required financial statements may be filed as an amendment to the report within the subsidiary's number of filing days, or within six months if the 50 percent or less owned person is a foreign business, after the end of such subsidiary's or person's fiscal year.

(3) The term registrant's number of filing days means:

(i) If the registrant is an accelerated filer:

(A) 90 days for fiscal years ending on or after December 15, 2002 and before December 15, 2003;

(B) 75 days for fiscal years ending on or after December 15, 2003 and before December 15, 2004; and

(C) 60 days for fiscal years ending on or after December 15, 2004; and

(ii) If the registrant is not an accelerated filer, 90 days.

(4) The term subsidiary's number of filing days means:

(i) If the 50 percent or less owned person is an accelerated filer:

(A) 90 days for fiscal years ending on or after December 15, 2002 and before December 15, 2003;

(B) 75 days for fiscal years ending on or after December 15, 2003 and before December 15, 2004; and

(C) 60 days for fiscal years ending on or after December 15, 2004; and

(ii) If the 50 percent or less owned person is not an accelerated filer, 90 days.

* * * * *

4. Section 210.3-12 is amended by:

a. Removing the phrase "135 days" and adding, in its place, the phrase "the number of days specified in paragraph (g) of this section" in both instances where it appears in the first sentence of paragraph (a);

b. Removing the phrase "90 days subsequent to the end of the fiscal year" and adding, in its place, the phrase "the number of days subsequent to the end of the fiscal year specified in paragraph (g) of this section" in the first sentence of paragraph (b); and

c. Adding paragraph (g) to read as follows:

§ 210.3-12 Age of financial statements at effective date of registration statement or at mailing date of proxy statement.

* * * * *

(g)(1) For purposes of paragraph (a) of this section, the number of days shall be:

(i) For accelerated filers (as defined in § 240.12b-2 of this chapter):

(A) 135 days for fiscal years ending on or after December 15, 2002 and before December 15, 2003;

(B) 130 days for fiscal years ending on or after December 15, 2004 and before December 15, 2004; and

(C) 125 days for fiscal years ending on or after December 15, 2004; and

(ii) 135 days for all other registrants.

(2) For purposes of paragraph (b) of this section, the number of days shall be:

(i) For accelerated filers (as defined in § 240.12b-2 of this chapter):

(A) 90 days for fiscal years ending on or after December 15, 2002 and before December 15, 2003;

(B) 75 days for fiscal years ending on or after December 15, 2003 and before December 15, 2004; and

(C) 60 days for fiscal years ending on or after December 15, 2004; and

(ii) 90 days for all other registrants.

¶ 1202 Regulation S-K

PART 229—STANDARD INSTRUCTIONS FOR FILING FORMS UNDER SECURITIES ACT OF 1933, SECURITIES EXCHANGE ACT OF 1934 AND ENERGY POLICY AND CONSERVATION ACT OF 1975—REGULATION S-K

5. The authority citation for Part 229 continues to read, in part, as follows:

Authority: 15 U.S.C. 77e, 77f, 77g, 77h, 77j, 77k, 77s, 77z-2, 77z-3, 77aa(25), 77aa(26), 77ddd, 77eee, 77ggg, 77hhh, 77iii, 77jjj, 77nnn, 77sss, 78c, 78i, 78j, 78l, 78m, 78n, 78o, 78u-5, 78w, 78ll(d), 78mm, 79e, 79n, 79t, 80a-8, 80a-29, 80a-30, 80a-31(c), 80a-37, 80a-38(a) and 80b-11, unless otherwise noted.

* * * * *

6. Section 229.101 is amended by revising paragraph (e) to read as follows:

§ 229.101 (Item 101) Description of business.

* * * * *

(e) Available information. Disclose the information in paragraphs (e)(1), (e)(2) and (e)(3) of this section in any registration statement you file under the Securities Act (15 U.S.C. 77a et seq.), and disclose the information in paragraphs (e)(3) and (e)(4) of this section if you are an accelerated filer (as defined in § 240.12b-2 of this chapter) filing an annual report on Form 10-K (§ 249.310 of this chapter):

(1) Whether you file reports with the Securities and Exchange Commission. If you are a reporting company, identify the reports and other information you file with the SEC.

(2) That the public may read and copy any materials you file with the SEC at the SEC's Public Reference Room at 450 Fifth Street, NW, Washington, DC 20549. State that the public may obtain information on the operation of the Public Reference Room by calling the SEC at 1-800-SEC-0330. If you are an electronic filer, state that the SEC maintains an Internet site that contains reports, proxy and information statements, and other information regarding issuers that file electronically with the SEC and state the address of that site (http://www.sec.gov).

(3) You are encouraged to give your Internet address, if available, except that if you are an accelerated filer filing your annual report on Form 10-K, you must disclose your Internet address, if you have one.

(4)(i) Whether you make available free of charge on or through your Internet website, if you have one, your annual report on Form 10-K, quarterly reports on Form 10-Q (§ 249.308a of this chapter), current reports on Form 8-K (§ 249.308 of this chapter), and amendments to those reports filed or furnished pursuant to Section 13(a) or 15(d) of the Exchange Act (15 U.S.C. 78m(a) or 78o(d)) as soon as reasonably practicable after you electronically file such material with, or furnish it to, the SEC;

(ii) If you do not make your filings available in this manner, the reasons you do not do so (including, where applicable, that you do not have an Internet website); and

(iii) If you do not make your filings available in this manner, whether you voluntarily will provide electronic or paper copies of your filings free of charge upon request.

* * * * *

¶ 1203 Exchange Act Rules

PART 240—GENERAL RULES AND REGULATIONS, SECURITIES EXCHANGE ACT OF 1934

7. The authority citation for Part 240 continues to read, in part, as follows:

Authority: 15 U.S.C. 77c, 77d, 77g, 77j, 77s, 77z-2, 77z-3, 77eee, 77ggg, 77nnn, 77sss, 77ttt, 78c, 78d, 78e, 78f, 78g, 78i, 78j, 78j-1, 78k, 78k-1, 78l, 78m, 78n, 78o, 78p, 78q, 78s, 78u-5, 78w, 78x, 78ll, 78mm, 79q, 79t, 80a-20, 80a-23, 80a-29, 80a-37, 80b-3, 80b-4 and 80b-11, unless otherwise noted.

* * * * *

8. Section 240.12b-2 is amended by adding the definition of "Accelerated filer" before the definition of "Affiliate" to read as follows:

§ 240.12b-2 Definitions.

* * * * *

Accelerated filer. (1) The term "accelerated filer" means an issuer after it first meets the following conditions as of the end of its fiscal year:

(i) The aggregate market value of the voting and non-voting common equity held by non-affiliates of the issuer is $75 million or more;

(ii) The issuer has been subject to the requirements of Section 13(a) or 15(d) of the Act (15 U.S.C. 78m or 78o(d)) for a period of at least twelve calendar months;

(iii) The issuer has filed at least one annual report pursuant to Section 13(a) or 15(d) of the Act; and

(iv) The issuer is not eligible to use Forms 10-KSB and 10-QSB (§ 249.310b and § 249.308b) for its annual and quarterly reports.

NOTE to paragraph (1): The aggregate market value of the issuer's outstanding voting and non-voting common equity shall be computed by use of the price at which the common equity was last sold, or the average of the bid and asked prices of such common equity, in the principal market for such common equity, as of the last business day of the issuer's most recently completed second fiscal quarter.

(2) Entering and Exiting Accelerated Filer Status. (i) The determination for whether a non-accelerated filer becomes an accelerated filer as of the end of the issuer's fiscal year governs the annual report to be filed for that fiscal year, the quarterly and annual reports to be filed for the subsequent fiscal year and all annual and quarterly reports to be filed thereafter while the issuer remains an accelerated filer.

(ii) Once an issuer becomes an accelerated filer, it will remain an accelerated filer unless the issuer becomes eligible to use Forms 10-KSB and 10-QSB for its annual and quarterly reports. In that case, the issuer will not become an accelerated filer again unless it subsequently meets the conditions in paragraph (1) of this definition.

* * * * *

9. Section 240.13a-10 is amended by:

a. Removing the phrase "90 days" and adding, in its place, the phrase "the number of days specified in paragraph (j) of this section" in the first sentence of paragraph (b) and the second sentence of paragraph (f);

b. Removing the phrase "45 days" and adding, in its place, the phrase "the number of days specified in paragraph (j) of this section" in the first sentence of paragraph (c), the second sentence of paragraph (e)(2), and the third sentence of paragraph (f); and

c. Adding paragraph (j) before the Note to read as follows:

§ 240.13a-10 Transition reports.

* * * * *

(j)(1) For transition reports to be filed on the form appropriate for annual reports of the issuer, the number of days shall be:

(i) For accelerated filers (as defined in § 240.12b-2):

(A) 90 days for fiscal years ending on or after December 15, 2002 and before December 15, 2003;

(B) 75 days for fiscal years ending on or after December 15, 2003 and before December 15, 2004; and

(C) 60 days for fiscal years ending on or after December 15, 2004; and

(ii) 90 days for all other issuers; and

(2) For transition reports to be filed on Form 10-Q or Form 10-QSB (§ 249.308a or § 249.308b of this chapter), the number of days shall be:

(i) For accelerated filers (as defined in § 240.12b-2):

(A) 45 days for fiscal years ending on or after December 15, 2002 and before December 15, 2004;

(B) 40 days for fiscal years ending on or after December 15, 2004 and before December 15, 2005; and

(C) 35 days for fiscal years ending on or after December 15, 2005; and

(ii) 45 days for all other issuers.

* * * * *

10. Section 240.15d-10 is amended by:

a. Removing the phrase "90 days" and adding, in its place, the phrase "the number of days specified in paragraph (j) of this section" in the first sentence of paragraph (b) and the second sentence of paragraph (f);

b. Removing the phrase "45 days" and adding, in its place, the phrase "the number of days specified in paragraph (j) of this section" in the first sentence of paragraph (c), the second sentence of paragraph (e)(2), and the third sentence of paragraph (f); and

c. Adding paragraph (j) before the Note to read as follows:

§ 240.15d-10 Transition reports.

* * * * *

(j)(1) For transition reports to be filed on the form appropriate for annual reports of the issuer, the number of days shall be:

(i) For accelerated filers (as defined in § 240.12b-2):

(A) 90 days for fiscal years ending on or after December 15, 2002 and before December 15, 2003;

(B) 75 days for fiscal years ending on or after December 15, 2003 and before December 15, 2004; and

(C) 60 days for fiscal years ending on or after December 15, 2004; and

(ii) 90 days for all other issuers; and

(2) For transition reports to be filed on Form 10-Q or Form 10-QSB (§ 249.308a or § 249.308b of this chapter), the number of days shall be:

(i) For accelerated filers (as defined in § 240.12b-2):

(A) 45 days for fiscal years ending on or after December 15, 2002 and before December 15, 2004;

(B) 40 days for fiscal years ending on or after December 15, 2004 and before December 15, 2005; and

(C) 35 days for fiscal years ending on or after December 15, 2005; and

(ii) 45 days for all other issuers.

* * * * *

¶ 1204 Exchange Act Forms

PART 249—FORMS, SECURITIES EXCHANGE ACT OF 1934

11. The authority citation for Part 249 continues to read, in part, as follows:

Authority: 15 U.S.C. 78a, et seq., unless otherwise noted.

* * * * *

12. Section 249.308a is revised to read as follows:

§ 249.308a Form 10-Q, for quarterly and transition reports under sections 13 or 15(d) of the Securities Exchange Act of 1934.

(a) Form 10-Q shall be used for quarterly reports under Section 13 or 15(d) of the Securities Exchange Act of 1934 (15 U.S.C. 78m or 78o(d)), required to be filed pursuant to § 240.13a-13 or § 240.15d-13 of this chapter. A quarterly report on this form pursuant to § 240.13a-13 or § 240.15d-13 of this chapter shall be filed within the following period after the end of the first three fiscal quarters of each fiscal year, but no quarterly report need be filed for the fourth quarter of any fiscal year:

(1) For accelerated filers (as defined in § 240.12b-2 of this chapter):

(i) 45 days after the end of the fiscal quarter for fiscal years ending on or after December 15, 2002 and before December 15, 2004;

(ii) 40 days after the end of the fiscal quarter for fiscal years ending on or after December 15, 2004 and before December 15, 2005; and

(iii) 35 days after the end of the fiscal quarter for fiscal years ending on or after December 15, 2005; and

(2) 45 days after the end of the fiscal quarter for all other registrants.

(b) Form 10-Q also shall be used for transition and quarterly reports filed pursuant to § 240.13a-10 or § 240.15d-10 of this chapter. Such transition or quarterly reports shall be filed in accordance with the requirements set forth in § 240.13a-10 or § 240.15d-10 of this chapter applicable when the registrant changes its fiscal year end.

13. Form 10-Q (referenced in § 249.308a) is amended by revising General Instruction A.1. and by adding a paragraph before the title "Applicable Only to Issuers Involved in Bankruptcy Proceedings During the Preceding Five Years:" on the cover page to read as follows:

Note: The text of Form 10-Q does not, and this amendment will not, appear in the Code of Federal Regulations.

UNITED STATES

SECURITIES AND EXCHANGE COMMISSION

Washington, D.C. 20549

FORM 10-Q

GENERAL INSTRUCTIONS

A. Rule as to Use of Form 10-Q.

1. Form 10-Q shall be used for quarterly reports under Section 13 or 15(d) of the Securities Exchange Act of 1934 (15 U.S.C. 78m or 78o(d)), filed pursuant to Rule 13a-13 (17 CFR 240.13a-13) or Rule 15d-13 (17 CFR 240.15d-13). A quarterly report on this form pursuant to Rule 13a-13 or Rule 15d-13 shall be filed within the following period after the end of each of the

first three fiscal quarters of each fiscal year, but no report need be filed for the fourth quarter of any fiscal year:

a. For accelerated filers (as defined in 17 CFR 240.12b-2):

(i) 45 days after the end of the fiscal quarter for fiscal years ending on or after December 15, 2002 and before December 15, 2004;

(ii) 40 days after the end of the fiscal quarter for fiscal years ending on or after December 15, 2004 and before December 15, 2005; and

(iii) 35 days after the end of the fiscal quarter for fiscal years ending on or after December 15, 2005; and

b. 45 days after the end of the fiscal quarter for all other issuers.

* * * * *

FORM 10-Q

* * * * *

Indicate by check mark whether the registrant is an accelerated filer (as defined in Rule 12b-2 of the Exchange Act). Yes ..... No ......

APPLICABLE ONLY TO ISSUERS INVOLVED IN BANKRUPTCY

PROCEEDINGS DURING THE PRECEDING FIVE YEARS:

* * * * *

14. Section 249.310 is revised to read as follows:

§ 249.310 Form 10-K, for annual and transition reports pursuant to sections 13 or 15(d) of the Securities Exchange Act of 1934.

(a) This form shall be used for annual reports pursuant to Sections 13 or 15(d) of the Securities Exchange Act of 1934 (15 U.S.C. 78m or 78o(d)) for which no other form is prescribed. This form also shall be used for transition reports filed pursuant to Section 13 or 15(d) of the Securities Exchange Act of 1934.

(b) Annual reports on this form shall be filed within the following period:

(1) For accelerated filers (as defined in § 240.12b-2 of this chapter):

(i) 90 days after the end of the fiscal year covered by the report for fiscal years ending on or after December 15, 2002 and before December 15, 2003;

(ii) 75 days after the end of the fiscal year covered by the report for fiscal years ending on or after December 15, 2003 and before December 15, 2004; and

(iii) 60 days after the end of the fiscal year covered by the report for fiscal years ending on or after December 15, 2004; and

(2) 90 days after the end of the fiscal year covered by the report for all other registrants.

(c) Transition reports on this form shall be filed in accordance with the requirements set forth in § 240.13a-10 or § 240.15d-10 of this chapter applicable when the registrant changes its fiscal year end.

(d) Notwithstanding paragraphs (b) and (c) of this section, all schedules required by Article 12 of Regulation S-X (§ § 210.12-01–210.12-29 of this chapter) may, at the option of the registrant, be filed as an amendment to the report not later than 30 days after the applicable due date of the report.

15. Form 10-K (referenced in § 249.310) is amended by revising General Instruction A. and the paragraph before the "Note" on the cover page to read as follows:

Note: The text of Form 10-K does not, and this amendment will not, appear in the Code of Federal Regulations.

UNITED STATES

SECURITIES AND EXCHANGE COMMISSION

Washington, D.C. 20549

FORM 10-K

* * * * *

GENERAL INSTRUCTIONS

A. Rule as to Use of Form 10-K.

(1) This Form shall be used for annual reports pursuant to Section 13 or 15(d) of the Securities Exchange Act of 1934 (15 U.S.C. 78m or 78o(d)) (the "Act") for which no other form is prescribed. This Form also shall be used for transition reports filed pursuant to Section 13 or 15(d) of the Act.

(2) Annual reports on this Form shall be filed within the following period:

(a) For accelerated filers (as defined in 17 CFR 240.12b-2):

(i) 90 days after the end of the fiscal year covered by the report for fiscal years ending on or after December 15, 2002 and before December 15, 2003;

(ii) 75 days after the end of the fiscal year covered by the report for fiscal years ending on or after December 15, 2003 and before December 15, 2004; and

(iii) 60 days after the end of the fiscal year covered by the report for fiscal years ending on or after December 15, 2004; and

(b) 90 days after the end of the fiscal year covered by the report for all other registrants.

(3) Transition reports on this Form shall be filed in accordance with the requirements set forth in Rule 13a-10 (17 CFR 240.13a-10) or Rule 15d-10 (17 CFR 240.15d-10) applicable when the registrant changes its fiscal year end.

(4) Notwithstanding paragraphs (2) and (3) of this General Instruction A., all schedules required by Article 12 of Regulation S-X (17 CFR 210.12-01–210.12-29) may, at the option of the registrant, be filed as an amendment to the report not later than 30 days after the applicable due date of the report.

* * * * *

FORM 10-K

* * * * *

Indicate by check mark whether the registrant is an accelerated filer (as defined in Rule 12b-2 of the Act). Yes ..... No ......

State the aggregate market value of the voting and non-voting common equity held by non-affiliates computed by reference to the price at which the common equity was last sold, or the average bid and asked price of such common equity, as of the last business day of the registrant's most recently completed second fiscal quarter.

* * * * *

Adopting Release: Additional Form 8-K Disclosure Requirements and Acceleration of Filing Date

Release Nos. 33-8400; 34-49424; File No. S7-22-02. March 16, 2004. Release in full text.

Additional Form 8-K Disclosure Requirements and Acceleration of Filing Date.

Agency: Securities and Exchange Commission.

Action: Final rules.

Summary: We are expanding the number of events that are reportable on Form 8-K under the Securities Exchange Act of 1934. These amendments add eight new items to the form, transfer two items from the periodic reports and expand disclosures under two existing Form 8-K items. Due to the increase in reportable events under the form, we are reorganizing the Form 8-K items into topical categories. The amendments also shorten the Form 8-K filing deadline for most items to four business days after the occurrence of an event triggering the disclosure requirements of the form. Finally, we are adopting a limited safe harbor from liability for failure to file certain of the required Form 8-K reports. These amendments are responsive to the "real time issuer disclosure" mandate in Section 409 of the Sarbanes-Oxley Act of 2002. They are intended to provide investors with better and faster disclosure of important corporate events.

Effective Date: August 23, 2004.

For Further Information: Ray Be, Special Counsel, or Julie A. Bell, Special Counsel, each at (202) 942-2910, Division of Corporation Finance, U.S. Securities and Exchange Commission, 450 Fifth Street, NW, Washington, DC 20549-0312.

Supplemenatary Information: We are adopting amendments to Form 8-K,[1] Form 10-K,[2] Form 10-KSB,[3] Form 10-Q,[4] Form 10-QSB,[5] Rule 12b-23,[6] Rule 13a-10,[7] Rule 13a-11,[8] Rule 15d-10,[9] and Rule 15d-11[10] under the Securities Exchange Act of 1934,[11] Form S-2[12], Form S-3[13] and Rule 144[14] under the Securities Act of 1933,[15] and Item 601[16] of Regulation S-B[17] and Item 601[18] of Regulation S-K.[19]

TABLE OF CONTENTS

---

[1] 17 CFR 249.308.

[2] 17 CFR 249.310.

[3] 17 CFR 249.310b.

[4] 17 CFR 249.308a.

[5] 17 CFR 249.308b.

[6] 17 CFR 249.12b-23.

[7] 17 CFR 249.13a-10.

[8] 17 CFR 240.13a-11.

[9] 17 CFR 240.15d-10.

[10] 17 CFR 240.15d-11.

[11] 15 U.S.C. 78a *et seq.*

[12] 17 CFR 239.12.

[13] 17 CFR 239.13.

[14] 17 CFR 230.144.

[15] 15 U.S.C. 77a *et seq.*

[16] 17 CFR 228.601.

[17] 17 CFR 228.10 et *seq.*

[18] 17 CFR 229.601.

[19] 17 CFR 229.10 et *seq.*

[¶ 2001]

I. BACKGROUND

On June 17, 2002, we proposed to increase the number of events required to be disclosed on Form 8-K.[20] Form 8-K is the Exchange Act form for current reports. Prior to the amendments being adopted today, Form 8-K required disclosure regarding nine different specified events.[21] At the time, the proposals would have increased the number of reportable events under the form to 22. The proposals also would have shortened the form's filing deadline from five business days or 15 calendar days, depending on the particular event, to two business days with an automatic two business day extension upon a company's filing of a Form 12b-25. In response to these proposals, we received approximately 85 comment letters from various constituencies, including investors, issuers, accounting firms, law firms and associations representing the interests of such constituencies.

Under the previous Form 8-K regime, companies were required to report very few significant corporate events. The limited number of Form 8-K disclosure items permitted a public company to delay disclosure of many significant events until the due date for its next periodic report. During such a delay, the market was unable to assimilate such undisclosed information into the value of a company's securities. The revisions that we adopt today will benefit markets by increasing the number of unquestionably or presumptively material events that must be disclosed currently. They will also provide investors with better and more timely disclosure of important corporate events.

On July 29, 2002, Congress enacted the Sarbanes-Oxley Act of 2002.[22] Section 409 of this Act requires public companies to disclose "on a rapid and current basis" material information regarding changes in a company's financial condition or operations as we, by rule, determine to be necessary or useful for the protection of investors and in the public interest. These amendments also further the goals of Section 409 of the Sarbanes-Oxley Act.

At the same time, we have taken into account a number of important comments on the proposals by adopting a modified version of the proposed Form 8-K amendments. We have addressed the commenters' concern regarding potential premature disclosure in a number of respects. We also have addressed the concerns raised by several commenters regarding the length of the Form 8-K filing period by extending it beyond the originally proposed two business day period and significantly reducing the amount of analysis required by the specific items of the form. Our general rules, however, prohibiting material omissions that make the contents of the disclosure mislead-

---

[20] Release No. 33-8106 (June 17, 2002) [67 FR 42914].

[21] In addition, three additional items of the form provided for voluntary disclosure of other significant events of a company, the filing of financial statements and exhibits, and disclosure of information pursuant to Regulation FD [17 CFR 243.100 *et seq.*]

[22] 15 U.S.C. 78m(*l*).

ing, of course, continue to apply.[23] We have also taken into account the concerns expressed by commenters regarding the liabilities that could arise for failure to make current disclosure of some events in what are still tight timeframes. In response to these comments, we have replaced the proposed safe harbor that would have afforded protection from potential Exchange Act Section 13(a) or 15(d) liability stemming from a company's failure to file a required Form 8-K to instead afford protection from potential liability arising under Exchange Act Section 10(b) and Rule 10b-5 thereunder.

[¶ 2002]

II. DISCUSSION OF AMENDMENTS

A. Shortened Form 8-K Filing Deadline and Availability of Form 12b-25

The amendments to Form 8-K require issuers that are subject to the reporting requirements of Section 13(a) and Section 15(d) of the Exchange Act, other than foreign private issuers that file annual reports on Form 20-F[24] or 40-F,[25] to file required current reports on Form 8-K within four business days of a triggering event.[26] These amendments do not affect the filing deadline for disclosures under Regulation FD (Item 7.01), voluntary disclosures (Item 8.01) and certain exhibits.

In the proposing release, we proposed a two business day deadline for Form 8-K, with provision for an automatic two business day extension upon a company's filing of Form 12b-25. Thus, the proposals would have permitted a four business day filing period whenever a company filed a Form 12b-25.

We received numerous comments and recommendations regarding appropriate filing deadlines.[27] The comments ranged from support of the two business day deadline to recommendations of as much as ten business days. Similarly, we received mixed comments on the Form 12b-25 proposal.[28] Some commenters noted that the Form 12b-25 proposal would complicate the process and that increased filings would reduce the significance of a Form 12b-25 filing.[29] We are persuaded by these commenters that modifications to the proposals are warranted. Thus, we are not adopting the proposal to extend the Form 8-K filing deadline via Form 12b-25. Rather, we are adopting a four business day deadline for Form 8-K, with no provision for extension under Rule 12b-25.[30] We believe that this change addresses commenters' concerns regarding the sufficiency of the filing period and simplifies the logistics of filing the four business day period.

B. Reorganization of Form 8-K Items

Because we are adding a number of new items to the form, we believe it is appropriate to organize the required reportable items into topical categories. Commenters generally supported such reorganization. The amendments organize the Form 8-K items under the following section headings and with the following new numbering system:

Section 1—Registrant's Business and Operations

Item 1.01 Entry into a Material Definitive Agreement

Item 1.02 Termination of a Material Definitive Agreement

Item 1.03 Bankruptcy or Receivership

Section 2—Financial Information

Item 2.01 Completion of Acquisition or Disposition of Assets

Item 2.02 Results of Operations and Financial Condition

Item 2.03 Creation of a Direct Financial Obligation or an Obligation under an Off-Balance Sheet Arrangement of a Registrant

Item 2.04 Triggering Events That Accelerate or Increase a Direct Financial Obligation or an Obligation under an Off-Balance Sheet Arrangement

Item 2.05 Costs Associated with Exit or Disposal Activities

Item 2.06 Material Impairments

Section 3—Securities and Trading Markets

Item 3.01 Notice of Delisting or Failure to Satisfy a Continued Listing Rule or Standard; Transfer of Listing

Item 3.02 Unregistered Sales of Equity Securities

Item 3.03 Material Modifications to Rights of Security Holders

---

[23] See, for example, Exchange Act Rule 12b-20 [17 CFR 240.12b-20].

[24] 17 CFR 249.220f.

[25] 17 CFR 249.240f.

[26] Instruction B.1. to Form 8-K.

[27] See, for example, the letters from American Institute of Certified Public Accountants ("AICPA"), City Bar of New York ("NY City Bar"), Deloitte & Touche, Dan Nguyen, Emerson Electric Co. ("Emerson"), Boeing Company ("Boeing"), Morgan Stanley and Perkins Coie.

[28] See, for example, the letters from the AICPA, KPMG, Cleary Gottlieb, Steen & Hamilton ("Cleary Gottlieb"), PriceWaterhouseCoopers ("PWC"), Intel Corporation ("Intel") and Ronald Stauber.

[29] See the letters from Cleary Gottlieb and PWC.

[30] For example, if a reportable event occurred on a Wednesday, the Form 8-K filing deadline would typically be the following Tuesday.

Section 4—Matters Related to Accountants and Financial Statements

Item 4.01 Changes in Registrant's Certifying Accountant

Item 4.02 Non-Reliance on Previously Issued Financial Statements or a Related Audit Report or Completed Interim Review

Section 5—Corporate Governance and Management

Item 5.01 Changes in Control of Registrant

Item 5.02 Departure of Directors or Principal Officers; Election of Directors; Appointment of Principal Officers

Item 5.03 Amendments to Articles of Incorporation or Bylaws; Change in Fiscal Year

Item 5.04 Temporary Suspension of Trading Under Registrant's Employee Benefit Plans

Item 5.05 Amendments to the Registrant's Code of Ethics, or Waiver of a Provision of the Code of Ethics

Section 6—[Reserved]

Section 7—Regulation FD

Item 7.01 Regulation FD Disclosure

Section 8—Other Events

Item 8.01 Other Events

Section 9—Financial Statements and Exhibits

Item 9.01 Financial Statements and Exhibits

This new numbering system avoids re-use of the former single-digit item numbering system previously used in Form 8-K to avoid confusion about the subject of particular items. For example, the Form 8-K item permitting voluntary disclosure of "other events" that was formerly designated as Item 5 now appears as Item 8.01. Thus, anyone searching the EDGAR database for such filings made before and after the change will need to search for both Items 5 and 8.01. In addition, a company amending a Form 8-K that it filed before the effective date of the rules we are adopting today must file the amendment using the form's new numbering system. For example, a company amending a Form 8-K previously filed under former Item 2, Acquisition or Disposition of Assets, to add the required financial statements must reference new Item 9.01, Financial Statements and Exhibits, when filing the amendment.

C. Expansion of Form 8-K Items

We are adding eight new items to the list of events that require a company to file a current report on Form 8-K and transferring, in part, two items from the periodic reports.[31] In addition, we are expanding two pre-existing Form 8-K items. Based on our review of Form 8-K filings, as well as public comment letters, we believe that these items represent events that unquestionably or presumptively have such significance that current disclosure should be required. These amendments will operate prospectively only.[32] The following is a discussion of the individual items in the revised Form 8-K.

Section 1—Registrant's Business and Operations

Item 1.01 Entry into a Material Definitive Agreement.

New Item 1.01 requires the disclosure of material definitive agreements entered into by a company that are not made in the ordinary course of business. The item parallels Items 601(b)(10) of Regulation S-K[33] with regard to the types of agreements that are material to a company, a standard already familiar to reporting companies.[34]

Under Item 1.01, a company must also disclose any material amendment to a material definitive agreement. Disclosure of a material amendment may be required under Item 1.01 even if the underlying agreement previously has not been disclosed by the company. This could occur if, for example, the agreement was entered into prior to the effective date of this Item 1.01, or the amendment results in the agreement becoming a material definitive agreement of the company.

A company must disclose the following information upon entry into, or material amendment of, a material definitive agreement:

- The date on which the agreement was entered into or amended, the identity of the parties to the agreement and a brief description of any material relationship between the company or its affiliates and any of the parties, other than in respect of the material definitive agreement or amendment; and

---

[31] The two items which we have modified from existing disclosure requirements in periodic reports and included in Form 8-K are Item 3.02 Unregistered Sales of Equity Securities and Item 3.03 Material Modifications to Rights of Security Holders, each of which previously was required to be reported pursuant to Forms 10-Q, 10-QSB, 10-K and 10-KSB, as applicable. As discussed more fully below, however, we have retained in these applicable periodic reports a requirement to disclose any sales of unregistered equity securities that do not meet the numeric thresholds of the new Form 8-K item.

[32] However, certain subsequent events, such as a material amendment to a material definitive agreement, may trigger a disclosure requirement even though the initial entry into the material definitive agreement occurred prior to the effectiveness of these amendments.

[33] Unless otherwise noted, throughout this release, where we refer to a particular item of Regulation S-K, we also refer to, and include, the comparable item under Regulation S-B.

[34] See Instruction 1 to Item 1.01.

- A brief description of the terms and conditions of the agreement or amendment that are material to the company.

We received substantial comment on this item at the proposing stage. In particular, many commenters opposed our proposal to require disclosure of letters of intent and other non-binding agreements in addition to disclosure of definitive agreements that are material to the company.[35] They noted that disclosure of non-binding agreements could cause significant competitive harm to the company and create excessive speculation in the market.[36] Several companies also stated that they use letters of intent extensively, but that few such letters culminate in a completed transaction.[37]

In response to the commenters, we eliminated the requirement that companies disclose their entry into non-binding agreements from this item.[38] We have further replaced the proposed definition of "agreement" with a definition of "material definitive agreement" and have moved this definition from a proposed instruction into Item 1.01(b). We have clarified that only agreements which provide for obligations that are material to and enforceable against a company, or rights that are material to the company and enforceable by the company against one or more other parties to the agreement by the company, are required to be disclosed pursuant to Item 1.01, regardless of whether the material definitive agreement is enforceable subject to stated conditions.[39]

We have also eliminated the specific requirements to disclose each party's rights and obligations under the material definitive agreement and the duration and termination provisions of the agreement. To the extent that any of these provisions is material to the company, it must be briefly described under paragraph (a)(2) of the item.

Filing of Exhibits

The proposals would have required a company to file a material agreement required to be disclosed under Item 1.01 as an exhibit to its Form 8-K. We received numerous comments on this proposal. A primary concern of commenters was that companies would not always be able to prepare and submit requests for confidential treatment of sensitive terms of the agreement within the short Form 8-K filing period.[40] They recommended several alternatives, including streamlined treatment of such requests, such as by creating a short-form confidential treatment request process,[41] and delaying the company's obligation to file the exhibit until it files its next periodic report.[42] In addition, some commenters were concerned that the process of preparing to submit such lengthy documents in proper EDGAR format would hinder the ability of a company to report the event promptly.

In response to these comments, we have eliminated the proposed requirement to file the material agreement as a Form 8-K exhibit. Prior to these amendments, material agreements did not need to be filed until the company's next periodic report as there was no Form 8-K item requiring disclosure of the event. Thus, the amendments do not change current requirements with regard to filing material agreements as exhibits, not do they affect the process for requesting confidential treatment of terms of those agreements. Given the initial disclosure of the agreement and its material terms, delayed filing of the exhibit should have minimal effect on the utility of the Item 1.01 disclosure. Pursuant to amended Item 601 of Regulation S-K, a company will have to file such agreement as an exhibit to the company's next periodic report or registration statement.[43] However, we encourage companies to file the exhibit with the Form 8-K when feasible, particularly when no confidential treatment is requested.

Considerations Regarding Business Combinations

New Item 1.01 requires disclosure of all material definitive agreements specified by the item,

---

[35] See, for example, the letters of the AICPA, American Bar Association, Section of Business Law ("ABA"), NY City Bar, Cleary Gottlieb, Financial Executives International ("FEI"), Intel and Morgan Stanley.

[36] See, for example, the letters of Compass Bancshares, Inc. ("Compass Bancshares"), NY City Bar and Hogan & Hartson.

[37] Many of these companies were real estate investment trusts. See, for example, the letter from the National Association of Real Estate Investment Trusts ("NAREIT").

[38] We note, however, that there may be instances under our other rules and regulations or applicable case law in which a company would be required to disclose such non-binding agreements, notwithstanding the absence of a Form 8-K requirement.

[39] Thus, for example, a material definitive agreement which is subject to customary closing conditions, such as the delivery of legal opinions or comfort letters, completion of due diligence or regulatory approval, must be disclosed under Item 1.01 when such agreement is enforceable against or by the company despite the fact that such conditions have not yet been satisfied. However, if a company enters into a non-binding letter of intent or memorandum of understanding that also contains some binding, but non-material elements, such as a confidentiality agreement or a no-shop agreement, the letter or memorandum does not need to be filed because the binding provisions are not material.

[40] See, for example, the letters from the ABA, NY City Bar and FEI.

[41] See the letter from the NY City Bar.

[42] See, for example, the letters from the AICPA, Compass Bancshares and Sullivan & Cromwell.

[43] See General Instruction B.4 to Form 8-K.

including business combination agreements and other agreements that relate to extraordinary corporate transactions. The filing of the Form 8-K may constitute the first "public announcement" for purposes of Rule 165[44] under the Securities Act and Rule 14d-2(b)[45] or Rule 14a-12[46] under the Exchange Act[47] and thereby trigger a filing obligation under those rules.

In the proposing release, we solicited comment on whether Form 8-K should include boxes on the cover page to enable the filer to indicate that the Form 8-K filing also satisfies a separate filing obligation under Rule 165, Rule 14d-2(b) and/or 14a-12.[48] We received favorable comments on this issue.[49] Thus, to avoid duplicative filings, we are amending Form 8-K to enable a company to check one or more boxes on the cover page to indicate that it is simultaneously satisfying its filing obligations under these rules, provided that the Form 8-K contains all of the information required by those rules.[50]

Item 1.02 Termination of a Material Definitive Agreement.

We are adopting a new Form 8-K item requiring disclosure if a material definitive agreement not made in the ordinary course of business to which a company is a party is terminated, other than by expiration of the agreement on a stated termination date or as a result of all parties completing their obligations under such agreement, and such termination of the agreement is material to the company. In such an event, the company must disclose the following information:

- The date of the termination of the material definitive agreement, the identity of the parties to the agreement and a brief description of any material relationship between the company or its affiliates and any of the parties other than in respect of the material definitive agreement;
- A brief description of the terms and conditions of the agreement that are material to the company;
- A brief description of the material circumstances surrounding the termination; and
- Any material early termination penalties incurred by the company.[51]

Several commenters believed that an agreement that terminates "by its terms" should not trigger disclosure.[52] We have addressed these concerns by excluding termination as a result of expiration of the agreement on its stated termination date or as a result of completion by all parties of their obligations.

Commenters also were concerned that one party to an agreement may use this item as a negotiation tool to induce another party to the agreement to modify the agreement on terms more favorable to the first party, or else potentially suffer a negative market reaction to disclosure about termination of the agreement.[53] We believe these comments are addressed by Instruction 1 to Item 1.02 which states that no disclosure is required under the item during negotiations or discussions regarding termination of a material definitive agreement unless and until the agreement has been terminated.

In addition, in response to commenters' concerns, we have further clarified in Instruction 2 to Item 1.02 that no disclosure is required under the item if the company believes, in good faith, that the agreement has not been terminated, unless the company has received a notice of termination pursuant to the terms of the agreement. If a

---

[44] 17 CFR 230.165.

[45] 17 CFR 240.14d-2(b).

[46] 17 CFR 240.14a-12.

[47] Rule 165 provides an exemption from Section 5 of the Securities Act for communications relating to the business combination made before the filing of a registration statement in connection with that business combination if all written communications are filed under Securities Act Rule 425 [17 CFR 230.425]. Rule 14d-2(b) allows communications by the bidder before the commencement of the tender offer provided that all written communications are filed. Rule 14a-12 allows solicitations to be made before a proxy statement meeting the requirements of Rule 14a-3(a) [17 CFR 240.14a-3(a)] is furnished to security holders if the written solicitations are filed.

[48] The Form 8-K filing must generally include the substantive information and legends required by those rules. The appropriate EDGAR tag (specifically, "425," "TO-C" or "DEFA14A") also will be necessary. An interpretation of the Division of Corporation Finance (see Q&A No. I.B.13, Manual of Publicly Available Telephone Interpretations, Third Supplement, July 2001) stated that a company that files information regarding a business combination on Form 8-K may be required to make a separate filing under Rule 425 [17 CFR 230.425]. As of the August 23, 2004 compliance date for these amendments, a separate filing no longer will be necessary if the company indicates on the cover of its Form 8-K report that the filing is intended to satisfy the requirements of Rule 425.

[49] See, for example, the letters from the ABA, NY City Bar, Compass Bancshares, and Sullivan & Cromwell.

[50] As Instruction A.2 to the Form 8-K indicates, however, because the information required by Rule 425(c) would otherwise be present in a Form 8-K report, such information need not be placed in the location specified by Rule 425(c).

[51] Disclosure of the termination of a material definitive agreement may be required under this item even if the agreement was not disclosed previously because, for example, the agreement was entered into prior to effectiveness of Item 1.01.

[52] See, for example, the letters from CIGNA Corporation ("CIGNA"), Cleary Gottlieb, John Deere Co. ("John Deere") and Shearman & Sterling.

[53] See, for example, the letters from Boeing, Intel, NY City Bar and Sullivan & Cromwell.

company believes in good faith that a material definitive agreement has not been terminated, but determines nevertheless to make disclosure under Item 1.02, the company could disclose under this item a statement of its good faith belief as to any relevant matter, including, for example, that not all conditions to termination have been satisfied or that a termination has otherwise not occurred. In such event, an amendment[54] under this Item 1.02 may be required if the company's conclusion as to termination changes due to a loss of, or change in, its good faith belief.

Other commenters were concerned about the proposed requirement to disclose management's analysis of the effect of the termination, which some referred to as a "mini-MD&A." [55] We agree with the commenters that in some cases such analysis may be difficult to provide within the abbreviated Form 8-K filing period and may be more relevant and complete when discussed in the context of full financial statements. Thus, we have removed this proposed requirement from specific required terms of the final rule. Nevertheless, any disclosure made in a report on Form 8-K must include all other material information, if any, that is necessary to make the required disclosure, in the light of the circumstances under which it is made, not misleading.[56]

Item 1.03 Bankruptcy or Receivership

This item retains the basic substantive requirements formerly included in Item 3 of Form 8-K regarding a company's entry into bankruptcy or receivership. As proposed, however, we are adopting minor changes to make the item more readable, such as breaking out embedded lists from the text and moving some language currently included in the text into an instruction to the item.

Section 2—Financial Information

Item 2.01 Completion of Acquisition or Disposition of Assets

This item retains most of the substantive requirements included in former Item 2 of Form 8-K. It requires disclosure if a company, or any of its majority-owned subsidiaries, has acquired or disposed of a significant amount of assets, otherwise than in the ordinary course of business.

We recognize that there will frequently be a relationship between the disclosure provided under this item and the disclosure required by new Item 1.01, "Entry into a Material Definitive Agreement." Typically, a company will report its entry into a material definitive agreement to acquire or dispose of assets under Item 1.01, and then later disclose the closing of the acquisition or disposition transaction under Item 2.01. However, a company will not necessarily be required to provide the Item 2.01 disclosure regarding every material definitive acquisition or disposition agreement disclosed under Item 1.01 as Item 2.01 includes a bright-line reporting threshold that is not included in Item 1.01. Under this threshold, a company need only report a completed acquisition or disposition of assets if the transaction meets the significant asset test as set forth in the item.[57]

We received several comments recommending harmonization between the reporting thresholds in Items 1.01 and 2.01.[58] It is our intention, however, that Item 1.01 address a different scope of agreements than those that will trigger disclosure under Item 2.01, which only applies to the acquisition or disposition of assets. We believe that the use of two different thresholds for these items will not cause undue confusion. Indeed, both items use existing thresholds, one from Item 601 of Regulation S-K, the other from former Item 2 of Form 8-K.

Several commenters believed that the disclosure requirements regarding the source of funding for an acquisition typically have not produced meaningful disclosure and should be limited to instances where a material relationship exists between the company and the source of the funding.[59] They suggested adding the same type of limitation regarding the disclosure that a company must provide about the formula or principle followed in determining the amount of the consideration involved in the acquisition or disposition. We agree with those commenters and have limited those disclosure requirements to instances in which such a relationship is present.

---

[54] In such event, the company will have to amend the Form 8-K to provide this updated information within four business days from the date that conclusion changes.

[55] These commenters likened the proposed analysis to Item 303 of Regulation S-K, which requires a company to include an MD&A section in periodic filings and registration statements containing financial statements. See the letter from Joseph Grundfest and seven Silicon Valley law firms ("Grundfest Group"), as well as the letters from the ABA, NY City Bar, and NAREIT.

[56] See Rule 12b-20 under the Exchange Act, as well as Exchange Act Section 10(b) [15 U.S.C. 78j(b)] and Rule 10b-5 [17 CFR 240.10b-5] thereunder.

[57] This test is the same as the test in former Item 2 of Form 8-K. It states that an acquisition or disposition is deemed significant if (1) the company's and its other subsidiaries' equity in the net book value of the assets or the amount paid or received for the assets exceeded 10% of the total assets of the company and its consolidated subsidiaries, or (2) the transaction involved a business that is significant under Regulation S-X.

[58] See the letters from Compass Bancshares, Kellogg, the New York State Bar Association ("NY State Bar"), Shearman & Sterling and Sullivan & Cromwell.

[59] See the letters from the NY State Bar and Sullivan & Cromwell.

As proposed, this item requires the same basic disclosure formerly required by Item 2 of Form 8-K, except that disclosure no longer is required regarding the nature of the business in which the acquired assets were used and whether the company acquiring the assets intends to continue such use. In addition, while we proposed revision of the disclosure regarding the source of funds used to effect a change in control, we believe that Congress intended for certain procedures to be present with regard to the disclosure of the identity of a bank involved in such a transaction when the bank is loaning funds in the ordinary course of its business.[60] Thus, we are not adopting the proposed changes to this aspect of the item.

Item 2.02 Results of Operations and Financial Condition

We have retained in new Item 2.02 all of the substantive requirements of former Item 12 of Form 8-K regarding public announcements or releases of material non-public information regarding a company's results of operations or financial condition.

Item 2.03 Creation of a Direct Financial Obligation or an Obligation under an Off-Balance Sheet Arrangement of a Registrant

This new item requires disclosure of the following information if the company becomes obligated under a direct financial obligation that is material to the company:

- the date on which the company becomes obligated on the direct financial obligation and a brief description of the transaction or agreement creating the obligation;
- the amount of the obligation, including the terms of its payment and, if applicable, a brief description of the material terms under which it may be accelerated or increased and the nature of any recourse provisions that would enable the company to recover from third parties; and
- a brief description of the other terms and conditions of the transaction or agreement that are material to the company.

In addition, if the company becomes directly or contingently liable for an obligation that is material to the company arising out of an off-balance sheet arrangement, it must provide the following information:

- the date on which the company becomes directly or contingently liable on the obligation and a brief description of the transaction or agreement creating the arrangement and obligation;
- a brief description of the nature and amount of the obligation of the company under the arrangement, including the material terms under which it may become a direct obligation, if applicable, or may be accelerated or increased and the nature of any recourse provisions that would enable the company to recover from third parties;
- the maximum potential amount of future payments (undiscounted) that the company may be required to make, if different;[61] and
- a brief description of the other terms and conditions of the obligation or arrangement that are material to the company.[62]

The item defines a "direct financial obligation" as any of the following:

- a long-term debt obligation, as defined in Item 303(a)(5)(ii)(A) of Regulation S-K (17 CFR 229.303(a)(5)(ii)(A));
- a capital lease obligation, as defined in Item 303(a)(5)(ii)(B) of Regulation S-K (17 CFR 229.303(a)(5)(ii)(B));
- an operating lease obligation, as defined in Item 303(a)(5)(ii)(C) of Regulation S-K (17 CFR 229.303(a)(5)(ii)(C)); or
- a short-term debt obligation that arises other than in the ordinary course of business.

The item refers to Item 303(a)(4)(ii) of Regulation S-K for the definition of the term "off-balance sheet arrangement." [63] It also defines the term "short-term debt obligation" as a payment obligation under a borrowing arrangement that is scheduled to mature within one year, or, for those companies that use the operating cycle concept of working capital, within a company's operating cycle that is longer than one year, as discussed in Accounting Research Bulletin No. 43, Chapter 3A, *Working Capital.*[64]

This new item also contains an instruction clarifying that a company need not file a report under this Item 2.03 until the company enters into an

---

[60] See 15 U.S.C. 13(d)(1)(B).

[61] Instruction 4 to Item 2.03 provides that the maximum amount of future payments may not be reduced by the effect of any amounts that may possibly be recovered by a company under recourse or collateralization provisions in any guarantee agreement, transaction or arrangement.

[62] See generally Financial Accounting Standards Board (FASB) Interpretation No. 45, *Guarantor's Accounting and Disclosure Requirements for Guarantees, Including Indirect Guarantees and Indebtedness of Others.*

[63] See paragraph (d) of Item 2.03 of Form 8-K.

[64] This definition is comparable to the definition of "short term obligation" in Statement of Financial Accounting Standards No. 6 (SFAS No. 6), *Classification of Short-Term Obligations Expected to Be Refinanced.* SFAS No. 6 defines "short term obligation" as those obligations that are scheduled to mature within one year after the date of an enterprise's balance sheet or, for those enterprises that use the operating cycle concept of working capital, within an enterprise's operating cycle that is longer than one year.

agreement enforceable against it, whether or not subject to conditions, under which the direct financial obligation will arise or be created or issued. If there is no such agreement, the company must provide the disclosure within four business days after the occurrence of the closing or settlement of the transaction or arrangement under which the direct financial obligation arises or is created.[65]

Another instruction clarifies that a company must provide the disclosure required regarding off-balance sheet arrangements, whether or not the company is also a party to the transaction or agreement creating the contingent obligation arising under the off-balance sheet arrangement.[66] In the event that neither the company nor any affiliate of the company is also a party to the transaction or agreement creating the contingent obligation arising under the off-balance arrangement in question, the four business day period for reporting the event under this Item 2.03 would begin on the earlier of (i) the fourth business day after the contingent obligation is created or arises, and (ii) the day on which an executive officer[67] of the company becomes aware of the contingent obligation.[68]

The third instruction clarifies that if the company enters into a facility, program or similar arrangement that creates or may give rise to direct financial obligations in connection with multiple transactions, the company must disclose the entering into of the facility, program or similar arrangement, and disclose its obligations, to the extent the obligations are material, as they arise or are created under the facility or program (including when a series of previously undisclosed individually immaterial obligations become material in the aggregate).[69]

A final instruction[70] provides that if the obligation required to be disclosed under this Item 2.03 is a security, or a term of a security, that has been or will be sold pursuant to an effective registration statement of the company, the company is not required to file a Form 8-K pursuant to the item, provided that the prospectus relating to the sale contains the information required by this item and is filed within the required time period under Securities Act Rule 424.[71]

We received numerous comments on this item. Many commenters requested clarification regarding the scope of obligations covered by this item.[72] Since we proposed the amendments, we have adopted new rules requiring a company to provide disclosure about its off-balance sheet arrangements.[73] Those rules define the term "off-balance sheet arrangement." Because these are the types of contingent obligations about which Item 2.03 seeks disclosure, new Item 2.03 incorporates the definition of "off-balance sheet arrangement" used in Item 303(a)(4)(ii) of Regulation S-K.

The new off-balance sheet arrangement disclosure rules also require disclosure of certain direct financial obligations in tabular form. We have revised the definition of "direct financial obligation" to refer to much of the same accounting literature used in these rules. We believe this approach will encourage consistency and reduce confusion regarding the scope of this item.

Item 2.04 Triggering Events That Accelerate or Increase a Direct Financial Obligation or an Obligation under an Off-Balance Sheet Arrangement.

This new item requires a company to file a Form 8-K report if a triggering event causing the increase or acceleration of a direct financial obligation of the company occurs and the consequences of the event are material to the company. In such case, the company must provide the following information:

- the date of the triggering event and a brief description of the agreement or transaction under which the direct financial obligation was created and is increased or accelerated;
- a brief description of the triggering event;
- the amount of the direct financial obligation, as increased if applicable, and the terms of payment or acceleration that apply; and

---

[65] See Instruction 1 to Item 2.03 of Form 8-K.

[66] For example, assume Company A enters into an agreement with Bank B pursuant to which Company A agrees with Bank B that Company C, an unconsolidated subsidiary of Company A, will maintain equity of at least $1. Six months later, Company C borrows $100 million from Bank B. Three months later, Company C defaults on its debt obligation to Bank B. In this fact pattern, upon entering into the initial agreement with Bank B, Company A would generally have no disclosure requirement under Item 2.03 on Form 8-K. However, when Company C borrows $100 million from Bank B, Company A will be required to file a Form 8-K under Item 2.03 as Company A has become contingently liable for an obligation arising out of an off-balance sheet arrangement, assuming such contingent obligation is material to Company A. Upon Company C's default on it debt obligation to Bank B, a further Form 8-K filing obligation will be required under Item 2.04, as discussed below, as a contingent obligation of Company A has become a direct financial obligation, assuming such direct financial obligation is material to Company A.

[67] The term "executive officer" is defined in Exchange Act Rule 3b-7 [17 CFR 240.3b-7].

[68] See Instruction 2 to Item 2.03 of Form 8-K.

[69] See Instruction 3 to Item 2.03 of Form 8-K.

[70] See Instruction 5 to Item 2.03 of Form 8-K.

[71] 17 CFR 230.424.

[72] See, for example, the letters from the ABA, Emerson, Intel, NY State Bar and Sullivan & Cromwell.

[73] Release No. 33-8182 (January 28, 2003) [68 FR 5982].

- any other material obligations of the company that may arise, increase, be accelerated or become direct financial obligations as a result of the triggering event or the increase or acceleration of the direct financial obligation.

Also, if a triggering event occurs causing a company's obligation under an off-balance sheet arrangement to increase or be accelerated, or causing a company's contingent obligation under an off-balance sheet arrangement to become a direct financial obligation of the company, and the consequences of such event are material to the company, it must disclose the following information:

- the date of the triggering event and a brief description of the off-balance sheet arrangement;
- a brief description of the triggering event;
- the nature and amount of the obligation, as increased if applicable, and the terms of payment or acceleration that apply; and
- any other material obligations of the company that may arise, increase, be accelerated or become direct financial obligations as a result of the triggering event or the increase or acceleration of the obligation under the off-balance sheet arrangement or its becoming a direct financial obligation of the company.

Item 2.04 defines the term "direct financial obligation" by reference to the definition provided in Item 2.03, but adds for purposes of Item 2.04 that such term includes an obligation arising out of an off-balance sheet arrangement that is accrued under the FASB Statement of Financial Accounting Standards No. 5, *Accounting for Contingencies*[74] (SFAS No. 5) as a probable loss contingency. "Off-balance sheet arrangement" is defined by reference to the definition provided in Item 2.03.[75] Finally, Item 2.04(e) defines the term "triggering event" as an event, including an event of default, event of acceleration or similar event, as a result of which a direct financial obligation of the company or an obligation of the company arising under an off-balance sheet arrangement is increased or becomes accelerated or as a result of which a contingent obligation of the company arising out of an off-balance sheet arrangement becomes a direct financial obligation of the company.

We have added four instructions to this item. Similar to Item 2.03, the first instruction clarifies that disclosure is required if a triggering event occurs in respect of the company's obligation under an off-balance sheet arrangement and the consequences are material to the company, whether or not the company is also a party to the transaction or agreement under which the triggering event occurs.[76] The second instruction states that no disclosure is required unless and until a triggering event has occurred in accordance with the terms of the relevant agreement, transaction or arrangement, including, if required, the sending to the company of notice of the occurrence of a triggering event pursuant to the terms of the agreement, transaction or arrangement and the satisfaction of all conditions to such occurrence, except the passage of time.

The third instruction provides that, similar to new Item 1.02 of Form 8-K, no disclosure is required if the company believes, in good faith, that no triggering event has occurred, unless the company has received a notice as described in Instruction 2 to Item 2.04. Similar to Item 1.02, a company may wish to disclose under this Item 2.04 a statement of its good faith belief as to any relevant matter, including, for example, that not all conditions to occurrence of a triggering event have been satisfied or that a triggering event otherwise has not occurred. In such event, an amendment under this Item 2.04 may be required if the company's conclusion as to the triggering event changes due to a loss of, or change in, its good faith.[77]

Finally, Instruction 4 to Item 2.04 explains that, if a company is subject to an obligation arising out of an off-balance sheet arrangement, whether or not disclosed pursuant to Item 2.03, if a triggering event occurs as a result of which under that obligation an accrual for a probable loss is required under SFAS No. 5, the obligation arising out of the off-balance sheet arrangement becomes a direct financial obligation for purposes of Item 2.04. In this situation, if the consequences as determined under Item 2.04(b) are material to the company, disclosure is required under Item 2.04.

Similar to those who objected to the proposed analysis provision in Item 1.02, one commenter opposed requiring disclosure of management's analysis of the effect of the triggering event on the company.[78] Again, we agree that it is appropriate to delete this requirement as a specific term of this Form 8-K item. We once again, however, remind companies that any disclosure made in a report on Form 8-K must include all other material information, if any, that is necessary to

---

[74] See Item 2.04(c).

[75] See Item 2.04(d).

[76] See, for example, note 66 above.

[77] In such event, the company would have to amend the Form 8-K to provide this updated information within four business days from the date that its conclusion changes.

[78] See the letter from the ABA.

make the required disclosure, in the light of the circumstances under which it is made, not misleading.[79]

Item 2.05 Costs Associated with Exit or Disposal Activities

This new item requires disclosure when the board of directors, a committee of the board of directors, or an authorized officer or officers if board action is not required, commits the company to an exit or disposal plan or otherwise disposes of a long-lived asset or terminates employees under a plan of termination described in paragraph 8 of FASB Statement of Financial Accounting Standards No. 146 *Accounting for Costs Associated with Exit or Disposal Activities* (SFAS No. 146), under which material charges will be incurred under generally accepted accounting principles applicable to the company. The item requires a company to disclose:

- the date of the commitment to the course of action and a description of the course of action, including the facts and circumstances leading to the expected action and the expected completion date;
- for each major type of cost associated with the course of action (for example, one-time termination benefits, contract termination costs and other associated costs), an estimate of the total amount or range of amounts expected to be incurred in connection with the action;
- an estimate of the total amount or range of amounts expected to be incurred in connection with the action; and
- the company's estimate of the amount or range of amounts of the charge that will result in future cash expenditures.

If at the time of filing the company is unable to make a good faith estimate of the amount of the charges, it need not disclose an estimate at that time, but must nevertheless file the Form 8-K report describing the company's commitment to a course of action under which it will incur a material charge. Within four business days after the company formulates an estimate, the company must amend its earlier Form 8-K filing to include the estimate.

We initially proposed that disclosure under Item 2.05 would have been triggered upon a "definitive" commitment of the company to a course of action. We have eliminated the term "definitive" because we believe that the tem "commitment" by itself adequately conveys the idea that a company has made a final determination regarding a course of action.

A number of commenters opposed this item. They noted that such events can occur over time, making it difficult to determine the exact date of the triggering event.[80] They suggested that it would be more appropriate for this type of disclosure to appear in a company's periodic reports. We believe that it is important for investors to receive this information on a current basis and that, by tying the Form 8-K filing requirement to the board's, committee's or officers' determination, the timing of the disclosure is sufficiently precise.

One commenter believed that a discussion of a single piece of financial information outside of the context of the complete financial statements would be difficult and potentially misleading.[81] Nonetheless, we believe that the occurrence of these events are important to investors making investment decisions. Others noted that a company often may not have estimated of the relevant charges at the time the plan is adopted.[82] We acknowledge this possibility and thus have revised the item to permit later disclosure of such estimates within four business days after they are determined.

Other commenters noted that, since we proposed this item, FASB has issued SFAS No. 146 which changed previous requirements regarding the timing of recognition of costs associated with exit or disposal activities.[83] SFAS No. 146, however, also requires disclosure of such events, prior to recognition, similar to that required in this item.[84] We have revised the disclosure requirements to more closely track the disclosures required in the footnotes to the financial statements required by SFAS No. 146. Thus, we do not believe that this item is inconsistent with current accounting literature, particularly in light of the added flexibility we have granted with regard to estimates.

Commenters were also concerned about the requirement that management provide an analysis,

---

[79] See Rule 12b-20 under the Exchange Act, as well as Exchange Act Section 10(b) and Rule 10b-5 thereunder.

[80] See the letters from the New York State Society of Certified Public Accountants ("NYSSCPA") and Radin, Glass & Co. ("Radin Glass").

[81] See the letter from Shearman & Sterling.

[82] See the letters from the AICPA, Cleary Gottlieb, Deloitte & Touche and FPL Group, Inc. ("FPL Group").

[83] See the letters from the AICPA, Compass Bancshares, FEI, Intel and PWC.

[84] Paragraph 20 of SFAS No. 146 requires companies to disclose specified information in the notes to financial statements to periodic reports covering periods in which an exit or disposal activity is initiated. Paragraph 21 of SFAS No. 146 states that an exit or disposal activity is initiated when management, having the authority to approve the action, commits to an exit or disposal plan or otherwise disposes of a long-lived asset.

or "mini-MD&A," of the effect of this event on the company.[85] Consistent with similar revisions that we have made to Items 1.02 and 2.04, we have eliminated this specific disclosure provision from the Item 2.05 disclosure requirements. Once again, we remind companies that any disclosure made in a report on Form 8-K must include all other material information, if any, that is necessary to make the required disclosure, in the light of the circumstances under which it is made, not misleading.[86]

Finally, commenters recommended that we not use the terms "write-off" or "restructuring" in Item 2.05 as such terms are not defined in the accounting literature.[87] We have revised the title and references in the item to reflect these comments and use terminology consistent with those used in the accounting literature.

Item 2.06 Material Impairments

This new item requires disclosure when a company's board of directors, a committee of the board of directors, or an authorized officer or officers if the company, if board action is not required, concludes that a material charge for impairment to one or more of its assets, including, without limitation, an impairment of securities or goodwill, is required under generally accepted accounting principles applicable to the company. Specifically, the company must:

- Disclose the date of the conclusion that a material charge is required and describe the impaired asset or assets and the facts and circumstances leading to the conclusion that the charge for impairment is required;
- Disclose the company's estimate of the amount or range of amounts of the impairment charge; and
- Disclose the company's estimate of the amount or range of amounts of the impairment charge that will result in future cash expenditures.

Comments on this item paralleled those on Item 2.05. We have made similar revisions to this item in response by providing greater flexibility regarding timing of the disclosure of estimates and eliminating the proposed "mini-MD&A" requirement.

We also recognize that tests for impairment or recoverability often occur in conjunction with the preparation, review or audit of financial statements. In light of the fact that a periodic report with complete financial statements will be made available to the public, we have added an instruction indicating that no Form 8-K disclosure is required pursuant to this item if the conclusion regarding the material charge is made in connection with the preparation, review or audit of financial statements at the end of a fiscal quarter or year and the plan is disclosed in the company's Exchange Act report for that period.[88]

Section 3—Securities and Trading Market

Item 3.01 Notice of Delisting or Failure to Satisfy a Continued Listing Rule or Standard; Transfer of Listing

New Item 3.01(a) requires a company to report its receipt of a notice from the national securities exchange or national securities association (or facility thereof) that maintains the principal listing for any class of the company's common equity,[89] indicating that:

- the company or such class of its securities does not satisfy a rule or standard for continued listing on the exchange or association;
- the exchange has submitted an application under Exchange Act Rule 12d2-2 to the Commission to delist such class of the company's securities; or
- the association has taken all necessary steps under its rules to delist the security from its automated inter-dealer quotation system.[90]

A company that receives this type of a notice must disclose the following information:

---

[85] See the letters from the FPL Group, PWC and Radin Glass.

[86] See Exchange Act Section 10(b) and Rule 10b-5 as well as Rule 12b-20 under the Exchange Act.

[87] See the letters from Ernst & Young and KPMG.

[88] See Instruction to Item 2.06.

[89] This term is defined in Exchange Act Rule 12b-2 [17 CFR 240.12b-2].

[90] We note that Instruction 3 to Item 3.01 provides that companies whose securities are quoted exclusively (i.e., the securities are not otherwise listed on an exchange or association) on automated inter-dealer quotation systems, such as the over-the-counter bulletin board, or OTCBB, and The Electronic Pink Sheets, are not subject to Item 3.01. Thus, these companies will not be required to file a Form 8-K pursuant to Item 3.01 if the securities cease to be quoted on such quotation system. These quotation systems do not provide companies with the ability to list their securities, but, rather, serve as a medium for the over-the-counter securities market by collecting and distributing market maker quotes to subscribers. These automated inter-dealer quotation systems do not maintain or impose listing standards, nor do they have a listing agreement or arrangement with the companies whose securities are quoted through them. Although market makers may be required to review and maintain specified information about a company and to furnish that information to the inter-dealer quotation system, the companies whose securities are quoted on such systems do not have any filing or reporting requirements imposed by the system. In some cases, however, a security that is listed on an exchange or association may also be quoted on such an automated inter-dealer quotation system. In that case, the company is be subject to Item 3.01 if any of the events specified in Item 3.01 occur.

- the date that it received the notice;
- the rule or standard for continued listing on the national securities exchange or national securities association that the company fails, or has failed, to satisfy; and
- any action or response that, at the time of filing, the company has determined to take in response to the notice.

In addition, under Item 3.01(b), if the company[91] has notified the national securities exchange or national securities association (or a facility thereof) that maintains the principal listing for any class of the company's common equity that the company is aware of any material noncompliance with a rule or standard for continued listing on the exchange or association, the company must disclose:

- the date that the company provided such notice to the exchange or association;
- a rule or standard for continued listing on the exchange or association that the registrant fails, or has failed, to satisfy; and
- any action or response that, at the time of filing, the company has determined to take regarding its noncompliance.

Furthermore, under Item 3.01(c), if a national securities exchange or national securities association (or a facility thereof) that maintains the principal listing for any class of the company's common equity, in lieu of suspending trading in or delisting such class of the company's securities, issues a public reprimand letter or similar communication indicating that the company has violated a rule or standard of the exchange or association, the company must state the date and summarize the contents of the letter or communication.

Finally, Item 3.01(d) requires that, if the company's board of directors, a committee of the board of directors or the officer or officers of the company authorized to take such action if board action is not required, has taken definitive action to cause the listing of a class of its common equity to be withdrawn from the national securities exchange, or terminated from the automated inter-dealer quotation system of a registered national securities association, where such exchange or association maintains the principal listing for such class of securities, the company must describe the action taken and state the date of the action.

This requirement includes disclosure of action taken by a company to transfer such a listing or quotation of its securities to another securities exchange or quotation system. The definitive action taken by the company may also include the adoption of a resolution by the board of directors, or committee of the board, to delist the class of securities.

Pursuant to Instruction 1 to Item 3.01, the company is not required to disclose any information required by paragraph (a) of Item 3.01 where, generally, the delisting is a result of one of the following:

- the entire class of the security has been called for redemption, maturity or retirement and, if required by the terms of the securities, funds sufficient for the payment of all such securities have been deposited with an agency authorized to make such payments and such funds have been made available to security holders;
- the entire class of the security has been redeemed or paid at maturity or retirement;
- the instruments representing the entire class of securities have come to evidence, by operation of law or otherwise, other securities in substitution therefor and represent no other right, except, if true, the right to receive an immediate cash payment; or
- all rights pertaining to the entire class of the security have been extinguished.

These exceptions are specifically referenced in Rule 12d2-2, the rule pursuant to which national securities exchanges file applications with the Commission to delist a security from the exchange.

In addition, Instruction 2 to Item 3.01 provides that a company must provide the disclosure required by paragraph (a) or (b) of this Item 3.01, as applicable, regarding any failure to satisfy a rule or standard for continued listing on the national securities exchange or national securities association (or a facility thereof) that maintains the principal listing for any class of the company's common equity even if the company has the benefit of a grace period or similar extension period during which it may cure the deficiency that triggers the disclosure requirement.

We had proposed to require companies to disclose notifications by an exchange or association of delisting or noncompliance with required listing requirements or standards. Since the time that the Form 8-K proposals were issued, we approved new rules[92] submitted by the New York Stock Exchange, the National Association of Securities

[91] Disclosure pursuant to this Item 3.01(b) is required if a particular exchange or association rule specifically provides that a particular officer or other authorized individual, such as the chief executive officer, must provide the notice to the exchange or association, rather than the company itself.

[92] See, for example, Release No. 34-48745 (November 4, 2003) [68 FR 64154].

Dealers, on behalf of The Nasdaq Stock Market, and the American Stock Exchange that require listed companies to notify the relevant market when an executive officer of the listed issuer becomes aware of any material noncompliance with the listing rules or standards relating to corporate governance.[93] In addition, as part of its recent amendments pertaining to corporate governance listing standards, the NYSE may issue a public reprimand letter to listed issuers that violate specified listing rules or standards.[94] This public reprimand letter is intended to serve as a lesser sanction than the delisting of the issuer's securities.

Furthermore, Exchange Act Rule 10A-3(a)(4)[95] requires an exchange or association to adopt standards requiring listed companies to notify the exchange or association promptly after an executive officer of the listed issuer becomes aware of any material noncompliance by the listed company with the requirements of the rule. In addition, under certain exchange or association listing standards or agreements, a listed company may be generally required to notify the exchange or association in the event they no longer comply with a particular listing standard. As a result, we believe the inclusion of Items 3.01(b) and (c) is necessary to ensure that all communications between a company and an exchange or association regarding delisting matters or noncompliance with a rule or standard for continued listing are disclosed.

In response to commenters, we have clarified that the relevant listing requirements or standards for this item are the rules or standards for continued listing on the exchange or association. Typically, exchanges and quotation systems have different standards for determining whether a security is qualified to enter the exchange or quotation system than for determining whether a security can remain listed. Because the entry standards are not relevant to whether the securities may continue trading on such exchange or quotation system, we have made this clarification.

Also, in response to commenters, we have revised the third element of the disclosure requirements regarding any action that the company has determined to take in response to a notice of delisting or failure to satisfy a listing standard. Commenters noted that, in light of the short Form 8-K filing deadline, a company may not have sufficient time to determine its course of action or to fully analyze the effect of such delisting on the company.[96] Thus, the item only requires identification of the company's anticipated action or response as of the Form 8-K filing date.[97] In addition, to clarify when an event triggering disclosure under new Item 3.01 occurs, we have revised the language in the item to more closely track and reference delisting rules and delisting procedures.[98]

Some commenters believed that the filing of a letter from the exchange or association as a Form 8-K exhibit would not significantly enhance the disclosures already required to be made by the company.[99] In response, we are not adopting the proposed provision that companies file the actual written notice received from the exchange or association as an exhibit.

One commenter requested clarification that "early warning" notices should not trigger disclosure.[100] While we agree with this commenter, we believe that the language of the item is clear in this regard. An early warning notice that merely informs the company that it is in danger of falling out of compliance with a rule or standard for continued listing on the exchange or association is not a notice that the company no longer satisfies that rule or standard. Thus, a company's receipt of such a notice will not trigger a disclosure obligation under the item. However, if the warning notice informs the company that it is out of compliance with a rule or standard for continued listing, but that the company will not be delisted if it cures the problem within a specified time, such a notice will trigger a Form 8-K filing requirement.

As a result, we generally anticipate two filings in the typical involuntary delisting process under Items 3.01(a) and (b). An initial filing will be made when the company receives the first notice that it does not comply with a rule or standard for continued listing, or when it notifies the exchange or association that it no longer complies with a

[93] See, for example, Rule 303A.12(b) of the NYSE Listing Manual and Rule 4350(m) of The Nasdaq Stock Market, Inc. Marketplace Rules.

[94] See Rule 303A.13 of the NYSE Listing Manual.

[95] 17 CFR 240.10A-3(a)(4). Rule 10A-3 requires the rules of each registered national securities exchange and national securities association to prohibit the initial or continued listing of any security of a company that is not in compliance with the audit committee requirements of Rule 10A-3.

[96] See the letters from the Grundfest Group and NY State Bar.

[97] A company may, of course, voluntarily file an amendment to the previously filed Form 8-K regarding any changes to the anticipated action or response.

[98] The item now specifically references provisions of Rule 12d2-2, pursuant to which national securities exchanges file applications with the Commission to delist a security from that exchange.

[99] See the letters from the ABA, Investment Counsel Association of America ("ICAA") and Shearman & Sterling.

[100] See the letter from the NY State Bar.

rule or standard for continued listing on the exchange or association.[101] A second Form 8-K filing will be required under Item 3.01(a) upon the company's receipt of a notice regarding the actual delisting of a class of the company's securities.[102]

Item 3.02 Unregistered Sales of Equity Securities

This new item requires a company to disclose the information specified in paragraphs (a) and (c) through (e) of Item 701 of Regulation S-K regarding the company's sale of equity securities in a transaction that is not registered under the Securities Act. This disclosure is currently required in Item 2(c) of Forms 10-Q and 10-QSB and Item 5(a) of Forms 10-K and 10-KSB.[103]

The amendments to Form 8-K will require earlier disclosure of certain issuances of unregistered equity securities, as discussed below. We believe that more timely disclosure of such issuances will benefit investors due to the fact that unregistered sales of equity securities can have a significant effect on the capital structure of the company and the security holdings of existing investors. Issuances not reported on Form 8-K, however, will continue to be required to be reported in periodic reports.

In response to concerns raised by commenters,[104] we have limited the disclosure of sale of unregistered equity securities required to be filed on Form 8-K. Under the new item, no Form 8-K need be filed if the equity securities sold in the aggregate since the company's last report filed under this item or last periodic report, whichever is more recent, constitute less than 1% of the company's outstanding securities of that class.[105] In the case of a small business issuer,[106] if the securities sold in the aggregate since the small business issuer's last report filed under this item or last periodic report, whichever is more recent, constitute less than 5% of the small business issuer's outstanding securities of that class, the information need not be disclosed on Form 8-K. We believe that these quantitative thresholds are appropriate given that companies will be required to continue to report all other unregistered sales of equity securities in their periodic reports.

For purposes of determining the required Form 8-K filing date under this item, we have provided that a company has no obligation to disclose information under Item 3.02 until the company enters into an agreement enforceable against it, whether or not subject to conditions, under which the equity securities are to be sold. If there is no such agreement, the company must provide the disclosure within four business days after the occurrence of the closing or settlement of the transaction or arrangement under which the equity securities are sold.

Commenters suggested that issuances of unreported equity securities through conversion and similar transactions should not require an Item 8-K filing. We believe that, given the 1% and 5% thresholds we have adopted and the importance of equity security issuances, these types of transactions should be covered.

Item 3.03 Material Modifications to Rights of Security Holders

This new item requires a company to disclose material modifications to the rights of the holders of any class of the company's registered securities and to briefly describe the general effect of such modifications on such rights. The substance of the disclosure is the same as previously required by Items 2(a) and (b) of Forms 10-Q and 10-QSB.[107]

We proposed to eliminate an existing instruction regarding working capital restrictions and other limitations upon the payment of dividends because we believed that it was clear that such restrictions and limitations constitute material modifications to the rights of security holders. One commenter disagreed and recommended that we keep the instruction.[108] To clarify that this item requires disclosure of such provisions, we are including the existing instruction in the new item.

The proposals would not have required disclosure about a particular material modification to the rights of security holders if the company previously had described the modification in its

---

[101] Instruction 3 to Item 3.01 states that subsequent notices or other communications that continue to indicate that the company does not comply with the same rule or standard for continued listing that was the subject of the initial notice are not required to be filed, but may be filed voluntarily.

[102] We note that Item 3.01 refers to a national securities exchange or a national securities association (or a facility thereof). Thus, for example, a notification by The Nasdaq Stock Market that a company does not satisfy a rule or standard for continued listing on Nasdaq, if Nasdaq maintains the principal listing of any class of the company's common equity, would be subject to Item 3.01.

[103] See 17 CFR 249.308a, 249.308b, 249.310 and 249.310a.

[104] See, for example, the letters from the ABA, Compass Bancshares, Deloitte & Touche and John Deere.

[105] Instruction 2 to Item 3.02 states that "the number of shares outstanding" refers to the actual number of shares of equity securities of the class outstanding and does not include outstanding securities convertible into or exchangeable for such equity securities.

[106] As defined under Item 10(a)(1) of Regulation S-B [17 CFR 228.10(a)(1)]. See Instruction 3 to Item 3.02.

[107] See 17 CFR 249.308a and 249.308b.

[108] See the letter from Shearman & Sterling.

proxy statement at the time it proposed the modification. One commenter noted that, although the proposed modification would have been disclosed, investors would not be informed as to whether the proposal had been approved by shareholders and ultimately adopted by the company until the company filed its next required periodic report.[109] In response to this comment, we have eliminated this exception from Item 3.02. In addition, once a company has reported a material modification to the rights of its security holders on Form 8-K, the company need not make any duplicative disclosure about the modification in any of its subsequently filed periodic reports.[110]

Section 4—Matters Related to Accountants and Financial Statements

Item 4.01 Changes in Registrant's Certifying Accountant

This item is substantively the same as former Item 4 of Form 8-K, requiring disclosure of the resignation, dismissal or engagement of an independent accountant. The only revision we have made to the substantive requirements of former Item 4 is to delete the phrase "and the related instructions to Item 304" as a company routinely needs to consider and comply with the instructions to all of our disclosure items containing instructions.

Item 4.02 Non-Reliance on Previously Issued Financial Statements or a Related Audit Report or Completed Interim Review

This new item requires a company to file a Form 8-K if and when its board of directors, a committee of the board of directors, or an authorized officer or officers if board action is not required, concludes that any of the company's previously issued financial statements covering one or more years or interim periods no longer should be relied upon because of an error in such financial statements as addressed in Accounting Principles Board Opinion No. 20 (APB Opinion No. 20). This item requires the company to disclose the following information:

- the date of the conclusion regarding the non-reliance and an identification of the financial statements and years or periods covered that should no longer be relied upon;
- a brief description of the facts underlying the conclusion to the extent known to the company at the time of filing; and
- a statement of whether the audit committee, or the board of directors in the absence of an audit committee, or authorized officer or officers, discussed with the company's independent accountant the subject matter giving rise to the conclusion.

Similarly, if the company is advised by, or receives notice from, its independent accountant that disclosure should be made or action should be taken to prevent future reliance on a previously issued audit report or completed interim review related to previously issued financial statements, it must disclose the following information:

- The date on which the company was so advised or notified;
- Identification of the financial statements that should no longer be relied upon;
- A brief description of the information provided by the accountant; and
- A statement of whether the audit committee, or the board of directors in the absence of an audit committee, or authorized officer or officers, discussed with the independent accountant the subject matter giving rise to the notice.

In addition, if the company receives such an advice or notice from its independent accountant, the company must provide the independent accountant with a copy of the disclosures it is making under Item 4.02(b) no later than the same day it files these disclosures with the Commission. The company also must request the independent accountant to furnish to the company as promptly as possible a letter addressed to the Commission stating whether the accountant agrees with the statements made by the company and, if not, stating the respects in which it does not agree. The company must then amend its previously filed Form 8-K by filing the independent accountant's letter as an exhibit to the filed Form 8-K within two business days of the company's receipt of the letter.

Commenters believed that the scope of the proposed item was too broad. Specifically, one commenter noted that there are some circumstances under which a company may need to restate its financial statements, or accountants may refuse to allow reliance on their reports, that do not implicate a problem with the financial statements.[111] For example, a company may be required to restate its financial statements as a result of the completion of a stock split.[112] In

---

[109] See the letter from the NY State Bar.

[110] See Instruction B.3 to Form 8-K.

[111] See the letter from the ABA.

[112] Another example would include a plan to discontinue operations (see Statement of Financial Accounting Standards No. 144, *Accounting for the Impairment or Disposal of Long-Lived Assets*). As these examples illustrate, certain events that occur after the end of a fiscal year may require retroactive restatement of that year's financial statements if such statements are reissued, but are not events that would trigger disclosure under Item 4.02.

response to these comments, we have modified this item to require disclosure under Item 4.02(a) where the company concludes that a prior statement should not be relied on because of an error or, under Item 4.02(b), where an independent accountant has notified a company that it should take action to prevent future reliance on previously issued financial statements audited or reviewed by the accountant.

Commenters also opposed the proposed requirement that a company disclose its plan to address the issue. They were concerned that, within the short Form 8-K filing timeframe, the company may not have sufficient time to complete its analysis regarding the impact of the error on the company's financial statements, which could require discussions with numerous parties, including the accountants.[113] We agree with those commenters and have revised this item to eliminate this proposed requirement.[114]

We have also separated the situation in which the company makes the determination internally regarding non-reliance on its financial statements from that in which the company's independent accountant notifies the company of non-reliance on a previously issued audit report or completed interim review by including them in two different paragraphs to clarify the requirements of the item.

Section 5—Corporate Governance and Management

Item 5.01 Changes in Control of Registrant

We are adopting this pre-existing item of Form 8-K substantially as proposed. We are not adopting the proposed revision regarding the source of funds used to effect a change in control due to the Congressional intent issue discussed under Item 2.01 above. We have, however, streamlined the language of the item to make it read more clearly. We have also not included the proposed instruction to Item 5.01 stating that disclosure pursuant to this item could be provided by incorporation by reference to a previous filing. We believe that Instruction B.3 to Form 8-K makes this clear.

Item 5.02 Departure of Directors or Principal Officers; Election of Directors; Appointment of Principal Officers

a. Disclosure under Item 5.02(a) when a director resigns or refuses to stand for reelection due to a disagreement or is removed for cause

Paragraph (a) of Item 5.02 broadens the scope of former Item 6 of Form 8-K. Former Item 6 required disclosure only if a director departed as a result of a disagreement, provided a letter to the company describing the disagreement and then requested that the company publicly disclose the matter. Thus, the action necessary to trigger disclosure pursuant to the former item rested solely with the director.

Under the revised item, if a director has resigned or refuses to stand for re-election to the board of directors since the date of the last annual meeting of shareholders because of a disagreement with the company, known to an executive officer of the company,[115] on any matter relating to the company's operations, policies or practices, or if a director has been removed for cause from the board of directors, the company must disclose:

- the date of the director's resignation, refusal to stand for re-election or removal;
- any positions held by the director on any committee of the board of directors at the time of the director's resignation, refusal to stand for re-election or removal; and
- a brief description of the circumstances representing the disagreement that management believes caused, in whole or in part, the director's resignation, refusal to stand for re-election or removal.

In addition, if the director furnishes the company with any written correspondence concerning the circumstances surrounding his or her resignation, refusal or removal, the company must file a copy of the correspondence as an exhibit to the report on Form 8-K regardless of whether the director requests that the company take such action. The company must provide the director with a copy of the disclosures it is making in response to this item no later than the day that the company files the disclosures with the Commission. The company must also provide the director with the opportunity to furnish a letter addressed to the company as promptly as possible stating whether he or she agrees with the company's disclosures in response to this item and, if not, the respects in which he or she does not agree. Finally, the company must file any letter it receives from the director with the Commission as an exhibit by amendment to the previously filed Form 8-K within two business days after receipt by the company.

Several commenters were concerned that the company may not be aware that the director

---

[113] See the letters from Foley Hoag and Radin Glass.

[114] Regarding the requirement of a company to disclose under Item 4.02(a) a brief description of the facts underlying the conclusion to the extent known to the company at the time of filing, a company may, of course, voluntarily file an amendment to the previously filed Form 8-K regarding any changes to the facts underlying the conclusion.

[115] The term "executive officer" is defined in Exchange Act Rule 3b-7.

departed because of a disagreement.[116] We believe that the phrase "known to an executive officer of the company" means that the company must be aware of the disagreement. As such, we have adopted this provision of Item 5.02(a) as proposed.

b. Disclosure under Item 5.02(b) when certain officers retire, resign or are terminated and disclosure when a director retires, resigns, is removed or refuses to stand for re-election for any reason other than as a result of a disagreement or for cause

Paragraph (b) of Item 5.02 requires disclosure when the company's principal executive officer, president, principal financial officer, principal accounting officer, principal operating officer or any person performing similar functions retires, resigns, or is terminated from that position. The item also requires disclosure when a director retires, resigns, is removed or declines to stand for re-election and the company is not required to provide disclosure under Item 5.02(a).

Several commenters were concerned about our proposal to require disclosure of the reasons for the departure of an officer.[117] They noted that requiring disclosure of reasons such as personal infirmity may cause unnecessary embarrassment to the departing officer. Some commenters similarly suggested that, if the officer leaves for reasons other than those disclosed by the company, such disclosure potentially could lead to a defamation action by the officer against the company. Other commenters believed that requiring disclosure of a disagreement regarding matters such as company policy or strategy between two officers would usurp the typical corporate decision-making process. We believe these concerns are valid and have therefore eliminated this proposed requirement.

c. Disclosure under Item 5.02(c) and (d) when the registrant appoints certain new officers or a new director is elected

Paragraph (c) of Item 5.02 requires disclosure if the company appoints a new principal executive officer, president, principal financial officer, principal accounting officer, principal operating officer or person performing similar functions. The company must disclose the officer's name, position, the date of the appointment, information regarding the background of the officer and certain related transactions with the company,[118] and a brief description of the material terms of any employment agreement between the company and the officer.

In addition, if a new director is elected to the board, except by a vote of security holders at an annual meeting or a special meeting convened for such purpose, paragraph (d) of Item 5.02 requires disclosure of the new director's name, the election date, a brief description of any arrangement or understanding pursuant to which the new director was selected as a director, any committees to which the new director has been, or at the time of the disclosure is expected to be, named, and information regarding certain related transactions between the new director and the company.[119]

Instruction 2 to Item 5.02 provides that, to the extent that information regarding an employment contract of a newly-appointed executive officer, or the board committee or related party transaction information associated with a newly-elected director, is not determined or is unavailable at the time of the required Form 8-K filing, a company must include a statement to this effect in the filing and then must file an amendment to the Item 5.02 Form 8-K filing containing the information within four business days after the information is determined or becomes available.

One commenter was concerned that requiring immediate disclosure of the appointment of an officer could interfere with the company's ability to plan for a smooth transition of authority.[120] It stated that companies need time to make proper introductions within the organization before publicly announcing such appointment. In response to this comment, we have inserted an instruction to Item 5.01(c) that permits a company to delay such disclosure until the day on which the company first makes public announcement of the appointment if the company intends to make a public announcement of the appointment other than by means of a report on Form 8-K.

One commenter believed that the departure or appointment of directors and officers of certain companies should not be reportable under this item.[121] We agree and have inserted an instruction to exclude a company that is a wholly-owned subsidiary of a reporting company from the reporting requirements of Item 5.02.[122]

---

[116] See the letters from Cleary Gottlieb, Radin Glass and Shearman & Sterling.

[117] See, for example, the letters from the ABA, Cleary Gottlieb, D'Ancona & Pflaum, Grundfest Group, Kellogg, Sullivan & Cromwell and Wells Fargo.

[118] Specifically, Item 5.02(c) requires disclosure of the information required by Items 401(b), 401(d), 401(e) and 404(a) of Regulation S-K [17 CFR 229.401(b), (d) and (e) and 229.404(a)], or, in the case of a small business issuer, Items 401(a)(4), 401(a)(5), 401(c) and 404(a) of Regulation S-B [17 CFR 228.401(a)(4), (a)(5) and (c), and 228.404(a) and (b)].

[119] Specifically, Item 5.02(d) requires disclosure of information required by Item 404(a) of Regulation S-K.

[120] See the letter from the ABA.

[121] See the letter from the ABA.

[122] See Instruction 1 to Item 5.02.

Item 5.03 Amendments to Articles of Incorporation or Bylaws; Change in Fiscal Year

This item requires a company with a class of equity securities registered under Section 12 of the Exchange Act to disclose any amendment to its articles of incorporation or bylaws if the company did not propose the amendment in a previously filed proxy statement or information statement. The item requires the company to disclose the effective date of the amendment and a description of the provision adopted or changed by amendment and, if applicable, the previous provision.

If the company determines to change the fiscal year from that used in its most recent filing with the Commission by means other than a submission to a vote of security holders through the solicitation of proxies or otherwise, or by an amendment to its articles of incorporation or bylaws, the company must state the date of that determination, the date of the new fiscal year end and the form on which the report covering the transition period will be filed.

One commenter noted that Item 601 of Regulation S-K requires a company to file a complete copy of its articles of incorporation or bylaws as amended.[123] The commenter was concerned that companies may not have sufficient time to prepare the restated copies for filing within the allotted timeframe. Thus, we have added an instruction to this item, as well as to Item 601 of Regulations S-K and S-B, clarifying that if an amendment to the articles of incorporation or bylaws is reported on Form 8-K, the company need only file the text of the amendment as an exhibit to the filing. If it does so, it must file the restated articles of incorporation or bylaws as an exhibit to its next periodic report.

One commenter suggested that the item be limited to companies with a class of equity securities registered under Section 12 of the Exchange Act.[124] Companies that do not have equity securities registered under the Exchange Act are typically debt issuers. The rights of holders of such securities are reflected in the debt documents and changes to those rights would typically be reflected under Item 3.03. We have revised this item accordingly in response to this comment.

D. Proposed Form 8-K Items Not Being Adopted

We proposed several additional new Form 8-K items which we are not adopting. First, we proposed an item that would have required disclosure of temporary suspension of trading under a company's employee benefit plans. Section 306 of the Sarbanes-Oxley Act required us to adopt rules requiring such disclosure on or before January 26, 2003. In response, we adopted Regulation BTR and former Item 11 of Form 8-K.[125] We have redesignated former Item 11 as Item 5.04 in the reorganized Form 8-K.[126]

Second, we proposed an item that would have required certain information regarding ratings received from rating agencies. On January 24, 2003, we issued a study on credit rating agencies and subsequently issued a concept release.[127] We continue to consider the appropriate regulatory approach for rating agencies.

Finally, we proposed an item that would have required disclosure regarding the termination or reduction of a business relationship with a customer. Many commenters opposed this item on the basis that it would be difficult for a company to determine when such a termination or reduction occurs. In addition, commenters were concerned about possible competitive harm caused by customers using such disclosure as a negotiation ploy. The proposed item would have some of the same types of concerns as are posed by new Item 1.02. In Item 1.02, we have sought to resolve the competitive harm issue by granting companies some latitude in determining when a contract has been terminated. We agree with commenters, however, that a reduction of customer orders can be difficult to discern as such reductions can happen over a period of time.[128] Thus, we have decided not to adopt this proposed item.[129]

E. Safe Harbor and Eligibility to Use Forms S-2 and S-3 and to Rely on Rule 144

Several commenters recommended that we adopt a safe harbor to protect a company against potential liability under Exchange Act Section

---

[123] See the letter from the ABA.

[124] See the letter from the ABA.

[125] Release No. 34-47225 (January 22, 2003) [68 FR 4337].

[126] As discussed more fully below, we have also changed the due date for the Form 8-K filing under Item 5.04 to, generally, four business days after the company receives the notice required by section 101(i)(2)(E) of the Employment Retirement Income Security Act of 1974 [29 U.S.C. 1021(i)(2)(E)].

[127] See Report on the Role and Function of Credit Rating Agencies in the Operation of the Securities Markets (January 24, 2003) [68 FR 35258], available at www.sec.gov/news/studies/creditratingreport0103.pdf, and Release No. 33-8236 (June 4, 2003) [68 FR 35258].

[128] See, for example, the letters from the NY City Bar, Cleary Gottlieb, Grundfest Group, PWC and Shearman & Sterling.

[129] However, we remind companies that Item 303 of Regulations S-K and S-B [17 CFR 229.303 and 17 CFR 228.303], Management's Discussion and Analysis of Financial Condition and Results of Operations, requires disclosure of known trends or uncertainties that have had, or that the company reasonably expects will have, a material favorable or unfavorable impact on net sales or revenues or income from continuing operations.

10(b) and Rule 10b-5 stemming from the company's failure to timely file a required Form 8-K.[130] While we are not convinced that we should extend a Section 10(b) and Rule 10b-5 safe harbor to all of the Form 8-K items, we recognize that several of the new Form 8-K disclosure items may require management to quickly assess the materiality of an event or to determine whether a disclosure obligation has been triggered. In this respect, these items raise issues analogous to those we considered in our adoption of the Section 10(b) and Rule 10b-5 safe harbor under Regulation FD.[131]

As a result, we have decided to adopt a new limited safe harbor from public and private claims under Exchange Act Section 10(b) and Rule 10b-5 for a failure to timely file a Form 8-K regarding the following items:

Item 1.01 Entry into a Material Definitive Agreement

Item 1.02 Termination of a Material Definitive Agreement

Item 2.03 Creation of a Direct Financial Obligation or an Obligation under an Off-Balance Sheet Arrangement of a Registrant

Item 2.04 Triggering Events that Accelerate or Increase a Direct Financial Obligation under an Off-Balance Sheet Arrangement

Item 2.05 Costs Associated with Exit or Disposal Activities

Item 2.06 Material Impairments

Item 4.02(a) Non-Reliance on Previously Issued Financial Statements or a Related Audit Report or Completed Interim Review (in the case where a company makes the determination and does not receive a notice described in Item 4.02(b) from its accountant)

In light of this new limited safe harbor under Section 10(b) and Rule 10b-5, we have eliminated the proposed safe harbor from liability under Section 13(a) or 15(d). As a result, the new safe harbor will not affect our ability to enforce any of the Form 8-K filing requirements under these sections.

The safe harbor for these items states that no failure to file a report on Form 8-K that is required solely pursuant to the provisions of Form 8-K shall be deemed to be a violation of Section 10(b) and Rule 10b-5 under the Exchange Act. The safe harbor only applies to a failure to file a report on Form 8-K. Thus, material misstatements or omissions in a Form 8-K will continue to be subject to Section 10(b) and Rule 10b-5 liability.

In addition, if the company has a duty to disclose information that is the subject of any of the Form 8-K items covered by the safe harbor for any reason apart from the Form 8-K requirement, the safe harbor will not provide protection from Section 10(b) and Rule 10b-5 that may arise from the company's failure to satisfy such separate disclosure obligation. For example, if a company publicly sells or repurchases its own securities while in possession of material non-public information that is required to be disclosed in a Form 8-K report pursuant to an item that is covered by the safe harbor, the safe harbor will not protect the company from Section 10(b) and Rule 10b-5 liability regarding its separate disclosure obligation pursuant to the offering of securities.

Furthermore, we are amending Forms 10-Q, 10-QSB, 10-K and 10-KSB to provide that the new safe harbor extends only until the due date of the periodic report of the company for the relevant period in which the Form 8-K was not timely filed. Thus, for example, if an event occurs that required the filing of a Form 8-K during a particular quarter, but the company fails to make the required timely disclosure on Form 8-K, the company must provide the disclosure prescribed by the relevant Form 8-K item in its Form 10-Q or 10-QSB filed for the quarter during which that event occurred. Failure to make such disclosure in the periodic report will subject a company to potential liability under Section 10(b) and Rule 10b-5, in addition to the potential liability under Section 13(a) or15(d).

Similarly, several commenters stated that failure to file all required Form 8-K reports in a timely manner should not disqualify companies from being eligible to use Securities Act Form S-2 and S-3 registration statements.[132] Under our current rules, to be eligible to use Form S-2 or S-3, among other things, a company must have timely filed all reports required to be filed under Exchange Act Section 13(a) or 15(d) during the 12 months prior to filing of the registration statement.[133]

[130] See the letters from Emerson, NAREIT, NY City Bar and Shearman & Sterling.

[131] Item 7.01, Regulation FD Disclosures, is already subject to a safe harbor from Section 10(b) and Rule 10b-5 pursuant to Regulation FD (17 CFR 243.100—243.103). Also, because Item 8.01, Other Events, is designated for voluntary filings, it does not, by itself, impose a duty to disclose for purposes of Section 10(b) and Rule 10b-5.

[132] See, for example, the letters from the ABA, AICPA, Ernst & Young, NAREIT, NY City Bar, NY State Bar, Shearman & Sterling, Sullivan & Cromwell and Wyrick Robbins.

[133] See General Instruction I.C to Form S-2, referenced in 17 CFR 239.12 and General Instruction I.A.3 to Form S-3, referenced in 17 CFR 239.13, respectively.

In response to these comments, we are revising the Form S-2 and S-3 eligibility requirements. Under the revised instructions to these forms,[134] companies that fail to file timely reports required by Items 1.01, 1.02, 2.03, 2.04, 2.05, 2.06 and 4.02(a) will not lose their eligibility to use Form S-2 and S-3 registration statements. These are the same items that are covered by the new limited safe harbor from Section 10(b) and Rule 10b-5 liability.

As stated above, we believe that these items may require management to make rapid materiality and similar judgments within the compressed Form 8-K filing timeframe. The potential significant burden that could result from a company's sudden loss of eligibility to use Form S-2 or S-3 under these circumstances could be a disproportionately large negative consequence of an untimely Form 8-K filing. We also believe that a carve-out of the same list of items as covered by the Section 10(b) and Rule 10b-5 safe harbor provides a beneficial measure of regulatory consistency.

We have clarified in the revised instructions, however, that a company must be current in its Form 8-K filings with respect to the items listed above at the actual time of a Form S-2 or S-3 filing. Thus, a company must have filed the disclosure required by any of these Form 8-K items on or before the date that it files a Form S-2 or Form S-3 registration statement to satisfy the eligibility requirements of these forms.[135] With respect to the other Form 8-K items not listed above, a company's failure to timely file Form 8-K pursuant to any of these items will result in a loss of Form S-2 or S-3 eligibility for the 12 months following the Form 8-K due date.[136] Many of these items are currently required Form 8-K disclosure items and are thus familiar to companies, while the other new Form 8-K items not included above generally do not require the same degree of analysis.

Commenters also recommended that we clarify that a company's failure to timely file a Form 8-K report would not affect a security holder's ability to rely on Securities Act Rule 144 to resell securities. Rule 144 eligibility is conditioned on, among other things, the availability of current public information about the company.[137] Because of the significant burden that would be placed on selling security holders if eligibility to rely on Rule 144 were conditioned on a company's satisfaction of the new Form 8-K requirements, we have amended Securities Act Rule 144 to clarify that a company need not have filed all required Form 8-K reports during the 12 months preceding a sale of securities pursuant to Rule 144 to satisfy the rule's "current public information" condition. As required by Rule 144(h),[138] however, a security holder will continue to be required to represent that he or she does not have inside information.[139]

F. Other Matters Related to Form 8-K Filings and Conforming Amendments

1. Events Falling under Multiple Items

We recognize that a company may need to report a given event under Item 1.01 as well as one or more other items, such as Item 2.03. We note that General Instruction D to Form 8-K permits a company to file a single Form 8-K to satisfy one or more disclosure items, provided that the company identifies by item number and caption all applicable items being satisfied and provides all of the substantive disclosure required by each of the items.

2. Amendments to Item 601 of Regulation S-K and Regulation S-B

Certain new Form 8-K items require new exhibits to be filed with the report. Exhibits to periodic filings are addressed by Item 601 of Regulation S-K. We are adding or modifying entries describing these exhibits to the Item 601 exhibit table. These new or modified exhibit entries include: (a) correspondence from an independent accountant regarding non-reliance on a previously issued audit report or completed interim review; (b) correspondence regarding the departure of director; (c) articles of incorporation; and (d) bylaws.

We are also adopting amendments to Item 601 to footnote the "8-K" column in the Exhibit Table to clarify that a company need only file the exhibits marked in the "8-K" column of the table that

---

[134] See revised General Instruction I.C to Form S-2 and revised General Instruction I.A.3 to Form S-3, as well as the revisions to 17 CFR 239.12 and 239.13.

[135] For example, if a company fails to file an Item 1.01 Form 8-K regarding the entry into a material definitive agreement, the company must include the disclosure required by Item 1.01 in the periodic report filed for the period in which the company failed to timely file the Form 8-K. This disclosure must be made before the company files a later Form S-3 registration statement (assuming that the registration statement is filed within 12 months of the missed Form 8-K) in order for the company to be current in its periodic reports and thus eligible to use Form S-3. If the company fails to include such disclosure in its quarterly report or annual report, as applicable, the company must amend the report to include the Item 1.01 information before filing the Form S-3 registration statement.

[136] For example, if a company fails to timely file an Item 3.01 Form 8-K regarding a delisting notice received from a national securities association, the company would be ineligible to use Form S-2 or S-3 for the next 12 months.

[137] See 17 CFR 230.144(c).

[138] 17 CFR 230.144(h).

[139] See generally Form 144 [17 CFR 239.144].

are relevant to a particular report on Form 8-K. Again, companies that have previously submitted an exhibit with another periodic filing may incorporate the exhibit by reference into the applicable Form 8-K report.

Finally, we are adopting a corrective amendment to eliminate the reference in Item 601 to submission of Financial Data Schedules.[140] We eliminated the requirement to file a Financial Data Schedule on May 30, 2000.[141]

3. Clarification of Filing Status of Exhibits

We have received several questions regarding whether an exhibit attached to a Form 8-K report furnished pursuant to Regulation FD is considered filed or furnished. In response to these questions, we have clarified General Instruction 2 to state clearly that if a report on Form 8-K contains disclosures under Item 2.02, Results of Operations and Financial Condition, or 7.01, Regulation FD Disclosure, whether or not the report contains disclosures regarding other items, all exhibits to that report relating to Item 2.02 or 7.01 will be deemed furnished, and not filed, unless the registrant specifies exhibits, or portions of exhibits, that are intended to be deemed filed rather than furnished. This amendment is intended only to clarify our position on this matter and does not change our existing position.

4. Revisions to Forms 10-Q, 10-QSB, 10-K and 10-KSB

As proposed, the amendments modify or eliminate several items in Forms 10-Q, 10-QSB, 10-K and 10-KSB. Portions of the disclosures called for in these items are no longer required in quarterly and annual reports because they will be more promptly reported on Form 8-K. We have revised or deleted, as applicable, the following items in Part II of Forms 10-Q and 10-QSB:

- revised the heading for Item 2 in Part II—Other Information;
- removed Items 2(a), 2(b) and 6(b);
- redesignated paragraphs (c), (d) and (e) in Item 2 as paragraphs (a), (b) and (c);
- revised newly redesignated paragraph (a) in Item 2;
- revised the Instructions to Item 3;
- revised Item 5;
- removed the words "and Reports on Form 8-K (§ 249.308 of this chapter)" from the heading of Item 6; and
- removed the paragraph (a) designation in Item 6.

We have also made the following changes to Form 10-K:

- revised paragraph (a) of Item 5, Market for Registrant's Common Equity and Related Stockholder Matters to require disclosure only of unregistered sales of equity securities not previously disclosed on Form 8-K;
- revised Item 9, Changes in and Disagreements With Accountants on Accounting and Financial Disclosure to require disclosure only of matters required by Item 304(b) of Regulation S-K[142];
- added Item 9A, Other Information;
- revised the heading of Item 15 to read "Exhibits and Financial Statement Schedules;"
- deleted paragraph (b) of Item 15, Exhibits, Financial Statement Schedules, and Reports on Form 8-K; and
- redesignated paragraphs (c) and (d) in Item 15 as paragraphs (b) and (c).

We have made the following changes to Form 10-KSB:

- revised paragraph (a) of Item 5, Market for Registrant's Common Equity and Related Stockholder Matters to require disclosure only of unregistered sales of equity securities not previously disclosed on Form 8-K;
- revised Item 8, Changes in and Disagreements With Accountants on Accounting and Financial Disclosure to require disclosure only of matters required by Item 304(b) of Regulation S-B[143];
- added Item 8B, Other Information;
- removed the words "and Reports on Form 8-K" from the heading to Item 13;
- deleted paragraph (b) of Item 13, Exhibits and Reports on Form 8-K;
- removed the paragraph (a) designation in Item 13;
- revised Item 3 in Part II of "Information Required in Annual Report of Transitional Small Business Issuers;" and
- removed Item 6 in Part II of "Information Required in Annual Report of Transitional Small Business Issuers."

As discussed above, however, we are adding an item to these forms that requires disclosure of any event required to be disclosed on a previous Form 8-K filing during the period covered by the forms

---

[140] See current Item 601(a)(1) of Regulations S-B and S-K [17 CFR 228.601(a)(1) and 229.601(a)(1)].

[141] Release No. 33-7855 (April 24, 2000) [65 FR 24788].

[142] 17 CRF 229.304(b).

[143] 17 CFR 228.304(b).

which was not disclosed on Form 8-K.[144] In addition, we have retained the requirement to disclose the information required pursuant to Item 304(b) of Regulation S-K in Form 10-K and 10-KSB as such information is not required pursuant to Item 4.01 of Form 8-K.

5. Certification under Section 906 of the Sarbanes-Oxley Act of 2002

In June of 2003, the Commission adopted rules requiring the public filing of both the Sarbanes-Oxley Act Sections 302 and 906 chief executive officer and chief financial officer certifications as exhibits to various Exchange Act periodic reports.[145] The adopting release noted that there had been questions raised about whether the certifications required by Section 906 of the Sarbanes-Oxley Act applied to Form 8-K. In that release, we noted our concern that extending Section 906 certifications to Form 8-K could potentially chill the disclosure of information by companies. The release also noted that we were considering the questions in consultation with the Department of Justice.

As a result of this review with the Department of Justice and representatives from the Department serving on the President's Corporate Fraud Task Force, the Department of Justice and we have jointly concluded that Section 906 does not apply to Form 8-K.[146]

6. Other Conforming Amendments

We have revised former Item 11 (new Item 5.04) of Form 8-K, regarding the temporary suspension of trading under company's employee benefit plans, to clarify that the required Form 8-K must be filed no later than the fourth business day after which the company receives the notice required by section 101(i)(2)(E) of the Employment Retirement Income Security Act of 1974[147] or, if such notice is not received by the company, on the same date on which the company transmits a timely notice to an affected officer or director within the time period prescribed by Rule 104(b)(2)(i)(B) or 104(b)(2)(ii) of Regulation BTR.[148] The former Item 11 provided that the Form 8-K must be filed not later than the date prescribed for transmission of the notice required by Rule 104(b)(2) of Regulation BTR. We have also provided for the filing of the updated notices under Rule 104(b)(2)(iii) of Regulation BTR.[149]

We have also amended the General Instructions to Form 8-K to combine Instruction B.6 with Instruction B.2. These two instructions are largely identical beyond the fact that they apply to different items. Therefore we have combined them into a single instruction addressing both items.

We have amended Note 1 at the end of Exchange Act Rules 13a-10 and 15d-10 regarding transition reports.[150] The previous note referred to Item 8 of Form 8-K, which has been re-designated as Item 5.03. Thus, we have conformed this reference accordingly. In addition, we have amended Item 9.01 of Form 8-K, Financial Statements and Exhibits, to ensure that financial statements required to be filed subsequent to an acquisition reported under Item 2.01 are due 71 days after the date the initial report on Form 8-K was required to be filed.

Finally, we have revised Exchange Act Rule 12b-23[151] to make clear that companies may incorporate by reference into their registration statements and reports information previously disclosed on Form 8-K without the requirement to file such Form 8-K reports as exhibits to the statements or reports.

[¶ 2003]

III. PAPERWORK REDUCTION ACT

A. Background

The amendments contain "collection of information" requirements within the meaning of the Paperwork Reduction Act of 1995 (PRA). We published a notice requesting comment on the collection of information requirements in the proposing release, and submitted requests to the Office of Management and Budget (OMB) for approval in accordance with the PRA. These requests were approved by the OMB.

The titles for the collections of information are:

- Form 8-K (OMB Control No. 3235-0060);
- Form 12b-25 (OMB Control No. 3235-0058);
- Form 10-K (OMB Control No. 3235-0063);
- Form 10-KSB (OMB Control No. 3235-0420);
- Form 10-Q (OMB Control No. 3235-0070);
- Form 10-QSB (OMB Control No. 3235-0416);
- Regulation S-K (OMB Control No. 3235-0071); and
- Regulation S-B (OMB Control No. 3235-0417).

---

[144] See Item 5 of Forms 10-Q and 10-QSB, new Item 9 of Form 10-K and new Item 8 of Form 10-KSB.

[145] Release No. 33-8238 (June 5, 2003) [68 FR 36636].

[146] Section 906 certifications also do not apply to filings on Form 6-K or Form 11-K [17 CFR 249.306 and 17 CFR 249.311].

[147] 29 U.S.C. 1021(i)(2)(E).

[148] 17 CFR 245.104(b)(2)(i)(B) and 17 CFR 245.104(b)(2)(ii), respectively.

[149] 17 CFR 245.104(b)(2)(iii).

[150] 17 CFR 240.13a-10 and 17 CFR 240.15d-10.

[151] 17 CFR 240.12b-23.

An agency may not conduct or sponsor, and a person is not required to respond to, a collection of information unless it displays a currently valid OMB control number.

B. Summary of Amendments

The amendments add eight new disclosure items to Form 8-K, transfer two existing items from the periodic reports and expand disclosures under two existing Form 8-K requirements. The amendments also reorganize the Form 8-K items into topical categories, shorten the Form 8-K filing deadline for most items to four business days after the occurrence of an event triggering the disclosure requirements of the form, provide a new limited safe harbor from liability under Exchange Act Section 10(b) and Rule 10b-5 for failure to file certain of the required Form 8-K reports, and provide limited relief from loss of eligibility to use Forms S-2 and S-3 stemming from a company's failure to timely file a Form 8-K report. These amendments are responsive to the "real time issuer disclosure" provision in Section 409 of the Sarbanes-Oxley Act of 2002. They are intended to provide investors with better and faster disclosure of important corporate events.

C. Summary of Comment Letters and Revisions to Proposals

We requested comment on the PRA analysis contained in the proposing release. Several commenters believed that the burdens would be higher than our estimates. One commenter believed that the burden and costs would be twice as much as our estimated burden and cost for complying with the proposed amendments.[152] Another commenter believed that it would have been required to file 15-20 more reports on Form 8-K during the past two years if the proposed requirements had been imposed during that period.[153] Neither commenter provided us with evidence to suggest that their estimates would apply to all companies.

We also received comments directed at the substance of the proposed Form 8-K items. In response to these comments, we have revised numerous items to simplify determinations of whether a reportable event has occurred. We also have reduced the amount of information and analysis that must be disclosed under many of the items. Furthermore, we are not adopting two of the proposed items.[154] Finally, in response to commenters' concerns regarding the difficulty of reporting events within two business days, as originally proposed, we have extended the filing deadline to four business days.

D. Revisions to PRA Reporting and Cost Burden Estimates

In response to the comments that we received on our estimates, we believe that companies may, on average, file more reports on revised Form 8-K than we previously estimated. In the proposing release, we estimated that a company would, on average, file two more reports on Form 8-K per year.[155] For purposes of the PRA, we now estimate that the amendments will cause, on average, an increase of five reports on Form 8-K per company per year. We recognize, however, that the actual number of reports a company must file is highly dependent on the nature of its activities. For example, a company with an active acquisition or financing program is more likely to be affected by these amendments than others. Thus, we expect that the amendments will impose a greater-than-average burden on some companies, and a less-than-average burden on others.

We estimate that each entity spends, on average, approximately five hours completing the form. We estimate that 75% of the burden is prepared by the company and that 25% of the burden is prepared by outside counsel retained by the company at an average cost of $300 per hour. We estimated the average number of hours each entity spends completing the form, and the average hourly rate for outside securities counsel, by contacting a number of law firms and other persons regularly involved in completing the forms and based on our experience with disclosure on Form 8-K.

As of the end of our 2003 fiscal year, we estimate that there were 11,800 companies filing reports on Form 8-K.[156] Based on our new estimate of five additional Form 8-K reports per company per year as a result of these amendments, we estimate an increase of 59,000 filings per year. This results in an estimate of 221,250 additional burden hours[157] and a cost of approxi-

---

[152] Letter of Radin, Glass & Co.

[153] Letter of John Deere. It was unclear whether this commenter included all routine financings in its estimate. Item 2.03 requires disclosure of short-term debt obligations only if they are made out of the ordinary course of business. We are uncertain as to whether the commenter's estimate would be the same under the adopted amendments.

[154] We are not adopting in this release proposed Item 1.03 Termination or Reduction of a Business Relationship with a Customer and proposed Item 3.01 Rating Agency Decisions.

[155] During our fiscal year ended September 30, 2003, we received approximately 58,400 Form 8-K reports from approximately 11,800 companies.

[156] 11,800 filers×5 additional Form 8-K filings per filer=59,000 additional filings.

[157] 59,000 filings×5 hours per filing×0.75=221,250 hours.

mately $22,125,000 for the services of outside professionals.[158]

Form 12b-25

The proposed rules would have permitted a company unable to timely file a Form 8-K to report the late filing on Form 12b-25 and to receive an automatic two business day filing extension. In the proposing release, we estimated that, of the expected 61,500 filings for which Form 12b-25 would be available, 6,700 would be late, resulting in an incremental Form 12b-25 burden of 16,750 hours and a total annual burden of 31,750 hours. These estimates were based on the current rate of late filings on Form 8-K. Because we have lengthened the proposed Form 8-K filing deadline to four business days, we are not adopting the proposed Form 12b-25 amendments.

Forms 10-Q, 10-QSB, 10-K and 10-KSB

We are transferring, in part, two disclosure requirements from Forms 10-Q, 10-QSB, 10-K and 10-KSB to Form 8-K. Because these items generally will be disclosed in the Form 8-K, companies do not have to repeat this disclosure in the annual and quarterly report. We estimate that these changes will result in a decrease of one burden hour per company per filing in connection with preparing and filing each quarterly report on Form 10-Q or 10-QSB and the annual report on Form 10-K or 10-KSB.

Item 601 of Regulation S-K and Regulation S-B

The revisions to Item 601 of Regulation S-K and Item 601 of Regulation S-B amend the exhibit tables to identify exhibits that must be filed with Form 8-K. We have incorporated the burden of actually submitting those exhibits in the estimated Form 8-K filing burden. These items do not, separate from the form, require any additional filing and thus do not add to the burden on companies. As a result, we do not expect any change in the total annual burden of reporting under these items. We assign one burden hour and no cost to Regulations S-B and S-K for administrative convenience to reflect the fact that these regulations do not impose any direct burden on companies.

Compliance with the revised disclosure requirements is mandatory. There is no mandatory retention period for the information disclosed, and responses to the disclosure requirements will not be kept confidential.

[¶ 2004]

IV. COSTS AND BENEFITS

A. Background

After we proposed the amendments to Form 8-K in June 2002, Congress enacted the Sarbanes-Oxley Act of 2002. Section 409 of that Act, entitled "Real Time Issuer Disclosures," states that "[e]ach issuer reporting under section 13(a) or 15(d) shall disclose to the public on a rapid and current basis such additional information concerning material changes in the financial condition or operations of the issuer ... as the Commission determines, by rule, is necessary or useful for the protection of investors and in the public interest." We believe these amendments are responsive to this provision of the Sarbanes-Oxley Act.

Prior to these amendments, Form 8-K required companies to disclose eight enumerated events within five business days or 15 calendar days, depending on the event. These amendments decrease this filing deadline to four business days after the event occurs for all events, other than Item 8.01 (current Item 5), which has no deadline, Item 7.01 (current Item 9), relating to Regulation FD disclosures and certain exhibits. The amendments also add 10 new events that would trigger a Form 8-K filing requirement, including two items transferred from the periodic reports. The amendments reorganize the Form 8-K items, create a limited safe harbor from liability under Exchange Act Section 10(b) and Rule 10b-5 for failure to file certain items, and provide limited relief from loss of eligibility to use Forms S-2 and S-3 for failure to file a Form 8-K on a timely basis. These changes will affect all companies reporting under Section 13(a) and 15(d) of the Exchange Act, other than foreign private issuers that file annual reports on Form 20-F[159] or 40-F.[160]

B. Benefits

Markets rely on timely dissemination of information to accurately and quickly value securities. These amendments increase the amount of significant information that a company must disclose to the public on a current basis, enhancing the ability of markets to respond to those corporate events. Under the prior system, predicated primarily on a periodic reporting system, the securities of a company could be trading on less complete information if an important corporate event has occurred but the company, under no duty to report that event, does not report the event on a timely basis. Such a delay in disclosure permits there to be significant time periods dur-

[158] 59,000 filings×5 hours per filing×0.25×$300 per hour=$22,125,000.

[159] 17 CFR 249.220f.

[160] 17 CFR 249.240f.

ing which important information is not disclosed to the market. These circumstances create opportunity for companies and those with access to nonpublic information to misuse that information. The amendments adopted today will reduce such opportunities for misuse.

Modern computer and communications systems enable current disclosure to be analyzed and incorporated into the price of a security quickly. By moving our rules towards a system emphasizing current reporting, our markets may become more effective as price discovery mechanisms during periods between periodic reports.

In addition, these amendments should enhance investor confidence in the financial markets. The requirement of enhanced, timely disclosure should raise investors' expectations regarding the amount and timing of information that reporting companies must make available to the public. Confidence in the expectation of such enhanced disclosure should provide more certainty to those investors that they are making investment decisions in a more transparent market, which should reduce market volatility as a result of uncertainty of the availability of accurate timely information about public companies.

C. Costs

Based on a review of approximately 68,000 Form 8-K filings, approximately 74% of those reports were filed within four business days of the reported event date. Although this review did not investigate whether filers reported the correct event date for each filing, it appears that most companies already file their Form 8-K reports within the new four-business-day timeframe. In addition, we believe that several of our recent rulemakings have caused companies to improve their internal processes for ensuring that material information is reported to management in a more timely manner. For example, we adopted rules requiring certain executive officers to certify that they have designed disclosure controls and procedures, or caused such controls and procedures to be designed, to ensure that material information about the company is reported to those executive officers.[161] Thus, we believe that companies will be able to comply with the four business day deadline without undue burden. Although we found, at the proposing stage, that the majority of filings were made within two calendar days, we recognize that some items may be more difficult to report in a timely manner. Rather than complicate the Form 8-K reporting framework by establishing multiple deadlines, we have decided to extend the proposed deadline to four business days.

We expect that the addition of new Form 8-K items will increase the number of Form 8-Ks that a company is required to file. Based on our estimates for purposes of the PRA, we expect approximately five additional filings per year per company. Assuming a value of $100 per hour for company time, we estimate an increase of approximately $44 million in filing costs associated with Form 8-K due to the adoption of these amendments.

Companies may experience some competitive or other strategic costs caused by the requirement to disclose more categories of information more quickly than they otherwise may have chosen to disclose. These costs are difficult to quantify. Further, we are sensitive to the argument that these enhanced disclosure requirements may increase a company's exposure to liability. Thus, we are adopting a new limited safe harbor from liability under Exchange Act Section 10(b) and Rule 10b-5 for failure to file a report on Form 8-K within the stated deadline for certain events. We are also eliminating any duplicative reporting requirements in annual and quarterly reports. In addition, developments such as EDGARLink that enable a company to file reports easily and directly with the Commission over the Internet,[162] without the added costs of using third parties to submit filings, as well as the industry's increased experience over the past several years using the EDGAR system, should minimize the cost to companies of filing more Form 8-K reports in a shorter timeframe.

[¶ 2005]

V. EFFECT ON EFFICIENCY, COMPETITION AND CAPITAL FORMATION

Section 23(a)(2)[163] of the Exchange Act requires us, when adopting rules under the Exchange Act, to consider the impact that any new rule would have on competition. In addition, Section 23(a)(2) prohibits us from adopting any rule that would impose a burden on competition not necessary or appropriate in furtherance of the purposes of the Exchange Act.

Section 2(b)[164] of the Securities Act and Section 3(f)[165] of the Exchange Act require us, when engaging in rulemaking where we are required to consider or determine whether an action is neces-

[161] Release No. 33-8124 (August 28, 2002) [67 FR 57276].

[162] EDGARLink is downloadable free of charge to filers from our website at https://www.edgarfiling.sec.gov.

[163] 15 U.S.C. 78w(a)(2).

[164] 15 U.S.C. 77b(b).

[165] 15 U.S.C. 78c(f).

sary or appropriate in the public interest, to consider, in addition to the protection of investors, whether the action will promote efficiency, competition and capital formation.

The amendments are intended to improve the amount, quality and timeliness of current information available to investors and the financial markets. This should improve the ability of investors to make informed investment and voting decisions. Informed investor decisions generally promote market efficiency and capital formation. Thus, we anticipate that these amendments will enhance the proper functioning of the capital markets. This increases the competitiveness of companies participating in the U.S. capital markets. Because only domestic companies subject to the reporting requirements of Sections 13 and 15 of the Exchange Act are required to make Form 8-K disclosures, competitors not subject to those reporting requirements potentially could gain an informational advantage. The possibility of these effects and their magnitude if they were to occur are difficult to quantify.

We requested comment on whether the proposed amendments, if adopted, would impose a burden on competition or, conversely, promote efficiency, competition and capital formation. Numerous commenters believed that a requirement to disclose non-binding agreements and letters of intent would cause companies competitive harm. Similarly, commenters believed that a disclosure requirement regarding the termination of a material agreement or loss of a significant customer may place the party required to make such disclosures at a competitive disadvantage to the counterparty.

In response to these comments, we have eliminated the proposed disclosure requirement regarding nonbinding agreements and letters of intent. We have also eliminated the proposed item regarding the loss of a significant customer due to the difficulty of identifying the particular date on which such loss occurs. With regard to the termination of a material agreement, we have revised the relevant item to provide a company with more flexibility if it believes that the counterparty is merely using a claim of termination as a negotiation ploy, contrary to the terms of the contract.

Several commenters recommended that we revise the eligibility rules under Forms S-2 and S-3 so that an untimely filing of a report on Form 8-K would not result in the loss of such eligibility. Loss of such eligibility can significantly restrict the ability of a company to raise capital and may be a disproportionately large negative consequence of an untimely filing of a Form 8-K. Although we believe it is important that a company provide full disclosure when it seeks to raise capital in public markets, we also recognize that the shortened timeframes for certain of the Form 8-K items may increase the number of companies that could lose eligibility under Forms S-2 and S-3. As a result, we have revised the form eligibility rules to allow a company to use Forms S-2 and S-3 despite the filing of an untimely Form 8-K for certain enumerated items of the form. A company would still need to be current in these Form 8-K reports, however, prior to the filing of a Form S-2 or Form S-3 registration statement. This ensures that when the company files its registration statement, required information under the enumerated items has been publicly disclosed.

Other commenters believed that the volume of reporting that would be required under the amendments may create a considerable distraction for management, which may hinder a company from operating efficiently. We have attempted to limit the new items required to be reported on Form 8-K to unquestionably or presumptively material events. For example, many of the items cover events that happen rarely to a company, such as delisting from an national securities exchange, bankruptcy and restatements of financial statements. Others items are limited by their terms. For example, Item 1.01 requires disclosure only of material definitive agreements outside the ordinary course of business, excluding many types of ordinary course contracts.

[¶ 2006]

VI. FINAL REGULATORY FLEXIBILITY ANALYSIS

This Final Regulatory Flexibility Analysis, or FRFA, has been prepared in accordance with the Regulatory Flexibility Act (RFA).[166] This FRFA involves amendments to shorten the filing deadline for Form 8-K and expand the events requiring disclosure on the form. An Initial Regulatory Flexibility Analysis (IRFA) was prepared in accordance with the Regulatory Flexibility Act in conjunction with the proposing release. The proposing release included and solicited comment on the IRFA.

A. Need for the Amendments

We are adopting the amendments to Form 8-K to provide investors and the securities markets with more timely access to a greater range of information concerning significant corporate events than is currently required by Form 8-K. The amendments to Form 8-K increase the list of events that trigger a Form 8-K filing requirement and require most Form 8-K reports to be filed no

---

[166] 5 U.S.C. 603.

later than the fourth business day following occurrence of the event to which the report relates. The amendments should enhance investor confidence in the fairness and integrity of the securities markets by requiring companies to provide more current disclosure about several significant corporate events. In addition to accelerating the filing deadlines for events that already trigger the Form 8-K filing requirements, the proposals would expand the types of information covered by Form 8-K.

B. Significant Issues Raised by Public Comment

No comments were raised specifically about the IRFA. However, several commenters recommended that small business issuers be afforded relief from the new reporting requirements, such as being granted longer filing deadlines because they do not have the same resources as larger issuers. Because we believe that different compliance or reporting requirements or timetables for small entities would interfere with the goal of making information about significant corporate events promptly available to investors and the markets, as discussed more fully below, we have generally not differentiated between small issuers and other issuers in the amendments to Form 8-K.

C. Small Entities Subject to the Amendments

The amendments to Form 8-K will affect issuers that are small entities. Exchange Act Rule 0-10(a)[167] defines an issuer, other than an investment company, to be a "small business" or "small organization" if it had total assets of $5 million or less on the last day of its most recent fiscal year. We estimate that there are approximately 2,500 issuers, other than investment companies, that may be considered small entities. The amendments to Form 8-K apply to any small entity that is subject to Exchange Act reporting requirements.

D. Reporting, Recordkeeping and Other Compliance Requirements

Form 8-K previously consisted of 12 disclosure items. The amendments add 10 new disclosure items, including two transferred from annual and quarterly reports. All small entities that are subject to the reporting requirements of Exhange Act Sections 13(a) or 15(d) are subject to these amendments. Because reporting companies already file Form 8-K for certain events, no additional professional skills beyond those currently possessed by these filers is necessary to prepare the form for the new disclosure items.

We expect that reporting of these new disclosure items will increase costs incurred by small entities because they will have to file Form 8-K more frequently. We have calculated for purposes of the PRA that each filer, including a small entity, will be subject to an added annual reporting burden of approximately 18.75 hours[168] and an estimated annual average cost of $1,875[169] for disclosure assistance from outside counsel as a result of the amendments.

E. Agency Action to Minimize Effect on Small Entities

The RFA directs us to consider significant alternatives that would accomplish the stated objective, while minimizing any significant adverse impact on small entity issuers. In connection with the proposed revisions to Form 8-K, we considered the following alternatives: (a) the establishment of differing compliance or reporting requirements or timetables that take into account the resources available to small entities; (b) the clarification, consolidation, or simplification of Form 8-K reporting requirements for small entities; (c) the use of performance rather than design standards; and (d) an exemption from coverage of the Form 8-K requirements, or any part thereof, for small entities.

We do not believe that small issuers will have to report more frequently than other issuers or disclose more information in their forms. We believe that different compliance or reporting requirements or timetables for small entities would interfere with achieving the primary goal of making information about significant corporate events promptly available to investors and the public securities markets. We also think that the current and proposed Form 8-K disclosure requirements are clear and straightforward. They generally require brief disclosure indicating that a specific significant corporate event has occurred. Thus, it does not seem necessary to develop separate requirements for small entities.

We recognize, however, that small entities are more likely to participate in securities offerings that constitute a relatively large percentage of their outstanding securities because such entities often do not have many securities outstanding. As a result, with regard to unregistered sales of equity securities, we are adopting a higher numeric threshold for disclosure. In the case of small business issuers, which include small entities, such issuers must disclose unregistered sales of equity securities if the sale represents a threshold of 5% of the company's outstanding shares, rather than the 1% threshold applied to other companies.

The nature of the required disclosures under other items do not generally lend themselves to

---

[167] 17 CFR 240.0-10(a).

[168] 5 filings×5 hours per filing×0.75=18.75 hours.

[169] 5 filings×5 hours/filing×0.25×$300/hour=$1,875.

numeric thresholds that can reliably represent presumptively material occurrences. Thus, similar distinctions have not been applied to other items. We have used design rather than performance standards in connection with the Form 8-K amendments. This is because we want this disclosure to appear in a specific type of disclosure filing so that investors will know where to find information about specific significant corporate events. We also want the Form 8-K information to be filed electronically using the EDGAR filing system to facilitate dissemination of information to markets and the public. We do not believe that performance standards for small entities would be consistent with the purpose of the amendments.

[¶ 2007]

VII. STATUTORY BASIS

We are adopting the amendments pursuant to Sections 7, 10 and 19 of the Securities Act, as amended, and Sections 10, 12, 13, 15 and 23 of the Securities Exchange Act, as amended.

TEXT OF THE AMENDMENTS

List of Subjects

17 CFR Part 228

Reporting and recordkeeping requirements, Securities, Small businesses.

17 CFR Parts 229, 230 and 239

Reporting and recordkeeping requirements, Securities.

17 CFR Part 240

Brokers, Confidential business information, Fraud, Reporting and recordkeeping requirements, Securities.

17 CFR Part 249

Brokers, Reporting and recordkeeping requirements, Securities.

For the reasons set out in the preamble, title 17, chapter II of the Code of Federal Regulations is amended as follows.

PART 228—INTEGRATED DISCLOSURE SYSTEM FOR SMALL BUSINESS ISSUERS

1. The authority citation for Part 228 continues to read in part as follows:

Authority: 15 U.S.C. 77e, 77f, 77g, 77h, 77j, 77k, 77s, 77z-2, 77z-3, 77aa(25), 77aa(26), 77ddd, 77eee, 77ggg, 77hhh, 77jjj, 77nnn, 77sss, 78*l*, 78m, 78n, 78o, 78u-5, 78w, 78*ll*, 78mm, 80a-8, 80a-29, 80a-30, 80a-37, 80b-11, and 7201 *et seq.*; and 18 U.S.C. 1350.

* * * * *

2. Amend § 228.601 by:

a. Revising the exhibit table;

b. Adding text to paragraph (b)(7); and

c. Revising paragraphs (b)(3) and (b)(17).

The revisions and addition read as follows:

§ 228.601 (Item 601) Exhibits.

(a) * * *

EXHIBIT TABLE

	Securities Act Forms					Exchange Act Forms			
	SB-2	S-2	S-3	S-4[3]	S-8	10-SB	8-K[5]	10-QSB	10-KSB
(1) Underwriting agreement	X	X	X	X			X		
(2) Plan of purchase, sale, reorganization, arrangement, liquidation or succession	X	X	X	X		X	X	X	X
(3) (i) Articles of Incorporation	X			X		X	X	X	X
(ii) Bylaws	X			X		X	X	X	X
(4) Instruments defining the rights of security holders, including indentures	X	X	X	X	X	X	X	X	X
(5) Opinion on legality	X	X	X	X	X				
(6) No exhibit required	N/A	N/A	N/A	N/A	N/A	N/A	N/A	N/A	N/A
(7) Correspondence from an independent accountant regarding non-reliance upon a previously issued audit report or completed interim review							X		
(8) Opinion on tax matters	X	X	X	X					
(9) Voting trust agreement and amendments	X			X		X			X
(10) Material contracts	X	X		X		X		X	X
(11) Statement re: computation of per share earnings	X	X		X		X		X	X
(12) No exhibit required	N/A	N/A	N/A	N/A	N/A	N/A	N/A	N/A	N/A
(13) Annual report to security holders for the last fiscal year, Form 10-Q or 10-QSB or quarterly report to security holders[1]	X	X		X					X
(14) Code of ethics							X		X
(15) Letter on unaudited interim financial information	X	X	X	X	X			X	
(16) Letter on change in certifying accountant[4]	X	X		X		X	X		X
(17) Letter on departure of director							X		
(18) Letter on change in accounting principles								X	X
(19) Reports furnished to security holders								X	
(20) Other documents or statements to security holders or any document incorporated by reference								X	X
(21) Subsidiaries of the small business issuer	X			X		X			X
(22) Published report regarding matters submitted to vote of security holders								X	X
(23) Consents of experts and counsel	X	X	X	X	X		X[2]	X[2]	X[2]
(24) Power of attorney	X	X	X	X	X	X	X	X	X
(25) Statement of eligibility of trustee	X	X	X	X					
(26) Invitations for competitive bids		X	X	X	X				
(27) through (30) [Reserved]									
(31) Rule 13a-14(a)/15d-14(a) Certifications								X	X

EXHIBIT TABLE

	Securities Act Forms					Exchange Act Forms			
	SB-2	*S-2*	*S-3*	*S-4* [3]	*S-8*	*10-SB*	*8-K* [5]	*10-QSB*	*10-KSB*
(32) Section 1350 Certifications								X	X
(33) through (98)[Reserved]									
(99) Additional exhibits	X	X	X	X	X	X	X	X	X

[1] Only if incorporated by reference into a prospectus and delivered to holders along with the prospectus as permitted by the registration statement; or in the case of a Form 10-KSB, where the annual report is incorporated by reference into the text of the Form 10-KSB.

[2] Where the opinion of the expert or counsel has been incorporated by reference into a previously filed Securities Act registration statement.

[3] An issuer need not provide an exhibit if: (1) an election was made under Form S-4 to provide S-2 or S-3 disclosure; and (2) the form selected (S-2 or S-3) would not require the company to provide the exhibit.

[4] If required under Item 304 of Regulation S-B.

[5] A Form 8-K exhibit is required only if relevant to the subject matter reported on the Form 8-K report. For example, if the Form 8-K pertains to the departure of a director, only the exhibit described in paragraph (b)(17) of this section need be filed. A required exhibit may be incorporated by reference from a previous filing.

(b) * * *

(3) *Articles of incorporation and bylaws.* (i) A complete copy of the articles of incorporation. Whenever the small business issuer files an amendment to its articles of incorporation, it must file a complete copy of the articles as amended. However, if such amendment is being reported on Form 8-K (§ 249.308 of this chapter), the small business issuer is required to file only the text of the amendment as a Form 8-K exhibit. In such case, a complete copy of the articles of incorporation as amended must be filed as an exhibit to the next Securities Act registration statement or periodic report filed by the small business issuer to which this exhibit requirement applies.

(ii) A complete copy of the bylaws. Whenever the small business issuer files an amendment to its bylaws, it must file a complete copy of the bylaws as amended. However, if such amendment is being reported on Form 8-K (§ 249.308 of this chapter), the small business issuer is required to file only the text of the amendment as a Form 8-K exhibit. In such cases, a complete copy of the bylaws as amended must be filed as an exhibit to the next Securities Act registration statement or periodic report filed by the small business issuer to which this exhibit requirement applies.

* * * * *

(7) *Correspondence from an independent accountant regarding non-reliance on a previously issued audit report or completed interim review.* Any written notice from the small business issuer's current or previously engaged independent accountant that the independent accountant is withdrawing a previously issued audit report or that a previously issued audit report or completed interim review, covering one or more years or interim periods for which the small business issuer is required to provide financial statements under this Regulation S-B, should no longer be relied upon. In addition, any letter, pursuant to Item 4.02(c) of Form 8-K (§ 249.308 of this chapter), from the independent accountant to the Commission stating whether the independent accountant agrees with the statements made by the small business issuer describing the events giving rise to the notice.

* * * * *

(17) *Correspondence on departure of director.* Any written correspondence from a former director concerning the circumstances surrounding the former director's retirement, resignation, refusal to stand for re-election or removal, including any letter from the former director to the small business issuer stating whether the former director agrees with statements made by the small business issuer describing the former director's departure.

* * * * *

PART 229—STANDARD INSTRUCTIONS FOR FILING FORMS UNDER SECURITIES ACT OF 1933, SECURITIES EXCHANGE ACT OF 1934 AND ENERGY POLICY AND CONSERVATION ACT OF 1975—REGULATION S-K

3. The general authority citation for Part 229 is revised to read as follows:

Authority: 15 U.S.C. 77e, 77f, 77g, 77h, 77j, 77k, 77s, 77z-2, 77z-3, 77aa(25), 77aa(26), 77ddd, 77eee, 77ggg, 77hhh, 77iii, 77jjj, 77nnn, 77sss, 78c, 78i, 78j, 78*l*, 78m, 78n, 78o, 78u-5, 78w, 78*ll*, 78mm, 79e, 79j, 79n, 79t, 80a-8, 80a-9, 80a-20, 80a-29, 80a-30, 80a-31(c), 80a-37, 80a-38(a), 80a-39, 80b-11, and 7201 *et seq.*; and 18 U.S.C. 1350, unless otherwise noted.

* * * * *

4. Amend § 229.601 by:

a. Revising the exhibit table;

b. Adding text to paragraph (b)(7); and

c. Revising paragraphs (b)(3) and (b)(17).

The revisions and addition read as follows:

§ 229.601 (Item 601) Exhibits.

(a) * * *

Instructions to the Exhibit Table

* * * * *

EXHIBIT TABLE

	Securities Act Forms										Exchange Act Forms			
	S-1	S-2	S-3	S-4[3]	S-8	S-11	F-1	F-2	F-3	F-4[3]	10	8-K[5]	10-Q	10-K
(1) Underwriting agreement	X	X	X	X	—	X	X	X	X	X	—	X	—	—
(2) Plan of acquisition, reorganization, arrangement, liquidation or succession	X	X	X	X	—	X	X	X	X	X	X	X	X	X
(3) (i) Articles of incorporation	X	—	—	X	—	X	X	—	—	X	X	X	X	X
(ii) Bylaws	X	—	—	X	—	X	X	—	—	X	X	X	X	X
(4) Instruments defining the rights of security holders, including indentures	X	X	X	X	X	X	X	X	X	X	X	X	X	X
(5) Opinion re legality	X	X	X	X	X	X	X	X	X	X	—	—	—	—
(6) [Reserved]	N/A	N/A	N/A	N/A	N/A	N/A	N/A	N/A	N/A	N/A	N/A	N/A	N/A	N/A
(7) Correspondence from an independent accountant regarding non-reliance on a previously issued audit report or completed interim review	—	—	—	—	—	—	—	—	—	—	—	X	—	—
(8) Opinion re tax matters	X	X	X	X	—	X	X	X	X	X	—	—	—	—
(9) Voting trust agreement	X	—	—	X	—	X	X	—	—	X	X	—	—	X
(10) Material contracts	X	X	—	X	—	X	X	—	—	X	X	—	X	X
(11) Statement re computation of per share earnings	X	X	—	X	—	X	X	X	—	X	X	—	X	X
(12) Statements re computation of ratios	X	X	X	X	—	X	X	X	—	X	X	—	—	X
(13) Annual report to security holders, Form 10-Q and 10-QSB, or quarterly report to security holders[1]	—	X	—	X	—	—	—	—	—	—	—	—	—	X
(14) Code of Ethics												X		X
(15) Letter re unaudited interim financial information	X	X	X	X	X	X	X	X	X	X	—	—	X	—
(16) Letter re change in certifying accountant[4]	X	X	—	X	—	X	—	—	—	—	X	X	—	X
(17) Correpondence on departure of director	—	—	—	—	—	—	—	—	—	—	—	X	—	—
(18) Letter re change in accounting principles	—	—	—	—	—	—	—	—	—	—	—	—	X	X
(19) Report furnished to security holders	—	—	—	—	—	—	—	—	—	—	—	—	X	—
(20) Other documents or statements to security holders	—	—	—	—	—	—	—	—	—	—	—	X	—	—
(21) Subsidiaries of the registrant	X	—	—	X	—	X	X	—	—	X	X	—	—	X
(22) Published report regarding matters submitted to vote of security holders	—	—	—	—	—	—	—	—	—	—	—	—	X	X
(23) Consents of experts and counsel	X	X	X	X	X	X	X	X	X	X	—	X[2]	X[2]	X[2]
(24) Power of attorney	X	X	X	X	X	X	X	X	X	X	X	X	X	X
(25) Statement of eligibility of trustee	X	X	X	X	—	X	X	X	X	X	—	—	—	—
(26) Invitations for competitive bids	X	X	X	X	—	—	X	X	X	X	—	—	—	—
(27) through (30) [Reserved]														
(31) Rule 13a-14(a)/15d-14(a) Certifications	—	—	—	—	—	—	—	—	—	—	—	—	X	X
(32) Section 1350 Certifications	—	—	—	—	—	—	—	—	—	—	—	—	X	X
(33) through (98) [Reserved]	N/A	N/A	N/A	N/A	N/A	N/A	N/A	N/A	N/A	N/A	N/A	N/A	N/A	N/A
(99) Additional exhibits	X	X	X	X	X	X	X	X	X	X	X	X	X	X

[1] Where incorporated by reference into the text of the prospectus and delivered to security holders along with the prospectus as permitted by the registration statement; or, in the case of the Form 10-K, where the annual report to security holders is incorporated by reference into the text of the Form 10-K.
[2] Where the opinion of the expert or counsel has been incorporated by reference into a previously filed Securities Act registration statement.

[3] An exhibit need not be provided about a company if: (1) With respect to such company an election has been made under Form S-4 or F-4 to provide information about such company at a level prescribed by Forms S-2, S-3, F-2 or F-3 and (2) the form, the level of which has been elected under Forms S-4 or F-4, would not require such company to provide such exhibit if it were registering a primary offering.

[4] If required pursuant to Item 304 of Regulation S-K.

[5] A Form 8-K exhibit is required only if relevant to the subject matter reported on the Form 8-K report. For example, if the Form 8-K pertains to the departure of a director, only the exhibit described in paragraph (b)(17) of this section need be filed. A required exhibit may be incorporated by reference from a previous filing.

(b) * * *

(3)(i) *Articles of incorporation.* The articles of incorporation of the registrant or instruments corresponding thereto as currently in effect and any amendments thereto. Whenever the registrant files an amendment to its articles of incorporation, it must file a complete copy of the articles as amended. However, if such amendment is being reported on Form 8-K (§ 249.308 of this chapter), the registrant is required to file only the text of the amendment as a Form 8-K exhibit. In such case, a complete copy of the articles of incorporation as amended must be filed as an exhibit to the next Securities Act registration statement or periodic report filed by the registrant to which this exhibit requirement applies. Where it is impracticable for the registrant to file a charter amendment authorizing new securities with the appropriate state authority prior to the effective date of the registration statement registering such securities, the registrant may file as an exhibit to the registration statement the form of amendment to be filed with the state authority. In such a case, if material changes are made after the copy is filed, the registrant must also file the changed copy.

(ii) *Bylaws.* The bylaws of the registrant or instruments corresponding thereto as currently in effect and any amendments thereto. Whenever the registrant files an amendment to the bylaws, it must file a complete copy of the amended bylaws. However, if such amendment is being reported on Form 8-K (§ 249.308 of this chapter), the registrant is required to file only the text of the amendment as a Form 8-K exhibit. In such case, a complete copy of the bylaws as amended must be filed as an exhibit to the next Securities Act registration statement or periodic report filed by the registrant to which this exhibit requirement applies.

* * * * *

(7) *Correspondence from an independent accountant regarding non-reliance on a previously issued audit report or completed interim review.* Any written notice from the registrant's current or previously engaged independent accountant that the independent accountant is withdrawing a previously issued audit report or that a previously issued audit report or completed interim review, covering one or more years or interim periods for which the registrant is required to provide financial statements under Regulation S-X (part 210 of this chapter), should no longer be relied upon. In addition, any letter, pursuant to Item 4.02(c) of Form 8-K (§ 249.308 of this chapter), from the independent accountant to the Commission stating whether the independent accountant agrees with the statements made by the registrant describing the events giving rise to the notice.

* * * * *

(17) *Correspondence on departure of director.* Any written correspondence from a former director concerning the circumstances surrounding the former director's retirement, resignation, refusal to stand for re-election or removal, including any letter from the former director to the registrant stating whether the former director agrees with statements made by the registrant describing the former director's departure.

* * * * *

PART 230—GENERAL RULES AND REGULATIONS, SECURITIES ACT OF 1933

5. The authority citation for part 230 continues to read in part as follows:

Authority: 15 U.S.C. 77b, 77c, 77d, 77f, 77g, 77h, 77j, 77r, 77s, 77z-3, 77sss, 78c, 78d, 78j, 78*l*, 78m, 78n, 78o, 78t, 78w, 78*ll*(d), 78mm, 79t, 80a-8, 80a-24, 80a-28, 80a-29, 80a-30, and 80a-37, unless otherwise noted.

* * * * * *

6. Amend § 230.144 by revising paragraph (c)(1) to read as follows:

§ 230.144 Persons deemed not to be engaged in a distribution and therefore not underwriters.

* * * * *

(c) * * *

(1) *Filing of reports.* The issuer has securities registered pursuant to section 12 of the Securities Exchange Act of 1934, has been subject to the reporting requirements of section 13 of that Act for a period of at least 90 days immediately preceding the sale of the securities and has filed all the reports required to be filed thereunder during the 12 months preceding such sale (or for such shorter period that the issuer was required to file such reports), other than Form 8-K reports (§ 249.308 of this chapter); or has securities registered pursuant to the Securities Act of 1933, has been subject to the reporting requirements of section 15(d) of the Securities Exchange Act of 1934 for a period of at least 90 days immediately preceding the sale of the securities and has filed all the reports required to be filed thereunder during the 12 months preceding such sale (or for such shorter period that the issuer was required to file such reports), other than Form 8-K reports (§ 249.308 of this chapter). The person for whose account the securities are to be sold shall be entitled to rely upon a statement in whichever is the most recent report, quarterly or annual, required to be filed and filed by the issuer that such issuer has filed all reports required to be filed by section 13 or 15(d) of the Securities Exchange Act of 1934 during the preceding 12 months (or for

such shorter period that the issuer was required to file such reports), other than Form 8-K reports (§ 249.308 of this chapter), and has been subject to such filing requirements for the past 90 days, unless he knows or has reason to believe that the issuer has not complied with such requirements. Such person shall also be entitled to rely upon a written statement from the issuer that it has complied with such reporting requirements unless he knows or has reasons to believe that the issuer has not complied with such requirements.

* * * * *

PART 239—FORMS PRESCRIBED UNDER THE SECURITIES ACT OF 1933

7. The authority citation for part 239 continues to read in part as follows:

Authority: 15 U.S.C. 77f, 77g, 77h, 77j, 77s, 77z-2, 77sss, 78c, 78*l*, 78m, 78n, 78o(d), 78u-5, 78w(a), 78*ll*(d), 79e, 79f, 79g, 79j, 79*l*, 79m, 79n, 79q, 79t, 80a-8, 80a-24, 80a-26, 80a-29, 80a-30, and 80a-37, unless otherwise noted.

* * * * *

8. Amend § 239.12 by revising paragraph (c)(2) to read as follows:

§ 239.12 Form S-2, for registration under the Securities Act of 1933 of securities of certain issuers.

* * * * *

(c) * * *

(2) Has filed in a timely manner all reports required to be filed during the twelve calendar months and any portion of a month immediately preceding the filing of the registration statement, other than a report that is required solely pursuant to Item 1.01, 1.02, 2.03, 2.04, 2.05, 2.06 or 4.02(a) of Form 8-K (§ 249.308 of this chapter). If the registrant has used (during the twelve calendar months and any portion of a month immediately preceding the filing of the registration statement) § 240.12b-25(b) of this chapter with respect to a report or a portion of a report, that report or portion thereof has actually been filed within the time period prescribed by that section; and

* * * * *

9. Amend Form S-2 (referenced in § 239.12) by revising General Instruction I.(C) to read as follows:

Note—The text of Form S-2 does not, and this amendment will not, appear in the Code of Federal Regulations.

FORM S-2

REGISTRATION STATEMENT UNDER THE SECURITIES ACT OF 1933

* * * * *

GENERAL INSTRUCTIONS

I. * * *

C. The registrant:

(1) has been subject to the requirements of Section 12 or 15(d) of the Exchange Act and has filed all the material required to be filed pursuant to Section 12, 14 or 15(d) for a period of at least thirty-six calendar months immediately preceding the filing of the registration statement on this Form; and

(2) has filed in a timely manner all reports required to be filed during the twelve calendar months and any portion of a month immediately preceding the filing of the registration statement, other than a report that is required solely pursuant to Item 1.01, 1.02, 2.03, 2.04, 2.05, 2.06 or 4.02(a) of Form 8-K (§ 249.308 of this chapter). If the registrant has used (during the twelve calendar months and any portion of a month immediately preceding the filing of the registration statement) Rule 12b-25(b) (§ 240.12b-25(b) of this chapter) under the Exchange Act with respect to a report or a portion of a report, that report or portion thereof has actually been filed within the time period prescribed by that rule.

* * * * *

10. Amend § 239.13 by removing the authority citation following the section and revising paragraph (a)(3)(ii) to read as follows:

§ 239.13 Form S-3, for registration under the Securities Act of 1933 of securities of certain issuers offered pursuant to certain types of transactions.

* * * * *

(a) * * *

(3) * * *

(ii) Has filed in a timely manner all reports required to be filed during the twelve calendar months and any portion of a month immediately preceding the filing of the registration statement, other than a report that is required solely pursuant to Item 1.01, 1.02, 2.03, 2.04, 2.05, 2.06 or 4.02(a) of Form 8-K (§ 249.308 of this chapter). If the registrant has used (during the twelve calendar months and any portion of a month immediately preceding the filing of the registration statement) § 240.12b-25(b) of this chapter with respect to a report or a portion of a report, that report or portion thereof has actually been filed within the time period prescribed by that section; and

* * * * *

11. Amend Form S-3 (referenced in § 239.13) by revising General Instruction I.A.3 to read as follows:

Note—The text of Form S-3 does not, and this amendment will not, appear in the Code of Federal Regulations.

FORM S-3

REGISTRATION STATEMENT UNDER THE SECURITIES ACT OF 1933

* * * * *

GENERAL INSTRUCTIONS

I. * * *

A. * * *

3. The registrant:

(a) has been subject to the requirements of Section 12 or 15(d) of the Exchange Act and has filed all the material required to be filed pursuant to Section 12, 14 or 15(d) for a period of at least twelve calendar months immediately preceding the filing of the registration statement on this Form; and

(b) has filed in a timely manner all reports required to be filed during the twelve calendar months and any portion of a month immediately preceding the filing of the registration statement, other than a report that is required solely pursuant to Item 1.01, 1.02, 2.03, 2.04, 2.05, 2.06 or 4.02(a) of Form 8-K (§ 249.308 of this chapter). If the registrant has used (during the twelve calendar months and any portion of a month immediately preceding the filing of the registration statement) Rule 12b-25(b) (§ 240.12b-25(b) of this chapter) under the Exchange Act with respect to a report or a portion of a report, that report or portion thereof has actually been filed within the time period prescribed by that rule.

* * * * *

PART 240—GENERAL RULES AND REGULATIONS, SECURITIES EXCHANGE ACT OF 1934

12. The authority citation for part 240 continues to read in part as follows:

Authority: 15 U.S.C. 77c, 77d, 77g, 77j, 77s, 77z-2, 77z-3, 77eee, 77ggg, 77nnn, 77sss, 77ttt, 78c, 78d, 78e, 78f, 78g, 78i, 78j, 78j-1, 78k, 78k-1, 78*l*, 78m, 78n, 78o, 78p, 78q, 78s, 78u-5, 78w, 78x, 78*ll*, 78mm, 79q, 79t, 80a-20, 80a-23, 80a-29, 80a-37, 80b-3, 80b-4, 80b-11, and 7201 *et seq.*; and 18 U.S.C. 1350, unless otherwise noted.

* * * * *

13. Amend § 240.12b-23 by revising paragraphs (a)(3)(i) and (ii) and adding paragraph (a)(3)(iii) to read as follows:

§ 240.12b-23 Incorporation by reference.

* * * * *

(a) * * *

(3) * * *

(i) A proxy or information statement incorporated by reference in response to Part III of Form 10-K and Form 10-KSB (17 CFR 249.310 and 249.310b);

(ii) A form of prospectus filed pursuant to 17 CFR 230.424(b) incorporated by reference in response to Item 1 of Form 8-A (17 CFR 249.208a); and

(iii) Information filed on Form 8-K (17 CFR 249.308) need not be filed as an exhibit.

* * * * *

14. Amend § 240.13a-10 by revising Note 1 at the end of the section to read as follows:

§ 240.13a-10 Transition reports.

* * * * *

Note 1: In addition to the report or reports required to be filed pursuant to this section, every issuer, except a foreign private issuer or an investment company required to file reports pursuant to § 270.30b1-1 of this chapter, that changes its fiscal closing date is required to file a Form 8-K (§ 249.308 of this chapter) report that includes the information required by Item 5.03 of Form 8-K within the period specified in General Instruction B.1. to that form.

* * * * *

15. Amend § 240.13a-11 by adding paragraph (c) to read as follows:

§ 240.13a-11 Current reports on Form 8-K (§ 249.308 of this chapter).

* * * * *

(c) No failure to file a report on Form 8-K that is required solely pursuant to Item 1.01, 1.02, 2.03, 2.04, 2.05, 2.06 or 4.02(a) of Form 8-K shall be deemed to be a violation of 15 U.S.C. 78j(b) and § 240.10b-5.

16. Amend § 240.15d-10 by revising Note 1 at the end of the section to read as follows:

§ 240.15d-10 Transition reports.

* * * * *

Note 1: In addition to the report or reports required to be filed pursuant to this section, every issuer, except a foreign private issuer or an investment company required to file reports pursuant to § 270.30b1-1 of this chapter, that changes its fiscal closing date is required to file a Form 8-K (§ 249.308 of this chapter) report that includes the information required by Item 5.03 of Form 8-K within the period specified in General Instruction B.1. to that form.

* * * * *

17. Amend § 240.15d-11 by adding paragraph (c) to read as follows:

§ 240.15d-11 Current reports on Form 8-K (§ 249.308 of this chapter).

* * * * *

(c) No failure to file a report on Form 8-K that is required solely pursuant to Item 1.01, 1.02, 2.03, 2.04, 2.05, 2.06 or 4.02(a) of Form 8-K shall be deemed to be a violation of 15 U.S.C. 78j(b) and § 240.10b-5.

PART 249—FORMS, SECURITIES EXCHANGE ACT OF 1934

18. The authority citation for part 249 continues to read in part as follows:

Authority: 15 U.S.C. 78a *et seq.* and 7201 *et seq.;* and 18 U.S.C. 1350, unless otherwise noted.

* * * * *

19. Amend Form 8-K (referenced in § 249.308) by:

a. Adding the "check the appropriate box" paragraph directly above the General Instructions on the cover page;

b. Revising the heading for General Instruction A, designating the current text as paragraph 1 and adding paragraph 2;

c. Revising General Instruction B; and

d. Revising all of the items appearing under the caption "Information to Be Included in the Report" after the General Instructions.

The revisions and addition read as follows:

Note—The text of Form 8-K does not, and this amendment will not, appear in the Code of Federal Regulations.

Form 8-K

Current Report

Pursuant to Section 13 or 15(d) of the Securities Exchange Act of 1934

* * * * *

Check the appropriate box below if the Form 8-K filing is intended to simultaneously satisfy the filing obligation of the registrant under any of the following provisions (*see* General Instruction A.2. below):

[ ] Written communications pursuant to Rule 425 under the Securities Act (17 CFR 230.425)

[ ] Soliciting material pursuant to Rule 14a-12(b) under the Exchange Act (17 CFR 240.14a-12(b))

[ ] Pre-commencement communications pursuant to Rule 14d-2(b) under the Exchange Act (17 CFR 240.14d-2(b))

GENERAL INSTRUCTIONS

A. Rules as to Use of Form 8-K.

1. * * *

2. Form 8-K may be used by a registrant to satisfy its filing obligations pursuant to Rule 425 under the Securities Act, regarding written communications related to business combination transactions, or Rules 14a-12(b) or Rule 14d-2(b) under the Exchange Act, relating to soliciting materials and pre-commencement communications pursuant to tender offers, respectively, provided that the Form 8-K filing satisfies all the substantive requirements of those rules (other than the Rule 425(c) requirement to include certain specified information in any prospectus filed pursuant to such rule). Such filing is also deemed to be filed pursuant to any rule for which the box is checked. A registrant is not required to check the box in connection with Rule 14a-12(b) or Rule 14d-2(b) if the communication is filed pursuant to Rule 425. Communications filed pursuant to Rule 425 are deemed filed under the other applicable sections. See Note 2 to Rule 425, Rule 14a-12(b) and Instruction 2 to Rule 14d-2(b)(2).

B. Events to be Reported and Time for Filing of Reports.

1. A report on this form is required to be filed or furnished, as applicable, upon the occurrence of any one or more of the events specified in the items in Sections 1 - 6 and 9 of this form. Unless otherwise specified, a report is to be filed or furnished within four business days after occurrence of the event. If the event occurs on a Saturday, Sunday or holiday on which the Commission is not open for business, then the four business day period shall begin to run on, and include, the first business day thereafter. A registrant either furnishing a report on this form under Item 7.01 (Regulation FD Disclosure) or electing to file a report on this form under Item 8.01 (Other Events) solely to satisfy its obligations under Regulation FD (17 CFR 243.100 and 243.101) must furnish such report or make such filing, as applicable, in accordance with the requirements of Rule 100(a) of Regulation FD (17 CFR 243.100(a)), including the deadline for furnishing or filing such report.

2. The information in a report furnished pursuant to Item 2.02 (Results of Operations and Financial Condition) or Item 7.01 (Regulation FD Disclosure) shall not be deemed to be "filed" for purposes of Section 18 of the Exchange Act or otherwise subject to the liabilities of that section, unless the registrant specifically states that the information is to be considered "filed" under the Exchange Act or incorporates it by reference into a filing under the Securities Act or the Exchange Act. If a report on Form 8-K contains disclosures under Item 2.02 or Item 7.01, whether or not the report contains disclosures regarding other items, all exhibits to such report relating to Item 2.02 or Item 7.01 will be deemed furnished, and not filed, unless the registrant specifies, under Item 9.01 (Financial Statements and Exhibits), which exhibits, or portions of exhibits, are intended to be deemed filed rather than furnished pursuant to this instruction.

3. If the registrant previously has reported substantially the same information as required by this form, the registrant need not make an addi-

tional report of the information on this form. To the extent that an item calls for disclosure of developments concerning a previously reported event or transaction, any information required in the new report or amendment about the previously reported event or transaction may be provided by incorporation by reference to the previously filed report. The term *previously reported* is defined in Rule 12b-2 (17 CFR 240.12b-2).

4. Copies of agreements, amendments or other documents or instruments required to be filed pursuant to Form 8-K are not required to be filed or furnished as exhibits to the Form 8-K unless specifically required to be filed or furnished by the applicable Item. This instruction does not affect the requirement to otherwise file such agreements, amendments or other documents or instruments, including as exhibits to registration statements and periodic reports pursuant to the requirements of Item 601 of Regulation S-K or Item 601 of Regulation S-B, as applicable.

5. When considering current reporting on this form, particularly of other events of material importance pursuant to Item 7.01 (Regulation FD Disclosure) and Item 8.01(Other Events), registrants should have due regard for the accuracy, completeness and currency of the information in registration statements filed under the Securities Act which incorporate by reference information in reports filed pursuant to the Exchange Act, including reports on this form.

6. A registrant's report under Item 7.01 (Regulation FD Disclosure) or Item 8.01 (Other Events) will not be deemed an admission as to the materiality of any information in the report that is required to be disclosed solely by Regulation FD.

* * * * *

Information to Be Included in the Report

Section 1—Registrant's Business and Operations

Item 1.01 Entry into a Material Definitive Agreement.

(a) If the registrant has entered into a material definitive agreement not made in the ordinary course of business of the registrant, or into any amendment of such agreement that is material to the registrant, disclose the following information:

(1) the date on which the agreement was entered into or amended, the identity of the parties to the agreement or amendment and a brief description of any material relationship between the registrant or its affiliates and any of the parties, other than in respect of the material definitive agreement or amendment; and

(2) a brief description of the terms and conditions of the agreement or amendment that are material to the registrant.

(b) For purposes of this Item 1.01, a *material definitive agreement* means an agreement that provides for obligations that are material to and enforceable against the registrant, or rights that are material to the registrant and enforceable by the registrant against one or more other parties to the agreement, in each case whether or not subject to conditions.

Instructions.

1. Any material definitive agreement of the registrant not made in the ordinary course of the registrant's business must be disclosed under this Item 1.01. An agreement is deemed to be not made in the ordinary course of a registrant's business even if the agreement is such as ordinarily accompanies the kind of business conducted by the registrant if it involves the subject matter identified in Item 601(b)(10)(ii)(A)—(D) of Regulation S-K (17 CFR 229.601(b)(10)(ii)(A)—(D)). An agreement involving the subject matter identified in Item 601(b)(10)(iii)(A) or (B) also must be disclosed unless Item 601(b)(10)(iii)(C) would not require the registrant to file a material agreement involving the same subject matter as an exhibit.

2. A registrant must provide disclosure under this Item 1.01 if the registrant succeeds as a party to the agreement or amendment to the agreement by assumption or assignment (other than in connection with a merger or acquisition or similar transaction).

Item 1.02 Termination of a Material Definitive Agreement.

(a) If a material definitive agreement which was not made in the ordinary course of business of the registrant and to which the registrant is a party is terminated otherwise than by expiration of the agreement on its stated termination date, or as a result of all parties completing their obligations under such agreement, and such termination of the agreement is material to the registrant, disclose the following information:

(1) the date of the termination of the material definitive agreement, the identity of the parties to the agreement and a brief description of any material relationship between the registrant or its affiliates and any of the parties other than in respect of the material definitive agreement;

(2) a brief description of the terms and conditions of the agreement that are material to the registrant;

(3) a brief description of the material circumstances surrounding the termination; and

(4) any material early termination penalties incurred by the registrant.

(b) For purposes of this Item 1.02, the term *material definitive agreement* shall have the same meaning as set forth in Item 1.01(b).

Instructions.

1. No disclosure is required solely by reason of this Item 1.02 during negotiations or discussions regarding termination of a material definitive agreement unless and until the agreement has been terminated.

2. No disclosure is required solely by reason of this Item 1.02 if the registrant believes in good faith that the material definitive agreement has not been terminated, unless the registrant has received a notice of termination pursuant to the terms of agreement.

Item 1.03 Bankruptcy or Receivership.

(a) If a receiver, fiscal agent or similar officer has been appointed for a registrant or its parent, in a proceeding under the Bankruptcy Act or in any other proceeding under state or federal law in which a court or governmental authority has assumed jurisdiction over substantially all of the assets or business of the registrant or its parent, or if such jurisdiction has been assumed by leaving the existing directors and officers in possession but subject to the supervision and orders of a court or governmental authority, disclose the following information:

(1) the name or other identification of the proceeding;

(2) the identity of the court or governmental authority;

(3) the date that jurisdiction was assumed; and

(4) the identity of the receiver, fiscal agent or similar officer and the date of his or her appointment.

(b) If an order confirming a plan of reorganization, arrangement or liquidation has been entered by a court or governmental authority having supervision or jurisdiction over substantially all of the assets or business of the registrant or its parent, disclose the following;

(1) the identity of the court or governmental authority;

(2) the date that the order confirming the plan was entered by the court or governmental authority;

(3) a summary of the material features of the plan and, pursuant to Item 9.01 (Financial Statements and Exhibits), a copy of the plan as confirmed;

(4) the number of shares or other units of the registrant or its parent issued and outstanding, the number reserved for future issuance in respect of claims and interests filed and allowed under the plan, and the aggregate total of such numbers; and

(5) information as to the assets and liabilities of the registrant or its parent as of the date that the order confirming the plan was entered, or a date as close thereto as practicable.

Instruction.

The information called for in paragraph (b)(5) of this Item 1.03 may be presented in the form in which it was furnished to the court or governmental authority.

Section 2—Financial Information

Item 2.01 Completion of Acquisition or Disposition of Assets.

If the registrant or any of its majority-owned subsidiaries has completed the acquisition or disposition of a significant amount of assets, otherwise than in the ordinary course of business, disclose the following information:

(a) the date of completion of the transaction;

(b) a brief description of the assets involved;

(c) the identity of the person(s) from whom the assets were acquired or to whom they were sold and the nature of any material relationship, other than in respect of the transaction, between such person(s) and the registrant or any of its affiliates, or any director or officer of the registrant, or any associate of any such director or officer;

(d) the nature and amount of consideration given or received for the assets and, if any material relationship is disclosed pursuant to paragraph (c) of this Item 2.01, the formula or principle followed in determining the amount of such consideration; and

(e) if the transaction being reported is an acquisition and if any material relationship is disclosed pursuant to paragraph (c) of this Item 2.01, the source(s) of the funds used *unless* all or any part of the consideration used is a loan made in the ordinary course of business by a bank as defined by Section 3(a)(6) of the Act, in which case the identity of such bank may be omitted provided the registrant:

(1) has made a request for confidentiality pursuant to Section 13(d)(1)(B) of the Act; and

(2) states in the report that the identity of the bank has been so omitted and filed separately with the Commission.

Instructions.

1. No information need be given as to:

(i) any transaction between any person and any wholly-owned subsidiary of such person;

(ii) any transaction between two or more wholly-owned subsidiaries of any person; or

(iii) the redemption or other acquisition of securities from the public, or the sale or other disposition of securities to the public, by the issuer of such securities or by a wholly-owned subsidiary of that issuer.

2. The term *acquisition* includes every purchase, acquisition by lease, exchange, merger, consolidation, succession or other acquisition, except that the term does not include the construction or development of property by or for the registrant or its subsidiaries or the acquisition of materials for such purpose. The term *disposition* includes every sale, disposition by lease, exchange, merger, consolidation, mortgage, assignment or hypothecation of assets, whether for the benefit of creditors or otherwise, abandonment, destruction, or other disposition.

3. The information called for by this Item 2.01 is to be given as to each transaction or series of related transactions of the size indicated. The acquisition or disposition of securities is deemed the indirect acquisition or disposition of the assets represented by such securities if it results in the acquisition or disposition of control of such assets.

4. An acquisition or disposition shall be deemed to involve a significant amount of assets:

(i) if the registrant's and its other subsidiaries' equity in the net book value of such assets or the amount paid or received for the assets upon such acquisition or disposition exceeded 10% of the total assets of the registrant and its consolidated subsidiaries; or

(ii) if it involved a business (see 17 CFR 210.11-01(d)) that is significant (see 17 CFR 210.11-01(b)).

Acquisitions of individually insignificant businesses are not required to be reported pursuant to this Item 2.01 unless they are related businesses (see 17 CFR 210.3-05(a)(3)) and are significant in the aggregate.

5. Attention is directed to the requirements in Item 9.01 (Financial Statements and Exhibits) with respect to the filing of:

(i) financial statements of businesses acquired;

(ii) *pro forma* financial information; and

(iii) copies of the plans of acquisition or disposition as exhibits to the report.

Item 2.02 Results of Operations and Financial Condition.

(a) If a registrant, or any person acting on its behalf, makes any public announcement or release (including any update of an earlier announcement or release) disclosing material non-public information regarding the registrant's results of operations or financial condition for a completed quarterly or annual fiscal period, the registrant shall disclose the date of the announcement or release, briefly identify the announcement or release and include the text of that announcement or release as an exhibit.

(b) A Form 8-K is not required to be furnished to the Commission under this Item 2.02 in the case of disclosure of material non-public information that is disclosed orally, telephonically, by webcast, by broadcast, or by similar means if:

(1) the information is provided as part of a presentation that is complementary to, and initially occurs within 48 hours after, a related, written announcement or release that has been furnished on Form 8-K pursuant to this Item 2.02 prior to the presentation;

(2) the presentation is broadly accessible to the public by dial-in conference call, by webcast, by broadcast or by similar means;

(3) the financial and other statistical information contained in the presentation is provided on the registrant's website, together with any information that would be required under 17 CFR 244.100; and

(4) the presentation was announced by a widely disseminated press release, that included instructions as to when and how to access the presentation and the location on the registrant's website where the information would be available.

Instructions.

1. The requirements of this Item 2.02 are triggered by the disclosure of material non-public information regarding a completed fiscal year or quarter. Release of additional or updated material non-public information regarding a completed fiscal year or quarter would trigger an additional Item 2.02 requirement.

2. The requirements of paragraph (e)(1)(i) of Item 10 of Regulation S-K (17 CFR 229.10(e)(1)(i)) (or paragraph (h)(1)(i) of Item 10 of Regulation S-B (17 CFR 228.10(h)(1)(i)) in the case of a small business issuer) shall apply to disclosures under this Item 2.02.

3. Issuers that make earnings announcements or other disclosures of material non-public information regarding a completed fiscal year or quarter in an interim or annual report to shareholders are permitted to specify which portion of the report contains the information required to be furnished under this Item 2.02.

4. This Item 2.02 does not apply in the case of a disclosure that is made in a quarterly report filed with the Commission on Form 10-Q (17 CFR 249.308a) (or Form 10-QSB (17 CFR 249.308b)) or an annual report filed with the Commission on Form 10-K (17 CFR 249.310) (or Form 10-KSB (17 CFR 249.310b)).

Item 2.03 Creation of a Direct Financial Obligation or an Obligation under an Off-Balance Sheet Arrangement of a Registrant.

(a) If the registrant becomes obligated on a direct financial obligation that is material to the registrant, disclose the following information:

(1) the date on which the registrant becomes obligated on the direct financial obligation and a brief description of the transaction or agreement creating the obligation;

(2) the amount of the obligation, including the terms of its payment and, if applicable, a brief description of the material terms under which it may be accelerated or increased and the nature of any recourse provisions that would enable the registrant to recover from third parties; and

(3) a brief description of the other terms and conditions of the transaction or agreement that are material to the registrant.

(b) If the registrant becomes directly or contingently liable for an obligation that is material to the registrant arising out of an off-balance sheet arrangement, disclose the following information:

(1) the date on which the registrant becomes directly or contingently liable on the obligation and a brief description of the transaction or agreement creating the arrangement and obligation;

(2) a brief description of the nature and amount of the obligation of the registrant under the arrangement, including the material terms whereby it may become a direct obligation, if applicable, or may be accelerated or increased and the nature of any recourse provisions that would enable the registrant to recover from third parties;

(3) the maximum potential amount of future payments (undiscounted) that the registrant may be required to make, if different; and

(4) a brief description of the other terms and conditions of the obligation or arrangement that are material to the registrant.

(c) For purposes of this Item 2.03, *direct financial obligation* means any of the following:

(1) a long-term debt obligation, as defined in Item 303(a)(5)(ii)(A) of Regulation S-K (17 CFR 229.303(a)(5)(ii)(A));

(2) a capital lease obligation, as defined in Item 303(a)(5)(ii)(B) of Regulation S-K (17 CFR 229.303(a)(5)(ii)(B));

(3) an operating lease obligation, as defined in Item 303(a)(5)(ii)(C) of Regulation S-K (17 CFR 229.303(a)(5)(ii)(C)); or

(4) a short-term debt obligation that arises other than in the ordinary course of business.

(d) For purposes of this Item 2.03, *off-balance sheet arrangement* has the meaning set forth in Item 303(a)(4)(ii) of Regulation S-K (17 CFR 229.303(a)(4)(ii)) or Item 303(c)(2) of Regulation S-B (17 CFR 228.303(c)(2)), as applicable.

(e) For purposes of this Item 2.03, *short-term debt obligation* means a payment obligation under a borrowing arrangement that is scheduled to mature within one year, or, for those registrants that use the operating cycle concept of working capital, within a registrant's operating cycle that is longer than one year, as discussed in Accounting Research Bulletin No. 43, Chapter 3A, *Working Capital.*

Instructions.

1. A registrant has no obligation to disclose information under this Item 2.03 until the registrant enters into an agreement enforceable against the registrant, whether or not subject to conditions, under which the direct financial obligation will arise or be created or issued. If there is no such agreement, the registrant must provide the disclosure within four business days after the occurrence of the closing or settlement of the transaction or arrangement under which the direct financial obligation arises or is created.

2. A registrant must provide the disclosure required by paragraph (b) of this Item 2.03 whether or not the registrant is also a party to the transaction or agreement creating the contingent obligation arising under the off-balance sheet arrangement. In the event that neither the registrant nor any affiliate of the registrant is also a party to the transaction or agreement creating the contingent obligation arising under the off-balance sheet arrangement in question, the four business day period for reporting the event under this Item 2.03 shall begin on the earlier of (i) the fourth business day after the contingent obligation is created or arises, and (ii) the day on which an executive officer, as defined in 17 CFR 240.3b-7, of the registrant becomes aware of the contingent obligation.

3. In the event that an agreement, transaction or arrangement requiring disclosure under this Item 2.03 comprises a facility, program or similar arrangement that creates or may give rise to direct financial obligations of the registrant in connection with multiple transactions, the registrant shall:

(i) disclose the entering into of the facility, program or similar arrangement if the entering into of the facility is material to the registrant; and

(ii) as direct financial obligations arise or are created under the facility or program, disclose the required information under this Item 2.03 to the extent that the obligations are material to the registrant (including when a series of previously undisclosed individually immaterial obligations become material in the aggregate).

4. For purposes of Item 2.03(b)(3), the maximum amount of future payments shall not be reduced by the effect of any amounts that may possibly be recovered by the registrant under re-

course or collateralization provisions in any guarantee agreement, transaction or arrangement.

5. If the obligation required to be disclosed under this Item 2.03 is a security, or a term of a security, that has been or will be sold pursuant to an effective registration statement of the registrant, the registrant is not required to file a Form 8-K pursuant to this Item 2.03, *provided* that the prospectus relating to that sale contains the information required by this Item 2.03 and is filed within the required time period under Securities Act Rule 424 (§ 230.424 of this chapter).

Item 2.04 Triggering Events That Accelerate or Increase a Direct Financial Obligation or an Obligation under an Off-Balance Sheet Arrangement.

(a) If a triggering event causing the increase or acceleration of a direct financial obligation of the registrant occurs and the consequences of the event, taking into account those described in paragraph (a)(4) of this Item 2.04, are material to the registrant, disclose the following information:

(1) the date of the triggering event and a brief description of the agreement or transaction under which the direct financial obligation was created and is increased or accelerated;

(2) a brief description of the triggering event;

(3) the amount of the direct financial obligation, as increased if applicable, and the terms of payment or acceleration that apply; and

(4) any other material obligations of the registrant that may arise, increase, be accelerated or become direct financial obligations as a result of the triggering event or the increase or acceleration of the direct financial obligation.

(b) If a triggering event occurs causing an obligation of the registrant under an off-balance sheet arrangement to increase or be accelerated, or causing a contingent obligation of the registrant under an off-balance sheet arrangement to become a direct financial obligation of the registrant, and the consequences of the event, taking into account those described in paragraph (b)(4) of this Item 2.04, are material to the registrant, disclose the following information:

(1) the date of the triggering event and a brief description of the off-balance sheet arrangement;

(2) a brief description of the triggering event;

(3) the nature and amount of the obligation, as increased if applicable, and the terms of payment or acceleration that apply; and

(4) any other material obligations of the registrant that may arise, increase, be accelerated or become direct financial obligations as a result of the triggering event or the increase or acceleration of the obligation under the off-balance sheet arrangement or its becoming a direct financial obligation of the registrant.

(c) For purposes of this Item 2.04, the term *direct financial obligation* has the meaning provided in Item 2.03 of this form, but shall also include an obligation arising out of an off-balance sheet arrangement that is accrued under FASB Statement of Financial Accounting Standards No. 5 *Accounting for Contingencies* (SFAS No. 5) as a probable loss contingency.

(d) For purposes of this Item 2.04, the term *off-balance sheet arrangement* has the meaning provided in Item 2.03 of this form.

(e) For purposes of this Item 2.04, a *triggering event* is an event, including an event of default, event of acceleration or similar event, as a result of which a direct financial obligation of the registrant or an obligation of the registrant arising under an off-balance sheet arrangement is increased or becomes accelerated or as a result of which a contingent obligation of the registrant arising out of an off-balance sheet arrangement becomes a direct financial obligation of the registrant.

Instructions.

1. Disclosure is required if a triggering event occurs in respect of an obligation of the registrant under an off-balance sheet arrangement and the consequences are material to the registrant, whether or not the registrant is also a party to the transaction or agreement under which the triggering event occurs.

2. No disclosure is required under this Item 2.04 unless and until a triggering event has occurred in accordance with the terms of the relevant agreement, transaction or arrangement, including, if required, the sending to the registrant of notice of the occurrence of a triggering event pursuant to the terms of the agreement, transaction or arrangement and the satisfaction of all conditions to such occurrence, except the passage of time.

3. No disclosure is required solely by reason of this Item 2.04 if the registrant believes in good faith that no triggering event has occurred, unless the registrant has received a notice described in Instruction 2 to this Item 2.04.

4. Where a registrant is subject to an obligation arising out of an off-balance sheet arrangement, whether or not disclosed pursuant to Item 2.03 of this form, if a triggering event occurs as a result of which under that obligation an accrual for a probable loss is required under SFAS No. 5, the obligation arising out of the off-balance sheet arrangement becomes a direct financial obligation as defined in this Item 2.04. In that situation, if the consequences as determined under Item

2.04(b) are material to the registrant, disclosure is required under this Item 2.04.

Item 2.05 Costs Associated with Exit or Disposal Activities.

If the registrant's board of directors, a committee of the board of directors or the officer or officers of the registrant authorized to take such action if board action is not required, commits the registrant to an exit or disposal plan, or otherwise disposes of a long-lived asset or terminates employees under a plan of termination described in paragraph 8 of FASB Statement of Financial Accounting Standards No. 146 *Accounting for Costs Associated with Exit or Disposal Activities* (SFAS No. 146), under which material charges will be incurred under generally accepted accounting principles applicable to the registrant, disclose the following information:

(a) the date of the commitment to the course of action and a description of the course of action, including the facts and circumstances leading to the expected action and the expected completion date;

(b) for each major type of cost associated with the course of action (for example, one-time termination benefits, contract termination costs and other associated costs), an estimate of the total amount or range of amounts expected to be incurred in connection with the action;

(c) an estimate of the total amount or range of amounts expected to be incurred in connection with the action; and

(d) the registrant's estimate of the amount or range of amounts of the charge that will result in future cash expenditures, *provided, however*, that if the registrant determines that at the time of filing it is unable in good faith to make a determination of an estimate required by paragraphs (b), (c) or (d) of this Item 2.05, no disclosure of such estimate shall be required; *provided further, however*, that in any such event, the registrant shall file an amended report on Form 8-K under this Item 2.05 within four business days after it makes a determination of such an estimate or range of estimates.

Item 2.06 Material Impairments.

If the registrant's board of directors, a committee of the board of directors or the officer or officers of the registrant authorized to take such action if board action is not required, concludes that a material charge for impairment to one or more of its assets, including, without limitation, impairments of securities or goodwill, is required under generally accepted accounting principles applicable to the registrant, disclose the following information:

(a) the date of the conclusion that a material charge is required and a description of the impaired asset or assets and the facts and circumstances leading to the conclusion that the charge for impairment is required;

(b) the registrant's estimate of the amount or range of amounts of the impairment charge; and

(c) the registrant's estimate of the amount or range of amounts of the impairment charge that will result in future cash expenditures, *provided, however*, that if the registrant determines that at the time of filing it is unable in good faith to make a determination of an estimate required by paragraphs (b) or (c) of this Item 2.06, no disclosure of such estimate shall be required; *provided further, however*, that in any such event, the registrant shall file an amended report on Form 8-K under this Item 2.06 within four business days after it makes a determination of such an estimate or range of estimates.

Instruction.

No filing is required under this Item 2.06 if the conclusion is made in connection with the preparation, review or audit of financial statements required to be included in the next periodic report due to be filed under the Exchange Act, the periodic report is filed on a timely basis and such conclusion is disclosed in the report.

Section 3—Securities and Trading Markets

Item 3.01 Notice of Delisting or Failure to Satisfy a Continued Listing Rule or Standard; Transfer of Listing.

(a) If the registrant has received notice from the national securities exchange or national securities association (or a facility thereof) that maintains the principal listing for any class of the registrant's common equity (as defined in Exchange Act Rule 12b-2 (17 CFR 240.12b-2)) that:

- the registrant or such class of the registrant's securities does not satisfy a rule or standard for continued listing on the exchange or association;
- the exchange has submitted an application under Exchange Act Rule 12d2-2 (17 CFR 240.12d2-2) to the Commission to delist such class of the registrant's securities; or
- the association has taken all necessary steps under its rules to delist the security from its automated inter-dealer quotation system, the registrant must disclose:

(i) the date that the registrant received the notice;

(ii) the a rule or standard for continued listing on the national securities exchange or national securities association that the registrant fails, or has failed to, satisfy; and

(iii) any action or response that, at the time of filing, the registrant has determined to take in response to the notice.

(b) If the registrant has notified the national securities exchange or national securities association (or a facility thereof) that maintains the principal listing for any class of the registrant's common equity (as defined in Exchange Act Rule 12b-2 (17 CFR 240.12b-2) that the registrant is aware of any material noncompliance with a rule or standard for continued listing on the exchange or association, the registrant must disclose:

(i) the date that the registrant provided such notice to the exchange or association;

(ii) the rule or standard for continued listing on the exchange or association that the registrant fails, or has failed, to satisfy; and

(iii) any action or response that, at the time of filing, the registrant has determined to take regarding its noncompliance.

(c) If the national securities exchange or national securities association (or a facility thereof) that maintains the principal listing for any class of the registrant's common equity (as defined in Exchange Act Rule 12b-2 (17 CFR 240.12b-2)), in lieu of suspending trading in or delisting such class of the registrant's securities, issues a public reprimand letter or similar communication indicating that the registrant has violated a rule or standard for continued listing on the exchange or association, the registrant must state the date, and summarize the contents of the letter or communication.

(d) If the registrant's board of directors, a committee of the board of directors or the officer or officers of the registrant authorized to take such action if board action is not required, has taken definitive action to cause the listing of a class of its common equity to be withdrawn from the national securities exchange, or terminated from the automated inter-dealer quotation system of a registered national securities association, where such exchange or association maintains the principal listing for such class of securities, including by reason of a transfer of the listing or quotation to another securities exchange or quotation system, describe the action taken and state the date of the action.

Instructions.

1. The registrant is not required to disclose any information required by paragraph (a) of this Item 3.01 where the delisting is a result of one of the following:

- the entire class of the security has been called for redemption, maturity or retirement; appropriate notice thereof has been given; if required by the terms of the securities, funds sufficient for the payment of all such securities have been deposited with an agency authorized to make such payments; and such funds have been made available to security holders;
- the entire class of the security has been redeemed or paid at maturity or retirement;
- the instruments representing the entire class of securities have come to evidence, by operation of law or otherwise, other securities in substitution therefor and represent no other right, except, if true, the right to receive an immediate cash payment (the right of dissenters to receive the appraised or fair value of their holdings shall not prevent the application of this provision); or
- all rights pertaining to the entire class of the security have been extinguished; *provided, however,* that where such an event occurs as the result of an order of a court or other governmental authority, the order shall be final, all applicable appeal periods shall have expired and no appeals shall be pending.

2. A registrant must provide the disclosure required by paragraph (a) or (b) of this Item 3.01, as applicable, regarding any failure to satisfy a rule or standard for continued listing on the national securities exchange or national securities association (or a facility thereof) that maintains the principal listing for any class of the registrant's common equity (as defined in Exchange Act Rule 12b-2 (17 CFR 240.12b-2)) even if the registrant has the benefit of a grace period or similar extension period during which it may cure the deficiency that triggers the disclosure requirement.

3. Notices or other communications subsequent to an initial notice sent to, or by, a registrant under Item 3.01(a), (b) or (c) that continue to indicate that the registrant does not comply with the same rule or standard for continued listing that was the subject of the initial notice are not required to be filed, but may be filed voluntarily.

4. Registrants whose securities are quoted exclusively (i.e., the securities are not otherwise listed on an exchange or association) on automated inter-dealer quotation systems are not subject to this Item 3.01 and such registrants are thus not required to file a Form 8-K pursuant to this Item 3.01 if the securities are no longer quoted on such quotation system. If a security is listed on an exchange or association and is also quoted on an automated inter-dealer quotation system, the registrant is subject to the disclosure obligations of Item 3.01 if any of the events specified in Item 3.01 occur.

Item 3.02 Unregistered Sales of Equity Securities.

(a) If the registrant sells equity securities in a transaction that is not registered under the Securities Act, furnish the information set forth in paragraphs (a) and (c) through (e) of Item 701 of Regulation S-K or Regulation S-B, as applicable (17 CFR 229.701(a) and (c) through (e) and

228.701(a) and (c) through (e), respectively). For purposes of determining the required filing date for the Form 8-K under this Item 3.02(a), the registrant has no obligation to disclose information under this Item 3.02 until the registrant enters into an agreement enforceable against the registrant, whether or not subject to conditions, under which the equity securities are to be sold. If there is no such agreement, the registrant must provide the disclosure within four business days after the occurrence of the closing or settlement of the transaction or arrangement under which the equity securities are to be sold.

(b) No report need be filed under this Item 3.02 if the equity securities sold, in the aggregate since its last report filed under this Item 3.02 or its last periodic report, whichever is more recent, constitute less than 1% of the number of shares outstanding of the class of equity securities sold. In the case of a small business issuer, no report need be filed if the equity securities sold, in the aggregate since its last report filed under this Item 3.02 or its last periodic report, whichever is more recent, constitute less than 5% of the number of shares outstanding of the class of equity securities sold.

Instructions.

1. For purposes of this Item 3.02, "the number of shares outstanding" refers to the actual number of shares of equity securities of the class outstanding and does not include outstanding securities convertible into or exchangeable for such equity securities.

2. Small business issuer is defined under Item 10(a)(1) of Regulation S-B (17 CFR 228.10(a)(1)).

Item 3.03 Material Modification to Rights of Security Holders.

(a) If the constituent instruments defining the rights of the holders of any class of registered securities of the registrant have been materially modified, disclose the date of the modification, the title of the class of securities involved and briefly describe the general effect of such modification upon the rights of holders of such securities.

(b) If the rights evidenced by any class of registered securities have been materially limited or qualified by the issuance or modification of any other class of securities by the registrant, briefly disclose the date of the issuance or modification, the general effect of the issuance or modification of such other class of securities upon the rights of the holders of the registered securities.

Instruction.

Working capital restrictions and other limitations upon the payment of dividends must be reported pursuant to this Item 3.03.

Section 4—Matters Related to Accountants and Financial Statements

Item 4.01 Changes in Registrant's Certifying Accountant.

(a) If an independent accountant who was previously engaged as the principal accountant to audit the registrant's financial statements, or an independent accountant upon whom the principal accountant expressed reliance in its report regarding a significant subsidiary, resigns (or indicates that it declines to stand for re-appointment after completion of the current audit) or is dismissed, disclose the information required by Item 304(a)(1) of Regulation S-K or Item 304(a)(1) of Regulation S-B, as applicable, including compliance with Item 304(a)(3) of Regulation S-K or Item 304(a)(3) of Regulation S-B (17 CFR 229.304(a)(1) and (a)(3) or 228.304(a)(1) and (a)(3), respectively).

(b) If a new independent accountant has been engaged as either the principal accountant to audit the registrant's financial statements or as an independent accountant on whom the principal accountant is expected to express reliance in its report regarding a significant subsidiary, the registrant must disclose the information required by Item 304(a)(2) of Regulation S-K or Item 304(a)(2) of Regulation S-B, as applicable (17 CFR 229.304(a)(2) or 228.304(a)(2), respectively).

Instruction.

The resignation or dismissal of an independent accountant, or its refusal to stand for re-appointment, is a reportable event separate from the engagement of a new independent accountant. On some occasions, two reports on Form 8-K are required for a single change in accountants, the first on the resignation (or refusal to stand for re-appointment) or dismissal of the former accountant and the second when the new accountant is engaged. Information required in the second Form 8-K in such situations need not be provided to the extent that it has been reported previously in the first Form 8-K.

Item 4.02 Non-Reliance on Previously Issued Financial Statements or a Related Audit Report or Completed Interim Review.

(a) If the registrant's board of directors, a committee of the board of directors or the officer or officers of the registrant authorized to take such action if board action is not required, concludes that any previously issued financial statements, covering one or more years or interim periods for which the registrant is required to provide financial statements under Regulation S-X (17 CFR 210) or Regulation S-B (17 CFR 228), should no longer be relied upon because of an error in such financial statements as addressed in Accounting

Principles Board Opinion No. 20, as may be modified, supplemented or succeeded, disclose the following information:

(1) the date of the conclusion regarding the non-reliance and an identification of the financial statements and years or periods covered that should no longer be relied upon;

(2) a brief description of the facts underlying the conclusion to the extent known to the registrant at the time of filing; and

(3) a statement of whether the audit committee, or the board of directors in the absence of an audit committee, or authorized officer or officers, discussed with the registrant's independent accountant the matters disclosed in the filing pursuant to this Item 4.02(a).

(b) If the registrant is advised by, or receives notice from, its independent accountant that disclosure should be made or action should be taken to prevent future reliance on a previously issued audit report or completed interim review related to previously issued financial statements, disclose the following information:

(1) the date on which the registrant was so advised or notified;

(2) identification of the financial statements that should no longer be relied upon;

(3) a brief description of the information provided by the accountant; and

(4) a statement of whether the audit committee, or the board of directors in the absence of an audit committee, or authorized officer or officers, discussed with the independent accountant the matters disclosed in the filing pursuant to this Item 4.02(b).

(c) If the registrant receives advisement or notice from its independent accountant requiring disclosure under paragraph (b) of this Item 4.02, the registrant must:

(1) provide the independent accountant with a copy of the disclosures it is making in response to this Item 4.02 that the independent accountant shall receive no later than the day that the disclosures are filed with the Commission;

(2) request the independent accountant to furnish to the registrant as promptly as possible a letter addressed to the Commission stating whether the independent accountant agrees with the statements made by the registrant in response to this Item 4.02 and, if not, stating the respects in which it does not agree; and

(3) amend the registrant's previously filed Form 8-K by filing the independent accountant's letter as an exhibit to the filed Form 8-K no later than two business days after the registrant's receipt of the letter.

Section 5—Corporate Governance and Management

Item 5.01 Changes in Control of Registrant.

(a) If, to the knowledge of the registrant's board of directors, a committee of the board of directors or authorized officer or officers of the registrant, a change in control of the registrant has occurred, furnish the following information:

(1) the identity of the person(s) who acquired such control;

(2) the date and a description of the transaction(s) which resulted in the change in control;

(3) the basis of the control, including the percentage of voting securities of the registrant now beneficially owned directly or indirectly by the person(s) who acquired control;

(4) the amount of the consideration used by such person(s);

(5) the source(s) of funds used by the person(s), *unless* all or any part of the consideration used is a loan made in the ordinary course of business by a bank as defined by Section 3(a)(6) of the Act, in which case the identity of such bank may be omitted provided the person who acquired control:

(1) has made a request for confidentiality pursuant to Section 13(d)(1)(B) of the Act; and

(2) states in the report that the identity of the bank has been so omitted and filed separately with the Commission.

(6) the identity of the person(s) from whom control was assumed; and

(7) any arrangements or understandings among members of both the former and new control groups and their associates with respect to election of directors or other matters.

(b) Furnish the information required by Item 403(c) of Regulation S-K (17 CFR 229.403(c)) or Item 403(c) of Regulation S-B (17 CFR 228.403(c)), as applicable.

Item 5.02 Departure of Directors or Principal Officers; Election of Directors; Appointment of Principal Officers.

(a)(1) If a director has resigned or refuses to stand for re-election to the board of directors since the date of the last annual meeting of shareholders because of a disagreement with the registrant, known to an executive officer of the registrant, as defined in 17 CFR 240.3b-7, on any matter relating to the registrant's operations, policies or practices, or if a director has been removed for cause from the board of directors, disclose the following information:

(i) the date of such resignation, refusal to stand for re-election or removal;

(ii) any positions held by the director on any committee of the board of directors at the time of the director's resignation, refusal to stand for re-election or removal; and

(iii) a brief description of the circumstances representing the disagreement that the registrant believes caused, in whole or in part, the director's resignation, refusal to stand for re-election or removal.

(2) If the director has furnished the registrant with any written correspondence concerning the circumstances surrounding his or her resignation, refusal or removal, the registrant shall file a copy of the document as an exhibit to the report on Form 8-K.

(3) The registrant also must:

(i) provide the director with a copy of the disclosures it is making in response to this Item 5.02 no later than the day the registrant file the disclosures with the Commission;

(ii) provide the director with the opportunity to furnish the registrant as promptly as possible with a letter addressed to the registrant stating whether he or she agrees with the statements made by the registrant in response to this Item 5.02 and, if not, stating the respects in which he or she does not agree; and

(iii) file any letter received by the registrant from the director with the Commission as an exhibit by an amendment to the previously filed Form 8-K within two business days after receipt by the registrant.

(b) If the registrant's principal executive officer, president, principal financial officer, principal accounting officer, principal operating officer or any person performing similar functions retires, resigns or is terminated from that position, or if a director retires, resigns, is removed, or refuses to stand for re-election (except in circumstances described in paragraph (a) of this Item 5.02), disclose the fact that the event has occurred and the date of the event.

(c) If the registrant appoints a new principal executive officer, president, principal financial officer, principal accounting officer, principal operating officer or person performing similar functions, disclose the following information with respect to the newly appointed officer:

(1) the name and position of the newly appointed officer and the date of the appointment;

(2) the information required by Items 401(b), (d), (e) and Item 404(a) of Regulation S-K (17 CFR 229.401(b), (d), (e) and 229.404(a)), or, in the case of a small business issuer, Items 401(a)(4), (a)(5), (c), and Items 404(a) and (b) of Regulation S-B (17 CFR 228.401(a)(4), (a)(5), (c), and 228.404(a) and (b), respectively); and

(3) a brief description of the material terms of any employment agreement between the registrant and that officer.

Instruction to paragraph (c).

If the registrant intends to make a public announcement of the appointment other than by means of a report on Form 8-K, the registrant may delay filing the Form 8-K containing the disclosures required by this Item 5.02(c) until the day on which the registrant otherwise makes public announcement of the appointment of such officer.

(d) If the registrant elects a new director, except by a vote of security holders at an annual meeting or special meeting convened for such purpose, disclose the following information:

(1) the name of the newly elected director and the date of election;

(2) a brief description of any arrangement or understanding between the new director and any other persons, naming such persons, pursuant to which such director was selected as a director;

(3) the committees of the board of directors to which the new director has been, or at the time of this disclosure is expected to be, named; and

(4) the information required by Item 404(a) of Regulation S-K or Item 404(a) of Regulation S-B, as applicable (17 CFR 229.404(a) or 228.404(a), respectively).

Instructions to Item 5.02.

1. The disclosure requirements of this Item 5.02 do not apply to a registrant that is a wholly-owned subsidiary of an issuer with a class of securities registered under Section 12 of the Exchange Act (15 U.S.C. 78l), or that is required to file reports under Section 15(d) of the Exchange Act (15 U.S.C. 78o(d)).

2. To the extent that any information called for in Item 5.02(c)(3) or Item 5.02(d)(3) or Item 5.02(d)(4) is not determined or is unavailable at the time of the required filing, the registrant shall include a statement this effect in the filing and then must file an amendment to its Form 8-K filing under this Item 5.02 containing such information within four business days after the information is determined or becomes available.

Item 5.03 Amendments to Articles of Incorporation or Bylaws; Change in Fiscal Year.

(a) If a registrant with a class of equity securities registered under Section 12 of the Exchange Act (15 U.S.C. 78l) amends its articles of incorporation or bylaws and a proposal for the amendment was not disclosed in a proxy statement or information statement filed by the registrant, disclose the following information:

(1) the effective date of the amendment; and

(2) a description of the provision adopted or changed by amendment and, if applicable, the previous provision.

(b) If the registrant determines to change the fiscal year from that used in its most recent filing with the Commission other than by means of:

(1) a submission to a vote of security holders through the solicitation of proxies or otherwise; or

(2) an amendment to its articles of incorporation or bylaws, disclose the date of such determination, the date of the new fiscal year end and the form (for example, Form 10-K, Form 10-KSB, Form 10-Q or Form 10-QSB) on which the report covering the transition period will be filed.

Instruction to Item 5.03.

Refer to Item 601(b)(3) of Regulation S-K or Regulation S-B (17 CFR 229.601(b)(3) and 228.601(b)(3)), as applicable, regarding the filing of exhibits to this Item 5.03.

Item 5.04 Temporary Suspension of Trading Under Registrant's Employee Benefit Plans.

(a) No later than the fourth business day after which the registrant receives the notice required by section 101(i)(2)(E) of the Employment Retirement Income Security Act of 1974 (29 U.S.C. 1021(i)(2)(E)), or, if such notice is not received by the registrant, on the same date by which the registrant transmits a timely notice to an affected officer or director within the time period prescribed by Rule 104(b)(2)(i)(B) or 104(b)(2)(ii) of Regulation BTR (17 CFR 245.104(b)(2)(i)(B) or 17 CFR 245.104(b)(2)(ii)), provide the information specified in Rule 104(b) (17 CFR 245.104(b)) and the date the registrant received the notice required by section 101(i)(2)(E) of the Employment Retirement Income Security Act of 1974 (29 U.S.C. 1021(i)(2)(E)), if applicable.

(b) On the same date by which the registrant transmits a timely updated notice to an affected officer or director, as required by the time period under Rule 104(b)(2)(iii) of Regulation BTR (17 CFR 245.104(b)(2)(iii)), provide the information specified in Rule 104(b)(3)(iii) (17 CFR 245.104(b)(2)(iii)).

Item 5.05 Amendments to the Registrant's Code of Ethics, or Waiver of a Provision of the Code of Ethics.

(a) Briefly describe the date and nature of any amendment to a provision of the registrant's code of ethics that applies to the registrant's principal executive officer, principal financial officer, principal accounting officer or controller or persons performing similar functions and that relates to any element of the code of ethics definition enumerated in Item 406(b) of Regulations S-K and S-B (17 CFR 229.406(b) and 228.406(b), respectively).

(b) If the registrant has granted a waiver, including an implicit waiver, from a provision of the code of ethics to an officer or person described in paragraph (a) of this Item 5.05, and the waiver relates to one or more of the elements of the code of ethics definition referred to in paragraph (a) of this Item 5.05, briefly describe the nature of the waiver, the name of the person to whom the waiver was granted, and the date of the waiver.

(c) The registrant does not need to provide any information pursuant to this Item 5.05 if it discloses the required information on its Internet website within four business days following the date of the amendment or waiver and the registrant has disclosed in its most recently filed annual report its Internet address and intention to provide disclosure in this manner. If the registrant elects to disclose the information required by this Item 5.05 through its website, such information must remain available on the website for at least a 12-month period. Following the 12-month period, the registrant must retain the information for a period of not less than five years. Upon request, the registrant must furnish to the Commission or its staff a copy of any or all information retained pursuant to this requirement.

Instructions.

1. The registrant does not need to disclose technical, administrative or other non-substantive amendments to its code of ethics.

2. For purposes of this Item 5.05:

(i) The term *waiver* means the approval by the registrant of a material departure from a provision of the code of ethics; and

(ii) The term *implicit waiver* means the registrant's failure to take action within a reasonable period of time regarding a material departure from a provision of the code of ethics that has been made known to an executive officer, as defined in Rule 3b-7 (17 CFR 240.3b-7) of the registrant.

Section 6—[Reserved]

Section 7—Regulation FD

Item 7.01 Regulation FD Disclosure.

Unless filed under Item 8.01, disclose under this item only information that the registrant elects to disclose through Form 8-K pursuant to Regulation FD (17 CFR 243.100 through 243.103).

Section 8—Other Events

Item 8.01 Other Events.

The registrant may, at its option, disclose under this Item 8.01 any events, with respect to which information is not otherwise called for by this form, that the registrant deems of importance to security holders. The registrant may, at its option, file a report under this Item 8.01 disclosing the nonpublic information required to be disclosed by Regulation FD (17 CFR 243.100 through 243.103).

Section 9—Financial Statements and Exhibits

Item 9.01 Financial Statements and Exhibits.

List below the financial statements, pro forma financial information and exhibits, if any, filed as a part of this report.

(a) *Financial statements of businesses acquired.*

(1) For any business acquisition required to be described in answer to Item 2.01 of this form, financial statements of the business acquired shall be filed for the periods specified in Rule 3-05(b) of Regulation S-X (17 CFR 210.3-05(b)).

(2) The financial statements shall be prepared pursuant to Regulation S-X except that supporting schedules need not be filed. A manually signed accountant's report should be provided pursuant to Rule 2-02 of Regulation S-X (17 CFR 210.2-02).

(3) With regard to the acquisition of one or more real estate properties, the financial statements and any additional information specified by Rule 3-14 of Regulation S-X (17 CFR 210.3-14) shall be filed.

(4) Financial statements required by this item may be filed with the initial report, or by amendment not later than 71 calendar days after the date that the initial report on Form 8-K must be filed. If the financial statements are not included in the initial report, the registrant should so indicate in the Form 8-K report and state when the required financial statements will be filed. The registrant may, at its option, include unaudited financial statements in the initial report on Form 8-K.

(b) *Pro forma financial information.*

(1) For any transaction required to be described in answer to Item 2.01 of this form, furnish any pro forma financial information that would be required pursuant to Article 11 of Regulation S-X (17 CFR 210).

(2) The provisions of paragraph (a)(4) of this Item 9.01 shall also apply to pro forma financial information relative to the acquired business.

(c) *Exhibits.* The exhibits shall be deemed to be filed or furnished, depending on the relevant item requiring such exhibit, in accordance with the provisions of Item 601 of Regulation S-K (17 CFR 229.601), or Item 601 of Regulation S-B (17 CFR 228.601) and Instruction B.2 to this form.

Instruction.

During the period after a registrant has reported a business combination pursuant to Item 2.01 of this form, until the date on which the financial statements specified by this Item 9.01 must be filed, the registrant will be deemed current for purposes of its reporting obligations under Section 13(a) or 15(d) of the Exchange Act (15 U.S.C. 78m or 78o(d)). With respect to filings under the Securities Act, however, registration statements will not be declared effective and post-effective amendments to registrations statements will not be declared effective unless financial statements meeting the requirements of Rule 3-05 of Regulation S-X (17 CFR 210.3-05) are provided. In addition, offerings should not be made pursuant to effective registration statements, or pursuant to Rules 505 and 506 of Regulation D (17 CFR 230.505 and 230.506) where any purchasers are not accredited investors under Rule 501(a) of that Regulation, until the audited financial statements required by Rule 3-05 of Regulation S-X (17 CFR 210.3-05) are filed; *provided, however,* that the following offerings or sales of securities may proceed notwithstanding that financial statements of the acquired business have not been filed:

(a) offerings or sales of securities upon the conversion of outstanding convertible securities or upon the exercise of outstanding warrants or rights;

(b) dividend or interest reinvestment plans;

(c) employee benefit plans;

(d) transactions involving secondary offerings; or

(e) sales of securities pursuant to Rule 144 (17 CFR 230.144).

* * * * *

20. Amend Form 10-Q (referenced in § 249.308a) by:

a. Revising the heading for Item 2 in Part II—Other Information;

b. Removing Items 2(a), 2(b) and 6(b);

c. Redesignating paragraphs (c), (d) and (e) in Item 2 as paragraphs (a), (b) and (c);

d. Revising newly redesignated paragraph (a) in Item 2;

e. Revising the Instructions to Item 3;

f. Revising Item 5;

g. Removing the words "and Reports on Form 8-K (§ 249.308 of this chapter)" from the heading of Item 6; and

h. Removing the paragraph (a) designation in Item 6.

The revisions read as follows:

Note—The text of Form 10-Q does not, and this amendment will not, appear in the Code of Federal Regulations.

Form 10-Q

* * * * *

PART II—OTHER INFORMATION

* * * * *

Item 2. Unregistered Sales of Equity Securities and Use of Proceeds.

(a) Furnish the information required by Item 701 of Regulation S-K (17 CFR 229.701) as to all equity securities of the registrant sold by the registrant during the period covered by the report that were not registered under the Securities Act. If the Item 701 information previously has been included in a Current Report on Form 8-K (17 CFR 249.308), however, it need not be furnished.

* * * * *

Item 3. Defaults Upon Senior Securities.

* * * * *

Instructions to Item 3

1. Item 3 need not be answered as to any default or arrearage with respect to any class of securities all of which is held by or for the account of the registrant or its totally held subsidiaries.

2. The information required by Item 3 need not be made if previously disclosed on a report on Form 8-K (17 CFR 249.308).

* * * * *

Item 5. Other Information.

The registrant must disclose under this item any information required to be disclosed in a report on Form 8-K during the period covered by this Form 10-Q, but not reported, whether or not otherwise required by this Form 10-Q. If disclosure of such information is made under this item, it need not be repeated in a report on Form 8-K which would otherwise be required to be filed with respect to such information or in a subsequent report on Form 10-Q.

* * * * *

21. Amend Form 10-QSB (referenced in § 249.308b) by:

a. Revising the heading for Item 2 in Part II—Other Information;

b. Removing Items 2(a), 2(b) and 6(b);

c. Redesignating paragraphs (c), (d) and (e) in Item 2 as paragraphs (a), (b) and (c);

d. Revising newly redesignated paragraph (a) in Item 2;

e. Revising the Instructions to Item 3;

f. Revising Item 5;

g. Removing the words "and Reports on Form 8-K" from the heading of Item 6; and

h. Removing the paragraph (a) designation in Item 6.

The revisions read as follows:

Note—The text of Form 10-QSB does not, and this amendment will not, appear in the Code of Federal Regulations.

Form 10-QSB

* * * * *

PART II—OTHER INFORMATION

* * * * *

Item 2. Unregistered Sales of Equity Securities and Use of Proceeds.

(a) Furnish the information required by Item 701 of Regulation S-B (17 CFR 228.701) as to all equity securities of the small business issuer sold by the small business issuer during the period covered by the report that were not registered under the Securities Act. If the Item 701 information previously has been included in a Current Report on Form 8-K (17 CFR 249.308), however, it need not be furnished.

* * * * *

Item 3. Defaults Upon Senior Securities.

* * * * *

Instructions to Item 3

1. Item 3 need not be answered as to any default or arrearage with respect to any class of securities all of which is held by or for the account of the small business issuer or its totally held subsidiaries.

2. The information required by Item 3 need not be made if previously disclosed on a report on Form 8-K (17 CFR 249.308).

* * * * *

Item 5. Other Information.

The small business issuer must disclose under this item any information required to be disclosed in a report on Form 8-K during the period covered by this Form 10-QSB, but not reported, whether or not otherwise required by this Form 10-QSB. If disclosure of such information is made under this item, it need not be repeated in a report on Form 8-K which would otherwise be required to be filed with respect to such information or in a subsequent report on Form 10-QSB.

* * * * *

22. Amend Form 10-K (referenced in § 249.310) by:

a. Revising Items 5(a) and 9;

b. Adding Item 9B;

c. Revising the heading of Item 15 to read "Exhibits and Financial Statement Schedules.";

d. Removing paragraph (b) of Item 15; and

e. Redesignating paragraphs (c) and (d) in Item 15 as paragraphs (b) and (c).

The revisions read as follows:

Note—The text of Form 10-K does not, and this amendment will not, appear in the Code of Federal Regulations.

Form 10-K

Annual Report Pursuant to Section 13 or 15(d) of the Securities Exchange Act of 1934

* * * * *

Item 5. Market for Registrant's Common Equity and Related Stockholder Matters.

(a) Furnish the information required by Item 201 of Regulation S-K (17 CFR 229.201) and Item 701 of Regulation S-K (17 CFR 229.701) as to all equity securities of the registrant sold by the registrant during the period covered by the report that were not registered under the Securities Act other than unregistered sales made in reliance on Regulation S (17 CFR 230.901 through 230.905). If the Item 701 information previously has been included in a Quarterly Report on Form 10-Q or 10-QSB (17 CFR 249.308a or 249.308b), or in a Current Report on Form 8-K (17 CFR 249.308), it need not be furnished.

* * * * *

Item 9. Changes in and Disagreements With Accountants on Accounting and Financial Disclosure.

Furnish the information required by Item 304(b) of Regulation S-K (§ 229.304(b) of this chapter).

* * * * *

Item 9B. Other Information.

The registrant must disclose under this item any information required to be disclosed in a report on Form 8-K during the fourth quarter of the year covered by this Form 10-K, but not reported, whether or not otherwise required by this Form 10-K. If disclosure of such information is made under this item, it need not be repeated in a report on Form 8-K which would otherwise be required to be filed with respect to such information or in a subsequent report on Form 10-K.

* * * * *

23. Amend Form 10-KSB (referenced in § 249.310a) by:

a. Revising Items 5(a) and 8 in Part II;

b. Adding Item 8B in Part II;

c. Removing the words "and Reports on Form 8-K" from the heading to Item 13;

d. Removing paragraph (b) of Item 13 in Part III;

e. Removing the paragraph (a) designation in Item 13;

f. Revising Item 3 in Part II of "Information Required in Annual Report of Transitional Small Business Issuers"; and

g. Removing Item 6 in Part II of "Information Required in Annual Report of Transitional Small Business Issuers".

The revisions read as follows:

Note—The text of Form 10-KSB does not, and this amendment will not, appear in the Code of Federal Regulations.

Form 10-KSB

(Check one)

[ ] Annual Report Pursuant to Section 13 or 15(d) of the Securities Exchange Act of 1934

* * * * *

PART II

Item 5. Market for Common Equity and Related Stockholder Matters.

(a) Furnish the information required by Item 201 of Regulation S-B and Item 701 of Regulation S-B as to all equity securities of the small business issuer sold by the small business issuer during the period covered by the report that were not registered under the Securities Act. If the Item 701 information previously has been included in a Quarterly Report on Form 10-Q or 10-QSB, or on a Current Report on Form 8-K, however, it need not be furnished.

* * * * *

Item 8. Changes In and Disagreements With Accountants on Accounting and Financial Disclosure.

Furnish the information required by Item 304(b) of Regulation S-B.

* * * * *

Item 8B. Other Information

The small business issuer must disclose under this item any information required to be disclosed in a report on Form 8-K during the fourth quarter of the year covered by this Form 10-KSB, but not reported, whether or not otherwise required by this Form 10-KSB. If disclosure of such information is made under this item, it need not be repeated in a report on Form 8-K which would otherwise be required to be filed with respect to such information or in a subsequent report on Form 10-KSB.

* * * * *

INFORMATION REQUIRED IN ANNUAL REPORT OF TRANSITIONAL SMALL BUSINESS ISSUERS

* * * * *

PART II

Item 3. Changes In and Disagreements With Accountants

Furnish the information required by Item 304(b) of Regulation S-B, if applicable.

* * * * *

By the Commission.
Jill M. Peterson

Assistant Secretary
March 16, 2004

Adopting Release: CEO/CFO Certification

Release Nos. 33-8124, 34-46427, IC-25722. File No. S7-21-02. August 28, 2002. Release in full text.

Certification of Disclosure in Companies' Quarterly and Annual Reports

Agency: Securities and Exchange Commission.

Action: Final rule; request for comments.

Summary: As directed by Section 302(a) of the Sarbanes-Oxley Act of 2002, we are adopting rules to require an issuer's principal executive and financial officers each to certify the financial and other information contained in the issuer's quarterly and annual reports. The rules also require these officers to certify that: they are responsible for establishing, maintaining and regularly evaluating the effectiveness of the issuer's internal controls; they have made certain disclosures to the issuer's auditors and the audit committee of the board of directors about the issuer's internal controls; and they have included information in the issuer's quarterly and annual reports about their evaluation and whether there have been significant changes in the issuer's internal controls or in other factors that could significantly affect internal controls subsequent to the evaluation. In addition, we are adopting previously proposed rules to require issuers to maintain, and regularly evaluate the effectiveness of, disclosure controls and procedures designed to ensure that the information required in reports filed under the Securities Exchange Act of 1934 is recorded, processed, summarized and reported on a timely basis.

Dates: Effective Date: August 29, 2002.

Comment Date: Comments on the extension of the certification requirement to definitive proxy and information statements should be received on or before 30 days after publication in the Federal Register.

Addresses: Comments should be submitted in triplicate to Jonathan G. Katz, Secretary, Securities and Exchange Commission, 450 Fifth Street, NW, Washington, DC 20549-0609. Comments also may be submitted electronically at the following electronic mail address: rule-comments@sec.gov. To help us process and review your comments more efficiently, comments should be submitted by one method only. All comment letters should refer to File No. S7-21-02; this file number should be included in the subject line if electronic mail is used. Comment letters will be available for public inspection and copying in the Commission's Public Reference Room, 450 Fifth Street, NW, Washington, DC 20549. Electronically submitted comment letters will be posted on the Commission's Internet website (http://www.sec.gov).[1]

For Further Information Contact: Mark A. Borges, Special Counsel, or Elizabeth M. Murphy, Chief, Office of Rulemaking, Division of Corporation Finance, at (202) 942-2910, or, with respect to issuers of asset-backed securities, Paula Dubberly, Chief Counsel, Division of Corporation Finance, at (202) 942-2900, or, with respect to investment companies, Tara L. Royal, Attorney, Office of Disclosure Regulation, Division of Investment Management, at (202) 942-0721, at the Securities and Exchange Commission, 450 Fifth Street, NW, Washington, DC 20549.

Supplementary Information: We are adopting new Item 307[2] of Regulation S-B,[3] new Item 307[4] of Regulation S-K,[5] new Rules 13a-14,[6] 13a-15,[7] 15d-14[8] and 15d-15[9] under the Securities Exchange Act of 1934 ("Exchange Act")[10] and new Rule 30a-2[11] under the Investment Company Act of 1940 ("Investment Company Act").[12] We also are adopting amendments to Rules 12b-15,[13] 13a-10[14] and 15d-10[15] and Forms 10-Q,[16] 10-QSB,[17] 10-K,[18] 10-KSB,[19] 20-F[20] and 40-F[21] under the Exchange Act, Rule 30b1-3 under the Investment Company Act,[22] Rule 302 of Regula-

---

[1] We do not edit personal identifying information, such as names and electronic mail addresses, from electronic submissions. You should submit only information that you wish to make available publicly.

[2] 17 CFR 228.307.

[3] 17 CFR 228.10 et seq.

[4] 17 CFR 229.307.

[5] 17 CFR 229.10 et seq.

[6] 17 CFR 240.13a-14.

[7] 17 CFR 240.13a-15.

[8] 17 CFR 240.15d-14.

[9] 17 CFR 240.15d-15.

[10] 15 U.S.C. 78a et seq.

[11] 17 CFR 270.30a-2.

[12] 15 U.S.C. 80a-1 et seq.

[13] 17 CFR 240.12b-15.

[14] 17 CFR 240.13a-10.

[15] 17 CFR 240.15d-10.

[16] 17 CFR 249.308a.

[17] 17 CFR 249.308b.

[18] 17 CFR 249.310.

[19] 17 CFR 249.310b.

[20] 17 CFR 249.220f.

[21] 17 CFR 249.240f.

[22] 17 CFR 270.30b1-3.

tion S-T[23] and Form N-SAR[24] under the Exchange Act and the Investment Company Act.

[¶ 2101]

I. Introduction

On July 30, 2002, the Sarbanes-Oxley Act of 2002 (the "Act") was enacted.[25] Section 302 of the Act, entitled "Corporate Responsibility for Financial Reports," requires the Commission to adopt final rules that must be effective by August 29, 2002, 30 days after the date of enactment, under which the principal executive officer or officers and the principal financial officer or officers, or persons providing similar functions, of an issuer each must certify the information contained in the issuer's quarterly and annual reports. Section 302 also requires these officers to certify that: they are responsible for establishing, maintaining and regularly evaluating the effectiveness of, the issuer's internal controls; they have made certain disclosures to the issuer's auditors and the audit committee of the board of directors about the issuer's internal controls; and they have included information in the issuer's quarterly and annual reports about their evaluation and whether there have been significant changes in the issuer's internal controls or in other factors that could significantly affect internal controls subsequent to the evaluation.

On June 14, 2002, we proposed rules that would have required a company's principal executive officer and principal financial officer to certify the contents of the company's quarterly and annual reports.[26] The June Proposals also would have required companies to maintain procedures to provide reasonable assurance that they are able to collect, process and disclose the information required in their Exchange Act reports. Finally, the June Proposals would have required companies to undertake an annual evaluation of these procedures under the supervision of management. Shortly after enactment of the Act, we provided supplemental information on the Act and the June Proposals.[27]

In light of Congress' directive in Section 302 of the Act, we are adopting rules that implement the certification mandated by the Act instead of the certification contained in the June Proposals. We received 102 comment letters in response to the June Proposals.[28] Although responding to the form of certification set forth in the June Proposals, a majority of the commenters supported a certification requirement for senior corporate officers.[29] In addition, the comment letters we have received since the enactment of the Act also express support for a certification requirement.[30] Because Section 302 of the Act prescribes the form of certification that we are to adopt, the new rules do not reflect many of the comments and suggestions that we received on the June Proposals.

While Section 302 of the Act requires an issuer's principal executive and financial officers to make specific certifications regarding their responsibilities to establish and maintain internal controls, it does not directly address the issuer's responsibility for controls and procedures related to the issuer's Exchange Act reporting obligations.[31] The June Proposals included requirements that companies maintain sufficient procedures to provide reasonable assurances that they are able to collect, process and disclose, within the time periods specified in the Commission's rules and forms, the information required to be disclosed in their Exchange Act reports.[32] We have adopted this requirement largely as proposed. Because of the broad scope of Section 302 of the Act, the new rules are applicable to all types of issuers that file reports under Section 13(a) or 15(d) of the Exchange Act, including foreign private issuers, banks and savings associations, issuers of asset-

---

23 17 CFR 232.302.

24 17 CFR 249.330; 17 CFR 274.101.

25 Pub. L. 107-204, 116 Stat. 745 (2002).

26 See Release No. 34-46079 (June 14, 2002) [67 FR 41877] (the "June Proposals").

27 See Release No. 34-46300 (Aug. 2, 2002) [67 FR 51508] notifying interested parties of the rules that we are required to adopt pursuant to Section 302 of the Act and highlighting some of the major differences between those rules and the June Proposals.

28 The commenters included 56 individual and institutional investors, 21 companies and company associations, one domestic governmental agency, one foreign governmental agency and 23 members of the accounting and legal communities. These comment letters and a summary of comments are available for public inspection and copying in our Public Reference Room, 450 Fifth Street, NW, Washington, DC 20549, in File No. S7-21-02. Public comments submitted electronically and the summary of comments are available on our website _http://www.sec.gov_.

29 See, for example, the Letter dated June 13, 2002 of Robert E. Jones, the Letter dated June 24, 2002 of Dan Jamieson and the Letter dated July 5, 2002 of T. Jeffrey Mangin.

30 See, for example, the Letter dated August 9, 2002 of the American Society of Corporate Securities and the Letter dated August 14, 2002 of the National Association of Real Estate Investment Trusts.

31 Separately, Section 404 of the Act directs the Commission to prescribe rules for issuers to state in their annual reports required by Section 13(a) or 15(d) of the Exchange Act the responsibility of management for establishing and maintaining an adequate internal control structure and procedures for financial reporting.

32 See proposed Exchange Act Rules 13a-15 and 15d-15.

backed securities, small business issuers and registered investment companies.[33]

[¶ 2102]

II. Certification of Quarterly and Annual Reports

A. Rule Requirements

As adopted, new Exchange Act Rules 13a-14 and 15d-14 require an issuer's principal executive officer or officers and the principal financial officer or officers, or persons performing similar functions, each to certify in each quarterly and annual report, including transition reports, filed or submitted by the issuer under Section 13(a) or 15(d) of the Exchange Act[34] that:

- he or she has reviewed the report;
- based on his or her knowledge, the report does not contain any untrue statement of a material fact or omit to state a material fact necessary in order to make the statements made, in light of the circumstances under which such statements were made, not misleading with respect to the period covered by the report;[35]
- based on his or her knowledge, the financial statements, and other financial information included in the report, fairly present in all material respects the financial condition, results of operations and cash flows of the issuer as of, and for, the periods presented in the report;
- he or she and the other certifying officers:

—are responsible for establishing and maintaining "disclosure controls and procedures" (a newly-defined term reflecting the concept of controls and procedures related to disclosure embodied in Section 302(a)(4) of the Act) for the issuer;

—have designed such disclosure controls and procedures to ensure that material information is made known to them, particularly during the period in which the periodic report is being prepared;

—have evaluated the effectiveness of the issuer's disclosure controls and procedures as of a date within 90 days prior to the filing date of the report; and

—have presented in the report their conclusions about the effectiveness of the disclosure controls and procedures based on the required evaluation as of that date;

- he or she and the other certifying officers have disclosed to the issuer's auditors and to the audit committee of the board of directors (or persons fulfilling the equivalent function):

—all significant deficiencies in the design or operation of internal controls (a pre-existing term relating to internal controls regarding financial reporting)[36] which could adversely affect the issuer's ability to record, process, summarize and report financial data and have identified for the issuer's auditors any material weaknesses in internal controls; and

—any fraud, whether or not material, that involves management or other employees who have a significant role in the issuer's internal controls; and

- he or she and the other certifying officers have indicated in the report whether or not there were significant changes in internal controls or in other factors that could significantly affect internal controls subsequent to the date of their evaluation, including any corrective actions with regard to significant deficiencies and material weaknesses.

For purposes of the new rules, "disclosure controls and procedures" are defined as controls and other procedures of an issuer that are designed to

[33] See Section IV below for a discussion of registered investment companies. Registered investment companies generally are required to file periodic reports under Section 13(a) or 15(d) of the Exchange Act on Form N-SAR and, therefore, would provide the certification required by Section 302 of the Act. However, because Section 302 of the Act only applies to issuers that file periodic reports under Section 13(a) or 15(d) of the Exchange Act, the rules we are adopting today will not apply to registered investment companies that do not file periodic reports under either Section 13(a) or 15(d).

[34] 15 U.S.C.78m(a) or 78o(d). Section 13(a) of the Exchange Act requires every issuer of a security registered pursuant to Section 12 of the Exchange Act [15 U.S.C. 78l] to file with the Commission such annual reports and such quarterly reports as the Commission may prescribe. Section 15(d) of the Exchange Act requires each issuer that has filed a registration statement that has become effective pursuant to the Securities Act of 1933 [15 U.S.C.77a et seq.] to file such supplementary and periodic information, documents and reports as may be required pursuant to Section 13 in respect of a security registered pursuant to Section 12. The duty of an issuer to file under Section 15(d) is automatically suspended for any fiscal year, other than a fiscal year in which its registration statement becomes effective or is required to be updated pursuant to Section 10(a)(3) of the Securities Act [15 U.S.C. 77j(a)(3)], if an issuer's securities are held of record by less than 300 persons. See Exchange Act Rule 12h-3(c) [17 CFR 240.12h-3(c)].

[35] As permitted under our rules, a registrant may satisfy its disclosure obligations under Part III of Forms 10-K and 10-KSB by incorporating the required information by reference from its definitive proxy or information statement, if that statement involves the election of directors and is filed not later than 120 days after the end of the fiscal year covered by the annual report. See General Instruction G(3) to Form 10-K and General Instruction E(3) to Form 10-KSB. For purposes of this provision, the certification in the annual report on Form 10-K or 10-KSB would be considered to cover the Part III information in a registrant's proxy or information statement as and when filed.

[36] See American Institute of Certified Public Accountants ("AICPA") Codification of Statements on Auditing Standards, AU 319.

ensure that information required to be disclosed by the issuer in the reports filed or submitted by it under the Exchange Act[37] is recorded, processed, summarized and reported, within the time periods specified in the Commission's rules and forms.[38] "Disclosure controls and procedures" include, without limitation, controls and procedures designed to ensure that information required to be disclosed by an issuer in its Exchange Act reports is accumulated and communicated to the issuer's management, including its principal executive and financial officers, as appropriate to allow timely decisions regarding required disclosure.

B. Discussion of Certification Requirement

1. Issuers Subject to Certification Requirement

Section 302 of the Act states that the certification requirement is to apply to each company filing periodic reports under Section 13(a) or 15(d) of the Exchange Act.[39] Accordingly, new Exchange Act Rules 13a-14 and 15d-14 apply to the principal executive officers and principal financial officers, or persons performing similar functions, of any issuer that files quarterly and annual reports with the Commission under either Section 13(a) or 15(d) of the Exchange Act, including foreign private issuers, banks and savings associations, issuers of asset-backed securities and small business issuers.[40]

a) Foreign Private Issuers

While the June Proposals would not have applied to foreign private issuers, [41] Section 302 of the Act makes no distinction between domestic and foreign issuers and, by its terms, clearly applies to foreign private issuers. New Exchange Act Rules 13a-14 and 15d-14, therefore, apply the certification requirement to the principal executive officers and principal financial officers of foreign private issuers that file reports under Section 13(a) or 15(d) of the Exchange Act.[42]

b) Banks and Saving Associations

The certification requirement of Section 302 of the Act also applies to principal executive officers and principal financial officers of banks and savings associations that file periodic reports under Section 13(a) or 15(d) of the Exchange Act. The Act amended Section 12(i) of the Exchange Act to make it clear that the federal banking agencies have the authority to administer and enforce various provisions of the Act, including the certification required by Section 302.[43]

c) Asset-Backed Securities Issuers

Issuers of asset-backed securities in public offerings have a reporting obligation under either Section 13(a) or 15(d) of the Exchange Act, at least for a period of time.[44] Because of the nature of asset-backed issuers, the staff of the Division of Corporation Finance has granted requests allowing asset-backed issuers to file modified reports under the Exchange Act.[45]

The modified reporting structure for asset-backed issuers allows issuers or depositors to file modified annual reports on Form 10-K and to file reports tied to payments on the underlying assets in the trust. These reports include a copy of the servicing or distribution report required by the issuer's governing documents and information on the performance of the assets, payments on the asset-backed securities and any other material developments that affect the issuer. Because the reported information for asset-backed issuers differs significantly from that for other issuers, the

---

[37] These reports include quarterly reports on Form 10-Q or 10-QSB, annual reports on Form 10-K, 10-KSB, 20-F or 40-F, current reports, definitive proxy materials filed under Section 14(a) of the Exchange Act [15 U.S.C. 78n(a)], definitive information statements filed under Section 14(c) of the Exchange Act [15 U.S.C. 78n(c)] and amendments to any of these reports or documents.

[38] See new Exchange Act Rules 13a-14(c) and 15d-14(c).

[39] See Section 302(a) of the Act.

[40] The new rules achieve the objective of Section 302(b) of the Act, which states that nothing in the provision is to be interpreted or applied in any way to allow any issuer to lessen the legal force of the certification requirement by an issuer that has reincorporated or engaged in any other transaction resulting in the transfer of the corporate domicile or offices of the issuer from inside of the United States to outside of the United States, because they are applicable to all issuers without regard to their jurisdiction of incorporation or domicile.

[41] For purposes of the Exchange Act, a "foreign private issuer" is any foreign issuer (other than a foreign government) except an issuer meeting the following conditions: (1) more than 50% of the issuer's outstanding voting securities are directly or indirectly held of record by residents of the U.S.; and (2) the majority of the executive officers or directors are U.S. citizens or residents; or more than 50% of the assets of the issuer are located in the U.S.; or the business of the issuer is administered principally in the U.S. See Exchange Act Rule 3b-4(c) [17 CFR 240.3b-4(c)]. We sought comment on whether to apply a certification requirement to foreign private issuers in the June Proposals.

[42] The new rules do not apply to foreign private issuers that furnish materials to the Commission pursuant to Exchange Act Rule 12g3-2(b) [17 CFR 240.12g3-2(b)].

[43] See Section 3(b)(4) of the Act.

[44] Asset-backed issuers also sometimes voluntarily file Exchange Act reports in order to comply with provisions in the indenture or pooling and servicing agreements.

[45] See, for example, Release No. 34-16520 (Jan. 23, 1980) (order granting application pursuant to Section 12(h) of the Exchange Act [15 U.S.C. 78l(h)] of Home Savings and Loan Association); Release No. 34-14446 (Feb. 6, 1978) (order granting application pursuant to Section 12(h) of the Exchange Act of Bank of America National Trust and Savings Association); Division of Corporation Finance no-action letters to Key Bank USA, N.A. (May 9, 1997) and Bay View Securitization Corp. (Jan. 15, 1998).

certification requirement of Section 302 of the Act must be specifically tailored for asset-backed issuers. The new rules require asset-backed issuers to certify their reports. The staff of the Division of Corporation Finance today is providing guidance for asset-backed issuers regarding compliance with the certification requirement.

d) Small Business Issuers

The June Proposals generally did not distinguish between large and small issuers. Similarly, Section 302 of the Act directs that the certification requirement apply to any company filing periodic reports under Section 13(a) or 15(d) of the Exchange Act. Accordingly, new Rules 13a-14 and 15d-14 apply to all issuers that file Exchange Act periodic reports regardless of their size. We note, however, that because many small business issuers do not file Exchange Act reports, not all small business issuers will be subject to the certification requirement.

2. Reports Subject to Certification Requirement

Section 302 of the Act states that the required certification is to be included in each annual or quarterly report filed or submitted under either Section 13(a) or 15(d) of the Exchange Act.[46] Accordingly, the certification requirement applies to annual reports on Forms 10-K, 10-KSB, 20-F and 40-F.[47] The certification requirement also applies to quarterly reports on Forms 10-Q and 10-QSB. Finally, the certification requirement applies to amendments to, and transition reports on, any of the foregoing reports.[48]

Reports that are current reports, such as reports on Forms 6-K[49] and 8-K, rather than periodic (quarterly and annual) reports are not covered by the certification requirement.[50] Disclosure controls and procedures, however, are required to be designed, maintained and evaluated to ensure full and timely disclosure in current reports, as well as definitive proxy materials and definitive information statements, even though there is no specific certification requirement relating to reports on those forms.[51]

The new rules apply the certification requirement to foreign private issuers filing annual reports on Form 20-F and Canadian issuers filing annual reports on Form 40-F under our Multijurisdictional Disclosure System. Although Form 20-F is not required to be signed by any specific executive officer of a foreign registrant,[52] we believe that it is the clear intent of Congress to require that the appropriate officers execute and submit the required certification in an annual report filed under the Exchange Act on Form 20-F or 40-F.

As we first indicated in the June Proposals, we continue to consider whether we should extend a certification requirement to other documents filed under the Exchange Act, such as registration statements on Forms 10 and 10-SB[53] and definitive proxy and information statements. We solicit comment on whether any or all of these documents, or any other documents, should be certified by an issuer's senior officers.

3. Content of Certification

Section 302 of the Act states that the required certification is to made by an issuer's principal executive officer or officers and principal financial officer or officers, or persons performing similar functions. The required certification contains several statements. The certification statement concerning the material accuracy and completeness of the periodic reports that are covered by the statement mirrors the existing statutory disclosure standards for "material" accuracy and completeness of information contained in reports.[54]

The certification statement regarding fair presentation of financial statements and other financial information included in the report was not part of the June Proposals. This statement separately addresses the presentation of an issuer's financial disclosure. This financial disclosure includes financial statements (including footnote disclosure), selected financial data, management's discussion and analysis of financial condition and results of operations and other financial informa-

---

[46] See Section 302(a) of the Act.

[47] The certification requirement does not apply to annual reports on Form 11-K [17 CFR 239.311].

[48] See amended Exchange Act Rules 12b-15, 13a-10 and 15d-10. In the case of the amendment on or after the compliance date of the new rules of a quarterly or annual report filed prior to August 29, 2002, the certification requirement will apply.

[49] 17 CFR 249.306.

[50] A foreign private issuer must furnish under cover of Form 6-K material information that it makes public or is required to make public under its home country laws or the rules of its home country stock exchange or that it distributes to security holders. While foreign private issuers may submit interim financial information under cover of Form 6-K, they do so pursuant to their home country requirements and not because of a Commission requirement to submit updated financial information for specified periods and according to specified standards. Therefore, we do not believe that a Form 6-K constitutes a "periodic" report analogous to a quarterly report on Form 10-Q or 10-QSB for which certification is required.

[51] See new Exchange Act Rules 13a-15 and 15d-15.

[52] See General Instruction D to Form 20-F.

[53] 17 CFR 249.210 and 249.210b.

[54] See Exchange Act Rules 10b-5(b) [17 CFR 230.10b-5(b)] and 12b-20 [17 CFR 240.12b-20.]. See also Basic, Inc. v. Levinson, 485 U.S. 224 (1988); TSC Industries, Inc. v. Northway, Inc., 426 U.S. (1976).

tion in a report. The certification, as adopted, states that the overall financial disclosure fairly presents, in all material respects, the company's financial condition, results of operations and cash flows. We have added a specific reference to cash flows even though Section 302 of the Act does not include such an explicit reference. We believe that it is consistent with Congressional intent to include both income or loss and cash flows within the concept of "fair presentation" of an issuer's results of operations.

The certification statement regarding fair presentation of financial statements and other financial information is not limited to a representation that the financial statements and other financial information have been presented in accordance with "generally accepted accounting principles" and is not otherwise limited by reference to generally accepted accounting principles. We believe that Congress intended this statement to provide assurances that the financial information disclosed in a report, viewed in its entirety, meets a standard of overall material accuracy and completeness that is broader than financial reporting requirements under generally accepted accounting principles.[55] In our view, a "fair presentation" of an issuer's financial condition, results of operations and cash flows encompasses the selection of appropriate accounting policies, proper application of appropriate accounting policies, disclosure of financial information that is informative and reasonably reflects the underlying transactions and events and the inclusion of any additional disclosure necessary to provide investors with a materially accurate and complete picture of an issuer's financial condition, results of operations and cash flows.[56]

Both of the foregoing certification statements are to be made based on the knowledge of the certifying officer. This is not meant to change the current obligations of corporate officers in connection with the discharge of their duties. Both of the foregoing statements are also made in the context of the requirements of the reports in which they are included. In particular, quarterly reports on Forms 10-Q and 10-QSB have less extensive disclosure and financial statement and footnote requirements than annual reports. The certification requirement is not intended to require expansion of quarterly reports to satisfy the requirements of annual reports. Rather, completeness of disclosure will be determined through application of standards derived from our existing rules, forms and interpretations.[57]

While the certification described in the June Proposals contained a statement regarding the completion of a review of an issuer's internal procedures and controls aimed at assuring adequate disclosure, the certification required by Section 302 of the Act includes several, more detailed, statements concerning an issuer's "internal controls" and the ongoing oversight of these controls. For purposes of the certification required by Section 302(a)(4) of the Act, we have defined the term "disclosure controls and procedures" to incorporate a broader concept of controls and procedures designed to ensure compliance with disclosure requirements generally. This definition is included in new Exchange Act Rules 13a-14 and 15d-14 and applies to the portion of the certification required by Section 302(a)(4) of the Act.[58]

We have defined the term "disclosure controls and procedures" to make it explicit that the controls contemplated by Section 302(a)(4) of the Act are intended to embody controls and procedures addressing the quality and timeliness of disclosure. We also have included this definition to differentiate this concept of disclosure controls and procedures from the pre-existing concept of "internal controls" that pertains to an issuer's financial reporting and control of its assets, as currently embodied in Section 13(b) of the Exchange Act[59] and as addressed in Sections 302(a)(5) and (a)(6) and Section 404 of the Act.

---

[55] Presenting financial information in conformity with generally accepted accounting principles may not necessarily satisfy obligations under the antifraud provisions of the federal securities laws. See United States v. Simon, 425 F.2d 796 (2d Cir. 1969). See also In re Caterpillar, Inc., Release No. 34-30532 (Mar. 31, 1992); Edison Schools, Inc., Release No. 34-45925 (May 14, 2002).

[56] See Exchange Act Rule 12b-20 and the case and proceedings referenced in n. 55 above. In addition, both International Accounting Standard IAS 1, 14 and 15 and AICPA, Codification of Statements on Auditing Standards, AU 411.04 speak to the essential elements that must be considered, within the framework of generally accepted accounting principles, in evaluating whether an issuer's financial statements fairly present its financial condition and results of operations. These statements, without being limited by reference to generally accepted accounting principles, provide guidance as to what elements should be considered in determining whether an issuer's financial information, taken as a whole, provides a fair presentation of its financial condition and results of operations. These elements include, without limitation, whether the accounting principles selected are appropriate in the circumstances and whether the disclosure is informative and reasonably reflects the underlying transactions and events.

[57] See, for example, In re Caterpillar, Inc., Release No. 34-30532 (Mar. 31, 1992); Exchange Act Rule 12b-20.

[58] See new Exchange Act Rules 13a-14(c) and 15d-14(c).

[59] 15 U.S.C. 78m(b). See also AICPA Professional Standards AU Section 319.06 ("Internal controls is a process—effected by an entity's board of directors, management and other personnel—designed to provide reasonable assurance regarding the achievement of objectives in the following categories: (a) reliability of financial reporting, (b) effectiveness and efficiency of operations and (c) compliance with applicable laws and regulations.").

We make this distinction based on our review of Section 302 of the Act as well as to effectuate what we believe to be Congress' intent - to have senior officers certify that required material non-financial information, as well as financial information, is included in an issuer's quarterly and annual reports. Under this interpretation, we maintain the pre-existing concept of internal controls without expanding it by relating it to non-financial information.

As discussed in the June Proposals, we are not requiring any particular procedures for conducting the required review and evaluation. Instead, we expect each issuer to develop a process that is consistent with its business and internal management and supervisory practices. We do recommend, however, that, if it has not already done so, an issuer create a committee with responsibility for considering the materiality of information and determining disclosure obligations on a timely basis.[60] As is implicit in Section 302(a)(4) of the Act, such a committee would report to senior management, including the principal executive and financial officers, who bear express responsibility for designing, establishing, maintaining, reviewing and evaluating the issuer's disclosure controls and procedures.

We believe that the concept of "internal controls" contemplated by Sections 302(a)(5) and (6) of the Act concern an issuer's controls and procedures for financial reporting purposes as required by Section 13(b) of the Exchange Act. They also relate to the "internal controls" addressed in Section 404 of the Act.[61] The certification required by new Exchange Act Rules 13a-14 and 15d-14 makes reference to certain disclosures regarding both disclosure controls and procedures and internal controls that must be made in the reports in which the certification is contained. These disclosure requirements appear in new Item 307 of Regulation S-K, Item 307 of Regulation S-B, Item 15 of Form 20-F and General Instruction B(6) of Form 40-F.

Because the statements involving disclosure controls and procedures and internal controls require the certifying officers to take certain specified actions, such as evaluating the effectiveness of the disclosure controls and procedures prior to the date of the report to which the certification relates, these statements will be required as part of the certification only with respect to any reports that cover periods ending on or after August 29, 2002, the effective date of the rules required by Section 302 of the Act.[62]

4. Form of Certification

The certification required by new Exchange Act Rules 13a-14 and 15d-14 must be in the exact form set forth in the amendments to the affected reports. The wording of the required certification may not be changed in any respect (even if the change would appear to be inconsequential in nature).[63]

5. Location of Certification

Section 302 of the Act states that the required certification is to be included "in" each quarterly or annual report filed or submitted under either Section 13(a) or 15(d) of the Exchange Act. To implement this directive, we have amended Forms 10-Q, 10-QSB, 10-K, 10-KSB, 20-F and 40-F under the Exchange Act to require that the certifications follow immediately after the signature sections of these reports.

The required certification is in addition to, and, thus, does not alter, the current signature requirements for quarterly and annual reports filed under the Exchange Act. The signatures required by the certifications will be part of these reports, and, therefore, also will be subject to the signature requirement of our rules.[64] We have amended Rule 302 of Regulation S-T[65] to make it clear that its requirements apply to the signatures appearing in these certifications.

6. Liability for False Certification

An issuer's principal executive and financial officers already are responsible as signatories for the issuer's disclosures under the Exchange Act liability provisions[66] and can be liable for material misstatements or omissions under general antifraud standards[67] and under our authority to seek

---

[60] Officers and employees of an issuer who have an interest in, and the expertise to serve on, the committee could include the principal accounting officer (or the controller), the general counsel or other senior legal official with responsibility for disclosure matters who reports to the general counsel, the principal risk management officer, the chief investor relations officer (or an officer with equivalent responsibilities) and such other officers or employees, including individuals associated with the issuer's business units, as the issuer deems appropriate.

[61] The rules called for under Section 404 of the Act will be the subject of separate Commission rulemaking. See n. 75 below.

[62] See Section V below.

[63] To further emphasize the importance of the required certification, a principal executive officer or principal financial officer is not permitted to have the certification signed on his or her behalf pursuant to a power of attorney or other form of confirming authority. See new Exchange Act Rules 13a-14(d) and 15d-14(d).

[64] See Exchange Act Rule 12b-11(d) [17 CFR 240.12b-11(d)].

[65] 17 CFR 232.302.

[66] See Sections 13(a) and 18 of the Exchange Act [15 U.S.C. 78m(a) and 78r].

[67] See, for example, Howard v. Everex Systems, Inc. 228 F.3d 1057 (9th Cir. 2000) (a corporate officer who signs a Commission filing containing representations

redress against those who cause or aid or abet securities law violations.[68] An officer providing a false certification potentially could be subject to Commission action for violating Section 13(a) or 15(d) of the Exchange Act and to both Commission and private actions for violating Section 10(b) of the Exchange Act[69] and Exchange Act Rule 10b-5.[70]

[¶ 2103]

III. Disclosure Controls and Procedures

A. Rule Requirements

As adopted, new Exchange Act Rules 13a-15 and 15d-15 require each issuer filing reports under Section 13(a) or Section 15(d) of the Exchange Act to maintain disclosure controls and procedures (as defined in new Exchange Act Rules 13a-14(c) and 15d-14(c)). We believe that, to assist principal executive and financial officers in the discharge of their responsibilities in making the required certifications, as well as to discharge their responsibilities in providing accurate and complete information to security holders, it is necessary for companies to ensure that their internal communications and other procedures operate so that important information flows to the appropriate collection and disclosure points in a timely manner.

B. Discussion of Disclosure Controls and Procedures

New Exchange Act Rules 13a-15 and 15d-15 complement existing requirements for reporting companies to establish and maintain systems of internal controls with respect to their financial information.[71] They are intended to ensure that an issuer maintains commensurate procedures for gathering, analyzing and disclosing all information that is required to be disclosed in its Exchange Act reports.

As discussed in the June Proposals, these procedures are intended to cover a broader range of information than is covered by an issuer's internal controls related to financial reporting. For example, the procedures should ensure timely collection and evaluation of information potentially subject to disclosure under the requirements of Regulation S-X,[72] Regulation S-K or S-B and Forms 20-F and 40-F. The procedures should capture information that is relevant to an assessment of the need to disclose developments and risks that pertain to the issuer's businesses.[73] They also should cover information that must be evaluated in the context of the disclosure requirement of Exchange Act Rule 12b-20. We believe that the new rules will help to ensure that an issuer's systems grow and evolve with its business and are capable of producing Exchange Act reports that are timely, accurate and reliable.[74]

New Exchange Act Rules 13a-15 and 15d-15 also are entirely complementary to the objectives of Section 302 of the Act. While Section 302 requires an issuer's principal executive and financial officers to make specific statements in their certifications and to take the actions satisfying the representations made in the statements as to the issuer's disclosure controls and procedures, it does not directly address the issuer's obligations with respect to these controls and procedures. The new rules will ensure that an issuer also has a responsibility to maintain adequate disclosure controls and procedures, so that its principal executive and financial officers can supervise and review these periodic evaluations and report the results to security holders through the issuer's Exchange Act reports.[75]

New Exchange Act Rules 13a-15 and 15d-15 also require the issuer, under the supervision of the principal executive and financial officers, to conduct an evaluation of the effectiveness of the

---

(Footnote Continued)

"makes" the statement in the filing and can be liable as a primary violator of Section 10(b) of the Exchange Act).

[68] See Sections 20, 21, 21C and 21D of the Exchange Act [15 U.S.C. 78t, 78u, 78u-3 and 78u-4].

[69] 15 U.S.C. 78j(b).

[70] A false certification also may have liability consequences under Sections 11 and 12(a)(2) of the Securities Act [15 U.S.C. 77k and 77l(a)(2)] where a quarterly or annual report is incorporated by reference into a registration statement on Form S-3 [17 CFR 239.13] or F-3 [17 CFR 239.33] or into a prospectus filed pursuant to Securities Act Rule 424(b) [17 CFR 230.424(b)].

[71] See Section 13(b)(2) of the Exchange Act [15 U.S.C. 78m(b)(2)] and Rules 13b2-1 and 13b2-2 [17 CFR 240.13b2-1 and 240.13b2-2].

[72] 17 CFR 210.1-01 et seq.

[73] For example, for some businesses, an assessment and evaluation of operational and regulatory risks may be necessary.

[74] Accordingly, a company that failed to maintain adequate procedures, review them and otherwise comply with the rule could be subject to Commission action for violating Section 13(a) of the Exchange Act even where the failure did not lead to flawed disclosure.

[75] We note that Section 404 of the Act directs us to prescribe rules requiring each annual report filed under Section 13(a) or 15(d) of the Exchange Act to contain an internal control report, which shall: (1) state the responsibility of management for establishing and maintaining an adequate internal control structure and procedures for financial reporting: and (2) contain an assessment, as of the end of the most recent fiscal year of the issuer, of the effectiveness of the internal control structure and procedures of the issuer for financial reporting. These rules will be the subject of a separate rulemaking project.

design and operation of the issuer's disclosure controls and procedures within 90 days of the filing date of any quarterly or annual report filed under the Exchange Act. While the new rules do not provide detailed procedures for such an evaluation, the evaluation must, at a minimum, address the matters specified by the rules. We expect that this evaluation would be carried out in a manner that would form the basis for the certification statements required by Section 302 of the Act regarding disclosure controls and procedures required by new Exchange Act Rules 13a-14(b)(4)(ii)-(iii) and 15d-14(b)(4)(ii)-(iii) in an issuer's quarterly and annual reports.

We noted in the June Proposals that mandatory requirements regarding disclosure controls and procedures may raise several issues for foreign private issuers. Section 302 of the Act, however, does not provide any exception to the certification requirement for foreign private issuers. Because we believe that the maintenance of disclosure controls and procedures is an important part of satisfying the certification requirement, it is appropriate to require foreign private issuers to comply with new Exchange Act Rules 13a-15 and 15d-15 with respect to the implementation of the controls and procedures outlined in Section 302(a)(4) of the Act.

[¶ 2104]

IV. Certification of Registered Investment Company Annual and Semi-Annual Reports

We are implementing Section 302 of the Act with respect to registered investment companies by adopting new Investment Company Act Rule 30a-2. This rule requires a registered investment company that files periodic reports under Section 13(a) or 15(d) of the Exchange Act (that is, Form N-SAR) to include the certification specified by Section 302 in those periodic reports. We are also amending the instructions to Form N-SAR, the annual and semi-annual reporting form for registered investment companies, to require the specified certification to be filed as an exhibit to Form N-SAR.[76]

Section 302 requires the specified certification to be included in "each annual or quarterly report filed or submitted" under either Section 13(a) or 15(d) of the Exchange Act.[77] Form N-SAR is the form designated for registered investment companies to comply with their reporting requirements under Sections 13(a) and 15(d) of the Exchange Act, as well as periodic reporting requirements under Sections 30(a) and 30(b)(1)[78] of the Investment Company Act.[79] Registered management investment companies are required to file annual and semi-annual reports on Form N-SAR not more than 60 calendar days after the close of each fiscal year and fiscal second quarter.[80] Registered unit investment trusts are required to file annual reports on Form N-SAR with respect to each calendar year, not more than 60 calendar days after the close of each year.[81]

Unlike Forms 10-K and 10-Q, Form N-SAR does not require the filing of financial statements. However, Form N-SAR requires management investment companies to provide certain financial information based on the financial statements as of the same date contained in the investment company's annual and semi-annual reports to shareholders.[82] Therefore, we are requiring the signing officers of a registered management investment company to certify under new Investment Company Act Rule 30a-2(b)(3) that the financial information included in the report and the financial statements on which the financial information is based fairly present, in all material respects, the financial condition, results of operations, changes in net assets and cash flows (if the financial statements are required to include a statement of cash flows) of the investment company.[83] We have added a specific reference to changes in net assets and cash flows even though Section 302 of the Act does not include such an explicit reference. We believe that it is consistent

---

[76] 17 CFR 249.330; 17 CFR 274.101; Item 133 and Instructions to Items 77Q3, 102P3 and 133 of Form N-SAR.

[77] See n. 34 above. Because Section 302 of the Sarbanes-Oxley Act only applies to companies that file periodic reports under Section 13(a) or 15(d) of the Exchange Act, the rules we are adopting today will not apply to registered investment companies that do not file periodic reports under Section 13(a) or 15(d).

[78] 15 U.S.C. 80a-30(a) and (b)(1).

[79] General Instruction A to Form N-SAR. See Release No. IC-14299 (Jan. 4, 1985) [50 FR 1442] (release adopting Form N-SAR).

[80] Investment Company Act Rule 30b1-1 [17 CFR 270.30b1-1]; General Instruction C to Form N-SAR.

[81] Investment Company Act Rule 30a-1 [17 CFR 270.30a-1]; General Instruction C to Form N-SAR. A unit investment trust is "an investment company which (A) is organized under a trust indenture, contract of custodianship or agency, or similar instrument, (B) does not have a board of directors, and (C) issues only redeemable securities, each of which represents an undivided interest in a unit of specified securities; but does not include a voting trust." Section 4(2) of the Investment Company Act [15 U.S.C. 80a-4(2)].

[82] See Items 72 and 74 of Form N-SAR and the Instructions to those items.

[83] In the case of a master-feeder fund, the report of the master fund on Form N-SAR would be expected to include a certification based upon the financial statements of the master fund included in the report to shareholders of the feeder fund.

with Congressional intent to include both income or loss, and changes in net assets and, in the case where the financial statements are required to include a statement of cash flows, within the concept of "fair presentation" of an investment company's results of operations.

The certification required by new Investment Company Act Rule 30a-2 must be in the exact form set forth in the amendments to Form N-SAR.[84] The wording of the required certification may not be changed in any respect (even if the change would appear to be inconsequential in nature).

Investment companies filing reports on Form N-SAR under Sections 13(a) and 15(d) of the Exchange Act will also be required to maintain disclosure controls and procedures under new Exchange Act Rules 13a-15 and 15d-15.[85] New Rules 13a-15 and 15d-15 also require an investment company, under the supervision and with the participation of the principal executive and financial officers, to conduct an evaluation of the effectiveness of the design and operation of the investment company's disclosure controls and procedures within 90 days of the filing date of each report requiring certification under new Investment Company Act Rule 30a-2. We expect that this evaluation would be carried out in a manner that would form the basis for the certification statements required by Section 302 of the Act regarding disclosure controls and procedures required by new Investment Company Act Rule 30a-2(b)(4)(i)-(iii) in an investment company's Form N-SAR.[86]

The certification required by new Investment Company Act Rule 30a-2 makes reference to certain disclosures regarding both disclosure controls and procedures and internal controls that must be made in the reports in which the certification is contained. These disclosure requirements appear in the new instructions to Form N-SAR.[87]

Unit investment trusts will be required to provide the specified certification with respect to the items of Form N-SAR specific to them, which include very limited financial information.[88] We recognize that unit investment trusts, which are unmanaged, fixed portfolios of securities, have no corporate management structure and hence will not have a principal executive officer or principal financial officer. Therefore, in the case of a unit investment trust, the required certification should be signed by personnel of the sponsor, trustee, depositor or custodian who perform functions similar to those of a principal executive officer and principal financial officer on behalf of the trust.[89]

Unit investment trusts and small business investment companies are not required to transmit reports to their shareholders containing their financial statements, and Form N-SAR does not require unit investment trusts and small business investment companies to report financial information based on their financial statements.[90] Therefore, the certification requirement applicable to these investment companies does not include the requirement of new Investment Company Act Rule 30a-2(b)(3) that the signing officers certify that the financial information included in the periodic report and the financial statements on which it is based fairly present, in all material respects, the financial condition, results of operations, changes in net assets and cash flows (if the financial statements are required to include a statement of cash flows) of the investment company.[91]

Business development companies and face-amount certificate companies file periodic reports

---

[84] The certification must be filed as an exhibit to the report on Form N-SAR. The EDGAR document type must be EX-99.77Q3 CERT for an Exhibit filed in response to the instructions to sub-item 77Q3, EX-99.102P3 CERT for an Exhibit filed in response to the instructions to sub-item 102P3 and EX-99.133 CERT for an Exhibit filed in response to the instructions to item 133 of this form.

[85] New Exchange Act Rule 13a-15 applies to every issuer that has a class of securities registered pursuant to Section 12 of the Exchange Act. New Exchange Act Rule 15d-15 applies to every issuer that is required to file reports pursuant to Section 15(d) of the Exchange Act.

[86] New Investment Company Act Rule 30a-2(c) incorporates the definition of "disclosure controls and procedures" contained in new Exchange Act Rules 13a-14(c) and 15d-14(c). We recognize that, in the case of a series fund or family of investment companies, the disclosure controls and procedures for each fund in the series or family may be the same. Therefore, for purposes of new Investment Company Act Rule 30a-2(b)(4)(ii) and (iii), a single evaluation of the effectiveness of the disclosure controls and procedures for the series or family could be used in multiple certifications for the funds in the series or family, as long as the evaluation has been performed within 90 days of the date of the report on Form N-SAR.

[87] Instructions (a)(i) and (ii) to sub-item 77Q3 of Form N-SAR.

[88] See Items 111 to 132 of Form N-SAR.

[89] Signing officers could include, for example, the officers of the depositor required to sign a registration statement on Form N-4 [17 CFR 239.17b; 17 CFR 274.11c] or N-6 [17 CFR 239.17c; 17 CFR 274.11d], or the officers of the depositor, trustee or custodian required to sign a registration statement on Form N-8B-2 [17 CFR 274.12].

[90] Cf. Investment Company Act Rule 30e-2 [17 CFR 270.30e-2] (requiring registered unit investment trusts substantially all of the assets of which consist of securities issued by a management investment company to transmit to their shareholders semi-annually a report containing all of the applicable information and financial statements or their equivalent required to be included in reports of the management investment company for the same fiscal period).

[91] Instruction to item 133 of Form N-SAR.

on Forms 10-K and 10-Q under the Exchange Act, and they are required to comply with the certification requirements applicable to these forms.[92]

We note that, in a companion release, we are proposing to require registered management investment companies to file certified shareholder reports with the Commission on new Form N-CSR and would designate these certified shareholder reports as reports that are required under Sections 13(a) and 15(d) of the Exchange Act. For registered management investment companies, the required reports to shareholders, rather than Form N-SAR, are the primary vehicle for providing financial statements to investors. We believe that the information in these reports to shareholders should be certified. In addition, we are proposing an amendment to Form N-SAR that would uniformly apply to all registered investment companies, and not just those subject to Section 13(a) or 15(d) of the Exchange Act, the requirement to include in Form N-SAR the certification required by Section 302 of the Act. We are also proposing a new rule to apply disclosure controls and procedures requirements, similar to those contained in Exchange Act Rules 13a-15 and 15d-15, uniformly to all registered investment companies.

[¶ 2105]

V. Transition Provisions

Paragraphs (b)(1), (2) and (3) of new Exchange Act Rules 13a-14 and 15d-14 apply to quarterly and annual reports, including transition reports, filed after the Effective Date. Paragraphs (b)(4), (5) and (6) of Rules 13a-14 and 15d-14 apply to quarterly and annual reports, including transition reports, filed for periods ending after the Effective Date. Paragraph (a) of Item 307 of Regulations S-B and S-K and paragraph (b) of new Exchange Act Rules 13a-15 and 15d-15 apply to quarterly and annual reports, including transition reports, filed for periods ending after the Effective Date.

Paragraphs (b)(1), (2) and (3) of new Investment Company Act Rule 30a-2 apply to annual and semi-annual reports, including transition reports, on Form N-SAR filed after the Effective Date. Paragraphs (b)(4), (5) and (6) of Rule 30a-2 apply to annual and semi-annual reports, including transition reports, filed for periods ending after the Effective Date. Paragraph (a)(i) of the Instruction to sub-item 77Q3 of Form N-SAR and paragraph (b) of new Exchange Act Rules 13a-15 and 15d-15 apply to annual and semi-annual reports, including transition reports, on Form N-SAR filed for periods ending after the Effective Date.

[¶ 2106]

VI. Paperwork Reduction Act

The new rules and amendments to existing rules and forms contain "collection of information" requirements within the meaning of the Paperwork Reduction Act of 1995 ("PRA").[93] We published a notice requesting comment on the collection of information requirements in the June Proposals, and submitted these requirements to the Office of Management and Budget ("OMB") for review in accordance with the PRA.[94] The titles for those collections of information are "Form 10-K," "Form 10-KSB," "Form 10-Q" and "Form 10-QSB."[95]

While we received only one comment letter specifically remarking on our PRA estimates included in the June Proposals,[96] we revised the proposed amendments in response to the directives in Section 302 of the Act. The revisions made to the rules and amendments do not alter the burden estimates for Forms 10-K (OMB Control No. 3235-0063), 10-KSB (OMB Control No. 3235-0420), 10-Q (OMB Control No. 3235-0070) and 10-QSB (OMB Control No. 3235-0416) previously submitted to and approved by OMB.

The new rules and form amendments that we are adopting cover the more expansive reach of Section 302 of the Act and contain additional "collection of information requirements" within the meaning of the PRA. Accordingly, we submitted additional materials to OMB for emergency

---

[92] Business development companies are a category of closed-end investment company that are not required to register under the Investment Company Act. See 15 U.S.C. 80a-2(a)(48) (defining business development companies). A face-amount certificate company is an investment company that engages or proposes to engage in the business of issuing certain face amount certificates. See 15 U.S.C. 80a-4(1). See Release No. IC-14080 (Aug. 6, 1984) [49 FR 32370, 32372] (business development companies and face-amount certificate companies are required to file reports on other forms prescribed under the Exchange Act rather than Form N-SAR).

[93] 44 U.S.C. 3501 et seq.

[94] 44 U.S.C. 3507(d) and 5 CFR 1320.11.

[95] The burden hour and cost estimates for these collections of information are as follows: with respect to Form 10-K (OMB Control No. 3235-0063) an increase in annual reporting and recordkeeping burden hours and cost of 35,190 hours and $3,519,000, respectively; with respect to Form 10-KSB (OMB Control No. 3235-0420) an increase in annual reporting and recordkeeping burden hours and cost of 14,209 hours and $1,421,000, respectively; with respect to Form 10-Q (OMB Control No. 3235-0070) an increase in annual reporting and recordkeeping burden hours and cost of 100,298 hours and $10,030,000, respectively; and respectively; with respect to Form 10-QSB (OMB Control No. 3235-0416) an increase in annual reporting and recordkeeping burden hours and cost of 43,530 hours and $4,353,000, respectively.

[96] See the Letter dated August 2, 2000 of Bernard E. Klein.

review in accordance with the PRA.[97] The titles for these collections of information are "Form 20-F" (OMB Control No. 3235-0288), "Form 40-F" (OMB Control No. 3235-0381) and "Form N-SAR" (OMB Control No. 3235-0330). An agency may not conduct or sponsor, and a person is not required to respond to, an information collection unless it displays a currently valid OMB control number.

Form 10-K prescribes information that registrants must disclose annually to the market about its business. Form 10-KSB prescribes information that registrants that are "small business issuers" as defined under our rules must disclose annually to the market about its business.

Form 10-Q prescribes information that registrants must disclose quarterly to the market about its business. Form 10-QSB prescribes information that registrants that are "small business issuers" as defined under our rules must disclose quarterly to the market about its business.

Form 20-F is used by foreign private issuers to either register a class of securities under the Exchange Act or provide an annual report required under the Exchange Act. Form 40-F is used by foreign private issuers to file reports under the Exchange Act after having registered securities under the Securities Act and by certain Canadian registrants. Form N-SAR is used by registered investment companies to file annual and semi-annual reports under the Exchange Act and the Investment Company Act.

New Exchange Act Rules 13a-14 and 15d-14[98] require an issuer's principal executive and financial officers to certify the information contained in the issuer's quarterly and annual reports and that they have taken certain actions with respect to the issuer's internal controls for the collection and reporting of financial and other information that is subject to disclosure in the issuer's quarterly and annual Exchange Act reports. This certification requirement would become part of the "collection of information" required in each quarterly and annual report.

New Exchange Act Rules 13a-15 and 15d-15[99] require an issuer to maintain disclosure controls and procedures to provide reasonable assurance that the issuer is able to record, process, summarize and report the information required in the issuer's Exchange Act reports. These procedures would become part of the "collection of information" required in these reports.

New Investment Company Act Rule 30a-2 requires an investment company's principal executive and financial officers to certify the information contained in the investment company's annual and semi-annual reports on Form N-SAR and that they have taken certain actions with respect to the investment company's internal controls for the collection and reporting of financial and other information that is subject to disclosure in the investment company's reports on Form N-SAR. This certification requirement would become part of the "collection of information" required in each report on Form N-SAR.

The purpose of the certification and disclosure controls and procedures requirements is to ensure that the information that is collected and disclosed in Exchange Act reports is complete and accurate. Consequently, the senior officer certification, as well as the periodic evaluations of internal reporting systems, required by the rules and amendments will become part of the process in which issuers engage to comply with the reporting requirements of the affected forms.

The compliance burden estimates for the collections of information are based on several assumptions.[100] The number of foreign private issuers that file annual reports on Form 20-F or 40-F is approximately 1,300 entities.[101] The number of registered investment companies that file Form N-SAR is approximately 4,450 entities.[102]

New Exchange Act Rule 13a-14 and new Investment Company Act Rule 30a-2 require an issuer's principal executive and financial officers to certify the information contained in the issuer's periodic reports. The compliance burden associated with new Exchange Act Rule 13a-14 and new Investment Company Act Rule 30a-2 is the burden associated with reading and thinking critically about each quarterly and annual report to be filed by the issuer so that the certifying officers can make the required certification. For purposes of the PRA, we estimate that the new certification requirement will result in an increase of five burden hours[103] per issuer in connection with pre-

[97] 44 U.S.C. 3507(j) and 5 CFR 1320.13.

[98] References to new Exchange Act Rule 13a-14 in this section also refer to new Exchange Act Rule 15d-14.

[99] References to new Exchange Act Rule 13a-15 in this section also refer to new Exchange Act Rule 15d-15.

[100] We have based our estimates of the effects that the new rules and amendments to existing rules and forms will have on these information collections primarily on our review of actual filings of these forms and the forms' requirements.

[101] This estimate is based on 1,200 foreign private issuers that file annual reports on Form 20-F and 100 Canadian issuers that file annual reports on Form 40-F.

[102] This estimate is based on 3,650 registered management investment companies and 800 registered unit investment trusts that file reports under Section 13(a) or 15(d) of the Exchange Act.

[103] This estimate is based on consultations with several law firms and other persons who regularly assist registrants in preparing and filing quarterly and annual reports with the Commission.

paring each annual report on Form 20-F or 40-F and an increase of five burden hours per issuer in connection with preparing each report on Form N-SAR.

New Exchange Act Rule 13a-15 requires an issuer to maintain sufficient procedures to collect, process and disclose the information required in its Exchange Act reports. We expect that issuers already maintain procedures, whether formal or informal, to comply with their Exchange Act disclosure obligations and for their own internal purposes. We do not believe that this requirement will result in any change in either the reporting or cost burden associated with preparing annual reports on Forms 20-F and 40-F or reports on Form N-SAR.

Based on a burden hour estimate of five hours per respondent per year, we estimate that the total burden hours of complying with Form 20-F and Form 40-F, revised to include the burden hours expected from the new rules, is estimated to be 586,248 hours for Form 20-F, an increase of 4,500 hours[104] from the current annual burden of 581,748 hours, and 525 hours for Form 40-F, an increase of 475 hours[105] from the current annual burden of 50 hours. The total burden hours of complying with Form N-SAR, revised to include the burden hours expected from the new rules, is estimated to be 154,450 hours,[106] an increase of 52,702 hours[107] from the current annual burden of 101,748 hours.

The total burden hours of complying with Forms 10-Q and 10-QSB, revised to include the burden hours expected from the new rules, is estimated to be 3,129,283 hours for Form 10-Q, an increase of 100,298 hours[108] from the current annual burden of 3,028,985 hours, and 1,288,488 hours for Form 10-QSB, an increase of 43,530 hours[109] from the current annual burden of 1,244,958 hours. The total burden hours of complying with Forms 10-K and 10-KSB, revised to include the burden hours expected from the new rules, is estimated to be 12,344,652 hours for Form 10-K, an increase of 35,190 hours[110] from the current annual burden of 12,309,462 hours, and 3,438,518 hours for Form 10-KSB, an increase of 14,209 hours[111] from the current annual burden of 3,424,309 hours.

In addition to the internal hours they will expend to comply with Forms 20-F and 40-F, we expect that respondents will retain outside professionals to assist in compliance with the information collection requirements. The total dollar cost of complying with Forms 20-F and 40-F, revised to include outside professional costs expected from the new rules, is estimated to be $523,596,000 for Form 20-F, an increase of $450,000[112] from the current annual burden of $523,146,000, and $52,500 for Form 40-F, an increase of $26,500[113] from the current annual burden of $26,000.

The total dollar cost of complying with Forms 10-Q and 10-QSB, revised to include outside pro-

[104] This estimate is based on the current annual burden per filing for each foreign private issuer. The estimate of 4,500 hours is calculated by 1,200 foreign private issuers x one filing per year x five burden hours x .75).

[105] This estimate is based on the current annual burden per filing for each Canadian issuer. The estimate of 475 hours is calculated by 100 Canadian issuers x one filing per year x five burden hours x .75 § 100 hours to reflect an adjustment in the distribution of burden hours and associated costs). The estimate has then been increased by 100 hours due to an adjustment to reflect a revised burden hour/cost allocation (75%/25%) for the report.

[106] This estimate is based on the current annual burden per filing for each investment company. With regard to Form N-SAR, the current estimated average burden hours per response for registered management investment companies and registered small business investment companies is 14.75 hours and the current estimated average burden hours per response for registered unit investment trusts is six hours. The estimated average burden hours per response, if new Investment Company Act Rule 30a-2 is adopted, for Form N-SAR would increase the average burden hours per response by five hours per filing that is required to be certified. We estimate that 50 registered management investment companies are not subject to Section 13(a) or 15(d) of the Exchange Act and hence would not be required to include the certification. Therefore, the estimate of 154,450 hours is calculated by: (3,650 registered management investment companies x two filings per year x 19.75 burden hours) § (50 registered management investment companies not subject to Section 13(a) or 15(d) of the Exchange Act x two filings per year x 14.75 burden hours) § (800 registered unit investment trusts x one filing per year x 11 burden hours).

[107] The increase in burden hours is attributed to an increase of 400 registered management investment companies and 67 registered unit investment trusts that are required to file reports pursuant to the Exchange Act from the previous number of these issuers calculated for the current annual burden, and the certification requirement required by the new rule.

[108] The estimate of 100,298 hours is calculated by 26,746 quarterly reports x five burden hours x .75.

[109] The estimate of 43,350 hours is calculated by 11,608 quarterly reports x five burden hours x .75.

[110] The estimate of 35,190 hours is calculated by 9,384 annual reports x five burden hours x .75.

[111] The estimate of 14,209 hours is calculated by 3,789 annual reports x five burden hours x .75.

[112] This estimate is based on the current annual burden per filing for each foreign private issuer. The estimate of $450,000 is calculated by 1,200 foreign private issuers x one filing per year x five burden hours x .25 x $300.00).

[113] This estimate is based on the current annual burden per filing for each foreign private issuer. The estimate of $26,500 is calculated by 100 foreign private issuers x one filing per year x five burden hours x .25 x $300.00). The estimate has then been reduced by $11,000 due to an adjustment to reflect a revised burden hour/cost allocation (75%/25%) for the report.

fessional costs expected from the new rules, is estimated to be $312,929,000 for Form 10-Q, an increase of $10,030,000[114] from the current annual burden of $302,899,000, and $128,849,000 for Form 10-QSB, an increase of $4,353,000[115] from the current annual burden of $124,496,000. The total dollar cost of complying with Forms 10-K and 10-KSB, revised to include outside professional costs expected from the new rules, is estimated to be $1,234,465,000 for Form 10-K, an increase of $3,519,000[116] from the current annual burden of $1,230,946,000, and $343,852,000 for Form 10-KSB, an increase of $1,421,000[117] from the current annual burden of $342,431,000.

Comments concerning the accuracy of these burden estimates, and any suggestions for reducing the burden, should be directed to the Commission. Compliance with the new rules is mandatory. Under our rules for the retention of manual signatures, issuers will be required to maintain the certifications for five years.[118] The information required by the new rules will not be kept confidential.

[¶ 2107]

VII. Cost-Benefit Analysis

The certification requirement that we are adopting today implements a Congressional mandate. We recognize that any implementation of the Sarbanes-Oxley Act will likely result in costs as well as benefits and have an effect on the economy. We are sensitive to the costs and benefits of our adoption of a rule that requires issuers to maintain disclosure controls and procedures. We discuss these costs and benefits below.

The new certification requirement may lead to some additional costs for issuers. The new rules require an issuer's principal executive and financial officers to review the issuer's periodic reports and to make the required certification. To the extent that corporate officers would need to spend additional time thinking critically about the overall context of their company's disclosure, issuers would incur costs (although investors would benefit from improved disclosure). The certification requirement creates a new legal obligation for an issuer's principal executive and financial officers, but does not change the standard of legal liability.

Issuers are already required to maintain reporting controls and procedures for identifying and processing the information needed to satisfy their disclosure obligations under the Exchange Act. The new rules do not dictate that issuers follow any particular procedure. By allowing issuers to determine what procedures are necessary to meet the obligation of the rules, we are mitigating the costs associated with compliance. Some issuers may need to institute appropriate controls and procedures. Other issuers may need to enhance existing informal or ad hoc controls and procedures. These incremental costs are difficult to quantify. While we requested comment and supporting data in connection with the June Proposals on the cost of implementing, or upgrading and strengthening existing, reporting controls and procedures, we received no specific comment letters in response to that request.

The required periodic evaluation of reporting controls and procedures likely will result in costs for issuers. The new certification requirement likely will require issuers to create or strengthen internal controls to enable their senior executive officers to meet their certification obligations under the new rules. Many issuers already regularly monitor and evaluate their controls and procedures. Because the size and scope of these internal reporting systems is likely to vary among issuers, it is difficult to provide an accurate cost estimate.

Conversely, the new rules are likely to provide significant benefits by ensuring that information about an issuer's business and financial condition is adequately reviewed by the issuer's principal executive and financial officers and the issuer's internal systems keep pace with the growth of the business.

We believe that investor confidence in corporate disclosure has suffered, in part, because of a belief that corporate officers may not devote sufficient attention to the preparation of their companies' periodic reports and to the disclosure controls and procedures that generate the data from which they are prepared.

The new rules should help to ensure that issuers maintain sufficient internal reporting controls and procedures to provide reasonable assurance that they can record, process, summarize and report the information that is required in all Exchange Act reports. To the extent that issuers do not maintain adequate controls and procedures, the new rules should lead to the development, or enhancement and modernization, of these controls

[114] The estimate of $10,030,000 is calculated by 26,746 quarterly reports x five burden hours x .25 x $300.00.

[115] The estimate of $4,353,000 is calculated by 11,608 quarterly reports x five burden hours x .25 x $300.00.

[116] The estimate of $3,519,000 is calculated by 9,384 annual reports x five burden hours x .25 x $300.00.

[117] The estimate of $1,421,000 is calculated by 3,789 annual reports x five burden hours x .25 x $300.00.

[118] See the amendment to Rule 302(b) of Regulation S-T [17 CFR 232.302(b)].

and procedures. The required periodic evaluation of these controls and procedures should ensure that issuers devote adequate resources and attention to the maintenance of their internal reporting systems. Additionally, the required evaluation should help to identify potential weaknesses and deficiencies in advance of a system breakdown, thereby ensuring the continuous, orderly and timely flow of information within the company and, ultimately, to investors and the marketplace.

[¶ 2108]

VIII. Final Regulatory Flexibility Analysis

This Final Regulatory Flexibility Analysis, or FRFA, has been prepared in accordance with the Regulatory Flexibility Act.[119] The FRFA pertains to new Exchange Act Rules 13a-15 and 15d-15 adopted for operating companies, for which we gave notice and sought comment. The Sarbanes-Oxley Act of 2002 directs us to adopt rules for registered investment companies. Because we find good cause to adopt those rules without notice and comment, we do not analyze them in the FRFA. New Exchange Act Rules 13a-15 and 15d-15 require an issuer to maintain disclosure controls and procedures to provide reasonable assurance that the issuer is able to record, process, summarize and report the information required in their Exchange Act reports.[120]

A. Reasons for, and Objectives of, New Rules

New Exchange Act Rules 13a-15 and 15d-15 complement existing requirements for reporting companies to establish and maintain systems of internal controls with respect to their financial information. They are intended to ensure that an issuer maintains commensurate procedures for gathering, analyzing and disclosing all information that is required to be disclosed in its Exchange Act reports.

B. Legal Basis

We are adopting the new rules under the authority set forth in Sections 10(b), 13, 15(d) and 23(a) of the Exchange Act and Sections 3(a) and 302 of the Act.

C. Small Entities Subject to the Final Rules

The new rules will affect small entities that are subject to the reporting requirements of Section 13(a) or 15(d) of the Exchange Act. For purposes of the Regulatory Flexibility Act, the Exchange Act[121] defines the term "small business," other than an investment company, to be an issuer that, on the last day of its most recent fiscal year, has total assets of $5 million or less.[122] We estimate that there are approximately 2,500 companies subject to the reporting requirements of Section 13(a) or 15(d) of the Exchange Act that are not investment companies and that have assets of $5 million or less.[123]

D. Significant Issues Raised by Public Comment

The IRFA appeared in the June Proposals.[124] We requested comment on any aspect of the IRFA, including the number of small businesses that would be affected by the proposals, the nature of the impact, how to quantify the number of small entities that would be affected and how to quantify the impact of the proposals. We received one comment letter responding to that request.[125] This commenter recommended that we provide a transition period for small businesses and that we clarify the need for small businesses to audit their internal controls quarterly. This release contains a transition provision that delays compliance with the certification requirement as it relates to disclosure controls and procedures and internal controls.[126] The requirements for periodic audit of an issuer's internal controls will be considered at a future date.

E. Reporting, Recordkeeping and Other Compliance Requirements

The new rules require issuers, including "small businesses," to maintain sufficient procedures to provide reasonable assurance that the issuer is able to record, process, summarize and report the information required in their Exchange Act reports filed with the Commission, and to periodically review and evaluate these procedures. We do not dictate the specifics of these procedures. The new rules may increase the costs associated with compliance with issuers' Exchange Act reporting obligations.

---

[119] 5 U.S.C. 603.

[120] The Initial Regulatory Flexibility Analysis ("IRFA") prepared in connection with the June Proposals also involved proposed rules under the Exchange Act that would have required an issuer's principal executive officer and principal financial officer to certify the information contained in their quarterly and annual reports That proposal has been superseded by the statutory mandate of Section 302 of the Act. The Act's directive to adopt rules for all issuers makes no distinction based on the size of the issuer. We, therefore, do not analyze the new rules adopted under the Exchange Act requiring certifications by an issuer's principal executive and financial officers.

[121] 17 CFR 240.0-10(a).

[122] A similar definition is provided under Securities Act Rule 157 [17 CFR 230.157].

[123] This estimate is based on filings with the Commission.

[124] See the June Proposals at Section V.

[125] See the Letter dated August19, 2002 of the Office of the Chief Counsel for Advocacy of the U.S. Small Business Administration.

[126] See Section V above.

F. Duplicative, Overlapping or Conflicting Federal Rules

Section 13(b)(2)(B) of the Exchange Act[127] requires issuers that are subject to the reporting requirements of Section 13(a) or 15(d) to devise and maintain a system of internal accounting controls sufficient to provide reasonable assurances that the transactions and information are recorded as necessary to permit the preparation of the issuer's financial statements. New Exchange Act Rules 13a-15 and 15d-15 are intended to address the issuer's controls and procedures for recording, processing summarizing and reporting the information that is required to be disclosed in Exchange Act reports.

G. Agency Action to Minimize Effect on Small Entities

The Regulatory Flexibility Act directs us to consider significant alternatives that would accomplish the stated objectives, while minimizing any significant adverse impact on small entities. In that regard, we considered the following alternatives: (a) establishing different compliance or reporting requirements that take into account the resources of small entities, (b) clarifying, consolidating or simplifying compliance and reporting requirements under the rules for small entities and (c) exempting small entities from all or part of the proposed rules. We solicited comment as to whether small business issuers should be excluded from the new rules. We received no comment letters responding to that request.

The periodic review and evaluation of information collection and reporting procedures required by the new rules involves a performance standard. The new rules do not mandate how issuers should conduct this review and evaluation. This flexibility will enable small and large entities to develop approaches for the review and evaluation that are appropriate to their individual circumstances. Because Congress has directed the senior officers of all issuers, regardless of size, to certify issuers' quarterly and annual reports, we do not believe it is consistent with that mandate to exempt small issuers from the new rules. We are not aware of any way to further clarify or simplify compliance for small entities.

[¶ 2109]

IX. Consideration of Burden on Competition and Promotion of Efficiency, Competition and Capital Formation

Section 23(a)(2) of the Exchange Act [128] requires us, when adopting rules under the Exchange Act, to consider the impact that any new rule would have on competition. In addition, Section 23(a)(2) prohibits us from adopting any rule that would impose a burden on competition not necessary or appropriate in furtherance of the purposes of the Exchange Act. Section 3(f) of the Exchange Act [129] and Section 2(c) of the Investment Company Act[130] requires us, when engaging in rulemaking where we are required to consider or determine whether an action is necessary or appropriate in the public interest, to consider, in addition to the protection of investors, whether the action will promote efficiency, competition and capital formation.

The new rules are intended to enhance investor confidence in the quality of the information available to them in quarterly and annual reports filed under the Exchange Act. We believe that by requiring an issuer's principal executive and financial officers to provide the required certification, investor confidence in the securities markets will be enhanced, thereby leading to a more efficient market.

We do not believe that the new rules will impose any burden on competition. Issuers will incur some costs in complying with the new rules. These costs will include conducting periodic evaluations of the issuer's internal controls and procedures to record, process, summarize and report, on a timely basis, the information required in periodic and current reports filed by the issuer under the Exchange Act. We requested comment in connection on the June Proposals on whether the proposed rules, if adopted, would impose a burden on competition. We received no comment letters in response to that request.

[¶ 2110]

X. Administrative Procedure Act

The Administrative Procedure Act, or APA, generally requires an agency to publish notice of a proposed rulemaking in the Federal Register.[131] The APA's notice and comment requirement does not apply, however, if the agency "for good cause finds . . . that notice and public procedure are impracticable, unnecessary, or contrary to the

[127] 15 U.S.C. 78m(b)(2)(B).

[128] 15 U.S.C. 78w(a)(2).

[129] 15 U.S.C. 78c(f).

[130] 15 U.S.C. 80a-2(c).

[131] See 5 U.S.C. 553(b).

public interest."[132] The Commission believes that it is appropriate to waive notice and comment for the portions of the new rules that were not included in the June Proposals and for the application of the new rules to investment companies. Congress has directed the Commission to implement Section 302 of the Act by rule within 30 days after the date of enactment.[133] It is impractical to provide notice and comment within the statutory deadline. It would be unnecessary and against the public interest to provide notice and opportunity for comment on a directive from Congress to implement specific rules. Accordingly, the Commission for good cause finds that delaying adoption of these rules until after a notice and comment period would be impractical, unnecessary and contrary to the public interest.

The APA also generally requires that an agency publish an adopted rule in the Federal Register 30 days before it becomes effective.[134] This requirement, however, does not apply if the agency finds good cause for making the rule effective sooner.[135] For the same reasons as it is waiving notice and comment, the Commission finds good cause to make the new Exchange Act Rules 13a-14 and 15d-14 and new Investment Company Act Rule 30a-2, and the amendments to related rules and forms, effective immediately. In addition, because new Exchange Act Rules 13a-15 and 15d-15 effectuate the purpose of the Section 302 certification requirement and might create a hardship if they did not become effective simultaneously with new Exchange Act Rules 13a-14 and 15d-14, the Commission finds good cause to make the rules effective immediately as to all issuers filing reports under Section 13(a) or 15(d) of the Exchange Act.[136]

[¶ 2111]

XI. Statutory Authority

The rules and amendments contained in this release are being adopted under the authority set forth in Sections 10(b), 13, 15(d) and 23(a) of the Exchange Act, Section 8, 30 and 38 of the Investment Company Act and Sections 3(a) and 302 of the Sarbanes-Oxley Act of 2002.

List of Subjects in 17 CFR Parts 228, 229, 232, 240, 249, 270 and 274

Securities.

Investment Companies.

Reporting and recordkeeping requirements.

TEXT OF FINAL RULES AND AMENDMENTS

In accordance with the foregoing, Title 17, Chapter II, of the Code of Federal Regulations is amended as follows:

Part 228 - INTEGRATED DISCLOSURE SYSTEM FOR SMALL BUSINESS ISSUERS

1. The authority citation for Part 228 is amended by adding the following citation to read as follows:

Authority: 15 U.S.C. 77e, 77f, 77g, 77h, 77j, 77k, 77s, 77z-2, 77z-3, 77aa(25), 77aa(26), 77ddd, 77eee, 77ggg, 77hhh, 77jjj, 77nnn, 77sss, 78l, 78m, 78n, 78o, 78u-5, 78w, 78ll, 78mm, 80a-8, 80a-29, 80a-30, 80a-37 and 80b-11.

Section 228.307 is also issued under secs. 3(a) and 302, Pub.L.No. 107-204, 116 Stat. 745.

2. By adding 228.307 to read as follows:

228.307 Controls and Procedures.

(a) Evaluation of disclosure controls and procedures. Disclose the conclusions of the small business issuer's principal executive officer or officers and principal financial officer or officers, or persons performing similar functions, about the effectiveness of the small business issuer's disclosure controls and procedures (as defined in §§ 240.13a-14(c) and 240.15d-14(c)) based on their evaluation of these controls and procedures as of a date within 90 days of the filing date of the quarterly or annual report that includes the disclosure required by this paragraph.

(b) Changes in internal controls. Disclose whether or not there were significant changes in the small business issuer's internal controls or in other factors that could significantly affect these controls subsequent to the date of their evaluation, including any corrective actions with regard to significant deficiencies and material weaknesses.

(c) Asset-Backed Issuers. A small business issuer that is an Asset-Backed Issuer (as defined in Rule 13a-14(g) and Rule 15d-14(g) under the Securities Exchange Act of 1934 [17 CFR 240.13a-14(g) and 17 CFR 240.15d-14(g)] is not

[132] Id. The Commission previously published notice and sought comment on a certification proposal that was somewhat similar to, but different in several material respects, from the new rules we are adopting today to implement Section 302 of the Sarbanes-Oxley Act. We did not propose rules that would apply to investment companies or foreign private issuers (although we sought comment on the latter).

[133] See Section 302 (a) and (c) of the Act.

[134] See 5 U.S.C. 553(d).

[135] Id.

[136] This finding also satisfies the requirements of 5 U.S.C. 808(2), allowing the rules to become immediately, effective notwithstanding the requirements of 5 U.S.C. 801 (if agency finds that notice and public comment procedure are "impractical, unnecessary, or contrary to the public interest," a rule "shall take effect at such time as the Federal agency promulgating the rule determines").

required to disclose the information required by this Item.

Part 229 - STANDARD INSTRUCTIONS FOR FILING FORMS UNDER SECURITIES ACT OF 1933, SECURITIES EXCHANGE ACT OF 1934 AND ENERGY POLICY AND CONSERVATION ACT OF 1975 - REGULATION S-K

3. The authority citation for Part 229 is amended by adding the following citation to read as follows:

Authority: 15 U.S.C. 77e, 77f, 77g, 77h, 77j, 77k, 77s, 77z-2, 77z-3, 77aa(25), 77aa(26), 77ddd, 77eee, 77ggg, 77hhh, 77iii, 77jjj, 77nnn, 77sss, 78c, 78i, 78j, 78l, 78m, 78n, 78o, 78u-5, 78w, 78ll(d), 78mm, 79e, 79n, 79t, 80a-8, 80a-29, 80a-30, 80a-31(c), 80a-37, 80a-38(a) and 80b-11, unless otherwise noted.

Section 229.307 is also issued under secs. 3(a) and 302, Pub.L.No. 107-204, 116 Stat. 745.

4. By adding § 229.307 to read as follows:

§ 229.307 Controls and Procedures.

(a) Evaluation of disclosure controls and procedures. Disclose the conclusions of the registrant's principal executive officer or officers and principal financial officer or officers, or persons performing similar functions, about the effectiveness of the registrant's disclosure controls and procedures (as defined in §§ 240.13a-14(c) and 240.15d-14(c)) based on their evaluation of these controls and procedures as of a date within 90 days of the filing date of the quarterly or annual report that includes the disclosure required by this paragraph.

(b) Changes in internal controls. Disclose whether or not there were significant changes in the registrant's internal controls or in other factors that could significantly affect these controls subsequent to the date of their evaluation, including any corrective actions with regard to significant deficiencies and material weaknesses.

(c) Asset-Backed Issuers. A registrant that is an Asset-Backed Issuer (as defined in §§ 240.13a-14(g) and 240.15d-14(g)) is not required to disclose the information required by this Item.

PART 232 - REGULATION S-T - GENERAL RULES AND REGULATIONS FOR ELECTRONIC FILINGS

5. The authority citation for Part 232 is amended by adding the following citation to read as follows:

Authority: 15 U.S.C. 77f, 77g, 77h, 77j, 77s(a), 77sss(a), 78c(b), 78l, 78m, 78n, 78o(d), 78w(a), 78ll(d), 79t(a), 80a-8, 80a-29, 80a-30 and 80a-37.

Section 232.302 is also issued under secs. 3(a) and 302, Pub.L.No. 107-204, 116 Stat. 745.

6. By amending 232.302 by revising paragraphs (a) and (b) to read as follows:

232.302 Signatures.

(a) Required signatures to, or within, any electronic submission (including, without limitation, signatories within the certifications required by §§ 240.13a-14, 240.15d-14 and 270.30a-2 of this chapter) must be in typed form rather than manual format. Signatures in an HTML document that are not required may, but are not required to, be presented in an HTML graphic or image file within the electronic filing, in compliance with the formatting requirements of the EDGAR Filer Manual. When used in connection with an electronic filing, the term "signature" means an electronic entry in the form of a magnetic impulse or other form of computer data compilation of any letters or series of letters or characters comprising a name, executed, adopted or authorized as a signature. Signatures are not required in unofficial PDF copies submitted in accordance with 232.104.

(b) Each signatory to an electronic filing (including, without limitation, each signatory to the certifications required by §§ 240.13a-14, 240.15d-14 and 270.30a-2 of this chapter) shall manually sign a signature page or other document authenticating, acknowledging or otherwise adopting his or her signature that appears in typed form within the electronic filing. Such document shall be executed before or at the time the electronic filing is made and shall be retained by the filer for a period of five years. Upon request, an electronic filer shall furnish to the Commission or its staff a copy of any or all documents retained pursuant to this section.

* * * * *

PART 240 - GENERAL RULES AND REGULATIONS, SECURITIES EXCHANGE ACT OF 1934

7. The authority citation for Part 240 is amended by adding the following citations in numerical order to read as follows:

Authority: 15 U.S.C. 77c, 77d, 77g, 77j, 77s, 77z-2, 77z-3, 77eee, 77ggg, 77nnn, 77sss, 77ttt, 78c, 78d, 78e, 78f, 78g, 78i, 78j, 78j-1, 78k, 78k-1, 78l, 78m, 78n, 78o, 78p, 78q, 78s, 78u-5, 78w, 78x, 78ll, 78mm, 79q, 79t, 80a-20, 80a-23, 80a-29, 80a-37, 80b-3, 80b-4 and 80b-11, unless otherwise noted.

* * * * *

Section 240.12b-15 is also issued under secs. 3(a) and 302, Pub.L.No. 107-204, 116 Stat. 745.

Section 240.13a-10 is also issued under secs. 3(a) and 302, Pub.L.No. 107-204, 116 Stat. 745.

Section 240.13a-14 is also issued under secs. 3(a) and 302, Pub.L.No. 107-204, 116 Stat. 745.

Section 240.13a-15 is also issued under secs. 3(a) and 302, Pub.L.No. 107-204, 116 Stat. 745.

Section 240.15d-10 is also issued under secs. 3(a) and 302, Pub.L.No. 107-204, 116 Stat. 745.

Section 240.15d-14 is also issued under secs. 3(a) and 302, Pub.L.No. 107-204, 116 Stat. 745.

Section 240.15d-15 is also issued under secs. 3(a) and 302, Pub.L.No. 107-204, 116 Stat. 745.

* * * * *

8. By revising § 240.12b-15 to read as follows:

§ 240.12b-15 Amendments.

All amendments must be filed under cover of the form amended, marked with the letter "A" to designate the document as an amendment, e.g., "10-K/A," and in compliance with pertinent requirements applicable to statements and reports. Amendments filed pursuant to this section must set forth the complete text of each item as amended. Amendments must be numbered sequentially and be filed separately for each statement or report amended. Amendments to a statement may be filed either before or after registration becomes effective. Amendments must be signed on behalf of the registrant by a duly authorized representative of the registrant. In addition, each principal executive officer and principal financial officer of the registrant must provide a new certification as specified in § 240.13a-14 or § 240.15d-14. The requirements of the form being amended will govern the number of copies to be filed in connection with a paper format amendment. Electronic filers satisfy the provisions dictating the number of copies by filing one copy of the amendment in electronic format. See Rule 309 of Regulation S-T (232.309 of this chapter).

9. By amending § 240.13a-10 to add an "Additional Note" after the "Note" at the end of the section to read as follows:

§ 240.13a-10 Transition reports.

* * * * *

Additional Note: The report or reports to be filed pursuant to this section must include the certification required by § 240.13a-14.

10. By adding § 240.13a-14 to read as follows:

§ 240.13a-14 Certification of disclosure in annual and quarterly reports.

(a) Each report, including transition reports, filed on Form 10-Q, Form 10-QSB, Form 10-K, Form 10-KSB, Form 20-F or Form 40-F (§ § 249.308a, 249.308b, 249.310, 249.310b, 249.220f and 249.240f of this chapter) under section 13(a) of the Act (15 U.S.C. 78m(a)), other than a report filed by an Asset-Backed Issuer (as defined in paragraph (g) of this section), must include a certification containing the information set forth in paragraph (b) of this section in the form specified in the report. Each principal executive officer or officers and principal financial officer or officers of the issuer, or persons performing similar functions, at the time of filing of the report must sign the certification.

(b) The certification included in each report specified in paragraph (a) of this section must be in the form specified in the report and consist of a statement of the certifying officer that:

(1) He or she has reviewed the report being filed;

(2) Based on his or her knowledge, the report does not contain any untrue statement of a material fact or omit to state a material fact necessary to make the statements made, in light of the circumstances under which such statements were made, not misleading with respect to the period covered by the report;

(3) Based on his or her knowledge, the financial statements, and other financial information included in the report, fairly present in all material respects the financial condition, results of operations and cash flows of the issuer as of, and for, the periods presented in the report;

(4) He or she and the other certifying officers are responsible for establishing and maintaining disclosure controls and procedures (as such term is defined in paragraph (c) of this section) for the issuer and have:

(i) Designed such disclosure controls and procedures to ensure that material information relating to the issuer, including its consolidated subsidiaries, is made known to them by others within those entities, particularly during the period in which the periodic reports are being prepared;

(ii) Evaluated the effectiveness of the issuer's disclosure controls and procedures as of a date within 90 days prior to the filing date of the report ("Evaluation Date"); and

(iii) Presented in the report their conclusions about the effectiveness of the disclosure controls and procedures based on their evaluation as of the Evaluation Date;

(5) He or she and the other certifying officers have disclosed, based on their most recent evaluation, to the issuer's auditors and the audit committee of the board of directors (or persons fulfilling the equivalent function):

(i) All significant deficiencies in the design or operation of internal controls which could adversely affect the issuer's ability to record, process, summarize and report financial data and have identified for the issuer's auditors any material weaknesses in internal controls; and

(ii) Any fraud, whether or not material, that involves management or other employees who have a significant role in the issuer's internal controls; and

(6) He or she and the other certifying officers have indicated in the report whether or not there were significant changes in internal controls or in other factors that could significantly affect internal controls subsequent to the date of their most recent evaluation, including any corrective actions with regard to significant deficiencies and material weaknesses.

(c) For purposes of this section and § 240.13a-15 of this chapter, the term "disclosure controls and procedures" means controls and other procedures of an issuer that are designed to ensure that information required to be disclosed by the issuer in the reports that it files or submits under the Act (15 U.S.C. 78a et seq.) is recorded, processed, summarized and reported, within the time periods specified in the Commission's rules and forms. Disclosure controls and procedures include, without limitation, controls and procedures designed to ensure that information required to be disclosed by an issuer in the reports that it files or submits under the Act is accumulated and communicated to the issuer's management, including its principal executive officer or officers and principal financial officer or officers, or persons performing similar functions, as appropriate to allow timely decisions regarding required disclosure.

(d) A person required to provide the certification specified in paragraph (a) of this section may not have the certification signed on his or her behalf pursuant to a power of attorney or other form of confirming authority.

(e) Each annual report filed by an Asset-Backed Issuer (as defined in paragraph (g) of this section) under section 13(a) of the Act (15 U.S.C. 78m(a)) must include a certification addressing the following items:

(1) Review by the certifying officer of the annual report and other reports containing distribution information for the period covered by the annual report;

(2) The absence in these reports, to the best of the certifying officer's knowledge, of any untrue statement of material fact or omission of a material fact necessary to make the statements made, in light of the circumstances under which such statements were made, not misleading;

(3) The inclusion in these reports, to the best of the certifying officer's knowledge, of the financial information required to be provided to the trustee under the governing documents of the issuer; and

(4) Compliance by the servicer with its servicing obligations and minimum servicing standards.

(f) With respect to Asset-Backed Issuers, the certification required by paragraph (e) of this section must be signed by the trustee of the trust (if the trustee signs the annual report) or the senior officer in charge of securitization of the depositor (if the depositor signs the annual report). Alternatively, the senior officer in charge of the servicing function of the master servicer (or entity performing the equivalent functions) may sign the certification.

(g) For purposes of this section, the term Asset-Backed Issuer means any issuer whose reporting obligation results from the registration of securities it issued that are primarily serviced by the cash flows of a discrete pool of receivables or other financial assets, either fixed or revolving, that by their terms convert into cash within a finite time period plus any rights or other assets designed to assure the servicing or timely distribution of proceeds to security holders.

11. By adding § 240.13a-15 to read as follows:

§ 240.13a-15 Issuer's disclosure controls and procedures related to preparation of required reports.

(a) Every issuer that has a class of securities registered pursuant to section 12 of the Act (15 U.S.C. 78l), other than an Asset-Backed Issuer (as defined in § 240.13a-14(g) of this chapter), must maintain disclosure controls and procedures (as defined in § 240.13a-14(c) of this chapter).

(b) Within the 90-day period prior to the filing date of each report requiring certification under § § 240.13a-14 and 270.30a-2 of this chapter, an evaluation must be carried out under the supervision and with the participation of the issuer's management, including the issuer's principal executive officer or officers and principal financial officer or officers, or persons performing similar functions, of the effectiveness of the design and operation of the issuer's disclosure controls and procedures.

12. By amending § 240.15d-10 to add an "Additional Note" after the "Note" at the end of the section to read as follows:

§ 240.15d-10 Transition reports.

* * * * *

Additional Note: The report or reports to be filed pursuant to this section must include the certification required by § 240.15d-14.

13. By adding § 240.15d-14 to read as follows:

§ 240.15d-14 Certification of disclosure in annual and quarterly reports.

(a) Each report, including transition reports, filed on Form 10-Q, Form 10-QSB, Form 10-K, Form 10-KSB, Form 20-F or Form 40-F (§ § 249.308a, 249.308b, 249.310, 249.310b, 249.220f and 249.240f of this chapter) under section 15(d) of the Act (15 U.S.C. 78o(d)), other than a report filed by an Asset-Backed Issuer (as defined in paragraph (g) of this section), must include a certification containing the information set forth in paragraph (b) of this section in the form specified in the report. Each principal executive officer or officers and principal financial officer or officers of the issuer, or persons performing similar functions, at the time of filing of the report must sign the certification.

(b) The certification included in each report specified in paragraph (a) of this section must be in the form specified in the report and consist of a statement of the certifying officer that:

(1) He or she has reviewed the report being filed;

(2) Based on his or her knowledge, the report does not contain any untrue statement of a material fact or omit to state a material fact necessary to make the statements made, in light of the circumstances under which such statements were made, not misleading with respect to the period covered by the report;

(3) Based on his or her knowledge, the financial statements, and other financial information included in the report, fairly present in all material respects the financial condition, results of operations and cash flows of the issuer as of, and for, the periods presented in the report;

(4) He or she and the other certifying officers are responsible for establishing and maintaining disclosure controls and procedures (as such term is defined in paragraph (c) of this section) for the issuer and have:

(i) Designed such disclosure controls and procedures to ensure that material information relating to the issuer, including its consolidated subsidiaries, is made known to them by others within those entities, particularly during the period in which the periodic reports are being prepared;

(ii) Evaluated the effectiveness of the issuer's disclosure controls and procedures as of a date within 90 days prior to the filing date of the report (the "Evaluation Date"); and

(iii) Presented in the report their conclusions about the effectiveness of the disclosure controls and procedures based on their evaluation as of the Evaluation Date;

(5) He or she and the other certifying officers have disclosed, based on their most recent evaluation, to the issuer's auditors and the audit committee of the board or directors (or persons fulfilling the equivalent function):

(i) All significant deficiencies in the design or operation of internal controls which could adversely affect the issuer's ability to record, process, summarize and report financial data and have identified for the issuer's auditors any material weaknesses in internal controls; and

(ii) Any fraud, whether or not material, that involves management or other employees who have a significant role in the issuer's internal controls; and

(6) He or she and the other certifying officers have indicated in the report whether or not there were significant changes in internal controls or in other factors that could significantly affect internal controls subsequent to the date of their most recent evaluation, including any corrective actions with regard to significant deficiencies and material weaknesses.

(c) For purposes of this section and § 240.15d-15 of this chapter, the term "disclosure controls and procedures" means controls and other procedures of an issuer that are designed to ensure that information required to be disclosed by the issuer in the reports that it files or submits under the Act (15 U.S.C. 78a et seq.) is recorded, processed, summarized and reported, within the time periods specified in the Commission's rules and forms. Disclosure controls and procedures include, without limitation, controls and procedures designed to ensure that information required to be disclosed by an issuer in the reports that it files or submits under the Act is accumulated and communicated to the issuer's management, including its principal executive officer or officers and principal financial officer or officers, or persons performing similar functions, as appropriate to allow timely decisions regarding required disclosure.

(d) A person required to provide the certification specified in paragraph (a) of this section may not have the certification signed on his or her behalf pursuant to a power of attorney or other form of confirming authority.

(e) Each annual report filed by an Asset-Backed Issuer (as defined in paragraph (g) of this section) under section 13(a) of the Act (15 U.S.C. 78m(a)) must include a certification addressing the following items:

(1) Review by the certifying officer of the annual report and other reports containing distribution information for the period covered by the annual report;

(2) The absence in these reports, to the best of the certifying officer's knowledge, of any untrue statement of material fact or omission of a material fact necessary to make the statements made, in light of the circumstances under which such statements were made, not misleading;

(3) The inclusion in these reports, to the best of the certifying officer's knowledge, of the financial information required to be provided to the trustee under the governing documents of the issuer; and

(4) Compliance by the servicer with its servicing obligations and minimum servicing standards.

(f) With respect to Asset-Backed Issuers, the certification required by paragraph (e) of this section must be signed by the trustee of the trust (if the trustee signs the annual report) or the senior officer in charge of securitization of the depositor (if the depositor signs the annual report). Alternatively, the senior officer in charge of the servicing function of the master servicer (or entity performing the equivalent functions) may sign the certification.

(g) For purposes of this section, the term Asset-Backed Issuer means any issuer whose reporting obligation results from the offering of securities it issued that are primarily serviced by the cash flows of a discrete pool of receivables or other financial assets, either fixed or revolving, that by their terms convert into cash within a finite time period plus any rights or other assets designed to assure the servicing or timely distribution of proceeds to security holders.

14. By adding § 240.15d-15 to read as follows:

§ 240.15d-15 Issuer's disclosure controls and procedures related to preparation of required reports.

(a) Every issuer that files reports under section 15(d) of the Act (15 U.S.C. 78o(d)), other than an Asset-Backed Issuer (as defined in § 240.15d-14(g) of this chapter), must maintain disclosure controls and procedures (as defined in § 240.15d-14(c) of this chapter).

(b) Within the 90-day period prior to the filing date of each report requiring certification under §§ 240.13a-14 and 270.30a-2 of this chapter, an evaluation must be carried out under the supervision and with the participation of the issuer's management, including the issuer's principal executive officer or officers and principal financial officer or officers, or persons performing similar functions, of the effectiveness of the design and operation of the issuer's disclosure controls and procedures.

PART 249 - FORMS, SECURITIES EXCHANGE ACT OF 1934

15. The authority citation for Part 249 is amended by adding the following citations in numerical order to read as follows:

Authority: 15 U.S.C. 78a et seq., unless otherwise noted.

* * * * *

Section 249.308a is also issued under secs. 3(a) and 302, Pub.L.No. 107-204, 116 Stat. 745.

Section 249.308b is also issued under secs. 3(a) and 302, Pub.L.No. 107-204, 116 Stat. 745.

Section 249.310 is also issued under secs. 3(a) and 302, Pub.L.No. 107-204, 116 Stat. 745.

Section 249.310b is also issued under secs. 3(a) and 302, Pub.L.No. 107-204, 116 Stat. 745.

Section 249.220f is also issued under secs. 3(a) and 302, Pub.L.No. 107-204, 116 Stat. 745.

Section 249.240f is also issued under secs. 3(a) and 302, Pub.L.No. 107-204, 116 Stat. 745.

* * * * *

16. By amending Form 10-Q (referenced in § 249.308a) by revising General Instruction G, by adding new Item 4 to "Part I - Financial Information" and by adding a "Certifications" section after the "Signatures" section to read as follows:

Note: The text of Form 10-Q does not, and this amendment will not, appear in the Code of Federal Regulations.

FORM 10-Q

* * * * *

GENERAL INSTRUCTIONS

* * * * *

G. Signature and Filing of Report.

If the report is filed in paper pursuant to a hardship exemption from electronic filing (see Item 201 et seq. of Regulation S-T (17 CFR 232.201 et seq.), three complete copies of the report, including any financial statements, exhibits or other papers or documents filed as a part thereof, and five additional copies which need not include exhibits must be filed with the Commission. At least one complete copy of the report, including any financial statements, exhibits or other papers or documents filed as a part thereof, must be filed with each exchange on which any class of securities of the registrant is registered. At least one complete copy of the report filed with the Commission and one such copy filed with each exchange must be manually signed on the registrant's behalf by a duly authorized officer of the registrant and by the principal financial or chief accounting officer of the registrant. (See Rule 12b-11(d) (17 CFR 240.12b-11(d).) Copies not manually signed must bear typed or printed signatures. In the case where the principal executive officer, principal financial officer or chief accounting officer is also duly authorized to sign on behalf of the registrant, one signature is acceptable provided that the registrant clearly indicates the dual responsibilities of the signatory. In addition, each principal executive officer and principal financial officer of the registrant must provide the certification required by Rule 13a-14 (17 CFR 240.13a-14) or Rule 15d-14 (17 CFR 240.15d-14) exactly as specified in this form.

* * * * *

PART I - FINANCIAL INFORMATION

* * * * *

Item 4. Controls and Procedures.

Furnish the information required by Item 307 of Regulation S-K (§ 229.307 of this chapter).

* * * * *

SIGNATURES

* * * * *

CERTIFICATIONS*

I, [identify the certifying individual], certify that:

1. I have reviewed this quarterly report on Form 10-Q of [identify registrant];

2. Based on my knowledge, this quarterly report does not contain any untrue statement of a material fact or omit to state a material fact necessary to make the statements made, in light of the circumstances under which such statements were made, not misleading with respect to the period covered by this quarterly report;

3. Based on my knowledge, the financial statements, and other financial information included in this quarterly report, fairly present in all material respects the financial condition, results of operations and cash flows of the registrant as of, and for, the periods presented in this quarterly report;

4. The registrant's other certifying officers and I are responsible for establishing and maintaining disclosure controls and procedures (as defined in Exchange Act Rules 13a-14 and 15d-14) for the registrant and we have:

a) designed such disclosure controls and procedures to ensure that material information relating to the registrant, including its consolidated subsidiaries, is made known to us by others within those entities, particularly during the period in which this quarterly report is being prepared;

b) evaluated the effectiveness of the registrant's disclosure controls and procedures as of a date within 90 days prior to the filing date of this quarterly report (the "Evaluation Date"); and

c) presented in this quarterly report our conclusions about the effectiveness of the disclosure controls and procedures based on our evaluation as of the Evaluation Date;

5. The registrant's other certifying officers and I have disclosed, based on our most recent evaluation, to the registrant's auditors and the audit committee of registrant's board of directors (or persons performing the equivalent function):

a) all significant deficiencies in the design or operation of internal controls which could adversely affect the registrant's ability to record, process, summarize and report financial data and have identified for the registrant's auditors any material weaknesses in internal controls; and

b) any fraud, whether or not material, that involves management or other employees who have a significant role in the registrant's internal controls; and

6. The registrant's other certifying officers and I have indicated in this quarterly report whether or not there were significant changes in internal controls or in other factors that could significantly affect internal controls subsequent to the date of our most recent evaluation, including any corrective actions with regard to significant deficiencies and material weaknesses.

Date:

[Signature]

[Title]

Provide a separate certification for each principal executive officer and principal financial officer of the registrant. See Rules 13a-14 and 15d-14. The required certification must be in the exact form set forth above.

17. By amending Form 10-QSB (referenced in § 249.308b) by revising General Instruction F, by adding new Item 3 to "Part I - Financial Information" and by adding a "Certifications" section after the "Signatures" section to read as follows:

Note: The text of Form 10-QSB does not, and this amendment will not, appear in the Code of Federal Regulations.

FORM 10-QSB

* * * * *

GENERAL INSTRUCTIONS

* * * * *

F. Signature and Filing of Report

1. If the report is filed in paper pursuant to a hardship exemption from electronic filing (see Item 201 et seq. of Regulation S-T (17 CFR 232.201 et seq.), file three "complete" copies and five "additional" copies of the report with the Commission and file at least one complete copy with each exchange on which any class of securities of the small business issuer is registered. A "complete" copy includes financial statements, exhibits and all other papers and documents. An "additional" copy excludes exhibits.

2. Manually sign at least one complete copy of the report filed with the Commission and with each exchange; other copies should have typed or printed signatures. (See Rule 12b-11(d) (17 CFR 240.12b-11(d).) In the case where the principal executive officer, principal financial officer or chief accounting officer is also duly authorized to sign on behalf of the small business issuer, one signature is acceptable provided that the issuer clearly indicates the dual responsibilities of the signatory. Each principal executive officer and principal financial officer of the small business issuer must provide the certification required by Rule 13a-14 (17 CFR 240.13a-14) or Rule 15d-14 (17 CFR 240.15d-14) exactly as specified in this form.

* * * * *

PART I - FINANCIAL INFORMATION

* * * * *

Item 3. Controls and Procedures.

Furnish the information required by Item 307 of Regulation S-B (228.307 of this chapter).

* * * * *

SIGNATURES

* * * * *

CERTIFICATIONS*

I, [identify the certifying individual], certify that:

1. I have reviewed this quarterly report on Form 10-QSB of [identify registrant];

2. Based on my knowledge, this quarterly report does not contain any untrue statement of a material fact or omit to state a material fact necessary to make the statements made, in light of the circumstances under which such statements were made, not misleading with respect to the period covered by this quarterly report;

3. Based on my knowledge, the financial statements, and other financial information included in this quarterly report, fairly present in all material respects the financial condition, results of operations and cash flows of the registrant as of, and for, the periods presented in this quarterly report;

4. The registrant's other certifying officers and I are responsible for establishing and maintaining disclosure controls and procedures (as defined in Exchange Act Rules 13a-14 and 15d-14) for the registrant and have:

a) designed such disclosure controls and procedures to ensure that material information relating to the registrant, including its consolidated subsidiaries, is made known to us by others within those entities, particularly during the period in which this quarterly report is being prepared;

b) evaluated the effectiveness of the registrant's disclosure controls and procedures as of a date within 90 days prior to the filing date of this quarterly report (the "Evaluation Date"); and

c) presented in this quarterly report our conclusions about the effectiveness of the disclosure controls and procedures based on our evaluation as of the Evaluation Date;

5. The registrant's other certifying officers and I have disclosed, based on our most recent evaluation, to the registrant's auditors and the audit committee of registrant's board of directors (or persons performing the equivalent functions):

a) all significant deficiencies in the design or operation of internal controls which could adversely affect the registrant's ability to record, process, summarize and report financial data and have identified for the registrant's auditors any material weaknesses in internal controls; and

b) any fraud, whether or not material, that involves management or other employees who have a significant role in the registrant's internal controls; and

6. The registrant's other certifying officers and I have indicated in this quarterly report whether or not there were significant changes in internal controls or in other factors that could significantly affect internal controls subsequent to the date of our most recent evaluation, including any corrective actions with regard to significant deficiencies and material weaknesses.

Date:

[Signature]

[Title]

Provide a separate certification for each principal executive officer and principal financial officer of the registrant. See Rules 13a-14 and 15d-14. The required certification must be in the exact form set forth above.

* * * * *

18. By amending Form 10-K (referenced in § 249.310):

a. by revising General Instruction D(2)(a),

b. by redesignating Item 14 as Item 15 in Part IV,

c. adding new Item 14 to Part III, and

d. by adding a "Certifications" section after the "Signatures" section and before the reference to "Supplemental information to be Furnished With Reports Filed Pursuant to Section 15(d) of the Act by Registrants Which Have Not Registered Securities Pursuant to Section 12 of the Act." The revisions read as follows:

Note: The text of Form 10-K does not, and this amendment will not, appear in the Code of Federal Regulations.

FORM 10-K

* * * * *

GENERAL INSTRUCTIONS

* * * * *

D. Signature and Filing of Report.

(1) * * *

(2)(a) The report must be signed by the registrant, and on behalf of the registrant by its principal executive officer or officers (who also must provide the certification required by Rule 13a-14 (17 CFR 240.13a-14) or Rule 15d-14 (17 CFR 240.15d-14) exactly as specified in this form), its principal financial officer or officers (who also must provide the certification required by Rule 13a-14 (17 CFR 240.13a-14) or Rule 15d-14 (17 CFR 240.15d-14) exactly as specified in this form), its controller or principal accounting officer, and by at least the majority of the board of directors or persons performing similar functions. Where the registrant is a limited partnership, the report must be signed by the majority of the board of directors of any corporate general partner who signs the report.

* * * * *

Annual Report Pursuant to Section 13 or 15(d) of the Securities Exchange Act of 1934

* * * * *

PART III

* * * * *

Item 14. Controls and Procedures.

Furnish the information required by Item 307 of Regulation S-K (§ 229.307 of this chapter).

* * * * *

SIGNATURES

* * * * *

CERTIFICATIONS*

I, [identify the certifying individual], certify that:

1. I have reviewed this annual report on Form 10-K of [identify registrant];

2. Based on my knowledge, this annual report does not contain any untrue statement of a material fact or omit to state a material fact necessary to make the statements made, in light of the circumstances under which such statements were made, not misleading with respect to the period covered by this annual report;

3. Based on my knowledge, the financial statements, and other financial information included in this annual report, fairly present in all material respects the financial condition, results of operations and cash flows of the registrant as of, and for, the periods presented in this annual report;

4. The registrant's other certifying officers and I are responsible for establishing and maintaining disclosure controls and procedures (as defined in Exchange Act Rules 13a-14 and 15d-14) for the registrant and have:

a) designed such disclosure controls and procedures to ensure that material information relating to the registrant, including its consolidated subsidiaries, is made known to us by others within those entities, particularly during the period in which this annual report is being prepared;

b) evaluated the effectiveness of the registrant's disclosure controls and procedures as of a date within 90 days prior to the filing date of this annual report (the "Evaluation Date"); and

c) presented in this annual report our conclusions about the effectiveness of the disclosure controls and procedures based on our evaluation as of the Evaluation Date;

5. The registrant's other certifying officers and I have disclosed, based on our most recent evaluation, to the registrant's auditors and the audit committee of registrant's board of directors (or persons performing the equivalent functions):

a) all significant deficiencies in the design or operation of internal controls which could adversely affect the registrant's ability to record, process, summarize and report financial data and have identified for the registrant's auditors any material weaknesses in internal controls; and

b) any fraud, whether or not material, that involves management or other employees who have a significant role in the registrant's internal controls; and

6. The registrant's other certifying officers and I have indicated in this annual report whether there were significant changes in internal controls or in other factors that could significantly affect internal controls subsequent to the date of our most recent evaluation, including any corrective actions with regard to significant deficiencies and material weaknesses.

Date:

[Signature]

[Title]

Provide a separate certification for each principal executive officer and principal financial officer of the registrant. See Rules 13a-14 and 15d-14. The required certification must be in the exact form set forth above.

* * * * *

19. By amending Form 10-KSB (referenced in § 249.310b):

a. by revising General Instruction C.2.,

b. by adding new Item 14 to Part III, and

c. by adding a "Certifications" section after the "Signatures" section and before the reference to "Supplemental information to be Furnished With Reports Filed Pursuant to Section 15(d) of the Exchange Act By Non-reporting Issuers." The revisions read as follows:

Note: The text of Form 10-KSB does not, and this amendment will not, appear in the Code of Federal Regulations.

FORM 10-KSB

* * * * *

GENERAL INSTRUCTIONS

* * * * *

PART III

* * * * *

Item 14. Controls and Procedures.

Furnish the information required by Item 307 of Regulation S-B (228.307 of this chapter).

* * * * *

C. Signature and Filing of Report.

1. * * *

2. Who must sign. The small business issuer, its principal executive officer or officers (who also must provide the certification required by Rule 13a-14 (17 CFR 240.13a-14) or Rule 15d-14 (17 CFR 240.15d-14) exactly as specified in this form), its principal financial officer (who also must provide the certification required by Rule 13a-14 (17 CFR 240.13a-14) or Rule 15d-14 (17 CFR 240.15d-14) exactly as specified in this form), its controller or principal accounting officer and at least a majority of the board of directors or persons performing similar functions. If the small business issuer is a limited partnership, then the general partner and a majority of its board of directors if a corporation must sign the report. Any person who occupies more than one of the specified positions must indicate each capacity in which he or she signs the report. See Rule 12b-11 concerning manual signatures under powers of attorney.

* * * * *

SIGNATURES

* * * * *

CERTIFICATIONS*

I, [identify the certifying individual], certify that:

1. I have reviewed this annual report on Form 10-KSB of [identify registrant];

2. Based on my knowledge, this annual report does not contain any untrue statement of a material fact or omit to state a material fact necessary to make the statements made, in light of the circumstances under which such statements were made, not misleading with respect to the period covered by this annual report;

3. Based on my knowledge, the financial statements, and other financial information included in this annual report, fairly present in all material respects the financial condition, results of operations and cash flows of the registrant as of, and for, the periods presented in this annual report;

4. The registrant's other certifying officers and I are responsible for establishing and maintaining disclosure controls and procedures (as defined in Exchange Act Rules 13a-14 and 15d-14) for the registrant and have:

a) designed such disclosure controls and procedures to ensure that material information relating to the registrant, including its consolidated subsidiaries, is made known to us by others within those entities, particularly during the period in which this annual report is being prepared;

b) evaluated the effectiveness of the registrant's disclosure controls and procedures as of a date within 90 days prior to the filing date of this annual report (the "Evaluation Date"); and

c) presented in this annual report our conclusions about the effectiveness of the disclosure controls and procedures based on our evaluation as of the Evaluation Date;

5. The registrant's other certifying officers and I have disclosed, based on our most recent evaluation, to the registrant's auditors and the audit committee of registrant's board of directors (or persons performing the equivalent functions):

a) all significant deficiencies in the design or operation of internal controls which could adversely affect the registrant's ability to record, process, summarize and report financial data and have identified for the registrant's auditors any material weaknesses in internal controls; and

b) any fraud, whether or not material, that involves management or other employees who have a significant role in the registrant's internal controls; and

6. The registrant's other certifying officers and I have indicated in this annual report whether there were significant changes in internal controls or in other factors that could significantly affect internal controls subsequent to the date of our most recent evaluation, including any corrective actions with regard to significant deficiencies and material weaknesses.

Date:

[Signature]

[Title]

Provide a separate certification for each principal executive officer and principal financial officer of the registrant. See Rules 13a-14 and 15d-14. The required certification must be in the exact form set forth above.

* * * *

20. By amending Form 20-F (referenced in § 249.220f):

a. by adding a new paragraph (e) to General Instruction B,

b. by adding new Item 15, and

c. by adding a "Certifications" section after the "Signatures" section and before the section referencing "Instructions as to Exhibits." The revisions read as follows:

Note: The text of Form 20-F does not, and this amendment will not, appear in the Code of Federal Regulations.

FORM 20-F

* * * * *

GENERAL INSTRUCTIONS

* * * * *

B. General Rules and Regulations That Apply to this Form.

* * * * *

(e) Where the Form is being used as an annual report filed under Section 13(a) or 15(d) of the Exchange Act, provide the certification required by Rule 13a-14 (17 CFR 240.13a-14) or Rule 15d-14 (17 CFR 240.15d-14) exactly as specified in this form.

* * * * *

PART II

* * * * *

Item 15. Controls and Procedures.

(a) Where the Form is being used as an annual report filed under Section 13(a) or 15(d) of the Exchange Act, disclose the conclusions of the registrant's principal executive officer or officers and principal financial officer or officers, or persons performing similar functions, about the effectiveness of the registrant's disclosure controls and procedures (as defined in §§240.13a-15(c) and 240.15d-15(c)) based on their evaluation the controls and procedures as of a date within 90 days prior to the filing date of the report.

(b) Where the Form is being used as an annual report filed under Section 13(a) or 15(d) of the Exchange Act, disclose whether or not there were significant changes in the registrant's internal controls or in other factors that could significantly affect these controls subsequent to the date of their evaluation, including any corrective actions with regard to significant deficiencies and material weaknesses.

* * * * *

SIGNATURES

* * * * *

CERTIFICATIONS*

I, [identify the certifying individual], certify that:

1. I have reviewed this annual report on Form 20-F of [identify registrant];

2. Based on my knowledge, this annual report does not contain any untrue statement of a material fact or omit to state a material fact necessary to make the statements made, in light of the circumstances under which such statements were made, not misleading with respect to the period covered by this annual report;

3. Based on my knowledge, the financial statements, and other financial information included in this annual report, fairly present in all material respects the financial condition, results of operations and cash flows of the registrant as of, and for, the periods presented in this annual report;

4. The registrant's other certifying officers and I are responsible for establishing and maintaining disclosure controls and procedures (as defined in Exchange Act Rules 13a-14 and 15d-14) for the registrant and have:

a) designed such disclosure controls and procedures to ensure that material information relating to the registrant, including its consolidated subsidiaries, is made known to us by others within those entities, particularly during the period in which this annual report is being prepared;

b) evaluated the effectiveness of the registrant's disclosure controls and procedures as of a date within 90 days prior to the filing date of this annual report (the "Evaluation Date"); and

c) presented in this annual report our conclusions about the effectiveness of the disclosure controls and procedures based on our evaluation as of the Evaluation Date;

5. The registrant's other certifying officers and I have disclosed, based on our most recent evaluation, to the registrant's auditors and the audit committee of registrant's board of directors (or persons performing the equivalent function):

a) all significant deficiencies in the design or operation of internal controls which could adversely affect the registrant's ability to record, process, summarize and report financial data and have identified for the registrant's auditors any material weaknesses in internal controls; and

b) any fraud, whether or not material, that involves management or other employees who have a significant role in the registrant's internal controls; and

6. The registrant's other certifying officers and I have indicated in this annual report whether or not there were significant changes in internal controls or in other factors that could significantly affect internal controls subsequent to the date of our most recent evaluation, including any corrective actions with regard to significant deficiencies and material weaknesses.

Date:

[Signature]

[Title]

Provide a separate certification for each principal executive officer and principal financial officer of the registrant. See Rules 13a-14 and 15d-14. The required certification must be in the exact form set forth above.

* * * * *

21. By amending Form 40-F (referenced in §249.240f) by adding a new paragraph (6) to General Instruction B and by adding a "Certifications" section after the "Signatures" section to read as follows:

Note: The text of Form 40-F does not, and this amendment will not, appear in the Code of Federal Regulations.

FORM 40-F

* * * * *

GENERAL INSTRUCTIONS

* * * * *

B. Information To Be Filed on this Form.

* * * * *

(6)Where the Form is being used as an annual report filed under Section 13(a) or 15(d) of the Exchange Act:

(a) Provide the certification required by Rule 13a-14 (17 CFR 240.13a-14) or Rule 15d-14 (17 CFR 240.15d-14) exactly as specified in this form.

(b) Disclose the conclusions of the registrant's principal executive officer or officers and principal financial officer or officers, or persons performing similar functions, about the effectiveness of the registrant's disclosure controls and procedures (as defined in §§240.13a-15(c) and 240.15d-15(c)) based on their evaluation the controls and procedures as of a date within 90 days prior to the filing date of the report.

(c) Disclose in the report whether or not there were significant changes in the registrant's internal controls or in other factors that could significantly affect these controls subsequent to the date of their evaluation, including any corrective actions with regard to significant deficiencies and material weaknesses.

* * * * *

SIGNATURES

* * * * *

CERTIFICATIONS*

I, [identify the certifying individual], certify that:

1. I have reviewed this annual report on Form 40-F of [identify registrant];

2. Based on my knowledge, this annual report does not contain any untrue statement of a material fact or omit to state a material fact necessary to make the statements made, in light of the circumstances under which such statements were made, not misleading with respect to the period covered by this annual report;

3. Based on my knowledge, the financial statements, and other financial information included in this annual report, fairly present in all material respects the financial condition, results of operations and cash flows of the registrant as of, and for, the periods presented in this annual report;

4. The registrant's other certifying officers and I are responsible for establishing and maintaining disclosure controls and procedures (as defined in Exchange Act Rules 13a-14 and 15d-14) for the registrant and have:

a) designed such disclosure controls and procedures to ensure that material information relating to the registrant, including its consolidated subsidiaries, is made known to us by others within those entities, particularly during the period in which this annual report is being prepared;

b) evaluated the effectiveness of the registrant's disclosure controls and procedures as of a date within 90 days prior to the filing date of this annual report (the "Evaluation Date"); and

c) presented in this annual report our conclusions about the effectiveness of the disclosure controls and procedures based on our evaluation as of the Evaluation Date;

5. The registrant's other certifying officers and I have disclosed, based on our most recent evaluation, to the registrant's auditors and the audit committee of registrant's board of directors (and persons performing the equivalent function):

a) all significant deficiencies in the design or operation of internal controls which could adversely affect the registrant's ability to record, process, summarize and report financial data and have identified for the registrant's auditors any material weaknesses in internal controls; and

b) any fraud, whether or not material, that involves management or other employees who have a significant role in the registrant's internal controls; and

6. The registrant's other certifying officers and I have indicated in this annual report whether there were significant changes in internal controls or in other factors that could significantly affect internal controls subsequent to the date of our most recent evaluation, including any corrective actions with regard to significant deficiencies and material weaknesses.

Date:

[Signature]

[Title]

Provide a separate certification for each principal executive officer and principal financial officer of the registrant. See Rules 13a-14 and 15d-14. The required certification must be in the exact form set forth above.

PART 270 - RULES AND REGULATIONS, INVESTMENT COMPANY ACT OF 1940

22. The authority citation for part 270 is amended by adding the following citation in numerical order to read as follows:

Authority: 15 U.S.C. 80a-1, et seq., 80a-34(d), 80a-37, 80a-39, unless otherwise noted;

* * * * *

Section 270.30a-2 is also issued under 15 U.S.C. 78m, 78o(d), and 80a-29, and secs. 3(a) and 302, Pub. L. No. 107-204, 116 Stat. 745.

* * * * *

23. By adding § 270.30a-2 to read as follows:

§ 270.30a-2 Certification of disclosure in annual and semi-annual reports.

(a) Each report, including transition reports, filed on Form N-SAR (referenced in § § 249.330 and 274.101) by a registered management investment company or unit investment trust must include a certification containing the information set forth in paragraph (b) of this section in the form specified in the report, except that a report of a unit investment trust or small business investment company on Form N-SAR may omit paragraph (b)(3) of this section. Each principal executive officer or officers and principal financial officer or officers of the investment company, or persons performing similar functions, at the time of filing of the report must sign the certification.

(b) The certification included in each report specified in paragraph (a) of this section must be in the form specified in the report and consist of a statement of the certifying officer that:

(1) He or she has reviewed the report being filed;

(2) Based on his or her knowledge, the report does not contain any untrue statement of a material fact or omit to state a material fact necessary to make the statements made, in light of the circumstances under which such statements were made, not misleading with respect to the period covered by the report;

(3) Based on his or her knowledge, the financial information included in the report, and the financial statements on which the financial information is based, fairly present in all material respects the financial condition, results of operations, changes in net assets, and cash flows (if the financial statements are required to include a statement of cash flows) of the investment company as of, and for, the periods presented in the report;

(4) He or she and the other certifying officers are responsible for establishing and maintaining disclosure controls and procedures (as such term is defined in paragraph (c) of this section) for the investment company and have:

(i) Designed such disclosure controls and procedures to ensure that material information relating to the investment company, including its consolidated subsidiaries, is made known to them by others within those entities, particularly during the period in which the periodic reports are being prepared;

(ii) Evaluated the effectiveness of the investment company's disclosure controls and procedures as of a date within 90 days prior to the filing date of the report (the "Evaluation Date"); and

(iii) Presented in the report their conclusions about the effectiveness of the disclosure controls and procedures based on their evaluation as of the Evaluation Date;

(5) He or she and the other certifying officers have disclosed, based on their most recent evaluation, to the investment company's auditors and the audit committee of the board of directors (or persons fulfilling the equivalent function):

(i) All significant deficiencies in the design or operation of internal controls which could adversely affect the investment company's ability to record, process, summarize, and report financial data and have identified for the investment company's auditors any material weaknesses in internal controls; and

(ii) Any fraud, whether or not material, that involves management or other employees who have a significant role in the investment company's internal controls; and

(6) He or she and the other certifying officers have indicated in the report whether or not there were significant changes in internal controls or in other factors that could significantly affect internal controls subsequent to the date of their most recent evaluation, including any corrective actions with regard to significant deficiencies and material weaknesses.

(c) For purposes of this section, the term "disclosure controls and procedures" means controls and other procedures of an investment company that are designed to ensure that information required to be disclosed by the investment company in the reports that it files or submits under the Securities Exchange Act of 1934 is recorded, processed, summarized, and reported, within the time periods specified in the Commission's rules and forms. Disclosure controls and procedures include, without limitation, controls and procedures designed to ensure that information required to be disclosed by an investment company in the reports that it files or submits under the Securities Exchange Act of 1934 is accumulated and communicated to the investment company's management, including its principal executive officer or officers and principal financial officer or officers, or persons performing similar functions, as appropriate to allow timely decisions regarding required disclosure.

(d) A person required to provide the certification specified in paragraph (a) of this section may not have the certification signed on his or her behalf pursuant to a power of attorney or other form of confirming authority.

24. Section 270.30b1-3 is amended by adding a sentence at the end of the section to read as follows:

§ 270.30b1-3 Transition reports.

* * * A report filed pursuant to this section must include the certification required by § 270.30a-2.

PART 249 - FORMS, SECURITIES EXCHANGE ACT OF 1934

PART 274 - FORMS PRESCRIBED UNDER THE INVESTMENT COMPANY ACT OF 1940

25. The authority citation for Part 274 is revised to read as follows:

Authority: 15 U.S.C. 77f, 77g, 77h, 77j, 77s, 78c(b), 78l, 78m, 78n, 78o(d), 80a-8, 80a-24, 80a-26, and 80a-29, and secs. 3(a) and 302, Pub. L. No. 107-204, 116 Stat. 745, unless otherwise noted.

26. By amending Form N-SAR (referenced in § § 249.330 and 274.101) by:

a. Revising the reference "132" in item 6 to read "133";

b. Adding item 133;

c. Revising the reference "132" in the fifth paragraph of General Instruction A to read "133";

d. Revising General Instructions D and G, and the Instructions to sub-items 77Q3 and 102P3;

e. Adding an Instruction to item 133; and

f. Revising the reference "132" in the Instructions to the Signature Page to read "133."

These additions and revisions read as follows:

Note: The text of Form N-SAR does not, and these amendments will not, appear in the Code of Federal Regulations.

FORM N-SAR

* * * * *

133. Include the certifications required by rule 30a-2 under the Investment Company Act (17 CFR 270.30a-2).

* * * * *

GENERAL INSTRUCTIONS

* * * * *

D. Preparation of Report

(1) No item of the form except items 77 and 102 shall be answered by incorporating any information by reference. No exhibits or supplemental information are required or permitted, except in response to these items and item 133.

* * * * *

G. Submitting an Amendment to Form N-SAR on Paper or Electronically

* * * * *

(5) In an exhibit to the amendment, each principal executive officer and principal financial officer must provide the certification required by Item 133, instruction (a) for sub-item 77Q3, and instruction (a) for sub-item 102P3. A registrant that is a unit investment trust or a small business investment company may omit paragraph 3 of the certification required by instruction 77Q3(a)(iii).

* * * * *

INSTRUCTIONS TO SPECIFIC ITEMS

* * * * *

SUB-ITEM 77Q3:

Subject to Rule 201.24 of the General Rules of Practice regarding incorporation by reference, the rules applicable to electronic submission of filings, and General Instruction F of this form, the following exhibits shall be filed as part of this form, if not previously filed:

(a) If the form is filed under Section 13(a) or 15(d) of the 1934 Act, include the following information:

(i) Disclose the conclusions of the registrant's principal executive officer or officers and principal financial officer or officers, or persons performing similar functions, about the effectiveness of the registrant's disclosure controls and procedures (as defined in rule 30a-2(c) under the Act (17 CFR 270.30a-2(c)) based on their evaluation of these controls and procedures as of a date within 90 days of the filing date of the report that includes the disclosure required by this paragraph.

(ii) Disclose whether or not there were significant changes in the registrant's internal controls or in other factors that could significantly affect these controls subsequent to the date of their evaluation, including any corrective actions with regard to significant deficiencies and material weaknesses.

(iii) Include the certification of each principal executive officer and principal financial officer required by Rule 30a-2 under the Act (17 CFR 270.30a-2). Provide a separate certification for each principal executive officer and principal financial officer, or person performing similar functions, in the exact form set forth below:

CERTIFICATIONS

I, [identify the certifying individual], certify that:

1. I have reviewed this report on Form N-SAR of [identify registrant];

2. Based on my knowledge, this report does not contain any untrue statement of a material fact or omit to state a material fact necessary to make the statements made, in light of the circumstances under which such statements were made, not misleading with respect to the period covered by this report;

3. Based on my knowledge, the financial information included in this report, and the financial statements on which the financial information is based, fairly present in all material respects the

financial condition, results of operations, changes in net assets, and cash flows (if the financial statements are required to include a statement of cash flows) of the registrant as of, and for, the periods presented in this report;

4. The registrant's other certifying officers and I are responsible for establishing and maintaining disclosure controls and procedures (as defined in rule 30a-2(c) under the Investment Company Act) for the registrant and have:

a) designed such disclosure controls and procedures to ensure that material information relating to the registrant, including its consolidated subsidiaries, is made known to us by others within those entities, particularly during the period in which this report is being prepared;

b) evaluated the effectiveness of the registrant's disclosure controls and procedures as of a date within 90 days prior to the filing date of this report (the "Evaluation Date"); and

c) presented in this report our conclusions about the effectiveness of the disclosure controls and procedures based on our evaluation as of the Evaluation Date;

5. The registrant's other certifying officers and I have disclosed, based on our most recent evaluation, to the registrant's auditors and the audit committee of the registrant's board of directors (or persons performing the equivalent functions):

a) all significant deficiencies in the design or operation of internal controls which could adversely affect the registrant's ability to record, process, summarize, and report financial data and have identified for the registrant's auditors any material weaknesses in internal controls; and

b) any fraud, whether or not material, that involves management or other employees who have a significant role in the registrant's internal controls; and

6. The registrant's other certifying officers and I have indicated in this report whether or not there were significant changes in internal controls or in other factors that could significantly affect internal controls subsequent to the date of our most recent evaluation, including any corrective actions with regard to significant deficiencies and material weaknesses.

Date:

[Signature]

[Title]

(b) Furnish any other information required to be included as an exhibit pursuant to such rules and regulations as the Commission may prescribe.

* * * * *

SUB-ITEM 102P3

See instructions for sub-item 77Q3. The registrant may omit paragraph 3 of the certification required by instruction (a)(iii).

* * * * *

ITEM 133

Include the exhibit required by instruction (a) for sub-item 77Q3. The registrant may omit paragraph 3 of the certification required by instruction (a)(iii).

By the Commission.

Margaret H. McFarland

Deputy Secretary

August 28, 2002

Adopting Release: Accelerated Filing Deadlines and Website Access

Release Nos. 33-8128, 34-46464, FR 63 File No. S7-08-02. August 29, 2002. Release in full text.

Acceleration of Periodic Report Filing Dates and Disclosure Concerning Website Access to Reports.

Agency: Securities and Exchange Commission.

Action: Final rules.

Summary: We are adopting amendments to our rules and forms to accelerate the filing of quarterly and annual reports under the Securities Exchange Act of 1934 by domestic reporting companies that have a public float of at least $75 million, that have been subject to the Exchange Act's reporting requirements for at least 12 calendar months and that previously have filed at least one annual report. The changes for these accelerated filers will be phased-in over three years. The annual report deadline will remain 90 days for year one and change from 90 days to 75 days for year two and from 75 days to 60 days for year three and thereafter. The quarterly report deadline will remain 45 days for year one and change from 45 days to 40 days for year two and from 40 days to 35 days for year three and thereafter. The phase-in period will begin for accelerated filers with fiscal years ending on or after December 15, 2002. We also are adopting amendments to require accelerated filers to disclose in their annual reports where investors can obtain access to their filings, including whether the company provides access to its Forms 10-K, 10-Q and 8-K reports on its Internet website, free of charge, as soon as reasonably practicable after those reports are electronically filed with or furnished to the Commission.

Dates: Effective Date: sixty days after publication in the Federal Register.

Compliance Dates: The phase-in period for accelerated deadlines of quarterly and annual reports will begin for reports filed by companies that meet the definition of "accelerated filer" as of the end of their first fiscal year ending on or after December 15, 2002. These accelerated filers must comply with the new disclosure requirements concerning website access to reports for their annual reports on Form 10-K to be filed for fiscal years ending on or after December 15, 2002. Registrants voluntarily may comply with the new filing deadlines and disclosure requirement before the compliance dates.

For Further Information Contact: Jeffrey J. Minton, Special Counsel, or Elizabeth M. Murphy, Chief, Office of Rulemaking, at (202) 942-2910, Division of Corporation Finance, U.S. Securities and Exchange Commission, 450 Fifth Street, NW, Washington, DC 20549-0312.

Supplementary Information: We are adopting amendments to Rules 3-01,[1] 3-09[2] and 3-12[3] of Regulation S-X[4] and Item 101[5] of Regulation S-K[6] under the Securities Act of 1933 ("Securities Act"),[7] Forms 10-Q[8] and 10-K[9] under the Securities Exchange Act of 1934 ("Exchange Act")[10] and Exchange Act Rules 12b-2,[11] 13a-10[12] and 15d-10.[13]

Table of Contents

---

[1] 17 CFR 210.3-01.

[2] 17 CFR 210.3-09.

[3] 17 CFR 210.3-12.

[4] 17 CFR 210.1-01 et seq.

[5] 17 CFR 229.101.

[6] 17 CFR 229.10 et seq.

[7] 15 U.S.C. 77a et seq.

[8] 17 CFR 249.308a.

[9] 17 CFR 249.310.

[10] 15 U.S.C. 78a et seq.

[11] 17 CFR 240.12b-2.

[12] 17 CFR 240.13a-10.

[13] 17 CFR 240.15d-10.

[¶ 2201]

I. Background and Overview of Rule Amendments

A. The Exchange Act Reporting System

The Exchange Act requires public companies to make information publicly available to investors on an ongoing basis to aid in their investment and voting decisions.[14] Issuers that have been subject to the reporting requirements for a certain period of time also can incorporate information from their Exchange Act reports into their registration statements under the Securities Act. Investors purchasing securities in public offerings therefore also rely on Exchange Act disclosure.

The Commission's rules under the Exchange Act now require disclosure at quarterly and annual intervals, with specified significant events reported on a more current basis.[15] Specifically, a domestic issuer subject to the Exchange Act must, among other obligations, file the following reports:[16]

An annual report on Form 10-K (or Form 10-KSB in the case of a small business issuer[17]) no later than 90 calendar days after the end of its fiscal year;[18]

---

[14] See Sections 13(a) and 15(d) of the Exchange Act [15 U.S.C. 78m(a) and 78o(d)]. The following types of companies are subject to the obligation to provide information to the secondary markets through reports filed with the Commission:

A company that has registered a class of equity or debt securities under Section 12(b) of the Exchange Act [15 U.S.C. 78l(b)] so that the securities can be listed and traded on a national securities exchange;

A company that has registered a class of equity securities under Section 12(g)(1) of the Exchange Act [15 U.S.C. 78l(g)(1)] and Exchange Act Rule 12g-1 [17 CFR 240.12g-1] because it had total assets of more than $10 million and the class of equity securities is held by more than 500 record holders as of the last day of the company's fiscal year (and cannot rely on an exemption from such registration);

A company that has voluntarily registered a class of equity securities under Section 12(g) of the Exchange Act;

Under Section 15(d) of the Exchange Act, a company that has filed a registration statement under the Securities Act that became effective and has not met the thresholds for suspension of the reporting requirements; and

Under Exchange Act Rules 12g-3 and 15d-5 [17 CFR 240.12g-3 and 240.15d-5], a company that has succeeded to the obligation of another reporting company.

[15] See, for example, Exchange Act Rules 13a-1, 13a-11, 13a-13, 15d-1, 15d-11 and 15d-13 [17 CFR 240.13a-1, 13a-11, 13a-13, 15d-1, 15d-11 and 15d-13]. In addition, Section 409 of the Sarbanes-Oxley Act of 2002 [Pub. L. No. 107-204, § 409, 116 Stat. 745 (2002)] added Section 13(l) of the Exchange Act [17 U.S.C. 78m(l)], which also requires disclosure on a rapid and current basis of such additional information concerning material changes in the financial condition or operations of the issuer as the Commission determines, by rule, is necessary or useful for the protection of investors and in the public interest.

[16] Reporting companies that are foreign private issuers, as defined in Exchange Act Rule 3b-4(c) [17 CFR 240.3b-4(c)], are subject to different requirements for periodic reports. They are not required to file quarterly reports. They file annual reports on Form 20-F [17 CFR 249.220f]. Instead of current reporting on Form 8-K, foreign issuers provide reports on Form 6-K [17 CFR 249.306]. Certain Canadian issuers may file different reports under the Multijurisdictional Disclosure System. Foreign government issuers, as defined in Exchange Act Rule 3b-4(c), also are subject to different reporting requirements. They file annual reports on Form 18-K [17 CFR 249.318]. Foreign private issuers may elect to file the forms used by domestic reporting companies. If they do so, they are subject to the same deadlines as domestic companies.

[17] The term "small business issuer" is defined in Exchange Act Rule 12b-2 as a U.S. or Canadian issuer with less than $25 million in revenues and public float that is not an investment company.

[18] Form 10-K (and Form 10-KSB [17 CFR 249.310b]) provides a comprehensive overview of the reporting company on an annual basis. The form currently consists of four parts (Form 10-KSB has three parts, but the categories of required information are similar). Part I requires disclosure regarding the company's business, its properties, legal proceedings and matters submitted to a security holder vote. Part II requires disclosure regarding the market for the company's common equity, sales of unregistered securities, the use of proceeds from recent sales of securities, specified financial statements and information, management's discussion and analysis of financial condition and results of operations and quantitative and qualitative disclosure about market risk. Part III requires disclosure regarding the company's directors and

Quarterly reports on Form 10-Q (or Form 10-QSB in the case of a small business issuer) no later than 45 calendar days after the end of the first three quarters of its fiscal year;[19] and

Current reports on Form 8-K for a number of specified events generally within five or 15 days after their occurrence.[20]In addition, a company may be required to file transition reports on Form 10-K or 10-KSB or Form 10-Q or 10-QSB when it changes its fiscal year.[21]

B. Proposing Release

In April 2002, we published for comment proposals to shorten the filing deadlines of quarterly and annual reports for many companies as a step in modernizing the periodic reporting system and improving the usefulness of periodic reports to investors.[22] The annual and quarterly report deadlines were last changed 32 years ago.[23] We proposed accelerating the deadline for annual reports from 90 days to 60 days after the end of the company's fiscal year and accelerating the deadline for quarterly reports from 45 days to 30 days after the end of the company's first three fiscal quarters. These proposals would have applied to companies that met the definition of an "accelerated filer" as of the end of their first fiscal year ending after October 31, 2002. We proposed the definition of an accelerated filer to include companies that had a public float[24] of at least $75 million, that had been reporting for at least 12 months and that previously had filed at least one annual report.

We also proposed to require a company subject to these accelerated filing deadlines to disclose in its annual report on Form 10-K where investors can obtain timely access to company filings, including whether the company provides access to its Forms 10-K, 10-Q and 8-K reports on its Internet website, free of charge, as soon as reasonably practicable after, and in any event on the same day as, these reports are electronically filed with or furnished to the Commission.[25] Under the proposals, a company that did not provide website access in this manner would have been required to disclose why it did not do so and where else investors could access these filings electronically immediately upon filing. The company also would be required to disclose its website address, if it has one.

We received responses to our proposals from 305 commenters.[26] 302 commented on the acceleration of periodic report deadlines. Generally, these commenters fell into two groups. The first group (20 commenters) represented primarily investors, institutional investors and other users of company reports who supported the proposals and our objective to provide investors with more timely access to company filings. The second group (282 commenters) represented primarily companies, business associations, law firms and

(Footnote Continued)

executive officers, executive compensation, security ownership and certain relationships and related party transactions. Part IV requires disclosure of exhibits, financial statement schedules and a list of current reports filed on Form 8-K.

[19] Form 10-Q (and Form 10-QSB [17 CFR 249.308b]) currently consists of two parts. Part I requires disclosure of specified financial statements, management's discussion and analysis of financial condition and results of operations and quantitative and qualitative disclosure about market risk. Part II requires disclosure regarding legal proceedings, changes in securities, sales of unregistered securities, the use of proceeds from recent sales of securities, defaults on senior securities, exhibits and a list of current reports filed on Form 8-K.

[20] 17 CFR 249.308. These events currently include change in control of the registrant, the acquisition or disposition of a significant amount of assets, the bankruptcy or receivership of the registrant, changes in the registrant's certifying accountant, the resignation of a member of the registrant's board of directors and any other event that the registrant deems of significance to security holders. Item 7 of Form 8-K states that financial statements and related pro forma financial information required to be included on Form 8-K when a company acquires a business may be filed with the initial report or by amendment not later than 60 days after the date that the initial Form 8-K to report the acquisition must be filed. See Item 7(a)(3) of Form 8-K. On June 17, 2002, we proposed adding 11 new items that would require a company to file Form 8-K, moving two items currently required to be included in annual and quarterly reports to Form 8-K, amending several existing Form 8-K disclosure items and shortening the filing deadline for most items to two business days after the triggering event. See Release No. 33-8106 (June 17, 2002) [67 FR 42914].

[21] See Exchange Act Rules 13a-10 and 15d-10.

[22] See Release No. 33-8089; 34-45741 (Apr. 12, 2002) [67 FR 19896] (the "Proposing Release").

[23] See Release No. 34-9000 (Oct. 21, 1970) [35 FR 16919] and Release No. 34-9004 (Oct. 28, 1970) [35 FR 17537].

[24] Public float is the aggregate market value of a company's outstanding voting and non-voting common equity (i.e., market capitalization) minus the value of common equity held by affiliates of the company. Public float also is one of the key determinants for eligibility for short-form registration under the Securities Act (Form S-3 [17 CFR 239.13] and Form F-3 [17 CFR 239.33]).

[25] Even if a company chooses not to make its reports available on its website, investors still would be able to access information about the company through our EDGAR system. A company's posting of its reports on its website is not a substitute for filing documents with the Commission. EDGAR is an acronym for the Electronic Data Gathering, Analysis and Retrieval system.

[26] The public comments we received, and a summary of the comments prepared by our staff (the "Comment Summary"), can be reviewed in our Public Reference Room at 450 Fifth Street, NW, Washington, DC 20549, in File No. S7-08-02. Public comments submitted by electronic mail and the Comment Summary also are available on our website, www.sec.gov.

accounting firms who opposed the extent of acceleration and length of transition period proposed because, in their view, preparing reports in the proposed timeframes would be too burdensome and could result in less accurate filings. However, many offered alternatives with longer transition periods or filing deadlines or alternative measures to limit the number of accelerated filers. Most of the 141 commenters expressing a view on the proposals concerning website access supported them, although some suggested refinements.

C. Final Rule Amendments

We have considered the commenters' views and have modified the proposed amendments to reflect these comments. A summary of the final rules follows:

1. Phase-In of Accelerated Deadlines

Commenters representing investors, investor groups and other users of financial information favored receiving reports within a shortened timeframe. Most of the commenters who objected to the proposals believed that the proposals were too aggressive in terms of the extent of acceleration and the speed with which we expected companies to begin complying with accelerated deadlines. These commenters offered alternatives to reduce the potential costs and burden to registrants and a possible inadvertent negative impact on disclosure quality. Also, while comments were mixed, the majority of commenters addressing the issue believed it would be more difficult to accelerate filing of the quarterly report than the annual report.

As we stated in our Proposing Release, in establishing the appropriate timeframes for filing periodic reports, we must balance the market's need for information with the time companies need to prepare that information without undue burden. Accordingly, in response to comments, we are phasing-in accelerated deadlines over a three year period, with no change in deadlines for the first year and a less extensive ultimate acceleration of the quarterly report deadline. For companies that meet our revised definition of accelerated filer as of the end of their first fiscal year ending on or after December 15, 2002, the annual report deadline will remain 90 days for year one and will then be reduced 15 days per year over two years to 60 days. The quarterly report deadline for these filers will remain 45 days for year one and will then be reduced five days per year over two years to 35 days. We also are making conforming amendments to transition reports filed by accelerated filers. These changes are summarized as follows:

For Fiscal Years Ending On or After December 15, 2002: Form 10-K Deadline Form is 90 days after fiscal year end. Form 10-Q deadline is 45 days after fiscal quarter end.

For Fiscal Years Ending On or After December 15, 2003: Form 10-K Deadline Form is 75 days after fiscal year end. Form 10-Q deadline is 45 days after fiscal quarter end.

For Fiscal Years Ending On or After December 15, 2004: Form 10-K Deadline Form is 60 days after fiscal year end. Form 10-Q deadline is 40 days after fiscal quarter end.

For Fiscal Years Ending On or After December 15, 2005: Form 10-K Deadline Form is 60 days after fiscal year end. Form 10-Q deadline is 35 days after fiscal quarter end.

2. Definition of Accelerated Filer

Comments were mixed on the proposed definition of accelerated filer. Several commenters believed all public companies should be subject to the same filing deadlines, regardless of a company's size or experience in preparing filings. Other commenters agreed with the notion of excluding smaller companies that may not have the necessary resources and infrastructure to report on an accelerated basis. Comments also were somewhat mixed on the proposed use of public float as a method to differentiate between companies. Several commenters thought the $75 million public float threshold was too low.

After evaluating the comments, we are adopting the proposals substantially as proposed with some minor clarifications. Under the final rules, accelerated deadlines will apply to a company after it first meets the following conditions as of the end of it fiscal year:

Its common equity public float was $75 million or more as of the last business day of its most recently completed second fiscal quarter;

The company has been subject to the reporting requirements of Section 13(a) or 15(d) of the Exchange Act for a period of at least 12 calendar months;

The company has previously filed at least one annual report pursuant to Section 13(a) or 15(d) of the Exchange Act; and

The company is not eligible to use Forms 10-KSB and 10-QSB.While we agree that there would be benefits from accelerating deadlines for all companies, we must balance the market's need for information with the ability of companies to prepare that information without undue burden. We are adopting the reporting history requirements and the $75 million public float threshold substantially as proposed, although we changed the determination date for the public float requirement to give companies more time to prepare for accelerated reporting. We believe that a public float test serves as a reasonable measure of size and market interest. A one-year reporting history requirement and a $75 million threshold excludes nearly half of all publicly traded companies from the category of accelerated filers. These requirements are based primarily on the current eligibility requirements for short-form registration and "shelf registration."[27] Further, we believe the adoption of a three-year phase-in period for accelerating deadlines and a less extensive acceleration of the quarterly report deadline militates against the need to raise the threshold.

3. Conforming Amendments for Other Commission Filings

In the Proposing Release, we requested comment on several possible conforming revisions to other Commission rules as a result of the proposals. Based on the responses we received, we are making several conforming amendments. We are adopting amendments to Regulation S-X to conform the timeliness requirements for the inclusion of financial information in other Commission filings, such as Securities Act and Exchange Act registration statements and proxy statements and information statements under Section 14 of the Exchange Act.[28] Under the conforming amendments, financial information included in these documents still will be required to be at least as current as financial information filed under the Exchange Act. However, in response to the concerns of commenters, separate financial statements of subsidiaries not consolidated and 50% or less owned persons required by Rule 3-09 of Regulation S-X will not be accelerated for inclusion in a company's annual report on Form 10-K if the subsidiary or 50% or less owned person is not an accelerated filer. Companies will be able to file these financial statements by amendment within the existing time periods.[29] We also are adopting as proposed conforming amendments to maintain an extra 30 days for companies to file schedules required by Article 12 of Regulation S-X[30] as an amendment to their annual report on Form 10-K, if needed.

As proposed, we are not shortening the period of time companies have to file their definitive proxy or information statements to allow the incorporation by reference of information required by Part III of Form 10-K. We also are not making conforming revisions to the financial statement filing requirements in Rule 3-05 of Regulation S-X[31] and Item 7 of Form 8-K for financial statements of businesses acquired.

4. Disclosure Concerning Website Access to Company Reports

The vast majority of commenters-representing investors, investor groups, companies and professional associations-supported the proposals that would require disclosure concerning website access to company reports. Accordingly, we are adopting the disclosure requirement substantially as proposed with minor modifications. Since the Proposing Release, we have arranged for real-time access to companies' electronically filed periodic reports through our Internet website.[32] Elimination of the 24-hour delay in accessing EDGAR reports on our website substantially facilitates provision by companies of free, real-time website access to their reports by hyperlinking to our website. We also have eliminated two of the proposed disclosure elements to minimize the amount of disclosure required.

As adopted, the amendments require accelerated filers to disclose the following in their annual reports on Form 10-K beginning with reports for fiscal years ending on or after December 15, 2002:

The company's website address, if it has one;

Whether the company makes available free of charge on or through its website, if it has one, its annual report on Form 10-K, quarterly reports on Form 10-Q, current reports on Form 8-K, and all amendments to those reports as soon as reasonably practicable after such material is electronically filed with or furnished to the Commission;

If the company does not make its filings available in this manner, the reasons it does not do so (including, where applicable, that it does not have an Internet website); and

If the company does not make its filings available in this manner, whether the company voluntarily will provide electronic or paper copies of its filings free of charge upon request.

[¶ 2202]

II. Discussion of Amendments

A. Reporting Deadlines for Annual and Quarterly Reports

1. Proposed Rules

The proposed rules would have shortened the filing due date of annual reports from 90 days to 60 days after the end of a company's fiscal year and the filing due date of quarterly reports on Form 10-Q from 45 days to 30 days after the end of a company's first three fiscal quarters for com-

---

[27] Shelf registration is the commonly used term for delayed offerings under Securities Act Rule 415 [17 CFR 230.415]. Rule 415 permits offerings to be delayed until some point determined by the registrant after effectiveness of the relevant registration statement.

[28] 15 U.S.C. 77n.

[29] See revisions to 17 CFR 210.3-09(b).

[30] 17 CFR 210.12-01 et seq.

[31] 17 CFR 210.3-05.

[32] See Press Release No. 2002-75 (May 30, 2002).

panies that met our proposed definition of "accelerated filer."[33] We proposed similar conforming amendments for transition reports filed on Forms 10-K and 10-Q by an accelerated filer when it changes its fiscal year.

As discussed in the Proposing Release, we believe that periodic reports contain valuable information for investors. While quarterly and annual reports at present generally reflect historical information, a lengthy delay before that information becomes available makes the information less valuable to investors. While the specific disclosure required in periodic reports has evolved over the past 30 years, and the integrated disclosure system has placed added emphasis on Exchange Act reporting, the basic structure and timeframes that were established in 1970 remain in place today.

The more extensive information in periodic reports is evaluated by investors and particularly analysts and institutional investors as a baseline for the incremental disclosures made by a company. These reports also contain more detailed information that is essential to conduct comparative analyses, as this information is often not contained in earnings releases or other incremental disclosures. Moreover, the information in Exchange Act reports, due to its required nature and the liability to which it is subject, provides a verification function against other statements made by the company in press releases and other public announcements. Investors and other users of the reports can judge previous informal statements by the company against the more extensive and mandated disclosure provided in the reports that have been reviewed by independent public accountants and other advisors.[34] Accelerating the availability of this information will enable this verification to occur at an earlier point in time. Accelerating the availability of these reports also may increase the relevance of the reports, as the timeliness of information has considerable value to investors and the markets.

In addition, many public companies issue press releases to announce quarterly and annual results well before they file their reports with us. These earnings announcements reflect the importance of financial information and investors' demand for it at the earliest possible time. Assuming that companies are collecting and evaluating information before they issue these announcements, the availability of this information also suggests that much of the process involved in preparing the financial information contained in periodic reports is substantially complete. However, these earnings announcements themselves are generally less complete in their disclosure than quarterly or annual reports, and they can emphasize information that is less prominent in quarterly or annual reports.[35] Investors often must wait for the periodic reports to receive financial statements and the accompanying notes prepared in accordance with generally accepted accounting principles, management's discussion and analysis, or MD&A, and other vitally important financial disclosures. These additional disclosures increase transparency for investors.

In establishing the appropriate timeframes for filing periodic reports, however, we must balance the market's need for information with the time companies need to prepare that information without undue burden. Significant technological advances over the last three decades have both increased the market's demand for more timely corporate disclosure and the ability of companies to capture, process and disseminate this information. However, we acknowledge that, while the deadlines for filing periodic reports have not changed in over 30 years, the disclosure requirements have changed and some companies, particularly those with widespread operations, face additional complexities in today's environment. Not all companies, particularly small and unseasoned companies, may have the resources and infrastructure in place to prepare their reports on a shorter timeframe without undue burden or expense. Our amendments must speed the flow of information to investors without sacrificing accuracy or completeness or imposing undue burden and expense on registrants.

2. Comments on the Proposal

We received responses from 302 commenters on the proposals to accelerate periodic report deadlines. Generally, these commenters fell into two groups. The first group (20 commenters) repre-

[33] As mentioned in the Proposing Release, the Commission previously had requested comment as to whether it should shorten the due dates for quarterly and annual reports for all issuers. See Release No. 33-7606A (Nov. 13, 1998) [63 FR 67174]. Comments received on that release are available through our Public Reference Room under File No. S7-30-98.

[34] In addition, the information in these reports must now be certified by the principal executive officer and principal financial officer of the company. See Sections 302 and 906 of the Sarbanes-Oxley Act of 2002 [Pub. L. No. 107-204, § § 302 and 906, 116 Stat. 745 (2002)].

[35] See Release No. 33-8039 (Dec. 4, 2001) [66 FR 63731]. In addition, Section 401(b) of the Sarbanes-Oxley Act of 2002 [Pub. L. No. 107-204, § 401(b), 116 Stat. 745 (2002)] directs the Commission to issue final rules providing that pro forma financial information included in any periodic or other report, or in any public disclosure or press or other release, shall be presented in a manner that reconciles it with the financial condition and results of operations of the issuer under generally accepted accounting principles.

sented primarily investors, institutional investors and financial analysts who supported the proposals and our objective to provide investors with more timely access to company filings. The second group (282 commenters) represented primarily companies, business associations, law firms and accounting firms who opposed the extent of acceleration and transition period proposed because, in their view, preparing reports in the proposed timeframes would be too burdensome and could result in less accurate filings. Most of these commenters believed that any incremental benefit from the speed and extent of acceleration proposed was insufficient to warrant the added burdens on registrants and the risk of diminished disclosure quality, although these commenters generally did not analyze the benefits from the perspective of users of the reports.

Many commenters representing investors, users of financial information and several companies believed that shortening deadlines will improve the delivery and flow of reliable information to investors and capital markets and assist in the efficient operation of the markets.[36] These commenters emphasized the importance of the extensive information in periodic reports and investors' demand for it at the earliest possible time.[37] Several other companies, accounting firms and professional associations agreed in concept that shortening due dates would improve the flow of information, but believed the due dates should reflect concerns about the quality of information to be filed.[38] A few companies, law firms and business organizations, however, believed that existing deadlines and market practices are sufficient to satisfy investors' needs.[39] These commenters did not think a significant benefit would result from shortening deadlines, but also generally did not attempt to address the question of possible benefits from the perspective of users of the reports.

While some companies commented that they could or already comply with the proposal without undue burden,[40] the group that objected to the proposal raised several common concerns over the extent of acceleration and transition period proposed. The most common concern was that the proposed deadlines would negatively affect the quality and accuracy of reports.[41] According to one professional association, two-thirds of its survey respondents expected a reduction in the precision of reported information under the original proposals.[42] Many commenters thought the proposals were contrary to other initiatives that the Commission has undertaken to increase the quantity and quality of company disclosure. Many believed that focusing on and improving accuracy and quality should be the objective, not speed.

Another common concern was that the proposed deadlines would impair the ability of management, external auditors, boards of directors and especially audit committees to scrutinize and review filings properly and give appropriate consideration to the form, substance and priority of

---

[36] See, for example, the Letters of the American Federal of Labor and Congress of Industrial Organizations ("AFL-CIO"); Association of Investment Management and Research ("AIMR"); AOL Time Warner Inc.; Adrienne Randle Bond; Corporate Communications Broadcast Network ("CCBN"); Council of Institutional Investors ("CII"); Comcast Corporation; CSX Corporation; Delphi Corporation; The Dow Chemical Company; EDGAR Online Inc.; Financial Executives Institute ("FEI"); IMC Global, Inc.; Maverick Capital Ltd.; McDonald's, Inc.; PepsiCo, Inc.; Pfizer Inc.; Pharmacia Corporation; SBC Communications Inc.; Scott H. Schulke; and Teachers Insurance and Annuity Association of America–College Retirement and Equities Fund ("TIAA-CREF"). In addition, one commenter provided the results of an unpublished study that argued that there is statistically reliable evidence of an investor response to periodic reports. See the Letter of Paul A. Griffin.

[37] In addition, according to a web-based survey on The Motley Fool's website, 67% of the 1,391 respondents thought that faster information was important to them.

[38] See, for example, the Letters of the American Electric Power; American Institute of Certified Public Accountants ("AICPA"); BDO Seidman, LLP; The Coca-Cola Company; Computer Sciences Corporation; Fidelity Management & Research Company; Investment Company Institute; J.P. Morgan Chase & Co.; KPMG LLP; PG&E Corporation; Sidley Austin Brown & Wood LLP ("Sidley"); and Toys R Us, Inc.

[39] See, for example, the Letters of the American Bar Association ("ABA"); AFLAC Incorporated; the Association of the Bar of the City of New York ("NYCBA"); BioReliance Corporation; Compass Bankshares, Inc.; Commercial Federal Corporation; Emerson Electric Co.; Greenberg Traurig, P.A.; HealthSouth Corporation; Kellogg Company; Kimball International, Inc.; and SCANA Corporation.

[40] See, for example, the Letters of Delphi Corporation; The Dow Chemical Company; Microsoft Corporation; Siebel Systems, Inc.; TIAA-CREF; United Technologies Corporation; and V. I. Technologies, Inc.

[41] See, for example, the Letters of the ABA; American Corporate Counsel Association ("ACCA"); Association of Financial Professionals ("AFP"); American Insurance Association ("AIA"); AICPA; American Society of Corporate Secretaries ("ASCS"); Ashland Inc.; AT&T Corp.; BDO Seidman, LLP; the Business Roundtable; The Chubb Corporation; Deloitte & Touche LLP; Dell Computer Corporation; Ernst & Young LLP; Eli Lilly and Company; Financial Institutions Accounting Committee ("FIAC"); Grant Thornton LLP; Joseph A. Grundfest; H&R Block, Inc.; Halliburton Company; HealthSouth Corporation; Kellogg Company; KPMG LLP; Liberty Media Corporation; Merck & Co., Inc.; New York State Bar Association ("NYSBA"); NYCBA; Papa John's International, Inc.; PepsiCo, Inc.; PricewaterhouseCoopers LLP; Securities Industry Association ("SIA"); Ronald S. Stowell; Sullivan & Cromwell; SCANA Corporation; Shearman & Sterling; Sidley; Sotheby's Holdings, Inc.; Washington Mutual, Inc.; The Williams Companies, Inc.; and Kathryn J. Wilson.

[42] See the Letter of the ASCS.

disclosures, especially MD&A disclosures and financial statement footnotes.[43] These commenters feared that disclosures could be reduced or become more boilerplate if companies have less time to prepare and review them. These commenters believed that accelerating deadlines in the manner proposed would also undermine the governance and review mechanisms that have been put in place to ensure quality. We have separately proposed and the Sarbanes-Oxley Act of 2002 establishes new requirements to ensure that procedures are in place to ensure that a company is able to collect, process and disclose the information required in its periodic reports and for senior officers to certify the accuracy of those reports.[44]

A third concern was that advances in technology over the past 30 years have been largely offset by increases in accounting and disclosure requirements.[45] Business operations have also become increasingly global and complex, further complicating report preparation. These commenters argued that technological advances that have allowed companies to generate earnings results quickly in an earnings release do not address the additional analysis necessary to prepare periodic reports. Processes and systems would need to be changed to report on an accelerated basis.

Commenters objecting to the original proposals also were concerned that companies would face an increased burden in preparing reports, particularly with respect to increased costs and audit fees. While a few commenters believed that the original proposals would not have a significant adverse effect on the cost of preparing reports,[46] most who addressed the subject mentioned that the original proposals would result in increased costs.[47] Many commenters outlined their process of preparing reports to demonstrate the difficulties of accelerating the process.[48] Several commenters provided detailed timelines. The particular steps and timing varied depending on the individual company, and not all companies appear to be at the same level of technological sophistication and staffing for preparing reports. Two professional associations noted that there are no current best practices for preparing reports.[49] As a result, the few cost estimates received varied widely, and many commenters were unable to provide estimates. One company believed it was not possible to put a dollar value on such costs, as it depends on the quality and flexibility of each registrant's present systems, processes and staff.[50] According to one professional association that surveyed its members, 52% of its survey respondents reported that they expected costs to increase in order to comply with the original proposals.[51] Forty-five percent of respondents indicated they would have to hire additional staff, and 27% of respondents indicated they would have to buy or develop additional systems. Other commenters were concerned that the original proposals would result in increased audit fees, particularly for companies with a calendar fiscal year-end, given a compression in the amount of time available for

---

[43] See, for example, the Letters of the ABA; American Counsel of Life Insurers ("ACLI"); ACCA; AFP; AICPA; ASCS; AT&T Corp.; BDO Seidman, LLP; The Bank of New York Company, Inc.; The Chubb Corporation; The Coca-Cola Company; Comcast Corporation; Deloitte & Touche LLP; Ernst & Young LLP; Eli Lilly and Company; FIAC; Grant Thornton LLP; Greenberg Traurig, P.A.; Joseph A. Grundfest; HealthSouth Corporation; KPMG LLP; Liberty Media Corporation; Simon M. Lorne; Marathon Oil Corporation; Merck & Co., Inc.; McGuireWoods LLP; NYCBA; NYSBA; Papa John's International, Inc.; PepsiCo, Inc.; PG&E Corporation; Pharmacia Corporation; PricewaterhouseCoopers LLP; Reed Smith LLP; Sullivan & Cromwell; SCANA Corporation; Shearman & Sterling; SIA; Sidley; Sotheby's Holdings, Inc.; Washington Mutual, Inc.; and The Williams Companies, Inc.

[44] See Release No. 34-46079 (June 14, 2002) [67 FR 41877]; Release No. 34-46300 (Aug. 2, 2002) [67 FR 51508]; Release No. 33-8124 (Aug. 29, 2002); and Sections 302, 404 and 906 of the Sarbanes-Oxley Act of 2002 [Pub. L. No. 107-204, §§302, 404 and 906, 116 Stat. 745 (2002)].

[45] See, for example, the Letters of the ABA; ACLI; ACCA; AICPA; ASCS; AT&T Corp.; BDO Seidman, LLP; The Bank of New York Company, Inc.; the Business Roundtable; The Coca-Cola Company; Comcast Corporation; Deloitte & Touche LLP; Ernst & Young LLP; Eli Lilly and Company; FIAC; Grant Thornton LLP; Greenberg Traurig, P.A.; Joseph A. Grundfest; H&R Block, Inc.; HealthSouth Corporation; Institute of Management Accountants; KPMG LLP; Liberty Media Corporation; Helen W. Melman; NYCBA; NYSBA; Papa John's International, Inc.; PepsiCo, Inc.; PG&E Corporation; PricewaterhouseCoopers LLP; Sullivan & Cromwell; SBC Communications Inc.; SIA; Sidley; The Southern Company; SunTrust Banks, Inc.; Washington Mutual, Inc.; and The Williams Companies, Inc.

[46] See, for example, the Letters of the AFL-CIO; AIMR; Delphi Corporation; The Dow Chemical Company; and TIAA-CREF.

[47] See, for example, the Letters of the ABA; ACLI; AFP; American Bankers Association; The Allstate Corporation; Deloitte & Touche LLP; Dollar Tree Stores, Inc.; Ernst & Young LLP; Halliburton Company; HealthSouth Corporation; KPMG LLP; National Association of Real Estate Companies ("NAREC"); National Association of Real Estate Investment Trusts ("NAREIT"); NYCBA; PricewaterhouseCoopers LLP; Southern Union Company; Ronald S. Stowell; and UnionBanCal Corporation.

[48] See, for example, the Letters of the ACCA; ASCS; BioReliance Corporation; Community Health Systems, Inc.; Constellation Energy Group, Inc.; Dean Foods Company; HealthSouth Corporation; Merrill Lynch & Co., Inc.; Nucor Corporation; Technitrol, Inc.; Veritas Software Corporation; and Zygo Corporation.

[49] See the Letters of the ASCS and the Business Roundtable.

[50] See the Letter of American Electric Power.

[51] See the Letter of the ASCS.

auditors to complete their work for these companies.

Objecting commenters mentioned additional concerns over the original proposals, such as an increased need to use estimates to prepare reports[52] or an increased risk of amendments or restatements because of rushed preparation.[53] Several commenters were especially concerned about accelerating deadlines now given recent events with Arthur Andersen LLP.[54] While comments were mixed, many commenters said that while most audit and review work is substantially complete before the earnings release or the proposed deadlines, the process of preparing reports, including the financial statements and footnotes, is not.[55] However, other commenters noted that the audit and review process is far from complete by the time a company issues an earnings release and little, if any, assurance can be ascribed to the publicly disclosed results.[56] While some commenters prepare their reports concurrently with the earnings release, most described the process as a series of sequential steps where the company first closes its financial books, then prepares and releases its earnings release and then turns its attention to the periodic reports. Some companies would need to revise their internal processes to prepare their reports on a more concurrent basis with the earnings release. Several companies expressed concern that the proposals would be difficult for companies that operate on a decentralized basis with many subsidiaries and operations to consolidate, especially when the subsidiaries and operations are located worldwide or in emerging markets.[57]

Slightly less than half of those objecting to the proposals (129 commenters) did not think any acceleration of deadlines was warranted.[58] However, slightly more than half of those objecting (153 commenters) objected because they believed the Commission was too aggressive in its proposal.[59] Many of these commenters generally supported the Commission's objective to provide investors with more timely access to company information and offered alternatives to reduce the potential costs and burden to registrants and any negative impact on disclosure quality. These alternatives fell roughly into three categories:

A more gradual phase-in or transition period than that proposed (e.g., reducing deadlines by a set number of days per year over several years or delaying the effective date of accelerated filing deadlines).[60]

Accelerating deadlines less extensively (e.g., 75 days for the annual report and 35 days for the quarterly report) or accelerating only the annual report deadline.[61] In this regard, while comments were mixed, the majority of commenters addressing the issue believed it would be more difficult to

---

[52] See, for example, the ABA; ACLI; AFLAC Incorporated; BioReliance Corporation; The Bank of New York Company, Inc.; ChevronTexaco Corporation; The Chubb Corporation; Crescent Real Estate Equities Company; Dean Foods Company; Deloitte & Touche LLP; Ernst & Young LLP; HealthSouth Corporation; J.C. Penney Company, Inc.; Mercury General Corporation; NAREC; NAREIT; PricewaterhouseCoopers LLP; and Washington Mutual, Inc.

[53] See, for example, the Letters of the ABA; AFLAC Incorporated; Cleary, Gottlieb, Steen & Hamilton; Halliburton Company; J.C. Penney Company, Inc.; Jones & Keller, P.C.; Perkins Coie LLP; PG&E Corporation; PricewaterhouseCoopers LLP; Sidley; and UnionBanCal Corporation.

[54] See, for example, the Letters of Brown-Forman Corporation; Caremark Rx, Inc.; Deloitte & Touche LLP; Joseph A. Grundfest; KPMG LLP; Liberty Media Corporation; NYCBA; PricewaterhouseCoopers LLP; and XTO Energy, Inc.

[55] See, for example, the Letters of the ACCA; ASCS; The Bank of New York Company, Inc.; Cleary, Gottlieb, Steen & Hamilton; Clifford Chance Rogers & Wells LLP; Crowe, Chizek and Company LLP; Greenberg Traurig, P.A.; Halliburton Company; J.P. Morgan Chase & Co.; Mellon Financial Corporation; PepsiCo, Inc.; Pfizer Inc.; SCANA Corporation; Shearman & Sterling; Southern Union Company; and Technitrol, Inc.

[56] See, for example, the Letters of BDO Seidman, LLP; Ernst & Young LLP; The Great Atlantic and Pacific Tea Company, Inc.; HealthSouth Corporation; KPMG LLP; Merrill Lynch & Co., Inc.; PricewaterhouseCoopers LLP; The Southern Company; and SunTrust Banks, Inc. We are surprised and concerned by these assertions given the importance of these announcements to investors and markets and are considering their implications.

[57] See, for example, the Letters of the ABA; AICPA; BDO Seidman, LLP; the Business Roundtable; ChevronTexaco Corporation; The Coca-Cola Company; Dean Foods Company; Deloitte & Touche LLP; Eli Lilly and Company; Grant Thornton LLP; HealthSouth Corporation; KPMG LLP; Marathon Oil Corporation; National Investor Relations Institute ("NIRI"); Perkins Coie LLP; PricewaterhouseCoopers LLP; Reed Smith LLP; Shearman & Sterling; Sidley; Southern Union Company; and Western Wireless Corporation.

[58] See the Comment Summary.

[59] Id.

[60] See, for example, the Letters of Abbott Laboratories; ACLI; AICPA; AOL Time Warner Inc.; ASCS; the Business Roundtable; Cabot Corporation; Cleary, Gottlieb, Steen & Hamilton; Deloitte & Touche LLP; Ernst & Young LLP; Joseph A. Grundfest; Halliburton Company; KPMG LLP; NYSBA; Pfizer Inc.; PricewaterhouseCoopers LLP; Sullivan & Cromwell; SIA; Sidley; and The Williams Companies, Inc.

[61] See, for example, the Letters of the ACCA; American Bankers Association; The Coca-Cola Company; Eli Lilly and Company; Harrah's Entertainment, Inc.; Lamar Advertising Company; Merck & Co., Inc.; Merrill Lynch & Co., Inc.; Michael McDonald; NAREC; NAREIT; NYCBA; Scholastic Inc.; Southern Union Company; Toys R Us, Inc.; TXU Corp.; UST Inc.; and Washington Mutual, Inc.

accelerate the quarterly report than the annual report.[62]

Linking the deadline for filing reports to a company's public announcement of earnings (e.g., the earlier of the existing deadlines or some period of time after a company's issuance of an earnings release).[63]In addition to the comments received on the Proposing Release, earlier this year we hosted an investor summit in Washington, DC.[64] The summit offered individual investors nationwide an opportunity to ask questions and offer comments about our regulatory agenda. Most participants at the investor summit mentioned their support for our proposals to accelerate the delivery of periodic reports to investors.[65]

As mentioned in the Proposing Release, we also hosted roundtable discussions in New York, Washington, DC, and Chicago earlier this year at which investor relations professionals, corporate executives, academics and experienced legal counsel discussed financial disclosure and auditor oversight.[66] Several participants at these roundtables indicated that reporting within the proposed shortened deadlines was feasible.[67] Some participants, however, referred to the comment letters on our 1998 request for comment on accelerating deadlines,[68] and were concerned about the ability of companies, and smaller companies in particular, to report in a shorter timeframe.[69] They thought that accelerating deadlines could cause the quality of reports to diminish.[70] One participant was concerned that shortened deadlines may present more problems for quarterly reports than for annual reports.[71]

3. Final Rules

After careful consideration of the comments received, we are adopting a phased-in approach of accelerated deadlines, with no change in deadlines for the first year and a less extensive ultimate acceleration of the deadline for quarterly reports. Specifically, we are phasing-in accelerated deadlines for accelerated filers according to the following schedule:

For Fiscal Years Ending On or After December 15, 2002: Form 10-K Deadline Form is 90 days after fiscal year end. Form 10-Q Deadline is 45 days after fiscal quarter end.

For Fiscal Years Ending On or After December 15, 2003: Form 10-K Deadline Form is 75 days after fiscal year end. Form 10-Q Deadline is 45 days after fiscal quarter end.

For Fiscal Years Ending On or After December 15, 2004: Form 10-K Deadline Form is 60 days after fiscal year end. Form 10-Q Deadline is 40 days after fiscal quarter end.

For Fiscal Years Ending On or After December 15, 2004: Form 10-K Deadline Form is 60 days after fiscal year end. Form 10-Q Deadline is 35 days after fiscal quarter end.

We also are accelerating the due dates for transition reports by accelerated filers on Form 10-K and 10-Q on the same schedule. These conforming changes will ensure that the deadlines for transition reports remain similar to the deadlines for periodic reports.[72] We also are making technical corrections to the codification of financial reporting policies to reflect our amendments.

---

[62] Compare, for example, the Letters of AFLAC Incorporated; Bank of America; Capital One Financial Corporation; CH Energy Group, Inc.; Clancy Systems International, Inc.; Constellation Energy Group, Inc.; Dollar Tree Stores, Inc.; FEI; Jefferson-Pilot Corporation; Lamar Advertising Company; Phillips Petroleum Company; The Southern Company; UnionBanCal Corporation and U.S. Bancorp with the Letters of American Electric Power; AOL Time Warner Inc.; Clifford Chance Rogers & Wells LLP; Long Aldridge & Norman LLP and United States Steel Corporation.

[63] See, for example, the Letters of the ABA; ACLI; AICPA; BDO Seidman, LLP; Comcast Corporation; Ernst & Young LLP; Grant Thornton LLP; Julia A. Harper; Hibernia Corporation; KPMG LLP; The Pepsi Bottling Group; PepsiCo, Inc.; PG&E Corporation; PricewaterhouseCoopers LLP; Stewart Information Services Corporation; UnumProvident Corporation; and Wild Oats Markets, Inc.

[64] See SEC Press Release No. 2002-59 (May 1, 2002). The summit was held on May 10, 2002. Archived broadcasts of the investor summit are available to the public on our Internet website (archived broadcast; transcript).

[65] See, for example, Joseph D. Borg, Bill Mann and Damon Silvers, Remarks at the Investor Summit in Washington, DC (May 10, 2002) (archived broadcast; transcript).

[66] See SEC Press Release Nos. 2002-28 (Feb. 22, 2002) and 2002-46 (Mar. 27, 2002). The New York roundtable was held on March 4, 2002. The Washington DC roundtable was held on March 6, 2002. The Chicago roundtable was held on April 4, 2002. Archived broadcasts and transcripts of the roundtables are available to the public on our Internet website.

[67] See, for example, Richard Carbone and Raymond Groves, Remarks at the Financial Disclosure and Auditor Oversight Roundtable in Washington, DC (Mar. 6, 2002) (archived broadcasts; transcripts).

[68] See, for example, John White, Remarks at the Financial Disclosure and Auditor Oversight Roundtable in New York, NY (Mar. 4, 2002); and James Cheek, Remarks at the Financial Disclosure and Auditor Oversight Roundtable in Washington, DC (Mar. 6, 2002) (archived broadcasts; transcripts).

[69] See, for example, Edward Nusbaum, Remarks at the Financial Disclosure and Auditor Oversight Roundtable in Chicago, IL (Apr. 4, 2002) (archived broadcast; transcript).

[70] See note 68 above.

[71] See, for example, Phil Livingston, Remarks at the Financial Disclosure and Auditor Oversight Roundtable in Washington, DC (Mar. 6, 2002) (archived broadcasts; transcripts).

[72] See, for example, Release No. 33-6823 (Mar. 13, 1989) [54 FR 10306] (Revising transition report rules to conform their filing requirements to those for periodic reports).

According to the amendments, if a company with a calendar year fiscal year-end determines it is an accelerated filer as of December 31, 2002 (its first fiscal year ending on or after December 15, 2002), its annual report on Form 10-K for that fiscal year will continue to have a 90 day filing deadline and will be due by March 31, 2003.[73] Each of the Form 10-Q reports for the first three quarters of its 2003 fiscal year will continue to have a 45-day deadline. For example, the Form 10-Q for the company's first fiscal quarter ending March 31, 2003 will continue to be due by May 15, 2003. The Form 10-K for the fiscal year ending December 31, 2003 will have a 75-day deadline and will be due by March 15, 2004. Each of the Form 10-Q reports for the first three quarters in the 2004 fiscal year will have a 40-day deadline. For example, the Form 10-Q for the company's first fiscal quarter ending March 31, 2004 will be due by May 10, 2004. The Form 10-K for the fiscal year ending December 31, 2004 will have a 60-day deadline and will be due by March 1, 2005. Each of the Form 10-Q reports for the first three quarters in the 2005 fiscal year will have a 35-day deadline. For example, the Form 10-Q for the company's first fiscal quarter ending March 31, 2005 will be due by May 5, 2005. All subsequent reports on Form 10-K and 10-Q by the accelerated filer will be subject to a 60 and 35-day deadline, respectively.

In establishing this schedule for accelerated deadlines, we agree with the suggestions of many commenters that appropriate focus should be directed toward report quality.[74] We also agree with investors and other users of financial information that timeliness of information is important. Increased quality and timeliness, with an appropriate balance between the two, assures that investors receive the full and reliable data they deserve at the speed in which they desire it. A phased-in approach of accelerated deadlines allows a greater transition period for companies to adjust their procedures and to develop efficiencies to ensure that the quality and accuracy of reported information will not be sacrificed. Under a phased-in approach, companies will have additional time to plan for and adjust their reporting schedules and processes to ensure that the necessary reviews will not be compromised. Given the recent enactment of the Sarbanes-Oxley Act of 2002, a phased-in approach also allows companies to adjust to significant new changes and requirements in the reporting system. At the same time, a phased-in approach allows investors to begin to experience the benefits of an accelerated flow of information. A phased-in approach also will provide the Commission with an opportunity to understand how each incremental change affects the disclosure process.

A phased-in approach helps to alleviate the immediate impact of any costs and burdens that may be imposed on certain registrants. While several commenters indicated that they could report on an accelerated timeframe today, several major business associations that surveyed their members reported that adjustment to accelerated deadlines would be easier with a longer phase-in period.[75] A longer transition may even help reduce costs as companies will have additional time to develop best practices, long-term processes and efficiencies to prepare reports, as opposed to having to take rushed and possibly inefficient measures to meet a more sudden acceleration.[76] Also, a longer transition period helps to smooth out any possible impact on the availability of third party advisors used by companies to prepare their reports.

A less extensive acceleration of the quarterly report deadline also will alleviate some of the burdens mentioned by commenters. There will be more time than proposed to gather the necessary data and complete the necessary reviews by company officials, the board of directors and outside advisors. One professional association commented that 80% of its survey respondents reported they could more easily meet a 35-day deadline than a 30-day deadline.[77] Further, we believe that by imposing a 40-day deadline before finally reducing it to 35 days, we are striking an adequate compromise between the benefits of reducing deadlines with the potential inconvenience, difficulty and cost that may be incurred by some companies.

We considered, but rejected, the alternative of tying the due date of reports to a company's announcement of earnings. Not all companies issue earnings releases or issue them on an accelerated basis. As a result, linking deadlines to earnings releases may not result in more accelerated reporting of information. We also were concerned that linking report deadlines to earnings announcements could delay earnings announce-

---

[73] A one-time extension of time to file a particular periodic report is available under certain circumstances under Exchange Act Rule 12b-25 [17 CFR 240.12b-25].

[74] For other proposals where we are specifically addressing the quality and content of information disclosed, see notes 20 and 44 above.

[75] See, for example, the Letters of the ASCS; the Business Roundtable; and FEI. These and other commenters also mentioned, and we are aware of other anecdotal reports that, many companies already are revising their systems and procedures to prepare for accelerated reporting.

[76] See, for example, the Letters of the ASCS and FEI.

[77] See the Letter of the ASCS. See also Letter of the Business Roundtable.

ments, as companies would know that the announcement would trigger the deadline to file reports. While market demand for earnings information could negate this risk, an approach linking deadlines to earnings announcements could have the effect of penalizing companies for early releases of information while rewarding companies that delay their earnings with extended time to file their reports.

Even with a phase-in period, accelerating filing deadlines may create the risk that more companies will file their reports late or need a filing extension. Moreover, if a company is late filing its reports, it will lose availability for short-form registration for at least one year from the date of the late filing. Being late also could render Securities Act Rule 144 temporarily unavailable for security holders' resales of restricted and control securities, and make new filings on Form S-8 temporarily unavailable for resales of employee benefit plan securities.[78] We considered the suggestions of some commenters to extend the filing extension periods in Exchange Act Rule 12b-25 as an additional method to alleviate any transition difficulties to shortened deadlines.[79] However, we think a lengthy phase-in period adequately addresses these concerns. A less dramatic acceleration of deadlines over a set schedule each year will provide companies with advance notice of the changes they will be expected to make and will smooth out some of the possible difficulties raised by commenters. Rule 12b-25 in its existing form still will provide companies that face extenuating circumstances the ability to gain a filing extension of five calendar days for quarterly reports and fifteen calendar days for annual reports.

While our proposals did not directly address the contents of earnings releases, many commenters supported additional efforts by the Commission in this area. Several recommended that earnings or other standardized earnings information be filed with the Commission, such as on Form 8-K.[80] Others thought the Commission should consider issuing or promoting minimum requirements or guidelines for the contents of earnings releases, such as a GAAP reconciliation.[81] While we will continue to explore ways to improve earnings releases, and the Sarbanes-Oxley Act of 2002 requires us to take steps in this area, we believe these are separate initiatives from the need to accelerate periodic report deadlines.[82] We recognize that the information in periodic reports is more extensive than that contained in earnings releases, and that it would be difficult to eliminate any gap between the earnings release and the filing of the report. As mentioned above, however, we believe periodic reports contain valuable information for investors, and comments received from the users of this information uniformly indicated their desire to receive the reports at the earliest time that is consistent with receiving quality information.[83]

B. Definition of "Accelerated Filer"

1. Proposed Rules

We proposed to accelerate the due dates for annual and quarterly reports only for companies with a common equity public float of $75 million or more, that have been reporting for at least 12 calendar months and that have filed at least one annual report. The public float and reporting history requirements are designed to include the companies that are least likely to find such a change overly burdensome and where investor interest in accelerated filing is likely to be highest. Other companies would continue to file under existing deadlines, including small business issuers that file on Forms 10-KSB and 10-QSB, foreign governments, foreign private issuers that elect to use Form 20-F and companies that do not have a common equity public float. Under the proposed rules, a company would determine its public float for purposes of determining whether it would become an accelerated filer as of a date no more than 60 and no less than 30 days before the end of its fiscal year. In addition, as proposed, a com-

---

[78] Securities Act Rule 144 [17 CFR 230.144] requires that for such a resale to be valid, the issuer of the securities must have made all filings required under the Exchange Act during the preceding 12 months. Form S-8 [17 CFR 239.16b] requires that an issuer be current in its reporting for the last 12 calendar months (or such shorter period that the issuer was required to file such reports and materials). If a company was late in filing its reports, the company would lose Rule 144 eligibility and eligibility to file a Form S-8 during the time that the company was not current in its reporting.

[79] See, for example, the Letters of the ASCS; Cleary, Gottlieb, Steen & Hamilton; CSX Corporation; Deloitte & Touche LLP; Ernst & Young LLP; NAREIT; NYSBA; Pharmacia Corporation; PricewaterhouseCoopers LLP; and Triarc Companies, Inc.

[80] See, for example, the Letters of the ABA; Deloitte & Touche LLP; FEI; Joseph A. Grundfest; Investment Company Institute; Intel Corporation; Merrill Lynch & Co., Inc.; Nucor Corporation; SCANA Corporation; SIA; The Southern Company; TIAA-CREF; and Trover Solutions, Inc.

[81] See, for example, the Letters of Ernst & Young LLP; FEI, Fidelity Management & Research Company; Investment Company Institute; KPMG LLP; NAREC; NAREIT; NIRI; Papa John's International, Inc.; Shearman & Sterling; SIA; and Valmont Industries, Inc.

[82] See, for example, Sections 401(b) and 409 of the Sarbanes-Oxley Act of 2002 [Pub. L. No. 107-204, §§401(b) and 409, 116 Stat. 745 (2002)].

[83] See, for example, the Letter of Fidelity Management & Research Company.

pany would become an accelerated filer at any time during the year if it met the public float test on a previous determination date and subsequently met the reporting requirements during the year.

2. Comments on the Proposal

Comments were mixed on the proposed definition of accelerated filer. Several commenters believed that all public companies should be required to adhere to the same filing deadlines, regardless of a company's size or experience in preparing filings.[84] These commenters thought it would be confusing to investors and companies to have differing filing deadlines. They also believed that investors in companies with a public float of less than $75 million should expect the same timely access to prompt disclosure as investors in larger companies. They argued that such prompt disclosure may be even more important for smaller companies. Several commenters also thought that while large firms may have more resources, they tend to have more complex and geographically widespread operations, numerous consolidated entities and segments and complicated financial transactions.[85]

Other commenters agreed with the notion of excluding smaller companies.[86] Smaller companies may have operations that are just as complicated as large companies. More importantly, accelerated reporting may be particularly burdensome for smaller companies because they may not have the necessary resources or infrastructure to report on an accelerated basis. Many of these issuers have small staffs and limited technological resources, so the imposition of accelerated deadlines may have a disproportionate impact on these companies. In addition, auditors may be more likely to postpone their reviews of smaller companies' financial statements until they have completed their work for larger clients. There also may not be sufficient market interest in these companies to justify the costs and burdens needed to accelerate a smaller company's reporting processes.[87]

Comments also were somewhat mixed on the use of public float as a method to differentiate between companies.[88] Several commenters questioned the use of public float as a measure indicative of a company's ability to file sooner. According to these commenters, smaller companies with limited operations and personnel could easily develop a significant public float. These commenters offered several alternative measures, including revenues, assets or some measure of trading volume. Other commenters thought the proposed $75 million public float threshold was too low.[89] These commenters recommended a number of alternative thresholds, ranging from $150 million to $10 billion. Several other commenters thought the proposed public float measurement date occurred too late in the fiscal year to give companies sufficient time to modify their systems and prepare for accelerated reporting.[90]

In the Proposing Release, we also requested comment on whether the deadline for annual reports of foreign private issuers on Form 20-F should be shortened. Comments were mixed on this request. Some commenters did not think there was a reason to not also shorten deadlines for foreign filers.[91] Others thought that the issues involving foreign issuers are sufficiently different as to warrant a separate study and rule proposal.[92] A few others thought the deadlines for foreign issuers should not be accelerated at all.[93]

3. Final Rules

After evaluating the comments on this aspect of the proposal, we are adopting the amendments substantially as proposed with some minor clarifications. Under the final rules, accelerated deadlines will apply to a company after it first meets

---

[84] See, for example, the Letters of the ABA; FEI; NYCBA; Caremark Rx, Inc.; Comcast Corporation; The Dow Chemical Company; Monsanto Company; and Troutman Sanders LLP.

[85] See, for example, the Letters of the ABA; American Electric Power; Cleary, Gottlieb, Steen & Hamilton; Grant Thornton, LLP; HealthSouth Corporation; and Union Planters Corporation.

[86] See, for example, the Letters of the AFL-CIO; Corning Incorporated; Crowe, Chizek and Company LLP; KPMG LLP; NAREC; NAREIT; NYSBA; and The Williams Companies, Inc.

[87] See, for example, the Letters of Community Bankshares, Inc; First Capital Bank Holding Corporation; and GrandSouth Bancorporation.

[88] Compare, for example, the Letters of the AFP; KPMG LLP; and Western Wireless Corporation with the Letters of the ABA; AICPA; American Bankers Association; Arris Group, Inc.; BDO Seidman, LLP; Ernst & Young LLP; Foley, Hoag & Eliot LLP; Grant Thornton LLP; Joseph A. Grundfest; NYCBA; NYSBA; PricewaterhouseCoopers LLP; Shearman & Sterling; Southern Union Company; and United States Steel Corporation.

[89] See, for example, the Letters of the AICPA; American Bankers Association; Arris Group, Inc.; Baldwin & Lyons, Inc.; Ernst & Young LLP; HealthSouth Corporation; KPMG LLP; NAREC; NYSBA; Perkins Coie LLP; Triarc Companies, Inc.; and Troutman Sanders LLP.

[90] See, for example, the Letters of the ABA; AICPA; Ernst & Young LLP; KMPG LLP; and Troutman Sanders LLP.

[91] See, for example, the Letters of the AIMR; Brown-Forman Corporation; Chevron Phillips Chemical Company LLP; Comcast Corporation; Deloitte & Touche LLP; The Dow Chemical Company; Markel Corporation; Maverick Capital Ltd.; and SBC Communications Inc.

[92] See, for example, the Letters of the AICPA; Ernst & Young LLP; Institute of Management Accountants; KMPG LLP; and PricewaterhouseCoopers LLP.

[93] See, for example, the Letters of Cleary, Gottlieb, Steen & Hamilton and NYCBA.

the following conditions as of the end of its fiscal year:

Its common equity public float was $75 million or more as of the last business day of its most recently completed second fiscal quarter;

The company has been subject to the reporting requirements of Section 13(a) or 15(d) of the Exchange Act for a period of at least 12 calendar months;

The company has previously filed at least one annual report pursuant to Section 13(a) or 15(d) of the Exchange Act; and

The company is not eligible to use Forms 10-KSB and 10-QSB.The public float and reporting history aspects of this definition are being adopted substantially as proposed. These requirements are based primarily on the current eligibility requirements for registration of primary offerings for cash on Form S-3.[94] These companies can take advantage of short-form registration, including the resultant benefits of incorporation by reference and quick access to the capital markets through "shelf registration." Shortening the periodic reporting deadline for these companies, coupled with our conforming revisions to the financial statement timeliness requirements discussed below, promises that investors will receive information about these companies sooner. This enhances the timeliness of information received for primary purchasers in these offerings in addition to secondary market purchasers. These changes also ensure that investors receive consistent financial information regardless of the particular registration form a company uses. In identifying companies that will be subject to this new requirement, we also thought it would be appropriate to use a pre-existing threshold to reduce regulatory complexity.

While we agree that investors in smaller companies value the timeliness of corporate disclosures, we must balance the market's need for information with the ability of companies to prepare that information without undue burden. The possible detrimental effects of accelerating the reporting process for companies least able to bear the burden of these changes may outweigh the potential advantages of acceleration if the quality of information suffers. We do not think that having two sets of reporting deadlines will be confusing. Some registrants, such as foreign private issuers, are already subject to different deadlines. We believe it is more important that companies of the same relative size, including the most actively followed companies, are subject to shortened deadlines. We agree that larger companies may have more complex operations, but they also are more likely than smaller companies to have the infrastructure and resources to report on an accelerated timeframe.

We believe that a public float test serves as a reasonable measure of company size and market interest. While several commenters urged raising the proposed threshold, we believe a longer phase-in period for accelerating deadlines and a less extensive acceleration of the quarterly report deadline militates against the need to raise the threshold. The definition of accelerated filer we are adopting today with a $75 million public float threshold excludes nearly half of all publicly traded companies, as well as all companies eligible for our small business issuer reporting system, all foreign private issuers that file on Form 20-F and all companies that do not have a common equity public float.[95]

A company that does not fall within the "accelerated filer" definition as of its first fiscal year ending on or after December 15, 2002 will have to re-evaluate its status at the end of each fiscal year. To address concerns raised by commenters, a company will determine its public float by looking back at the last business day of its most recently completed second fiscal quarter. This allows companies to know further in advance whether they will become an accelerated filer at the end of their fiscal year and allow them to begin making the appropriate preparations.

As explained in the new definition of "accelerated filer," the determination of whether a non-accelerated filer becomes an accelerated filer as of the end of its fiscal year governs the annual report to be filed for that fiscal year, the quarterly reports to be filed for the subsequent fiscal year and annual and quarterly reports to be filed thereafter. Under the final rules, a company would not need to determine whether it would become an accelerated filer other than at the end of its fiscal year. We believe this provides increased notice to a company for planning purposes. It also lessens any potential confusion to investors by a sudden change in deadlines.

---

[94] See General Instructions I.A.3 and I.B.1 of Form S-3.

[95] We arrived at this estimate by dividing the number of companies in Standard & Poors Research Insight Compustat Database with a market capitalization below $75 million as of November, 2001 (4,622) by the total number of companies in the Compustat Database with a reported market capitalization for that period (9,325). It is our understanding that the data in the Compustat Database is derived principally from larger companies, so our estimate may understate the actual percentage of companies that would be excluded by the proposals. Further, this figure does not include many additional companies that would not be affected by the amendments, including foreign private issuers that file on Form 20-F and issuers that do not have a common equity public float.

For example, if a calendar year-end company meets the public float requirement, but has not filed its first annual report as of December 31, 2002, it does not become an accelerated filer and remains subject to existing deadlines for its 2002 annual report and its 2003 quarterly reports. However, if on December 31, 2003, the company meets the public float test as of the last business day of its second fiscal quarter ending June 30, 2003 and meets the other requirements of the accelerated filer definition, the company becomes an accelerated filer subject to the accelerated deadlines for its 2003 annual report, 2004 quarterly reports and all periodic reports thereafter.

As proposed, once a company becomes an accelerated filer, it remains an accelerated filer subject to shortened deadlines unless and until it subsequently becomes eligible to use Forms 10-KSB and 10-QSB for its annual and quarterly reports.[96] In that case, the issuer ceases to be an accelerated filer unless and until it again meets the accelerated filer criteria. A few commenters thought that the use of different standards for entering and exiting accelerated filer status would be confusing and potentially unfair compared to companies that never had their public float exceed $75 million, especially for companies that cross the threshold for a certain period of time and then fall back below the threshold but do not otherwise meet the criteria to become a small business issuer.[97] However, it is our view that, once a company meets the accelerated filer threshold, it is reasonable to minimize a company's fluctuation in and out of accelerated filer status while still allowing the company to exit if it becomes so small for so long that it becomes eligible to file its reports as a small business issuer. Accordingly, we are adopting the provisions to exit accelerated filer status as proposed.

Currently, companies are required to disclose on the cover page of their annual report on Form 10-K their public float as of a specified date within 60 days before filing. To assist investors and the Commission in evaluating whether a company is subject to accelerated deadlines, we are revising this requirement. We are requiring every company, regardless of whether it is an accelerated filer, to disclose its public float as computed on the last business day of the company's most recently completed second fiscal quarter. We recognize that this will reduce the currency of this disclosure, but we believe such a change will simplify the burdens companies face by requiring them to calculate only one public float amount. Also, to clarify further a company's filing status, we are requiring each company to check a box on the cover of its quarterly and annual reports to indicate whether it is an accelerated filer.

We are not adopting changes today to the deadline for annual reports by foreign private issuers on Form 20-F. As we mentioned in the Proposing Release, we are continuing to consider this issue and Exchange Act filing requirements generally for foreign issuers. We recognize that with the adoption of today's amendments, the discrepancy between the filing deadlines for larger seasoned U.S. issuers and those for foreign private issuers will increase. We will consider the comments received in our continuing review of the issue.

C. Conforming Amendments

In the Proposing Release, we requested comment on several possible conforming revisions to other Commission rules as a result of the proposals. Our decisions on these requests are discussed in this section.

1. Timeliness Requirements in Other Commission Filings

We mentioned in the Proposing Release that we were considering making conforming revisions to accelerate the timeliness requirements in Regulation S-X for the inclusion of financial statements by accelerated filers in other Commission filings, such as Securities Act and Exchange Act registration statements and proxy and information statements under Section 14 of the Exchange Act. We requested comment on whether these changes should be made. Most of the commenters that responded to this request suggested we should make conforming changes if we change the periodic report deadlines.[98] We agree.

When the Commission made extensive revisions to its rules, forms and regulations in 1980 to further the integrated disclosure system, it adopted amendments regarding the inclusion of financial information in registration statements and proxy statements that parallel the requirements for financial data in Exchange Act periodic reports.[99] Parallel requirements facilitate the in-

[96] See Item 10(a)(2) of Regulation S-B [17 CFR 228.10(a)(2)] for the conditions for entering and exiting the small business reporting system. A reporting company that is not a small business issuer must meet the definition of a small business issuer at the end of two consecutive fiscal years before it will be considered a small business issuer for purposes of Form 10-KSB and Form 10-QSB.

[97] See, for example, the Letters of the ABA and NAREIT.

[98] See, for example, the Letters of American Electric Power; Comcast Corporation; The Dow Chemical Company; Ernst & Young LLP; Eli Lilly and Company; and HealthSouth Corporation.

[99] See Release No. 33-6234 (Sept. 2, 1980) [45 FR 63682].

tegrated reporting system by simplifying existing rules. They also improve overall disclosure as investors are assured consistent requirements as to the timeliness of information regardless of the document received. If conforming amendments are not made to keep these requirements parallel, a filing could conceivably be filed under the Securities Act with financial information less current than that filed under the Exchange Act. Accordingly, to facilitate uniform requirements, we are adopting amendments to Regulation S-X to conform the timeliness requirements. Under the conforming amendments we are adopting today, financial statements included in a registration statement or proxy statement still will be required to be at least as current as any financial statements filed under the Exchange Act.

We recognize that in making these conforming changes, for some short period of time, accelerated filers may be prevented from going to market.[100] However, it is our view that, when a company is an accelerated filer and is attempting to raise capital in the marketplace after audited financial information would be required to be filed under the Exchange Act, it is reasonable to delay registration until such financial statements become available. We believe this change is in the best interest of the investing public and will not create any additional burden on the large majority of accelerated filers because the required financial information already will be required to have been filed. Also, as in the past, we will consider waivers to the rules where unusual circumstances dictate the need for them.[101]

a. Filings Within 90 Days of Year-End

Currently, a reporting issuer is not required to include audited financial statements for its most recent fiscal year until the 90th day after the end of the fiscal year if it satisfies three conditions:

The company has filed all required Exchange Act reports;

The company reasonably, and in good faith, expects income, after taxes but before extraordinary items and a cumulative effect of a change in accounting principle, for its most recent fiscal year; and

For at least one of the two immediately preceding fiscal years, the company has reported income, after taxes but before extraordinary items and cumulative effect of a change in accounting principle. Unless all three conditions are met, registration statements filed or declared effective or proxy statements mailed after the 45th day following the fiscal year end must include audited financial statements for the most recent fiscal year end.[102]

We are shortening the 90-day deadline to conform to the phase-in periods for accelerated filers to keep this requirement parallel to the requirement to file an annual report under the Exchange Act. In year one of the phase-in period, the deadline will remain at 90 days. In year two of the phase-in period, the deadline will be reduced to 75 days. For year three and subsequent years, the deadline will be reduced to 60 days.

One commenter suggested we eliminate the distinctions among registrants that meet the conditions in Rule 3-01(c) of Regulation S-X.[103] We are not changing the 45-day deadline for companies that do not meet the three required conditions. This deadline was not previously linked to an Exchange Act reporting requirement, and we continue to think that this shorter deadline is sufficient. This deadline will continue to require audited financial information more current than that required by the Exchange Act reporting requirements for companies that have not reported, and do not expect to report, income.

b. Filings After 134 Days of Year-End

The existing rules require interim financial information in registration statements filed by registrants after 134 days subsequent to the end of the registrant's fiscal year-the period after audited financial statements for the most recently completed fiscal year are already required to be filed by most registrants on Form 10-K or 10-KSB and on or after the date most registrants are required to have filed interim financial statements for the first quarter on Form 10-Q or 10-QSB. Under the conforming amendments, in year one of the phase-in period, the period will remain at 134 days for accelerated filers. In year two of the phase-in period, the period will be reduced from 134 to 129 days for accelerated filers. When a registration statement is filed or is to be declared effective during this period, updated financial statements will now be required as of an interim date within 130 days of the date of filing. For year three and subsequent years, the period will be reduced to 124 days for accelerated filers. Registration statements filed or to be declared effective during this period will be required to include updated financial statements as of an interim date within 125 days of the date of filing.

[100] For example, after the phase-in period is complete, an accelerated filer would need to include updated financial statements in its registration statements up to 30 days earlier than under the current rules.

[101] See, for example, Rule 3-13 of Regulation S-X [17 CFR 210.3-13].

[102] If the audited financial statements for the most recently completed fiscal year are available or become available before effectiveness or mailing, they must be included in the filing.

[103] See the Letter of Ernst & Young LLP.

Here again, the amended rules parallel the requirements for filing interim information under the Exchange Act.

c. Age at Effective Date of Filing

Under the existing rules, where financial statements in a filing are as of a date 135 days or more before the date the filing is expected to become effective, or proposed mailing date in the case of a proxy statement, the financial statements must be updated with a balance sheet as of an interim date within 135 days and with statements of income and cash flows on a comparative basis for the interim period between the end of the most recent fiscal year and the date of the interim balance sheet provided.[104] Two exceptions exist under the current rule. First, where the registrant meets the conditions in Rule 3-01 of Regulation S-X and the anticipated effective date or proposed mailing date in the case of a proxy statement falls after 45 days but within 90 days of the end of the fiscal year, the filing need not be updated with financial statements more current than as of the end of the third fiscal quarter of the most recently completed fiscal year provided audited financial statements for such fiscal year are not available. Second, where the registrant does not meet the prescribed conditions referred to above and the anticipated effective date or proposed mailing date falls after 45 days but within 90 day of the end of the fiscal year, the filing must include audited financial statements for the most recent fiscal year. Both exceptions are consistent with the rules governing financial statements as of the date of filing.

The conforming amendments revise the updating rule to parallel the requirements for filing financial information under the Exchange Act. In year one of the phase-in period, the general updating period will remain at 135 days for accelerated filers. In year two of the phase-in period, the general updating period will be reduced from 135 days to 130 days for accelerated filers. For year three and subsequent years, the period will be reduced to 125 days. For each of the exceptions, the 90 day period will remain at 90 days for year one and then be reduced to 75 days in year two and 60 days in year three and subsequent years for accelerated filers. We will maintain the two existing exceptions in the rule.[105]

d. Unconsolidated Subsidiaries and 50% or Less Owned Persons

Several commenters did not think that the due date in Rule 3-09 of Regulation S-X regarding the inclusion of financial statements of significant equity investees, joint ventures and subsidiaries not consolidated should be accelerated to conform to that of the investor registrant.[106] Accelerating the filing of these financial statements could require a company that does not meet the definition of an accelerated filer to file its financial statements before it would otherwise be required to do so solely because of a minority ownership stake by the investor registrant. In addition, the investor registrant may have difficulty in obtaining these financial statements from these non-wholly owned entities in the appropriate timeframe. This may lead a registrant to either sell its investment, not for business reasons, but in order to remain timely and current in its filing requirements, or cause the investor registrant to be not timely, which could have a number of adverse effects, including the loss of short-form registration.

As part of our conforming amendments, we are amending Rule 3-09 of Regulation S-X to address these concerns. Separate financial statements of subsidiaries not consolidated and 50% or less owned persons required by Rule 3-09 of Regulation S-X will not be accelerated for inclusion in a company's annual report on Form 10-K if the subsidiary or 50% or less owned person is not an accelerated filer. In that instance, the financial statements of the subsidiary or 50% or less owned person can be filed by amendment within the existing time periods. In addition, we are making conforming amendments to still provide companies with additional time to file the required financial statements if the fiscal years of the investor registrant and the subsidiary or 50% or less owned person differ.

2. Time Allowed to Incorporate Form 10-K Information From Definitive Proxy or Information Statements

In the Proposing Release, we did not propose to make a conforming change to the 120-day period companies have to file their definitive proxy or information statements involving the election of directors to allow the incorporation by reference of the information required by Part III of Form 10-K.[107] We requested comment on whether this period should be shortened. While two commenters supported accelerating the filing of definitive proxy or information statements to ensure

[104] See Rule 3-12 of Regulation S-X.

[105] As with the existing rules, the revised updating rule also includes a general provision that if a filing is made near the end of a fiscal year and the audited financial statements for that fiscal year are not included in the original filing, the filing must be updated with those audited financial statements if they become available before the anticipated effective date, or proposed mailing date in the case of a proxy statement.

[106] See, for example, the Letters of the AICPA; Corning Incorporated; Ernst & Young LLP; and KPMG LLP.

[107] See General Instruction I.G.(3) of Form 10-K.

that investors have timely information,[108] the majority of commenters that responded to our request objected to a conforming change.[109] The objecting commenters thought that a shortened deadline would be overly burdensome. We see no significant reason to shorten the deadline at this time.

Some commenters were concerned that a reduction of the filing deadline for Form 10-K without a corresponding change in the deadline for incorporating the Part III information by reference from the proxy statement would interfere with the ability of some companies to file new short-form registration statements for securities offerings during the period between the Form 10-K filing date and the filing of the proxy statement.[110] This is because these issuers would be required to include the Part III information in the registration statement, either directly or through incorporation by reference from another document, before the proxy statement is filed. As the ability to incorporate the Part III information from the proxy statement is voluntary and is designed for the benefit of registrants, we do not believe this concern warrants either a change to the deadline to incorporate Part III information from the proxy statement or the Form 10-K deadline. Companies will retain the flexibility to choose the alternative that best suits their individual circumstances.

3. Form 10-K Schedules Required by Article 12 of Regulation S-X

We did propose to make a conforming change to the date by which all schedules required by Article 12 of Regulation S-X may be filed as an amendment to the annual report. We proposed to change this date from 120 calendar days to 90 calendar days for accelerated filers to maintain a 30-day period after the due date of the report to file the amendment. We requested comment on this change.

The majority of commenters responding to this request supported this change.[111] Several commenters supported eliminating any delay and requiring these schedules to be filed with the Form 10-K.[112] However, we understand that in some instances additional time may be necessary to prepare these schedules. As a result, we are adopting conforming amendments to maintain a 30-day period after the due date of the report to file the schedules.

4. Financial Statement Filing Requirements in Rule 3-05 of Regulation S-X and Item 7 of Form 8-K

In the Proposing Release, we requested comment on whether we should make conforming revisions to the financial statement filing requirements in Item 7 of Form 8-K and Rule 3-05[113] of Regulation S-X for financial statements of businesses acquired. The commenters who responded to this request uniformly objected to such a change.[114] Many of these commenters believed that the ability to obtain audited financial statements of a significant acquired business generally is unrelated to any circumstances of the acquirer that cause it to be an accelerated filer for purposes of its own financial statements. We see no significant reason to shorten the deadline at this time, and therefore we are not adopting conforming amendments to these provisions.

D. Website Access to Information

*1. Proposed Rules*We proposed to require accelerated filers to provide additional disclosure in their annual reports of where investors can obtain access to company filings. This would have included disclosure regarding the availability of information from the Commission, the company's website address and whether the company makes available free of charge on its website, if it has one, its annual, quarterly and current reports, and all amendments to those reports, as soon as reasonably practicable after, and in any event on the same day as, such material is electronically filed with or furnished to the Commission. If a company chose not to make its filings available on its website in this manner, the proposals would have required it to disclose why it does not do so and where else the public can access these filings immediately upon filing and whether there is a fee for such access. Companies also would have to disclose whether they voluntarily will provide electronic or paper copies of its filings upon request.

---

[108] See the Letters of the AIMR and Maverick Capital Ltd.

[109] See, for example, the Letters of American Electric Power; AFLAC Incorporated; ASCS; The Coca-Cola Company; Comcast Corporation; The Dow Chemical Company; Ernst & Young LLP; Intel Corporation; LeBoeuf, Lamb, Green & MacRae; McGuireWoods LLP; NYSBA; PepsiCo, Inc.; PricewaterhouseCoopers LLP; The Southern Company; and Technitrol, Inc.

[110] See, for example, the Letters of J.P. Morgan Chase & Co. and NYCBA.

[111] See, for example, the Letters of American Electric Power; ASCS; The Dow Chemical Company; Ernst & Young LLP; and United States Steel Corporation. But see the Letter of Triarc Companies, Inc.

[112] See, for example, the Letters of the AIMR; Maverick Capital Ltd.; and PricewaterhouseCoopers LLP.

[113] 17 CFR 210.3-05.

[114] See, for example, the Letters of the AICPA; ASCS; Cleary, Gottlieb, Steen & Hamilton; Deloitte & Touche LLP; Ernst & Young LLP; KPMG LLP; NYCBA; and PricewaterhouseCoopers LLP.

Widespread access to timely corporate information promotes the efficient functioning of the secondary markets by enabling investors to make informed investment and voting decisions. Further, ready access to Exchange Act information is critical to short-form registration of securities offerings by seasoned issuers under the Securities Act.[115] This form of registration allows certain information about the company conducting the offering to be incorporated by reference from the company's Exchange Act reports without, in many instances, separate delivery of those reports. One rationale for this method of registration is that the information in the company's Exchange Act reports already has been adequately disseminated and evaluated by the marketplace.

The development of the Internet has revolutionized information production, availability, and dissemination.[116] The increased availability of information has helped to promote transparency, liquidity and efficiency in our capital markets. One of the key benefits of the Internet is that companies can make information available to many investors and the financial markets quickly and in a cost-effective manner. Online access to Internet information also helps to democratize the capital markets by enabling many small investors to access corporate information.[117]

We have taken a number of steps to encourage the dissemination of information electronically via the Internet. For 18 years, we have been continually improving and modernizing electronic access to companies' Exchange Act reports through our EDGAR system, including by providing Internet access to these reports.[118] We now provide electronic access to the public on a real-time basis through our Internet website.[119]

Without regard to EDGAR, an efficient and economical method for companies to make information available about themselves to many investors is through their Internet websites. In addition to other existing sources of company information, such as our website, a company's website is often an obvious place for investors to find information about a company. A company also may use different formats and other approaches to making information available in ways it believes are useful to investors. Most companies, realizing the benefits of this technology for information dissemination, already provide access to their Commission filings through their websites. A study by our Office of Economic Analysis revealed that approximately 83% of companies with a public float of at least $75 million provide some form of access to their Commission filings through their websites, either via a hyperlink with a third-party service providing real-time access to the filings (45%), by posting the filings directly on their websites (29%) or via a hyperlink to our EDGAR database (15%).

Modernizing the disclosure system under the federal securities laws involves recognizing the importance of the Internet in fostering prompt and more widespread dissemination of information.[120] We believe company disclosure should be more readily available to investors on a timely basis in a variety of locations to facilitate investor access to that information. We believe it is important for companies to make investors aware of the different sources that provide access to company information. We applaud those that already provide access to their Commission filings through their websites, and encourage every reporting company to do so.

2. Comments on the Proposal

We received responses from 141 commenters on the proposals for disclosure concerning access to company filings. The vast majority of commenters representing investors, investor groups, companies and professional associations were supportive of the proposals. Sixty commenters supported the requirement as proposed and concurred with our objective to provide investors with information on where they can access company reports.[121] These

---

[115] Short-form registration is available in varying degrees for domestic issuers on Forms S-2 [17 CFR 239.12], S-3, S-4 [17 CFR 239.25] and S-8.

[116] See, for example, Report to the Congress: The Impact of Recent Technological Advances on the Securities Markets, (Sept. 1997). That report, like all Commission reports issued after 1996, is available on our Internet website (http://www.sec.gov).

[117] See, for example, Ianthe Jeanne Dugan, "Small Investors United by Web Find New Power," The Washington Post, May 30, 1999, at A01.

[118] Numerous third-party vendors also make information filed with the Commission electronically available to investors, but many charge fees for this service.

[119] See note 32 above.

[120] Congress has already recognized the importance of utilizing the Internet to disseminate information. For example, Section 403(a) of the Sarbanes-Oxley Act of 2002 [Pub. L. No. 107-204, §403(a), 116 Stat. 745 (2002)] added Section 16(a)(4) of the Exchange Act [15 U.S.C. 78p(a)(4)] requiring companies to provide Section 16(a) filings on their corporate websites. Other countries also have begun to recognize the importance of the Internet to disseminate information. For example, the listing standards for the S.T.A.R. Market segment of the Italian Exchange (Borsa Italiana) require listed companies to post their periodic reports on their websites. See Article 2.2.3, paragraph 3.e) of Regolamento Dei Mercati Organizzati E Gestiti Da Borsa Italiana S.P.A. [Rules of the Markets Organized and Managed by the Italian Exchange] (July 15, 2002).

[121] See, for example, the Letters of the AFP; AIA; AIMR; The Allstate Corporation; AOL Time Warner Inc.; Armstrong World Industries, Inc.; BDO Seidman, LLP; the Business Roundtable; CCBN; CII; Jason Cook; Deloitte & Touche LLP; Delphi Corporation; Dollar Tree Stores, Inc.; The Dow Chemical Company; EDGAR On-

commenters believed the proposal would aid in encouraging companies to make information available in a variety of locations and hence make corporate information more widely accessible and disseminated. One professional association mentioned that almost 90% of companies in its survey expected to accomplish the objectives of the proposal with ease.[122] The commenter also referred to other studies demonstrating that corporate websites are a significant source of information to investors and the media.

Forty commenters concurred with our objective but offered modifications to the proposal, such as recommending that we allow additional time for companies to post the reports on their websites and suggesting that a permanent statement regarding availability of the company's filings on a web page referring to EDGAR or a standing hyperlink to EDGAR should suffice.[123] Twenty other commenters offered similar suggestions to modify the proposal.[124] Some of the commenters requested interpretive clarifications for complying with the proposals.[125]

Twenty-one commenters questioned the utility of the proposal, especially considering the existence of the Commission's EDGAR website and the Commission's recent announcement that its website now provides real-time access to filings.[126] Some of these commenters thought the proposal unnecessarily duplicated the Commission's EDGAR system.[127] One commenter did not agree that a variety of electronic sources provides any more widespread access to information than a single source.[128] Ten companies suggested that the desired improvement the Commission seeks in instant accessibility of information could be best accomplished by modernizing the EDGAR system, including by making filings immediately available to the public on its website, which we have now done.[129]

3. Final Rules

After evaluating the comments received, we are adopting the proposals with minor revisions. These amendments require accelerated filers to disclose in their annual reports on Form 10-K the following:[130]

The company's website address, if it has one;

Whether the company makes available free of charge on or through its website, if it has one, its annual report on Form 10-K, quarterly reports on Form 10-Q, current reports on Form 8-K, and all amendments to those reports as soon as reasonably practicable after such material is electronically filed with or furnished to the Commission;

If the company does not make its filings available in this manner, the reasons it does not do so (including, where applicable, that it does not have an Internet website);[131] and

If the company does not make its filings available in this manner, whether the company voluntarily will provide electronic or paper copies of its filings free of charge upon request.

Accelerated filers must begin complying with the new disclosure requirement starting with their annual reports on Form 10-K to be filed for fiscal years ending on or after December 15, 2002.

In response to comment, we have eliminated the proposed requirement that registrants disclose that filings are available on our website and in our public reference room as unnecessary. We have also eliminated the proposed disclosure relating to

---

(Footnote Continued)

line; Eli Lilly and Company; Grant Thornton LLP; Investment Company Institute; Jefferson-Pilot Corporation; NIRI; Pharmacia Corporation; Principal Financial Group, Inc.; SunTrust Banks, Inc.; TIAA-CREF; UnionBanCal Corporation; UnumProvident Corporation; and XTO Energy Inc.

122 See the Letter of the NIRI.

123 See, for example, the Letters of the ACCA; American Electric Power; AFLAC Incorporated; Amerada Hess Corporation; the American Bankers Association; Capital One Financial Corporation; The Chubb Corporation; CIGNA Corporation; Cleary, Gottlieb, Steen & Hamilton; Dell Computer Corporation; Ernst & Young LLP; FEI; Halliburton Company; Merrill Lynch & Co., Inc.; NAREC; PepsiCo, Inc.; PG&E Corporation; and UniSource Energy Corporation.

124 See, for example, the Letters of the ABA; J.P. Morgan Chase & Co.; McDonald's, Inc.; Mellon Financial Corporation; NAREIT; PricewaterhouseCoopers LLP; and Sullivan & Cromwell.

125 See, for example, the Letters of the ABA; Capital One Financial Corporation; and Reed Smith LLP.

126 See, for example, the Letters of American Financial Group, Inc.; Allegheny Energy, Inc.; Aztar Corporation; Caremark Rx, Inc.; Chevron Phillips Chemical Company LLP; Compass Bankshares, Inc.; Community Bankshares, Inc.; Edison Electric Institute; First Capital Bank Holding Corporation; GrandSouth Bancorporation; International Bancshares Corporation; J.C. Penney Company, Inc.; M&T Bank Corporation; Marathon Oil Corporation; MDU Resources, Inc.; Pinnacle West Capital Corporation; and Sinclair Broadcast Group, Inc.

127 See, for example, the Letters of Allegheny Energy, Inc.; Compass Bankshares, Inc.; Commercial Federal Corporation; Edison Electric Institute; and Pinnacle West Capital Corporation.

128 See the Letter of Compass Bankshares, Inc.

129 See, for example, the Letters of American Financial Group, Inc.; Caremark Rx, Inc.; Community Bankshares, Inc.; First Capital Bank Holding Corporation; GrandSouth Bancorporation; International Bancshares Corporation; J.C. Penney Company, Inc.; M&T Bank Corporation; Marathon Oil Corporation; and MDU Resources, Inc.

130 See revisions to Item 101(e) of Regulation S-K.

131 This requirement relates to the company's experience during the period covered by the report, or since the effective date of the amendments if a company has not completed a full fiscal year before its next annual report is due.

where else the public can access company filings immediately upon filing if the company does not provide real-time website access as real-time access to filings is now available through our website.

We understand that companies provide website access to their Exchange Act reports in a variety of ways, including by establishing a hyperlink to its Exchange Act reports via a third-party service in lieu of maintaining the reports themselves.[132] For purposes of the disclosure element for website access to reports, hyperlinking to a third-party service is acceptable so long as the reports are made available in the appropriate time frame and access to the reports is free of charge to the user. To clarify that hyperlinking to a third party website is acceptable, we have slightly modified the proposed language to specify that a company can provide access on or through its website. A company should hyperlink directly to its reports (or to a list of its reports) instead of just to the home page or general search page of the third-party service.[133] We note that many companies already provide this level of specificity in their hyperlinks as a matter of best practice.

As we now provide real-time access to Exchange Act reports through our website, hyperlinking directly to a company's reports (or to a list of its reports) on our EDGAR website will allow a company to state that it provides website access to its reports as soon as reasonably practicable after those reports are filed. This will help to decrease further any incremental burdens or costs caused by the new requirement. Despite the availability of these reports through our website, we concluded that disclosure regarding company website access is still desirable as one of our objectives is to encourage the availability of information in a variety of locations and foster best practices for making that information broadly accessible. Hyperlinking through EDGAR will now allow a company to state in all cases that it provides website access as soon as reasonably practicable.[134]

In reference to comments concerned about technical and other obstacles that might lead to violating the "same day" requirement, we have eliminated that requirement. However, we interpret the "as soon as reasonably practicable" standard to mean that the report would be available, barring unforeseen circumstances, on the same day as filing. We could revisit this requirement if posting on the same day does not generally occur.

Whether a company provides access to its Exchange Act reports either directly or through a third-party service, we recognize that some companies display the reports in electronic formats (for example, PDF) other than the official electronic format used to transmit the filing to our EDGAR system. In fact, we encourage companies to do so if alternative formats enhance readability and accessibility of the reports, so long as all of the information in the reports remains retrievable. However, the use of a particular medium to access the reports should not be so burdensome that the intended recipients cannot effectively access the information provided.[135]

The website access contemplated by the amendments includes access to all exhibits and supplemental schedules electronically filed with the reports or amendments. Information incorporated by reference is not required to be separately posted, although we encourage companies to do so if it will aid investor access to the information.

While the amendments do not cover how long a company's report must be made available on or through its website, we encourage companies to provide ongoing website access to their reports. At a minimum, we suggest companies provide website access to their previous reports for at least a 12 month period. It would be desirable for companies to provide access to their previous reports on an appropriately archived portion of their website over an even longer timeframe. Finally, we encourage companies to provide website access to all of their filings with the Commission, including their filings under the proxy rules and their Securities Act filings.

Regarding the requirement that a company disclose its website address in its annual report on Form 10-K, some commenters were concerned as to whether including the website address in the filing constitutes incorporation by reference of

---

[132] In Release No. 33-7856 (Apr. 28, 2000) [65 FR 25843] (the "2000 Release"), we provided interpretive guidance on the possible effects of hyperlinking to a third party website. See the 2000 Release, at n.48 and the accompanying text.

[133] Companies could present the viewer with an intermediate screen stating that the visitor is leaving the company's website. Also, a disclaimer of responsibility for the accuracy of the third party service will not make the website posting ineffective for purposes of the disclosure requirement.

[134] Several companies already hyperlink to our EDGAR website to provide website access to their reports. As a result of adding real-time EDGAR filing data to our website, new searches located on new webpages are now available on our website that provide access to this real-time data. For companies that currently hyperlink to our website, they will need to revise their hyperlink scripts if they have not already done so to refer to the new search pages providing real-time data. The older search pages will be eliminated in the near future.

[135] See, for example, Release No. 33-7233 (Oct. 6, 1995) [60 FR 53458], at n. 24 and the accompanying text.

any website information into the filing.[136] If a company is complying with this disclosure item in its annual report on Form 10-K, the inclusion of the company's website address will not, by itself, include or incorporate by reference the information on the site into the company's Commission filing, unless the company otherwise acts to incorporate the information by reference.[137]

We understand that a company may have multiple websites that it uses for various purposes, such as investor relations, product information and business-to-business activities. We interpret the requirement to disclose the company's website address to mean the website the company normally uses for its investor relations functions.

The revisions we adopt today create new disclosure obligations that are designed to create duties only under Sections 13(a) and 15(d) of the Exchange Act. The new disclosure is not an antifraud rule, and it is not designed to create new duties under the antifraud provisions of the federal securities laws or in private rights of action or to alter any existing liability provisions. The new disclosure also does not separately create or otherwise affect a company's duty to update its prior statements.

As proposed, we are initially limiting the amendments to accelerated filers. Commenters were nearly unanimous in thinking that we should extend the amendments to all filers, including smaller issuers and foreign issuers.[138] According to these commenters, the utility of information about report access is likely to be just as great or even greater for these issuers compared to the minimal incremental cost that may be associated with the proposals. We will continue to study this issue and consider extending the requirement to all reporting companies after evaluating our initial experience with the requirement by accelerated filers.

[¶ 2203]

III. Paperwork Reduction Act

The amendments contain "collection of information" requirements within the meaning of the Paperwork Reduction Act of 1995 ("PRA").[139] We published a notice requesting comment on the collection of information requirements in the Proposing Release, and we submitted these requirements to the Office of Management and Budget ("OMB") for review.[140] Subsequently, OMB approved the proposed information collection requirements.

The titles for the collection of information are "Form 10-K" and "Form 10-Q." An agency may not conduct or sponsor, and a person is not required to respond to, a collection of information unless it displays a currently valid OMB control number.

Form 10-K (OMB Control No. 3235-0063) prescribes information that a registrant must disclose annually to the market about its business. Preparing and filing an annual report on Form 10-K is a collection of information.

Form 10-Q (OMB Control No. 3235-0070) prescribes information that a registrant must disclose quarterly to the market about its business. Preparing and filing a quarterly report on Form 10-Q is a collection of information.

We currently estimate that Form 10-K results in a total annual compliance burden of 12,105,360 hours and an annual cost of $1,210,536,000. The burden was calculated by multiplying the estimated number of respondents filing Form 10-K annually (9,384) by the estimated average number of hours each entity spends completing the form (1,720 hours). We estimate that 75% of the burden is carried by the respondent internally (9,384 x 1,720 x 0.75 = 12,105,360), and we estimate that 25% of the burden is carried by outside advisors retained by the respondent at an average cost of $300 per hour (9,384 x 1,720 x 0.25 x $300 = $1,210,536,000).[141] The portion of the burden carried by outside advisors is reflected as a cost.

We currently estimate that Form 10-Q results in a total annual compliance burden of 2,728,092 hours and an annual cost of $272,809,200. The burden was calculated by multiplying the estimated number of reports on Form 10-Q filed annually (26,746) by the estimated average number of hours each entity spends completing the form

136 See, for example, the Letters of the ABA; ASCS; Caremark Rx, Inc.; NYCBA; NYSBA; PricewaterhouseCoopers LLP; and Sullivan & Cromwell.

137 In the 2000 Release, we provided interpretive guidance on the effect of including a website address in other situations. See the 2000 Release, note 132 above, at n.41 and the accompanying text. We are not changing that guidance for those other situations.

138 See, for example, the Letters of the ABA; ASCS; Comcast Corporation; Deloitte & Touche LLP; The Dow Chemical Company; Institute of Management Accountants; PricewaterhouseCoopers LLP; and TIAA-CREF.

139 44 U.S.C. 3501 et seq.

140 Publication and submission were in accordance with 44 U.S.C. 3507(d) and 5 CFR 1320.11.

141 Our allocation of the burden for Form 10-K and Form 10-Q is a departure from the Proposing Release and our past PRA submissions for Exchange Act periodic reports, for which we estimated that the company carried 25% of the burden internally and 75% of the burden was carried by outside professionals retained by the company. See also Release No. 33-3098 (May 10, 2002) [67 FR 35620]. We believe that this new allocation more accurately reflects current practice for annual and quarterly reports.

(136 hours). We estimate that 75% of the burden is prepared by the respondent (26,746 x 136 x 0.75 = 2,728,092). We estimate that 25% of the burden is prepared by outside advisors retained by the respondent at an average cost of $300 per hour (26,746 x 136 x 0.25 x $300 = $272,809,200). This portion of the burden is reflected as a cost.

A. Summary of Amendments

The amendments will accelerate the filing deadlines of quarterly reports on Form 10-Q and annual reports on Form 10-K by companies subject to specified public float and reporting history requirements. The amendments also require those companies to disclose in their annual reports on Form 10-K where investors can obtain access to company filings, including whether the company provides access to its Exchange Act reports free of charge on its Internet website as soon as reasonably practicable after those reports are electronically filed with or furnished to the Commission. If a company does not provide website access in this manner, it must also disclose the reasons it does not do so. We also require companies to disclose their website address if they have one. We believe that the revisions will promote direct, uniform and more widespread dissemination of timely information to investors and the markets and further the purposes of short-form registration under the Securities Act.

B. Summary of Comment Letters and Revisions to Proposals

We requested comment on the PRA analysis contained in the Proposing Release. We received responses from two companies addressing the Commission's overall estimates for preparing reports.[142] Both commenters questioned our original estimate of the allocation of the burden between the company (25% of the burden) and outside professionals retained by the company (75% of the burden). Both believed the estimate for the amount of work prepared in-house should be much higher.[143] Subsequent to the Proposing Release, we have changed our estimates of the allocation of the burden between the company and outside advisors to 75% for in-house work and 25% for outside advisors.[144] We recognize that not all companies may utilize in-house resources to the extent mentioned by the commenters, but we believe the new allocation more accurately reflects current practice for annual and quarterly reports.

One of the commenters believed the Commission's estimate of the average number of hours each entity spends completing Form 10-Q (136 hours) is too low.[145] The commenter also believed that the Commission's estimate of the average number of hours each entity spends completing the Form 10-K (1,720 hours) was more accurate. We have not concluded that our estimates should be changed as a result of this comment, although we will continue to monitor registrant response to our burden hour estimates.

In addition to the concerns raised by commenters, we have made several modifications to the proposals, although the modifications do not affect our estimate of the incremental burden of the amendments. The amendments will change the calculation date for determining the disclosure of a company's common equity public float that appears on the cover page of its Form 10-K. In addition, companies will be required to check a box on their Form 10-K and 10-Q indicating whether they are an accelerated filer. We believe these changes are minimal and do not affect the total amount of burden hours for preparing the forms.

In addition, we have made several changes to the proposal for disclosure concerning access to company reports in response to comments on the substance of the proposal and to avoid unnecessarily lengthening reports. These changes include revising or eliminating some of the proposed disclosure elements. We do not believe these changes will significantly change our previous estimates of the burden on registrants from this new disclosure item.

C. Revisions to Reporting and Cost Burden Estimates

We estimate that approximately 59% of Form 10-K and Form 10-Q respondents, or 5,494 respondents, will satisfy our proposed definition of accelerated filer, and thus will be subject to accelerated deadlines and the requirement to make the enhanced disclosure in their Form 10-K regarding website access to their Exchange Act reports.[146]

---

[142] See the Letters of PPL Corporation and Southern Union Company.

[143] One commenter believed the estimate should be 90% for in-house work and 10% for outside professionals. See the Letter of PPL Corporation. The other commenter mentioned it prepares over 95% of its reports by in-house personnel. See the Letter of Southern Union Company.

[144] See note 141 above.

[145] The commenter provided an estimate of 400 hours. See the Letter of PPL Corporation.

[146] We arrived at this estimate by multiplying the approximate number of respondents that file on Form 10-K that do not only have a class of securities registered under Section 15(d) of the Exchange Act (and hence are less likely to have listed equity and therefore a public float) (7,384) by 74.4%, which represents the percentage of companies in Standard & Poors Research Insight Compustat Database with a market capitalization above $75 million out of the total number of companies in the Compustat Database with a market capitalization above $25 million (the upper limit for small business filers on Form 10-KSB). It is our understanding that the data in the Compustat Database is derived principally from larger companies, so our estimate may overstate the

For our amendments regarding filing deadlines, the amount of information required to be included in Exchange Act reports will remain the same. Accordingly, solely for purposes of the Paperwork Reduction Act, our estimate is that the amount of time necessary to prepare the reports, and hence, the total amount of burden hours, will not change.

As proposed, we estimate that the preparation of the required disclosure regarding information access in a respondent's Form 10-K will add 0.50 burden hours to each annual report on Form 10-K. Thus, we estimate this aspect of the amendments will add an additional 2,747 burden hours to the current Form 10-K (0.50 hours x 5,494 respondents). We estimate that 75% of the burden is carried by the respondent (0.50 x 5,494 x 0.75 = 2,060).[147] We estimate that 25% of the burden is prepared by outside advisors retained by the respondent at an average cost of $300 per hour (0.50 x 5,494 x 0.25 x $300 = $206,025). This portion of the burden is reflected as a cost.

As a result, we estimate the total annual compliance burden for Form 10-K after our revisions to be 12,107,420 hours and an annual cost of $1,210,742,025, an increase of 2,060 hours and $206,025 in cost. Compliance with the disclosure requirement will be mandatory. There will be no mandatory retention period for the information disclosed, and responses to the disclosure requirements will not be kept confidential. We do not believe that the imposition of this disclosure requirement will alter significantly the number of respondents that file on Form 10-K.

[¶ 2204]

IV. Cost-Benefit Analysis

The amendments are part of our initiative to modernize and improve the regulatory system for periodic disclosure under the Exchange Act. We are sensitive to the costs and benefits that result from our rules. In this section, we examine the benefits and costs of our amendments.

The rule and form changes will enhance the timeliness and availability of disclosure to investors in two ways:

Shorten the due dates of quarterly and annual reports (and transition reports) for domestic reporting companies that meet certain public float and reporting history requirements;[148] and

Require companies to disclose in their annual reports on Form 10-K where investors can obtain access to company filings, including whether companies provide access to their Exchange Act reports on their Internet websites.

A. Acceleration of Quarterly and Annual Report Due Dates

1. Benefits

The due dates for quarterly and annual reports by domestic issuers have not changed in over 30 years, despite enormous advances in information technology and productivity. We believe that periodic reports contain valuable information for investors. Shortening the due dates for quarterly, annual and transition reports will provide many benefits. Most importantly, it will accelerate the delivery of information to investors and the capital markets, enabling them to make more informed investment and valuation decisions more quickly.[149] This helps the capital markets function more efficiently, which implies more efficient valuation and pricing. While quarterly and annual reports at present generally reflect historical information, a lengthy delay before that information becomes available makes the information less valuable to investors.

The more extensive information in periodic reports is evaluated by investors and particularly analysts and institutional investors as a baseline for the incremental disclosures made by a company. These reports also contain more detailed information that is essential to conduct comparative analyses, as this information is often not contained in earnings releases or other incremental disclosures. Moreover, the information in Exchange Act reports, due to its required nature and the liability to which it is subject, provides a verification function against other statements made by the company in press releases and other public announcements. Investors and other users of the reports can judge previous informal statements by the company against the more extensive

(Footnote Continued)

actual percentage of companies that would be affected by the proposals.

147 As discussed in note 141 above, this allocation of the burden is a departure from the Proposing Release, for which we estimated that the respondent carried 25% of the burden internally and 75% of the burden was carried by outside advisors retained by the respondent. We believe that this new allocation more accurately reflects current practice for annual and quarterly reports.

148 We also are making conforming amendments to the timeliness requirements for the inclusion of financial information in proxy statements, information statements and Securities Act and Exchange Act registration statements.

149 Some academic evidence shows that annual reports on Form 10-K filed through the EDGAR system provide incremental information to the market even after the firm has made an earnings announcement. See, for example, Daqing Qi, Woody Wu, and In-Mu Haw, 2000, "The Incremental Information Content of SEC 10-K Reports Filed Under the EDGAR System," *Journal of Accounting, Auditing, and Finance* 15 (Winter): 25-45. See also the Letter of Paul A. Griffin.

and mandated disclosure provided in the reports that have been reviewed by independent public accountants and other advisors. Accelerating the availability of this information will enable this verification to occur at an earlier point in time. Accelerating the availability of these reports also may increase the relevance of these reports, as the timeliness of information has considerable value to investors and the markets. Moreover, seasoned issuers incorporate information from their Exchange Act reports in their Securities Act registration statements. Hence, investors buying in these public offerings, particularly in on-going shelf offerings, also may benefit from more timely disclosure.

Many companies now routinely release quarterly and annual results well before they file their formal reports with us. These earnings announcements reflect the importance of financial information and investors' demand for it at the earliest possible time. Assuming that companies are collecting and evaluating information before they issue these announcements, the availability of this information also suggests that much of the process involved in preparing the financial information contained in periodic reports is substantially complete. However, these earnings announcements are generally less complete in their disclosure than quarterly or annual reports, and they can emphasize information that is less prominent in quarterly or annual reports. Investors often must wait for the periodic reports to receive financial statements and the accompanying notes prepared in accordance with generally accepted accounting principles, MD&A and other vitally important financial disclosures. These additional disclosures increase transparency for investors.

We also are making conforming amendments to accelerate the timeliness requirements in Regulation S-X for the inclusion of financial statements by accelerated filers in other Commission filings, such as Securities Act and Exchange Act registration statements and proxy and information statements under Section 14 of the Exchange Act. When the Commission made extensive revisions to its rules, forms and regulations in 1980 to further the integrated disclosure system, it adopted amendments regarding the inclusion of financial information in registration statements and proxy statements that parallel the requirements for financial data in Exchange Act periodic reports. Parallel requirements facilitate the integrated reporting system by simplifying existing rules. They also improve overall disclosure as investors are assured consistent requirements as to the timeliness of information regardless of the document received. If conforming amendments are not made to keep these requirements parallel, a filing could conceivably be made under the Securities Act with financial information less current than that filed under the Exchange Act. Accordingly, to facilitate uniform requirements, we are adopting amendments to Regulation S-X to conform the timeliness requirements. Under the conforming amendments we are adopting today, financial statements included in a registration statement or proxy statement still will be required to be at least as current as any financial statements filed under the Exchange Act.

Many commenters representing investors, users of financial information and several companies concurred with our assessment of the benefits of the proposals. These commenters believed that shortening deadlines will improve the delivery and flow of reliable information to investors and capital markets and assist in the efficient operation of the markets. These commenters emphasized the importance of the extensive information in periodic reports and investors' demand for it at the earliest possible time. Several other companies, accounting firms and professional associations agreed in concept that shortening due dates would improve the flow of information, but believed the due dates should reflect concerns about the quality of information to be filed.

A small minority of companies, law firms and business organizations, however, believed that existing deadlines and market practices are sufficient to satisfy investors' needs and believed we over-emphasized the importance of periodic reports. These commenters did not think a significant benefit would result from shortening deadlines, but also generally did not attempt to address the question of possible benefits from the perspective of users of the reports. While we recognize that investors and the markets rely on information from a variety of sources in formulating their investment decisions, we agree with the near unanimous view of commenters representing the users of reports that the financial and other information in periodic reports is important to them, and that accelerating the delivery of the reports will provide benefits to investors and the markets.

2. Costs

The amendments will increase costs to some affected reporting companies, although companies may, and some already do, report within the new deadlines voluntarily. Specifically, the amendments may increase the costs of preparing reports because although companies already must prepare the reports, some may have to delay other projects or use additional resources, including in-house personnel, outside legal counsel and outside auditors to prepare the information in a shorter timeframe. Some companies may need to make additional capital investments, such as in additional information systems, to prepare their reports in a shorter timeframe.

While a few commenters believed that the original proposals would not have a significant adverse effect on the cost of preparing reports, most who addressed the subject mentioned that the original proposals would result in some increased costs. Many outlined their process of preparing reports to demonstrate the difficulties of accelerating the process. The particular steps and timing varied depending on the individual company, and not all companies appear to be at the same level of technological sophistication and staffing for preparing reports. Two professional associations noted that there are no current best practices for preparing reports.[150] As a result, the few cost estimates received varied widely, and many commenters were unable to provide estimates. One company believed it was not possible to put a dollar value on such costs, as it depends on the quality and flexibility of each registrant's present systems, processes and staff.[151] According to one professional association that surveyed its members, 52% of its survey respondents reported that they expected costs to increase in order to comply with the original proposals.[152] Forty-five percent of respondents indicated they would have to hire additional staff, and 27% of respondents indicated they would have to buy or develop additional systems. Other commenters were concerned that accelerating deadlines would result in increased audit fees, particularly for companies with a calendar fiscal year-end, given a compression in the amount of time available for auditors to complete their work for these companies.

The amendments may have indirect effects as well. While some companies commented that they could or already comply with the proposal without undue burden, the group that objected to the proposal raised several common concerns over the extent of acceleration and transition period proposed. The most common concern was that the proposed deadlines would negatively affect the quality and accuracy of reports. According to one professional association, two-thirds of its survey respondents expected a reduction in the precision of reported information under the original proposals.[153] We are not changing the liability standards for reports, nor are we decreasing the amount of information required. Investors and the capital markets may suffer if quality or accuracy diminished, causing the markets to function less efficiently and investment decisions to be impaired.

Another common concern was that the proposed deadlines would impair the ability of management, external auditors, boards of directors and especially audit committees to scrutinize and review filings properly and give appropriate consideration to the form, substance and priority of disclosures, especially MD&A disclosures and financial statement footnotes. These commenters feared that disclosures could be reduced or become more boilerplate if companies have less time to prepare and review them. The commenters believed that accelerating deadlines in the manner proposed would also undermine the governance and review mechanisms that have been put in place to ensure quality. Several other commenters mentioned additional concerns over the proposals, such as an increased need to use estimates or an increased risk of amendments or restatements because of rushed preparation. Several commenters were especially concerned about accelerating deadlines now given recent events with Arthur Andersen LLP.

We have limited direct data on which to base cost estimates of the amendments. However, we reviewed cost estimates provided by respondents to a survey conducted by the American Society of Corporate Secretaries. These estimates were based on the original proposal. We attempted to determine if the survey results were related to issuer characteristics. The cost estimates did not appear to be related to market capitalization, revenues, industry or number of reporting segments of the underlying company. Based on 46 companies with over $75 million in public float that provided estimates, 17% reported that they did not expect any additional costs from the proposals. 43.4% expected initial costs to prepare for the proposals. These estimates ranged from $12,500 to $5,000,000, with a median value of $125,000. 50% expected on-going annual costs to comply with the proposals. These estimates ranged from $27,500 to $250,000, with a median value of $90,000. 11% of respondents expected both initial and on-going costs to comply with the proposals. Assuming these estimates are representative of all affected companies, we estimate that initial costs of the original proposal for all affected companies would range from $29,862,500 to $11,945,000,000, with a median value of $298,625,000.[154] Aggregate on-going, annual costs of the original proposal for all affected companies would range from $75,524,500 to $686,750,000, with a median value of $247,230,000.

---

[150] See the Letters of the ASCS and the Business Roundtable.

[151] See the Letter of American Electric Power.

[152] See the Letter of the ASCS.

[153] Id.

[154] This estimate is based on our estimate of the probable number of affected reporting companies determined for purposes of the Paperwork Reduction Act (5,494).

These estimates may overstate the actual costs from the amendments we are adopting today, however, as we are making several accommodations to address commenters' concerns and to ease compliance, including:

A gradual phase-in of the new deadlines over three years, with no change in deadlines for the first year;

A less extensive ultimate acceleration of quarterly reports than proposed;

Revisions to the definition of accelerated filer to give companies more advance notice and time to prepare for accelerated deadlines; and

Conforming amendments that allow certain financial statements of subsidiaries to be filed by later amendment if the subsidiary is not an accelerated filer.

A phased-in approach helps to alleviate the immediate impact of any costs and burdens that may be imposed on certain registrants. While several commenters indicated that they could report on an accelerated timeframe today, several major business associations that surveyed their members reported that adjustment to accelerated deadlines would be easier with a phase-in period.[155] A longer transition may even help reduce costs as companies will have additional time to develop best practices, long-term processes and efficiencies to prepare reports, as opposed to having to take rushed and possibly inefficient measures to meet a more sudden acceleration. Also, a longer transition period helps to smooth out any possible impact on the availability of third party advisors used by companies to prepare their reports.

A less extensive acceleration of the quarterly report deadline also will alleviate some of the burdens mentioned by commenters. There will be more time than proposed to gather the necessary data and complete the necessary reviews by company officials, the board of directors and outside advisors. One professional association commented that 80% of its survey respondents reported they could more easily meet a 35-day deadline than a 30-day deadline.[156] Further, we believe that by imposing a 40-day deadline before finally reducing it to 35 days, we are striking an adequate compromise between the benefits of reducing deadlines with the potential inconvenience, difficulty and cost that may be incurred by some companies.

Regarding our conforming changes to the timeliness requirements in other Commission filings, we recognize that for some short period of time, accelerated filers may be prevented from going to market. However, it is our view that, when a company is an accelerated filer and is attempting to raise capital in the marketplace after audited financial information would be required to be filed under the Exchange Act, it is reasonable to delay registration until such financial statements become available. We believe this change is in the best interest of the investing public and will not create any additional burden on the large majority of accelerated filers because the required financial information already will be required to have been filed. Also, as in the past, we will consider waivers to the rules where unusual circumstances dictate the need for them.

We considered several regulatory alternatives in formulating the final amendments. We considered, but rejected, the alternative of tying the due date of reports to a company's announcement of earnings. Not all companies issue earnings releases or issue them on an accelerated basis. As a result, linking deadlines to earnings releases may not result in more accelerated reporting of information. We also were concerned that linking report deadlines to earnings announcements could delay earnings announcements, as companies would know that the announcement would trigger the deadline to file reports. While market demand for earnings information could negate this risk, an approach linking deadlines to earnings announcements could have the effect of penalizing companies for early releases of information while rewarding companies that delay their earnings with extended time to file their reports.

Even with a phase-in period, accelerating filing deadlines may create the risk that more companies will file their reports late or need a filing extension. Moreover, if a company is late filing its reports, it will lose availability for short-form registration for at least one year from the date of the late filing. Being late also could render Securities Act Rule 144 temporarily unavailable for security holders' resales of restricted and control securities, and make new filings on Form S-8 temporarily unavailable for resales of employee benefit plan securities. We considered the suggestions of some commenters to extend the filing extension periods in Exchange Act Rule 12b-25 as an additional method to alleviate any transition difficulties to shortened deadlines. However, we think a lengthy phase-in period adequately addresses these concerns. A less dramatic acceleration of deadlines over a set schedule each year will provide companies with advance notice of the changes they will be expected to make and will smooth out some of the possible difficulties raised by commenters. Rule 12b-25 in its existing form

155 See, for example, the Letters of the ASCS; the Business Roundtable; and FEI.

156 See the Letter of the ASCS. See also Letter of the Business Roundtable.

still will provide companies that face extenuating circumstances the ability to gain a filing extension.

While our proposals did not directly address the contents of earnings releases, many commenters supported additional efforts by the Commission in this area. Several recommended that earnings or other standardized earnings information be filed with the Commission, such as on Form 8-K. Others thought the Commission should consider issuing or promoting minimum requirements or guidelines for the contents of earnings releases, such as a GAAP reconciliation. While we will continue to explore ways to improve earnings releases, and the Sarbanes-Oxley Act of 2002 requires us to take steps in this area, we believe these are separate initiatives from the need to accelerate periodic report deadlines. As mentioned above, we believe periodic reports contain valuable information for investors, and comments received from the users of this information uniformly indicated their desire to receive the reports at the earliest time that is consistent with receiving quality information.

We also considered shorter and longer phase-in periods and deadlines. While several commenters indicated they could report on an accelerated timeframe today, several major business associations that surveyed their members reported that adjustment to accelerated deadlines would be easier with a phase-in period. Also, while comments were mixed, the majority of commenters addressing the issue believed it would be more difficult to accelerate the quarterly report than the annual report. Accordingly, the quarterly deadline will only be reduced to a 35-day deadline at the end of the phase-in period, which is five days longer than originally proposed. We think any concerns over possible confusion over changing deadlines during the phase-in period will be temporary and justified by the benefits of giving companies additional time to adjust their reporting schedules.

We considered shortening filing deadlines for all companies. Comments were mixed over excluding smaller issuers. Although we believe investors in less large or unseasoned companies may want and benefit from more timely disclosures just as much as investors in larger, listed companies, we are concerned that this may impose undue burden and expense on these companies. Smaller companies are likely to be more sensitive to any increased costs in preparing their reports. These entities may not have the infrastructure and resources available or necessary to prepare their reports on a shorter timeframe. Accordingly, we are only shortening the filing deadlines for companies with a minimum public float or reporting history as proposed. Of course, smaller companies may file their reports earlier voluntarily.

Comments also were mixed on the proposed $75 million public float threshold. We considered several different thresholds for shortening deadlines, including thresholds based on revenue, measures of trading volume and listing status. However, based on our past experience, we believe the public float test currently used in Form S-3 is consistent with our purposes. We believe that a public float test serves as a reasonable measure of company size and market interest. While several commenters urged raising the threshold, we believe a longer phase-in period and a less extensive acceleration of the quarterly report deadline militates against the need to raise the threshold. The definition of accelerated filer we are adopting today excludes nearly half of all publicly traded companies, as well as all companies eligible for our small business issuer reporting system, all foreign private issuers that file on Form 20-F and all companies that do not have a common equity public float. Selecting a $75 million public float threshold also is consistent with our conforming amendments to the timeliness requirements for other Commission filings. By using the same threshold as in Form S-3, investors are assured of receiving the most up-to-date information regardless of the particular registration form a company chooses.

B. Website Access to Information

1. Benefits

Widespread access to timely company information promotes the efficient functioning of the capital markets. Also, ready access to Exchange Act information is critical to short-form registration of securities offerings. Many aspects of our disclosure system were adopted well before the revolutions in information technology brought about by the Internet. In modernizing and improving our disclosure system, we recognize the benefits of the Internet in promoting more widespread dissemination of information. An efficient and cost effective method for companies to make information available about themselves is through their Internet website. In addition to other existing sources of company information, such as our website, a company's website is one obvious place for many investors to find information about a company. A company also may use different formats and other approaches to making information available in ways it believes are useful to investors. We believe company disclosure should be more readily available to investors on a timely basis in a variety of locations to facilitate investor access to that information. We believe it is important for investors to know of additional sources where they can access company information.

Providing this disclosure and encouraging companies to post their Exchange Act reports on their websites will provide many benefits, and the vast majority of commenters concurred and were supportive of the proposals. The amendments protect investors by alerting them to sources where they can obtain direct and easy access to the information they should have to make informed investment and valuation decisions. The amendments will help promote consistent, direct, timely and more widespread access of information to investors and the markets, and further the proper functioning of the integrated disclosure and short-form registration system. An efficiently functioning registration system facilitates capital formation. Not all reporting companies now make their Exchange Act filings available through their websites, and not all the ones that do make information available provide access in real-time. The amendments encourage uniform best practices to aid in an investor's search for timely information, thereby potentially reducing the costs to gather such information.

2. Costs

The amendments may increase the costs to some affected companies, although we seek to minimize those costs. Companies will be required to include minimal additional disclosure in their annual report on Form 10-K. We estimate this will result in a total cost of $463,525 for all affected companies.[157] The disclosure requirement only will apply to companies that meet specified public float and reporting history requirements, which will help to minimize the impact on companies potentially less able to bear additional costs. The amendments also will not require a company to provide website access, although we encourage all companies to do so. Commenters were nearly unanimous in their belief that the proposal would result in no or minimal additional costs and would not be unduly burdensome to implement, particularly since it is limited only to accelerated filers.[158] One professional association mentioned that the majority of its survey respondents expected that the proposal would incur no additional costs.[159] Another professional association mentioned that almost 90% of companies in its survey expected to accomplish the objectives of the proposal with ease.[160]

Also, as we now provide real-time access to Exchange Act reports through our website, hyperlinking directly to our EDGAR website will allow a company to state that it provides website access in the required timeframe. This will help to decrease further any incremental burdens or costs caused by the amendments. Some commenters thought the proposal was duplicative of EDGAR, particularly considering that we now provide real-time Internet access to reports. Despite the availability of reports through our website, we concluded that disclosure regarding company website access is still desirable as one of our objectives is to encourage the availability of information in a variety of locations and foster best practices for making that information broadly accessible. In response to comments concerned about the technical and other obstacles that might lead to violating the proposed "same day" requirement, we have eliminated that requirement.

We considered several additional regulatory alternatives. Many companies already voluntarily provide at least some access to their filings on their websites, but not all provide access to all of their filings or in real-time. We considered requiring website access to company reports as an additional eligibility requirement for short-form registration. However, we were concerned that the potential loss of form eligibility from non-compliance with the requirement would be overly burdensome on companies. We are considering the suggestions by many commenters to extend the disclosure requirement to non-accelerated filers.

[¶ 2205]

V. Consideration of Burden on Competition, and Promotion of Efficiency, Competition and Capital Formation

Section 23(a)(2) of the Exchange Act[161] requires us, when adopting rules under the Exchange Act, to consider the impact that any new rule would have on competition. In addition, Section 23(a)(2) prohibits us from adopting any rule that would impose a burden on competition not necessary or appropriate in furtherance of the purposes of the Exchange Act. We have considered the amendments in light of the standards in Section 23(a)(2).

The amendments are intended to improve the timeliness and accessibility of Exchange Act reports to investors and the financial markets. We anticipate these amendments will enhance the proper functioning of the capital markets. This increases the competitiveness of companies par-

[157] The estimate is based on the burden hour estimates calculated under the Paperwork Reduction Act. For purposes of the Paperwork Reduction Act, we estimate that the additional disclosure will result in 2,060 internal burden hours and $206,025 in external costs. Assuming a cost of $125/hour for in-house professional staff, the total cost for the internal burden hours would be $257,500. Hence the aggregate cost estimate is $463,525 ($257,500 § $206,025).

[158] See, for example, the Letters of the ASCS; Dow Chemical Company; Hibernia Corporation; PricewaterhouseCoopers LLP; and TIAA-CREF.

[159] See the Letter of the ASCS.

[160] See the Letter of the NIRI.

[161] 15 U.S.C. 78w(a)(2).

ticipating in the U.S. capital markets. The amendments will affect certain companies and not others, so the impacts of the proposal may not be equally distributed. Also, if not all competitors in a given industry are subject to accelerated deadlines, information about some competitors may be disclosed ahead of other competitors (for example, the filing of material contracts).[162] This could potentially give some competitors an informational advantage. If the amendments to shorten filing deadlines increased the number of companies who filed their reports late, this could reduce the number of companies eligible for short-form and delayed shelf registration. For our amendments relating to website access, companies that will be subject to accelerated deadlines may incur increased costs from providing additional disclosure that will not be incurred by companies not subject to these deadlines. However, we believe these costs are not significant.

We requested comment on any anti-competitive effects of the proposals. A few commenters suggested that the proposals to accelerate filing deadlines might have some effects on competition. For example, one law firm thought that differing reporting deadlines for accelerated and non-accelerated filers could adversely affect competition.[163] Non-accelerated filers would enjoy a competitive advantage against accelerated filers who are forced to incur the incremental costs imposed by accelerated deadlines. While we recognize that the impacts of the amendments will not be equally distributed, we also must balance the market's need for information with the ability of companies to report on an accelerated timeframe without undue burden. Not all companies, particularly small and unseasoned companies, may have the resources and infrastructure in place to prepare their reports on a shorter timeframe without undue burden or expense. While any dividing line we ultimately choose could have a possible disproportionate affect at the margin, we believe separating small and large companies balances the needs of investors against the constraints facing smaller issuers. In doing so, the amendments could actually encourage competition because they are designed to avoid imposing onerous burdens and expenses on those companies that are least able to bear them. We will continue to study whether acceleration of deadlines for a broader class of issuers is appropriate.

Several other commenters believed we should not exclude foreign private issuers from our definition of accelerated filer.[164] These commenters believe foreign filers should be subject to the same rules to create a level playing field for all companies that access the U.S. capital markets. Other commenters thought that the issues involving foreign issuers are sufficiently different as to warrant separate study and rule proposals.[165] We agree with the latter group. We do recognize that with the amendments we adopt today, the discrepancy between the filing deadlines for larger seasoned U.S. issuers and those for foreign private issuers will increase. Foreign issuers are subject to similar obligations as to the information to be reported. There are some categories of information, for example executive compensation, where requirements for foreign issuers are less onerous. Foreign issuers that do not prepare their financial statements in accordance with U.S. GAAP, however, must go through the additional step of preparing a reconciliation of their financial statements to U.S. GAAP. These companies also may have additional home country reporting requirements. We are continuing to consider this issue and Exchange Act filing requirements generally for foreign issuers. However, given that a current filing lag already exists, we do not believe the relative increase in the lag created by the amendments is significant enough to warrant a delay in their adoption. To the extent any anti-competitive effect may arise from the increase in this lag, we believe any such burden would be necessary and appropriate for the protection of investors.

Section 2(b) of the Securities Act[166] and Section 3(f) of the Exchange Act[167] requires us, when engaging in rulemaking where we are required to consider or determine whether an action is necessary or appropriate in the public interest, to consider, in addition to the protection of investors, whether the action will promote efficiency, competition, and capital formation. We have considered the amendments in light of the standards in these provisions.

The amendments will enhance our reporting requirements in light of technological advances. The purpose of the amendments is to promote

---

[162] The Commission does have rules in place that allow for the non-disclosure of certain limited information filed with the Commission. See, for example, Exchange Act Rule 24b-2 [17 CFR 240.24b-2].

[163] See, for example, the Letter of Troutman Sanders LLP.

[164] See, for example, the Letters of Chevron Phillips Chemical Company LLP; Eastman Kodak Company; and Maverick Capital Ltd.

[165] See, for example, the Letters of the AICPA; Ernst & Young LLP; Institute of Management Accountants; KPMG LLP; and PricewaterhouseCoopers LLP.

[166] 17 U.S.C. 77b(b).

[167] 15 U.S.C. 78c(f).

greater timeliness and accessibility of this information so that investors can more easily make informed investment and voting decisions. Informed investor decisions generally promote market efficiency and capital formation. As noted above, however, the proposals could have certain indirect negative effects, such as discouraging or precluding some companies near the threshold from using short-form registration, which could adversely impact their ability to raise capital.

We also are adopting conforming amendments to the timeliness requirements for the inclusion of financial statements in proxy statements, information statements and Securities Act and Exchange Act registration statements. We recognize that in making these conforming changes, for some short period of time, accelerated filers may be prevented from going to market. However, it is our view that, when a company is an accelerated filer and is attempting to raise capital in the marketplace after audited financial information would be required to be filed under the Exchange Act, it is reasonable to delay registration until such financial statements become available. We believe this change is in the best interest of the investing public and will not create any additional burden on the large majority of accelerated filers because the required financial information already will be required to have been filed. Also, as in the past, we will consider waivers to the rules where unusual circumstances dictate the need for them.

We requested comment on how the proposals would affect efficiency, competition and capital formation. Many commenters representing investors, investor organizations as well as some companies believed that shortening deadlines will improve the delivery and flow of reliable information to investors and capital markets and assist in the efficient operation of the markets. A larger group of commenters representing primarily companies, business associations, law firms and accounting firms objected to the extent of acceleration and transition period proposed because, in their view, preparing reports in the proposed time frame could result in less accurate filings, which could stifle efficiency. Some commenters also were concerned that the proposed deadlines may increase the number of late filings. In addition to adverse market reaction, filing late could cause companies to lose eligibility to use short-form registration statements for at least one year, which could raise the cost of capital.

In response to these concerns, we are phasing-in deadlines over a three-year period and adopting a less extensive acceleration of the quarterly report deadline. A phased-in approach of accelerated deadlines allows a greater transition period for companies to adjust their procedures and develop efficiencies to ensure that the quality and accuracy of reported information will not be sacrificed. With a less extensive acceleration of the quarterly report deadline, there will be more time than proposed to gather the necessary data and complete the necessary reviews by company officials, the board of directors and outside advisors. Also, Exchange Rule 12b-25 in its existing form still will provide companies that face extenuating circumstances the ability to gain a filing extension.

[¶ 2206]

VI. Final Regulatory Flexibility Analysis

This Final Regulatory Flexibility Analysis, or FRFA, has been prepared in accordance with the Regulatory Flexibility Act.[168] This FRFA relates to amendments to the rules and forms under the Securities Act and the Exchange Act to:

Shorten the due dates of quarterly and annual reports (and transition reports) for domestic reporting companies that meet certain public float and reporting history requirements;[169] and

Require companies to disclose in their annual reports on Form 10-K where investors can obtain access to company filings, including whether companies provide access to their Exchange Act reports on their Internet websites.

A. Need for the Amendments

The amendments have two primary objectives. First, we are accelerating the disclosure of information to investors and the capital markets by shortening the due dates of quarterly and annual periodic reports and transition reports for domestic reporting companies that meet certain minimum public float and reporting history requirements. These due dates have not changed in over 30 years, despite advances in information technology and productivity and increases in the pace of and need for communications in the capital markets. Accelerating the delivery of information to the capital markets will help enhance the efficient functioning of those markets. The more extensive information in periodic reports is evaluated by investors and particularly analysts and institutional investors as a baseline for the incremental disclosures made by a company, and these reports also contain more detailed information that is essential to conduct comparative financial analyses. Many companies routinely release quarterly and annual financial results before they file

---

[168] 5 U.S.C. 603.

[169] We also are making conforming amendments to the timeliness requirements for the inclusion of financial information in proxy statements, information statements and Securities Act and Exchange Act registration statements.

their formal reports with us. However, these earnings announcements are generally less complete in their disclosure than periodic reports, and they can emphasize information that is less prominent than in the reports. Shortening the deadlines will shorten this information gap, thereby increasing the relevance of those reports. Investors buying in public offerings of issuers that incorporate their Exchange Act reports in their Securities Act registration statements also will benefit from more timely disclosure.

Second, we wish to encourage more direct and widespread accessibility and dissemination of timely information to investors and the capital markets in a variety of locations. Accordingly, we are requiring companies subject to the accelerated filing deadlines to disclose in their annual reports on Form 10-K where investors can obtain access to company filings, including whether the company provides access to its Exchange Act reports free of charge on its Internet website as soon as reasonably practicable after those reports are electronically filed with or furnished to the Commission. These amendments will help promote consistent, direct, timely and more widespread access of information to investors and the markets and further the proper functioning of the integrated disclosure and short-form registration system. Not all public companies currently make their filings available on their websites, and not all provide access to all of their reports or in real-time. The amendments will thus promote greater access for investors.

B. Significant Issues Raised by Public Comment

The Initial Regulatory Flexibility Analysis, or IRFA, appeared in the Proposing Release.[170] We requested comment on any aspect of the IRFA, including the number of small entities that would be affected by the proposals, the nature of the impact, how to quantify the number of small entities that would be affected and how to quantify the impact of the proposals. We received no comment letters responding to that request.

C. Small Entities Subject to the Amendments

The amendments will affect certain small entities that are required to file quarterly and annual periodic reports and transition reports under the Exchange Act, but only if those small entities meet the definition of an "accelerated filer" that we are adopting today. For purposes of the Regulatory Flexibility Act, Exchange Act Rule 0-10(a)[171] defines the term "small business" to be an issuer, other than an investment company, that, on the last day of its most recent fiscal year, has total assets of $5 million or less. The Securities Act defines a "small business" issuer, other than investment companies, to be an issuer that, on the last day of its most recent fiscal year, has total assets of $5 million or less and is engaged in or proposes to engage in an offering of securities of $5 million or less.[172]

We estimate that there are approximately 2,500 companies, other than investment companies, subject to the reporting requirements of Sections 13 or 15(d) of the Exchange Act that have assets of $5 million or less. The amendments to shorten the deadlines for annual and quarterly periodic and transition reports and the amendments regarding access to Exchange Act reports will apply to these small entities if they have a public float of $75 million or more, have been subject to the Exchange Act's reporting requirements for at least one year, have filed at least one annual report and are not eligible for our small business issuer reporting system. We have no way to determine exactly how many small entities meet these requirements, although it is likely that only a very small number of these entities will meet the public float requirement. In addition, small entities are not affected if they are eligible to use our small business issuer reporting system.

According to the Standard & Poors Research Insight Compustat Database, of the 711 reporting companies listed with assets of $5 million or less, 10, or 1.4%, had a market capitalization greater than $75 million.[173] Assuming that this sample is representative of all small entities, the public float requirement will have the effect of almost completely excluding all small entities.

D. Projected Reporting, Recordkeeping, and Other Compliance Requirements

For reporting companies that meet the public float and reporting history requirements, we are phasing-in shortened due dates for annual reports on Form 10-K and quarterly reports on Form 10-Q over three years. The Form 10-K deadline will be reduced over three years from the current deadline of 90 days after the end of the company's fiscal year to 60 days after the end of the company's fiscal year. The Form 10-Q deadline will be reduced over three years from the current deadline of 45 days after the end of the company's first three fiscal quarters to 35 days after the end of the first three fiscal quarters. We are making

[170] See the Proposing Release at Section VI

[171] 17 CFR 240.0-10(a).

[172] 17 CFR 230.157.

[173] It is our understanding that the data in the Compustat Database is derived principally from larger companies, so our estimate could understate the actual percentage of companies that would be affected by the proposals.

similar changes to transition reports these companies must file when they change their fiscal year and the timeliness requirements for financial information that must be included in other Commission filings such as proxy statements, information statements and Securities Act and Exchange Act registration statements. We are not changing the filing deadlines for other companies, including small business issuers eligible to rely on our small business reporting system, at this time.

While the amount of information required to be included in Exchange Act reports, and hence the amount of time necessary to prepare them, will remain the same, affected companies may be required to use additional resources, including in-house personnel, in preparing their reports on a shorter timeframe. Small entities that meet the public float and reporting history requirements may incur additional costs in seeking the help of outside experts, particularly outside legal counsel and auditors, or in making any necessary technological investments to speed their reporting process.

Companies that are late in filing their reports will lose eligibility for short-form registration for at least one year, and Securities Act Rule 144 and new filings on Form S-8 will be temporarily unavailable during the period of noncompliance.[174] On the margin, affected small entities that are unable, or cannot afford, to prepare their reports on a shorter timeframe may be discouraged from remaining public companies or accessing the public markets. This may adversely affect their ability to raise capital.

We also are requiring accelerated filers to disclose in their annual reports on Form 10-K where investors can obtain access to company filings, including whether the company provides access to its Exchange Act reports free of charge on its Internet website as soon as reasonably practicable after those reports are electronically filed with or furnished to the Commission. If a company does not provide such access, it must also disclose why it does not do so. In formulating these amendments, we have sought to minimize its costs, particularly on small entities. The requirement will apply only to companies that met the public float and reporting history requirements. Companies will not be required to establish an Internet website for purposes of this requirement if they did not otherwise have one. Also, a company can elect not to provide website access to their reports as long as it disclosed that it has elected not to do so and the reasons it has elected not to do so. Accordingly, these elements of the amendments, coupled with the fact that almost all small entities will be effectively excluded from the proposal, lead us to believe that the requirement will not have a disproportionate effect on small entities.

E. Agency Action to Minimize Effect on Small Entities

As required by the Regulatory Flexibility Act, we have considered alternatives that would accomplish our stated objectives, while minimizing any significant adverse impact on small entities. In connection with the amendments, we considered several alternatives, including:

Establishing different compliance or reporting requirements or timetables that take into account the resources available to small entities;

Clarifying, consolidating or simplifying compliance and reporting requirements under the rules for small entities;

Using performance rather than design standards; and

Exempting small entities from all or part of the requirements. Our amendments to shorten the filing deadlines will apply only to entities that meet minimum public float and reporting history requirements, which should serve to exclude almost all small entities. As a result, different timetables will apply for almost all small entities. We strive to strike a balance between timely delivery of information to investors and giving companies enough time to prepare their reports. We considered the alternative of only shortening the filing deadlines for companies whose securities are listed on the NYSE or AMEX or quoted on Nasdaq National Market System or Small Cap Market. However, we believe investors in companies that are not as large or listed but nevertheless meet the public float or reporting history requirements may want and benefit from more timely disclosures just as much as investors in larger, listed companies. Accordingly, we rejected exempting small entities in their entirety from the coverage of the amendments.

In addition, we are not aware of how to further clarify, consolidate or simply these proposals for small entities. In this regard, we already are limiting the shortened deadlines to entities that meet minimum public float and reporting history requirements. We do not consider using performance rather than design standards to be consistent with our statutory mandate of investor protection in the present context. Because specified information in Exchange Act reports must be reported in a timely manner to be useful, design standards are necessary to achieve the objectives of the

[174] One-time extensions of due dates are available under certain circumstances under Exchange Act Rule 12b-25. Also, companies that are not timely will not meet the timeliness requirements for their proxy statements, information statements and Securities Act and Exchange Act registration statements.

amendments. Accelerating the delivery of mandated information is one of the goals of the amendments.

Our amendments regarding disclosure of website access to company reports are designed to enhance the accessibility and dissemination of information to investors. These amendments also will apply only to entities that meet minimum public float and reporting history requirements, which should serve to exclude almost all small entities. We believe our amendments strike a balance between providing investor access to information and giving companies alternatives in providing this access. Different compliance or reporting requirements for affected small entities or exemptions for all affected small entities are not considered warranted at this time because it is just as important that information be adequately disseminated and easily available for affected small entities as it is for large entities, if not more so. We have made a number of changes to the proposal that we believe decrease further the impact on all issuers, including small entities. First, we have narrowed the scope of disclosure required. Second, we now provide real-time access to EDGAR filings through our website for free, which allows companies an easy and low cost method to provide real-time access if they choose to do so. The expected low costs of complying with the proposal, as well as the effect of the public float requirement in lessening the impact on small entities, also contributed to our decision not to exclude small entities in their entirety.

Companies can choose whether to provide website access and therefore the disclosure that will be necessary in their annual report on Form 10-K. This allows companies, including small entities, the flexibility to choose the alternative that best suits their individual circumstances. We believe this freedom should apply to all entities, large and small. We are not aware of ways to further clarify, consolidate or simply these proposals for small entities.

[¶ 2207]

VII. Update to Codification of Financial Reporting Policies

The Commission amends the "Codification of Financial Reporting Policies" announced in Financial Reporting Release No. 1 (April 15, 1982) as follows:

1. By amending Section 102.05.(2) to read as follows:

(2) Conforming the Filing Requirements of Transition Reports to the Current Requirements for Forms 10-Q and 10-K

To conform to the current filing periods for reports on Forms 10-K and 10-Q, the filing period for transition reports on Form 10-K is 90, 75 or 60 days for accelerated filers, as applicable depending on the issuer's fiscal year specified in Rules 13a-10 and 15d-10, and 90 days for other issuers after the close of the transition period or the date of the determination to change the fiscal year, whichever is later, and for transition reports on Form 10-Q, the filing period is 45, 40 or 35 days for accelerated filers, as applicable depending on the issuer's fiscal year specified in Rules 13a-10 and 15d-10, or 45 days for other issuers after the later of these two events.

2. By amending Section 102.05. to add the following preliminary note to the "Appendix" to Section 102.05.:

Preliminary Note: The following examples are applicable if the issuer is not an accelerated filer. If the issuer is an accelerated filer, substitute 75 or 60 days, as applicable depending on the issuer's fiscal year specified in Rules 13a-10 and 15d-10, for 90 days in the examples for transition reports on Form 10-K, and substitute 40 or 35 days, as applicable depending on the issuer's fiscal year specified in Rules 13a-10 and 15d-10, for 45 days in the examples for transition reports on Form 10-Q.

3. By amending Section 302.01.a. to:

a. Replace the phrase "after 45 days but within 90 days of the end of the registrant's fiscal year" with the phrase "after 45 days but within 90, 75 or 60 days of the end of the registrant's fiscal year for accelerated filers, as applicable depending on the registrant's fiscal year (or after 45 days but within 90 days of the end of the registrant's fiscal year for other registrants)" in the second paragraph of Section 302.01.a.; and

b. Replace the phrase "after 45 days but within 90 days of the end of its fiscal year (i.e., February 16 to March 31 for calendar year companies)" with the phrase "after 45 days but within 90, 75 or 60 days of the end of its fiscal year if the registrant is an accelerated filer, as applicable depending on the company's fiscal year (i.e., February 16 to March 31, 15 or 1 for calendar year companies) (or after 45 days but within 90 days of the end of its fiscal year for other registrants (i.e., February 16 to March 31 for calendar year companies))" in the first sentence of the fourth paragraph of Section 302.01.a.

4. By amending Section 302.01.b. to:

a. Replace the phrase "134 days subsequent to the end of a registrant's fiscal year" with the phrase "134, 129 or 124 days subsequent to the end of a registrant's fiscal year if the registrant is an accelerated filer, as applicable depending on the registrant's fiscal year (or 134 days subsequent to the end of a registrant's fiscal year for other registrants)" in the first sentence of Section 302.01.b.;

b. Replace the phrase "135 days of the date of the filing" with the phrase "135, 130 or 125 days of the date of the filing if the registrant is an accelerated filer, as applicable depending on the registrant's fiscal year (or 135 days of the date of the filing for other registrants)" in the second sentence of Section 302.01.b.; and

c. Removing the words "135 day" in the footnote to the fourth sentence of Section 302.01.b.

5. By amending Section 302.01.c. to:

a. Replace the phrase "135 days or more" with the phrase "135, 130 or 125 days or more, if the registrant is an accelerated filer, as applicable depending on the registrant's fiscal year (or 135 days or more for other registrants)" in the first paragraph of Section 302.01.c.;

b. Replace the phrase "as of an interim date within 135 days" with the phrase "as of an interim date within 135, 130 or 125 days, if the registrant is an accelerated filer, as applicable depending on the registrant's fiscal year (or 135 days for other registrants)" in the first paragraph of Section 302.01.c.; and

c. Replace the phrase "after 45 days but within 90 days of the end of the fiscal year" with the phrase "after 45 days but within 90, 75 or 60 days of the end of the fiscal year if the registrant is an accelerated filer, as applicable depending on the registrant's fiscal year (or after 45 days but within 90 days of the end of the fiscal year for other registrants)" in the second and third sentences of the second paragraph of Section 302.01.c.

The Codification is a separate publication of the Commission. It will not be published in the Federal Register or Code of Federal Regulations.

[¶ 2208]

VIII. Statutory Authority and Text of Rule Amendments

The amendments contained in this document are being adopted under the authority set forth in Sections 3(b) and 19(a) of the Securities Act and Sections 12, 13, 15(d) and 23(a) of the Exchange Act.

TEXT OF RULE AMENDMENTS

List of Subjects in 17 CFR Parts 210, 229, 240 and 249

Reporting and recordkeeping requirements, Securities.

In accordance with the foregoing, Title 17, Chapter II of the Code of Federal Regulations is amended as follows.

PART 210—FORM AND CONTENT OF AND REQUIREMENTS FOR FINANCIAL STATEMENTS, SECURITIES ACT OF 1933, SECURITIES EXCHANGE ACT OF 1934, PUBLIC UTILITY HOLDING COMPANY ACT OF 1935, INVESTMENT COMPANY ACT OF 1940, INVESTMENT ADVISERS ACT OF 1940, AND ENERGY POLICY AND CONSERVATION ACT OF 1975

1. The authority citation for Part 210 continues to read as follows:

Authority: 15 U.S.C. 77f, 77g, 77h, 77j, 77s, 77z-2, 77z-3, 77aa(25), 77aa(26), 78c, 78j-1, 78l, 78m, 78n, 78o(d), 78q, 78u-5, 78w(a), 78ll, 78mm, 79e(b), 79j(a), 79n, 79t(a), 80a-8, 80a-20, 80a-29, 80a-30, 80a-37(a), 80b-3, 80b-11 unless otherwise noted.

2. Section 210.3-01 is amended by:

a. Removing the phrase "90 days of the end of the registrant's fiscal year" and adding, in its place, the phrase "the number of days of the end of the registrant's fiscal year specified in paragraph (i) of this section" in the introductory text of paragraph (c) and paragraph (d); and

b. Revising paragraph (e) and adding paragraph (i) to read as follows:

§ 210.3-01 Consolidated balance sheets.

* * * * *

(e) For filings made after the number of days specified in paragraph (i) of this section, the filing shall also include a balance sheet as of an interim date within the following number of days of the date of filing:

(1) For accelerated filers (as defined in § 240.12b-2 of this chapter):

(i) 135 days for fiscal years ending on or after December 15, 2002 and before December 15, 2004;

(ii) 130 days for fiscal years ending on or after December 15, 2004 and before December 15, 2005; and

(iii) 125 days for fiscal years ending on or after December 15, 2005; and

(2) 135 days for all other registrants.

* * * * *

(i)(1) For purposes of paragraph (c) and (d) of this section, the number of days shall be:

(i) For accelerated filers (as defined in § 240.12b-2 of this chapter):

(A) 90 days for fiscal years ending on or after December 15, 2002 and before December 15, 2003;

(B) 75 days for fiscal years ending on or after December 15, 2003 and before December 15, 2004; and

(C) 60 days for fiscal years ending on or after December 15, 2004; and

(ii) 90 days for all other registrants.

(2) For purposes of paragraph (e) of this section, the number of days shall be:

(i) For accelerated filers (as defined in § 240.12b-2 of this chapter):

(A) 134 days subsequent to the end of the registrant's most recent fiscal year for fiscal years ending on or after December 15, 2002 and before December 15, 2004;

(B) 129 days subsequent to the end of the registrant's most recent fiscal year for fiscal years ending on or after December 15, 2004 and before December 15, 2005; and

(C) 124 days subsequent to the end of the registrant's most recent fiscal year for fiscal years ending on or after December 15, 2005; and

(ii) 134 days subsequent to the end of the registrant's most recent fiscal year for all other registrants.

3. Section 210.3-09 is amended by:

a. Removing the authority citation following § 210.3-09;

b. Removing the phrase "§ 210.1-02(v)" and adding, in its place, the phrase "§ 210.1-02(w)" in the first sentence of paragraph (a); and

c. Revising the last sentence of paragraph (b) and adding paragraphs (b)(1), (b)(2), (b)(3) and (b)(4) to read as follows:

§ 210.3-09 Separate financial statements of subsidiaries not consolidated and 50 percent or less owned persons.

* * * * *

(b) * * * For purposes of a filing on Form 10-K (§ 249.310 of this chapter):

(1) If the registrant is an accelerated filer (as defined in § 240.12b-2 of this chapter) but the 50 percent or less owned person is not an accelerated filer, the required financial statements may be filed as an amendment to the report within 90 days, or within six months if the 50 percent or less owned person is a foreign business, after the end of the registrant's fiscal year.

(2) If the fiscal year of any 50 percent or less owned person ends within the registrant's number of filing days before the date of the filing, or if the fiscal year ends after the date of the filing, the required financial statements may be filed as an amendment to the report within the subsidiary's number of filing days, or within six months if the 50 percent or less owned person is a foreign business, after the end of such subsidiary's or person's fiscal year.

(3) The term registrant's number of filing days means:

(i) If the registrant is an accelerated filer:

(A) 90 days for fiscal years ending on or after December 15, 2002 and before December 15, 2003;

(B) 75 days for fiscal years ending on or after December 15, 2003 and before December 15, 2004; and

(C) 60 days for fiscal years ending on or after December 15, 2004; and

(ii) If the registrant is not an accelerated filer, 90 days.

(4) The term subsidiary's number of filing days means:

(i) If the 50 percent or less owned person is an accelerated filer:

(A) 90 days for fiscal years ending on or after December 15, 2002 and before December 15, 2003;

(B) 75 days for fiscal years ending on or after December 15, 2003 and before December 15, 2004; and

(C) 60 days for fiscal years ending on or after December 15, 2004; and

(ii) If the 50 percent or less owned person is not an accelerated filer, 90 days.

* * * *

4. Section 210.3-12 is amended by:

a. Removing the phrase "135 days" and adding, in its place, the phrase "the number of days specified in paragraph (g) of this section" in both instances where it appears in the first sentence of paragraph (a);

b. Removing the phrase "90 days subsequent to the end of the fiscal year" and adding, in its place, the phrase "the number of days subsequent to the end of the fiscal year specified in paragraph (g) of this section" in the first sentence of paragraph (b); and

c. Adding paragraph (g) to read as follows:

§ 210.3-12 Age of financial statements at effective date of registration statement or at mailing date of proxy statement.

* * * * *

(g)(1) For purposes of paragraph (a) of this section, the number of days shall be:

(i) For accelerated filers (as defined in § 240.12b-2 of this chapter):

(A) 135 days for fiscal years ending on or after December 15, 2002 and before December 15, 2004;

(B) 130 days for fiscal years ending on or after December 15, 2004 and before December 15, 2005; and

(C) 125 days for fiscal years ending on or after December 15, 2005; and

(ii) 135 days for all other registrants.

(2) For purposes of paragraph (b) of this section, the number of days shall be:

(i) For accelerated filers (as defined in § 240.12b-2 of this chapter):

(A) 90 days for fiscal years ending on or after December 15, 2002 and before December 15, 2003;

(B) 75 days for fiscal years ending on or after December 15, 2003 and before December 15, 2004; and

(C) 60 days for fiscal years ending on or after December 15, 2004; and

(ii) 90 days for all other registrants.

PART 229—STANDARD INSTRUCTIONS FOR FILING FORMS UNDER SECURITIES ACT OF 1933, SECURITIES EXCHANGE ACT OF 1934 AND ENERGY POLICY AND CONSERVATION ACT OF 1975-REGULATION S-K

5. The authority citation for Part 229 continues to read, in part, as follows:

Authority: 15 U.S.C. 77e, 77f, 77g, 77h, 77j, 77k, 77s, 77z-2, 77z-3, 77aa(25), 77aa(26), 77ddd, 77eee, 77ggg, 77hhh, 77iii, 77jjj, 77nnn, 77sss, 78c, 78i, 78j, 78l, 78m, 78n, 78o, 78u-5, 78w, 78ll(d), 78mm, 79e, 79n, 79t, 80a-8, 80a-29, 80a-30, 80a-31(c), 80a-37, 80a-38(a) and 80b-11, unless otherwise noted.

* * * * *

6. Section 229.101 is amended by revising paragraph (e) to read as follows:

§ 229.101 (Item 101) Description of business.

* * * * *

(e) Available information. Disclose the information in paragraphs (e)(1), (e)(2) and (e)(3) of this section in any registration statement you file under the Securities Act (15 U.S.C. 77a et seq.), and disclose the information in paragraphs (e)(3) and (e)(4) of this section if you are an accelerated filer (as defined in § 240.12b-2 of this chapter) filing an annual report on Form 10-K (§ 249.310 of this chapter):

(1) Whether you file reports with the Securities and Exchange Commission. If you are a reporting company, identify the reports and other information you file with the SEC.

(2) That the public may read and copy any materials you file with the SEC at the SEC's Public Reference Room at 450 Fifth Street, NW, Washington, DC 20549. State that the public may obtain information on the operation of the Public Reference Room by calling the SEC at 1-800-SEC-0330. If you are an electronic filer, state that the SEC maintains an Internet site that contains reports, proxy and information statements, and other information regarding issuers that file electronically with the SEC and state the address of that site (http://www.sec.gov).

(3) You are encouraged to give your Internet address, if available, except that if you are an accelerated filer filing your annual report on Form 10-K, you must disclose your Internet address, if you have one.

(4)(i) Whether you make available free of charge on or through your Internet website, if you have one, your annual report on Form 10-K, quarterly reports on Form 10-Q (§ 249.308a of this chapter), current reports on Form 8-K (§ 249.308 of this chapter), and amendments to those reports filed or furnished pursuant to Section 13(a) or 15(d) of the Exchange Act (15 U.S.C. 78m(a) or 78o(d)) as soon as reasonably practicable after you electronically file such material with, or furnish it to, the SEC;

(ii) If you do not make your filings available in this manner, the reasons you do not do so (including, where applicable, that you do not have an Internet website); and

(iii) If you do not make your filings available in this manner, whether you voluntarily will provide electronic or paper copies of your filings free of charge upon request.

* * * * *

PART 240—GENERAL RULES AND REGULATIONS, SECURITIES EXCHANGE ACT OF 1934

7. The authority citation for Part 240 continues to read, in part, as follows:

Authority: 15 U.S.C. 77c, 77d, 77g, 77j, 77s, 77z-2, 77z-3, 77eee, 77ggg, 77nnn, 77sss, 77ttt, 78c, 78d, 78e, 78f, 78g, 78i, 78j, 78j-1, 78k, 78k-1, 78l, 78m, 78n, 78o, 78p, 78q, 78s, 78u-5, 78w, 78x, 78ll, 78mm, 79q, 79t, 80a-20, 80a-23, 80a-29, 80a-37, 80b-3, 80b-4 and 80b-11, unless otherwise noted.

* * * * *

8. Section 240.12b-2 is amended by adding the definition of "Accelerated filer" before the definition of "Affiliate" to read as follows:

§ 240.12b-2 Definitions.

* * * * *

Accelerated filer. (1) The term "accelerated filer" means an issuer after it first meets the following conditions as of the end of its fiscal year:

(i) The aggregate market value of the voting and non-voting common equity held by non-affiliates of the issuer is $75 million or more;

(ii) The issuer has been subject to the requirements of Section 13(a) or 15(d) of the Act (15 U.S.C. 78m or 78o(d)) for a period of at least twelve calendar months;

(iii) The issuer has filed at least one annual report pursuant to Section 13(a) or 15(d) of the Act; and

(iv) The issuer is not eligible to use Forms 10-KSB and 10-QSB (§ 249.310b and § 249.308b) for its annual and quarterly reports.

NOTE to paragraph (1): The aggregate market value of the issuer's outstanding voting and non-voting common equity shall be computed by use of the price at which the common equity was last sold, or the average of the bid and asked prices of such common equity, in the principal market for such common equity, as of the last business day of the issuer's most recently completed second fiscal quarter.

(2) Entering and Exiting Accelerated Filer Status. (i) The determination for whether a non-accelerated filer becomes an accelerated filer as of the end of the issuer's fiscal year governs the annual report to be filed for that fiscal year, the quarterly and annual reports to be filed for the subsequent fiscal year and all annual and quarterly reports to be filed thereafter while the issuer remains an accelerated filer.

(ii) Once an issuer becomes an accelerated filer, it will remain an accelerated filer unless the issuer becomes eligible to use Forms 10-KSB and 10-QSB for its annual and quarterly reports. In that case, the issuer will not become an accelerated filer again unless it subsequently meets the conditions in paragraph (1) of this definition.

* * * *

Section 240.13a-10 is amended by:

a. Removing the phrase "90 days" and adding, in its place, the phrase "the number of days specified in paragraph (j) of this section" in the first sentence of paragraph (b) and the second sentence of paragraph (f);

b. Removing the phrase "45 days" and adding, in its place, the phrase "the number of days specified in paragraph (j) of this section" in the first sentence of paragraph (c), the second sentence of paragraph (e)(2), and the third sentence of paragraph (f); and

c. Adding paragraph (j) before the Note to read as follows:

§ 240.13a-10 Transition reports.

* * * * *

(j)(1) For transition reports to be filed on the form appropriate for annual reports of the issuer, the number of days shall be:

(i) For accelerated filers (as defined in § 240.12b-2):

(A) 90 days for fiscal years ending on or after December 15, 2002 and before December 15, 2003;

(B) 75 days for fiscal years ending on or after December 15, 2003 and before December 15, 2004; and

(C) 60 days for fiscal years ending on or after December 15, 2004; and

(ii) 90 days for all other issuers; and

(2) For transition reports to be filed on Form 10-Q or Form 10-QSB (§ 249.308a or § 249.308b of this chapter), the number of days shall be:

(i) For accelerated filers (as defined in § 240.12b-2):

(A) 45 days for fiscal years ending on or after December 15, 2002 and before December 15, 2004;

(B) 40 days for fiscal years ending on or after December 15, 2004 and before December 15, 2005; and

(C) 35 days for fiscal years ending on or after December 15, 2005; and

(ii) 45 days for all other issuers.

* * * * *

10. Section 240.15d-10 is amended by:

a. Removing the phrase "90 days" and adding, in its place, the phrase "the number of days specified in paragraph (j) of this section" in the first sentence of paragraph (b) and the second sentence of paragraph (f);

b. Removing the phrase "45 days" and adding, in its place, the phrase "the number of days specified in paragraph (j) of this section" in the first sentence of paragraph (c), the second sentence of paragraph (e)(2), and the third sentence of paragraph (f); and

c. Adding paragraph (j) before the Note to read as follows:

§ 240.15d-10 Transition reports.

* * * * *

(j)(1) For transition reports to be filed on the form appropriate for annual reports of the issuer, the number of days shall be:

(i) For accelerated filers (as defined in § 240.12b-2):

(A) 90 days for fiscal years ending on or after December 15, 2002 and before December 15, 2003;

(B) 75 days for fiscal years ending on or after December 15, 2003 and before December 15, 2004; and

(C) 60 days for fiscal years ending on or after December 15, 2004; and

(ii) 90 days for all other issuers; and

(2) For transition reports to be filed on Form 10-Q or Form 10-QSB (§ 249.308a or § 249.308b of this chapter), the number of days shall be:

(i) For accelerated filers (as defined in § 240.12b-2):

(A) 45 days for fiscal years ending on or after December 15, 2002 and before December 15, 2004;

(B) 40 days for fiscal years ending on or after December 15, 2004 and before December 15, 2005; and

(C) 35 days for fiscal years ending on or after December 15, 2005; and

(ii) 45 days for all other issuers.

* * * * *

PART 249—FORMS, SECURITIES EXCHANGE ACT OF 1934

11. The authority citation for Part 249 continues to read, in part, as follows:

Authority: 15 U.S.C. 78a, et seq., unless otherwise noted.

* * * * *

12. Section 249.308a is revised to read as follows:

§ 249.308a Form 10-Q, for quarterly and transition reports under sections 13 or 15(d) of the Securities Exchange Act of 1934.

(a) Form 10-Q shall be used for quarterly reports under Section 13 or 15(d) of the Securities Exchange Act of 1934 (15 U.S.C. 78m or 78o(d)), required to be filed pursuant to § 240.13a-13 or § 240.15d-13 of this chapter. A quarterly report on this form pursuant to § 240.13a-13 or § 240.15d-13 of this chapter shall be filed within the following period after the end of the first three fiscal quarters of each fiscal year, but no quarterly report need be filed for the fourth quarter of any fiscal year:

(1) For accelerated filers (as defined in § 240.12b-2 of this chapter):

(i) 45 days after the end of the fiscal quarter for fiscal years ending on or after December 15, 2002 and before December 15, 2004;

(ii) 40 days after the end of the fiscal quarter for fiscal years ending on or after December 15, 2004 and before December 15, 2005; and

(iii) 35 days after the end of the fiscal quarter for fiscal years ending on or after December 15, 2005; and

(2) 45 days after the end of the fiscal quarter for all other registrants.

(b) Form 10-Q also shall be used for transition and quarterly reports filed pursuant to § 240.13a-10 or § 240.15d-10 of this chapter. Such transition or quarterly reports shall be filed in accordance with the requirements set forth in § 240.13a-10 or § 240.15d-10 of this chapter applicable when the registrant changes its fiscal year end.

13. Form 10-Q (referenced in § 249.308a) is amended by revising General Instruction A.1. and by adding a paragraph before the title "Applicable Only to Issuers Involved in Bankruptcy Proceedings During the Preceding Five Years:" on the cover page to read as follows:

Note: The text of Form 10-Q does not, and this amendment will not, appear in the Code of Federal Regulations.

UNITED STATES SECURITIES AND EXCHANGE COMMISSION

Washington, D.C. 20549

FORM 10-Q

GENERAL INSTRUCTIONS

A. Rule as to Use of Form 10-Q.

1. Form 10-Q shall be used for quarterly reports under Section 13 or 15(d) of the Securities Exchange Act of 1934 (15 U.S.C. 78m or 78o(d)), filed pursuant to Rule 13a-13 (17 CFR 240.13a-13) or Rule 15d-13 (17 CFR 240.15d-13). A quarterly report on this form pursuant to Rule 13a-13 or Rule 15d-13 shall be filed within the following period after the end of each of the first three fiscal quarters of each fiscal year, but no report need be filed for the fourth quarter of any fiscal year:

a. For accelerated filers (as defined in 17 CFR 240.12b-2):

(i) 45 days after the end of the fiscal quarter for fiscal years ending on or after December 15, 2002 and before December 15, 2004;

(ii) 40 days after the end of the fiscal quarter for fiscal years ending on or after December 15, 2004 and before December 15, 2005; and

(iii) 35 days after the end of the fiscal quarter for fiscal years ending on or after December 15, 2005; and

b. 45 days after the end of the fiscal quarter for all other issuers.

* * * * *

FORM 10-Q

* * * * *

Indicate by check mark whether the registrant is an accelerated filer (as defined in Rule 12b-2 of the Exchange Act). Yes ..... No ......

APPLICABLE ONLY TO ISSUERS INVOLVED IN BANKRUPTCY

PROCEEDINGS DURING THE PRECEDING FIVE YEARS:

* * * * *

14. Section 249.310 is revised to read as follows:

§ 249.310 Form 10-K, for annual and transition reports pursuant to sections 13 or 15(d) of the Securities Exchange Act of 1934.

(a) This form shall be used for annual reports pursuant to Sections 13 or 15(d) of the Securities Exchange Act of 1934 (15 U.S.C. 78m or 78o(d)) for which no other form is prescribed. This form also shall be used for transition reports filed pursuant to Section 13 or 15(d) of the Securities Exchange Act of 1934.

(b) Annual reports on this form shall be filed within the following period:

(1) For accelerated filers (as defined in § 240.12b-2 of this chapter):

(i) 90 days after the end of the fiscal year covered by the report for fiscal years ending on or after December 15, 2002 and before December 15, 2003;

(ii) 75 days after the end of the fiscal year covered by the report for fiscal years ending on or after December 15, 2003 and before December 15, 2004; and

(iii) 60 days after the end of the fiscal year covered by the report for fiscal years ending on or after December 15, 2004; and

(2) 90 days after the end of the fiscal year covered by the report for all other registrants.

(c) Transition reports on this form shall be filed in accordance with the requirements set forth in § 240.13a-10 or § 240.15d-10 of this chapter applicable when the registrant changes its fiscal year end.

(d) Notwithstanding paragraphs (b) and (c) of this section, all schedules required by Article 12 of Regulation S-X (§ § 210.12-01–210.12-29 of this chapter) may, at the option of the registrant, be filed as an amendment to the report not later than 30 days after the applicable due date of the report.

15. Form 10-K (referenced in § 249.310) is amended by revising General Instruction A. and the paragraph before the "Note" on the cover page to read as follows:

Note: The text of Form 10-K does not, and this amendment will not, appear in the Code of Federal Regulations.

UNITED STATES SECURITIES AND EXCHANGE COMMISSION

Washington, D.C. 20549

FORM 10-K

* * * * *

GENERAL INSTRUCTIONS

A. Rule as to Use of Form 10-K.

(1) This Form shall be used for annual reports pursuant to Section 13 or 15(d) of the Securities Exchange Act of 1934 (15 U.S.C. 78m or 78o(d)) (the "Act") for which no other form is prescribed. This Form also shall be used for transition reports filed pursuant to Section 13 or 15(d) of the Act.

(2) Annual reports on this Form shall be filed within the following period:

(a) For accelerated filers (as defined in 17 CFR 240.12b-2):

(i) 90 days after the end of the fiscal year covered by the report for fiscal years ending on or after December 15, 2002 and before December 15, 2003;

(ii) 75 days after the end of the fiscal year covered by the report for fiscal years ending on or after December 15, 2003 and before December 15, 2004; and

(iii) 60 days after the end of the fiscal year covered by the report for fiscal years ending on or after December 15, 2004; and

(b) 90 days after the end of the fiscal year covered by the report for all other registrants.

(3) Transition reports on this Form shall be filed in accordance with the requirements set forth in Rule 13a-10 (17 CFR 240.13a-10) or Rule 15d-10 (17 CFR 240.15d-10) applicable when the registrant changes its fiscal year end.

(4) Notwithstanding paragraphs (2) and (3) of this General Instruction A., all schedules required by Article 12 of Regulation S-X (17 CFR 210.12-01–210.12-29) may, at the option of the registrant, be filed as an amendment to the report not later than 30 days after the applicable due date of the report.

* * * * *

FORM 10-K

* * * * *

Indicate by check mark whether the registrant is an accelerated filer (as defined in Rule 12b-2 of the Act). Yes ..... No ......

State the aggregate market value of the voting and non-voting common equity held by non-affiliates computed by reference to the price at which the common equity was last sold, or the average bid and asked price of such common equity, as of the last business day of the registrant's most recently completed second fiscal quarter.

* * * * *

By the Commission.

Margaret H. McFarland

Deputy Secretary

Topical Index

References are to paragraph numbers